Course   Elements of Business

Course Number   **BUGN 295**

MONTCLAIR STATE UNIVERSITY

SCHOOL OF BUSINESS

http://create.mheducation.com

ISBN-10: 1259713679   ISBN-13: 9781259713675

Contents

Credits

2

Understanding Economics and How It Affects Business

Learning Objectives

AFTER YOU HAVE READ AND STUDIED THIS CHAPTER, YOU SHOULD BE ABLE TO

LO 2-1   Explain basic economics.

LO 2-2   Explain what capitalism is and how free markets work.

LO 2-3   Compare socialism and communism.

LO 2-4   Analyze the trend toward mixed economies.

LO 2-5   Describe the economic system of the United States, including the significance of key economic indicators (especially GDP), productivity, and the business cycle.

LO 2-6   Contrast fiscal policy and monetary policy, and explain how each affects the economy.

Getting to Know **Matt Flannery**

People talk about the state of "*the* economy" so much that it can seem as if economics deals only with big, world-shaking financial issues. In reality, though, economics can be found all around us in daily life. From a family saving money for the future to a major corporation measuring its revenue, the world is full of economies both large and small.

It's these small economies that are the major concern of Matt Flannery, co-founder and CEO of the microlending company Kiva.org. His company offers small loans to entrepreneurs working in developing countries in Africa, Asia and South America. Unlike businesspeople operating in the U.S., these entrepreneurs don't need thousands upon thousands of dollars to see their dreams become reality. Instead, many loans issued by Kiva are little more than a few hundred dollars.

But it's not the size of the loans that makes Flannery's work notable. In fact, microlending has been a common source of financing for the developing world since the early 1980s. What sets Kiva apart from the rest is the company's approach. Kiva operates in a similar way to crowdfunding sites like Kickstarter or Indiegogo. These companies rely on small donations from many people in order to fund a larger goal. At Kiva, users first go to the site to select the person or family they'd like to fund. Next, they lend $25 to the entrepreneur of their choice. If the borrowers reach their funding goal, then Kiva grants the loans. The borrowers gradually make repayments that are sent back to Kiva, which then distributes the money back to the lenders. Although lenders don't earn any interest, the satisfaction of helping another human being thousands of miles away is enough to ensure that 70 percent of all lenders make another loan.

Flannery took a winding road to reach this point in his career. Interestingly enough, other than Kiva, he doesn't have any previous background in either financing or the nonprofit sector. After getting a degree from Stanford University, Flannery got a job developing software at Tivo, but he really wanted a business of his own. "I tried to start maybe ten companies," says Flannery. "It was like I had a midlife crisis at 22." For example, Flannery attempted to start a DVD-rental machine business years before Redbox existed. He also tried his hand at starting an online luxury clothes rental company. "A lot of those other ideas for me were a little empty . . . they weren't proactive movements towards something I loved. This idea is different. The actual content of the idea I enjoy every day . . . this is my dream job."

The inspiration for Kiva didn't hit him until he spent a few months working in rural communities throughout Africa. The impact of small businesses on the communities Flannery visited made a profound impression on him. Kiva launched in 2005, after he spent a year researching the aid industry and talking with experts. Today Kiva has distributed more than $500 million in loans to entrepreneurs throughout the world. "Small loans used for business growth encourage self-respect, accountability, and hope among loan recipients," says Flannery. "Primarily, the challenges they [entrepreneurs in Africa] face are very similar to the challenges we face . . . a story about a woman selling fish on the side of the street in Uganda, you can get into profit margins, inventory management, the same things that businesses here think about. There's a commonality that can unify people. Which is exciting."

Many people don't realize the importance of the economic environment to the success of business. That is what this chapter is all about. You will learn to compare different economic systems to see the benefits and the drawbacks of each. You will learn how the free-market system of the United States works. And you will learn more about what makes some countries rich and other countries poor. By the end of the chapter, you should understand the direct effect economic systems have on the wealth and happiness of communities throughout the world.

Sources: Mohana Ravindranath, "Microfinance Nonprofit Kiva Launches in D.C.," *The Washington Post*, January 8, 2013; Interview, "Why Purpose Matters For Matt Flannery of Kiva.org," *Yscouts*, September 11, 2013; Charles Blass, "Matt Flannery: Co-Founder and CEO, Kiva Microfunds," *Thefuturemakers.net*, May 2, 2013; and www.kiva.org, accessed January 2014.

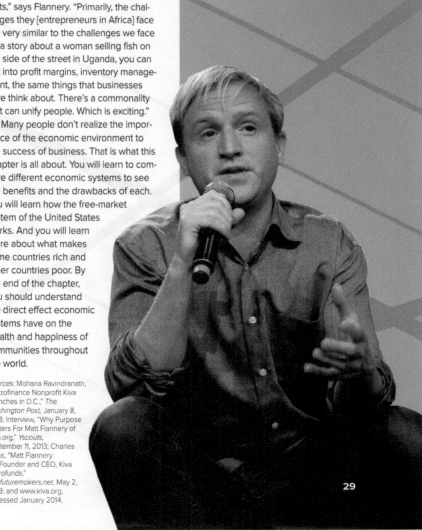

Matt Flannery
Co-Founder and CEO of Kiva.org
- From software developer to microlender
- Provides small loans to build businesses

www.kiva.org
twitter.com/kiva

name that **company**

This privately funded organization provides funds to support world health and education. This organization was founded and is managed by one of the most famous U.S. entrepreneurs and his wife. What is the name of this organization? (Find the answer in the chapter.)

LO 2–1   Explain basic economics.

HOW ECONOMIC CONDITIONS AFFECT BUSINESSES

Compared to, say, Mexico, the United States is a relatively wealthy country. Why? Why is South Korea comparatively wealthy and North Korea suffering economically, with many of its people starving? Such questions are part of the subject of economics. In this chapter, we explore the various economic systems of the world and how they either promote or hinder business growth, the creation of wealth, and a higher quality of life for all.

A major part of the United States' business success in the past was due to an economic and social climate that allowed most businesses to operate freely. People were free to start a business anywhere, and just as free to fail and start again. That freedom motivated people to try until they succeeded because the rewards were often so great.[1]

Any change in the U.S. economic or political system has a major influence on the success of the business system.[2] For example, the recent increase in government involvement in business will have an economic effect. What that effect will be in the long run, however, remains to be seen.

Global economics and global politics also have a major influence on businesses in the United States. For example, there is even some talk today about having a one-time global wealth tax.[3] This is a tax that was proposed by the International Monetary Fund (IMF). The idea is to tax the wealth of individuals around the world by 10 percent to bring the debt of nations closer to the pre-recession levels. Think of how such a tax would affect businesses and workers in the United States. Clearly, to understand business, you must also understand basic economics and politics. This is especially true of new college graduates looking for jobs.

What Is Economics?

Economics is the study of how society chooses to employ resources to produce goods and services and distribute them for consumption among various competing groups and individuals. There are two major branches of economics: **macroeconomics** looks at the operation of a nation's economy as a whole (the whole United States), and **microeconomics** looks at the behavior of people and organizations in markets for particular products or services.[4] A question in macroeconomics might be: What should the United States do to lower its national debt?[5] Macroeconomic topics in this chapter include gross domestic product (GDP), the unemployment rate, and price indexes. Recently, there has been some question about macroeconomic policies and how effective they really are.[6] A question in microeconomics might be: Why do people buy smaller cars when gas prices go up? Such questions seem easier to answer.

economics
The study of how society chooses to employ resources to produce goods and services and distribute them for consumption among various competing groups and individuals.

macroeconomics
The part of economics study that looks at the operation of a nation's economy as a whole.

microeconomics
The part of economics study that looks at the behavior of people and organizations in particular markets.

The economic contrast is remarkable. Business is booming in Seoul, South Korea (as shown in the top photo). But North Korea, a communist country, is not doing well, as the picture on the bottom shows. What do you think accounts for the dramatic differences in the economies of these two neighboring countries?

Some economists define economics as the study of the allocation of *scarce* resources. They believe resources need to be carefully divided among people, usually by the government. However, there's no way to maintain peace and prosperity in the world by merely dividing the resources we have today among the existing nations. There aren't enough known resources to do that. **Resource development** is the study of how to increase resources (say, by getting oil and gas from shale and tar sands) and create conditions that will make better use of them (like recycling and conservation).[7]

Businesses can contribute to an economic system by inventing products that greatly increase available resources. For example, they can discover new energy sources (natural gas for autos), new ways of growing food (hydroponics), and new ways of creating needed goods and services such as nanotechnology

resource development
The study of how to increase resources and to create the conditions that will make better use of those resources.

and 4D technology (moving 3D, with time as the fourth dimension). Maricul-ture, or raising fish in pens out in the ocean, could lead to more food for every-one and more employment. It is believed that the United States could monopolize the shrimp industry using aquaculture. Now we import about a billion pounds of shrimp a year.

The Secret to Creating a Wealthy Economy

Imagine the world when kings and other rich landowners had most of the wealth, and the majority of the people were peasants. The peasants had many children, and it may have seemed a natural conclusion that if things went on as usual there would soon be too many people and not enough food and other

resources. Economist Thomas Malthus made this argument in the late 1700s and early 1800s, lead-ing the writer Thomas Carlyle to call economics "the dismal science."

Followers of Malthus today (who are called neo-Malthusians) still believe there are too many people in the world and that the solution to pov-erty is radical birth control, including forced abor-tions and sterilization.[8] The latest world statistics, however, show population growing more slowly than expected. In some industrial countries—such as Japan, Germany, Italy, Russia, and the United States—population growth may be so slow that eventually there will be too many old people and too few young people to care for them.[9] In the developing world, on the other hand, population will climb relatively quickly and may lead to greater poverty and more unrest. Studies about the effects of population growth on the economy are part of macroeconomics.

New ways of producing goods and services add resources to the economy and create more employment. Fish farms, for instance, create both food and jobs. Can you think of other innovations that can help increase economic development?

Some macroeconomists believe that a large population, especially an edu-cated one, can be a valuable resource. You've probably heard the saying "Give a man a fish and you feed him for a day, but teach a man to fish and you feed him for a lifetime." You can add to that: "Teach a person to start a fish farm, and he or she will be able to feed a village for a lifetime." *The secret to economic develop-ment is contained in this last statement.* Business owners provide jobs and eco-nomic growth for their employees and communities as well as for themselves.[10]

The challenge for macroeconomists is to determine what makes some countries relatively wealthy and other countries relatively poor, and then to implement policies and programs that lead to increased prosperity for every-one in all countries. One way to begin understanding this challenge is to con-sider the theories of Adam Smith.

Adam Smith and the Creation of Wealth

Rather than believing fixed resources had to be divided among competing groups and individuals, Scottish economist Adam Smith envisioned creating more resources so that everyone could become wealthier. Smith's book *An Inquiry into the Nature and Causes of the Wealth of Nations* (often called simply *The Wealth of Nations*) was published in 1776.

Smith believed *freedom* was vital to the survival of any economy, especially the freedom to own land or property and to keep the profits from working the land or running a business.[11] He believed people will work long and hard if they have incentives for doing so—that is, if they know they'll be rewarded. As a result of those efforts, the economy will prosper, with plenty of food and all kinds of products available to everyone. Smith's ideas were later challenged by Malthus and others who believed economic conditions would only get worse, but Smith, not Malthus, is considered the father of modern economics.

How Businesses Benefit the Community

In Adam Smith's view, businesspeople don't necessarily deliberately set out to help others. They work primarily for their own prosperity and growth. Yet as people try to improve their own situation in life, Smith said, their efforts serve as an "invisible hand" that helps the economy grow and prosper through the production of needed goods, services, and ideas. Thus, the phrase **invisible hand** is used to describe the process that turns self-directed gain into social and economic benefits for *all*.

How do people working in their own self-interest produce goods, services, and wealth for others? The only way farmers can become wealthy is to sell some of their crops to others. To become even wealthier, they have to hire workers to produce more food. So the farmers' self-centered efforts to become wealthy lead to jobs for some and food for almost all. Think about that process for a minute, because it is critical to understanding economic growth in the United States and other free countries. The same principles apply to everything from clothing to houses to iPhones.

Smith assumed that as people became wealthier, they would naturally reach out to help the less fortunate in the community. That has not always happened. In fact, today the poverty rate in the United States is quite high and there is a great disparity between the amount of money the wealthy have and the amount of money poor people have.[12] This is called "inequality" and is the central concern of many political, religious, and social leaders today.[13] Many businesspeople are becoming more concerned about social issues and their obligation to return to society some of what they've earned.[14] The economic question is: What can and should we do about poverty and unemployment in the United States and around the world?

As we mentioned in Chapter 1, it is important for businesses to be ethical as well as generous. Unethical practices undermine the whole economic system. The Making Ethical Decisions box explores the effects of corruption.

invisible hand
A phrase coined by Adam Smith to describe the process that turns self-directed gain into social and economic benefits for all.

According to Adam Smith's theory, business owners are motivated to work hard because they know they will earn, and keep, the rewards of their labor. When they prosper, as the owner of this restaurant has, they are able to add employees and grow, indirectly helping the community and the larger economy grow in the process. What might motivate you to start your own business?

making **ethical decisions**

How Corruption Harms the Economy

There are numerous forces in poor countries that hinder economic growth and development. One of those forces is corruption. In many countries, a businessperson must bribe government officials to get permission to own land, build on it, and conduct normal business operations. The United States has seen much corruption among businesspeople, such as use of prostitutes, illegal drug use, alcohol addiction, and gambling. Imagine you need a permit to add liquor to your restaurant menu to increase your profit. You have tried for years to get one, with no results. You have a friend in the government who offers to help you if you make a large contribution to his or her reelection campaign. Would you be tempted to make a campaign contribution? What are your alternatives? What are the consequences of each?

Use LearnSmart to help retain what you have learned. Access your instructor's Connect course to check out LearnSmart, or go to learnsmartadvantage.com for help.

LEARNSMART

test **prep**

- **What is the difference between macroeconomics and microeconomics?**
- **What is better for an economy than teaching a man to fish?**
- **What does Adam Smith's term *invisible hand* mean? How does the invisible hand create wealth for a country?**

LO 2–2   Explain what capitalism is and how free markets work.

UNDERSTANDING FREE-MARKET CAPITALISM

Basing their ideas on free-market principles such as those of Adam Smith, businesspeople in the United States, Europe, Japan, Canada, and other countries began to create more wealth than ever before. They hired others to work on their farms and in their factories, and their nations began to prosper as a result. Businesspeople soon became the wealthiest people in society.

However, great disparities in wealth remained or even increased. Many businesspeople owned large homes and fancy carriages while most workers lived in humble surroundings. Nonetheless, there was always the promise of better times. One way to be really wealthy was to start a successful business of your own. Of course, it wasn't that easy—it never has been. Then and now, you have to accumulate some money to buy or start a business, and you have to work long hours to make it grow. But the opportunities are there.[15]

capitalism
An economic system in which all or most of the factors of production and distribution are privately owned and operated for profit.

The economic system that has led to wealth creation in much of the world is known as capitalism. Under **capitalism** all or most of the factors of production and distribution—such as land, factories, railroads, and stores—are owned by individuals. They are operated for profit, and businesspeople, not government officials, decide what to produce and how much, what to charge, and how much to pay workers. They also decide whether to produce goods in their own countries or have them made in other countries. No country is purely capitalist, however. Often the government gets involved in issues such as determining minimum wages, setting farm prices, and lending money to some failing businesses—as it does in the United States. But capitalism is the *foundation* of the U.S. economic system, and of the economies of England, Australia, Canada, and most other industrialized nations.

Capitalism, liked all economic systems has its faults. For example, income inequality is a major issue that concerns many today. However, John Mackey,

CEO of Whole Foods, believes that "conscious capitalism," that is, capitalism based on businesses that serve all major stakeholders, is the best system in the world.[16] Here is what he says about capitalism: "In the long arc of history, no human creation has had a greater positive impact on more people more rapidly than free-enterprise capitalism. . . . This system has afforded billions of us the opportunity to join in the great enterprise of earning our sustenance and finding meaning by creating value for each other."[17]

Some countries have noticed the advantages of capitalism and have instituted what has become known as state capitalism.[18] **State capitalism** is a combination of freer markets and some government control. China, for example, has had rapid growth over the last few years as a result of state capitalism—that is, freer markets and less government control.[19] We shall discuss the Chinese system in more detail when we look at communism.

state capitalism
A combination of freer markets and some government control.

The Foundations of Capitalism

Under free-market capitalism people have four basic rights:

1. *The right to own private property.* This is the most fundamental of all rights under capitalism. Private ownership means that individuals can buy, sell, and use land, buildings, machinery, inventions, and other forms of property. They can also pass property on to their children. Would farmers work as hard if they didn't own the land and couldn't keep the profits from what they earned?

2. *The right to own a business and keep all that business's profits.* Recall from Chapter 1 that profits equal revenues minus expenses (salaries, materials, taxes). Profits act as important incentives for business owners.

3. *The right to freedom of competition.* Within certain guidelines established by the government, individuals are free to compete with other individuals or businesses in selling and promoting goods and services.

4. *The right to freedom of choice.* People are free to choose where they want to work and what career they want to follow. Other choices people are free to make include where to live and what to buy or sell.

The right to own private property and the right to own a business and keep its profits are two of the fundamental rights that exist in the economic system called free-market capitalism. Would either of these rights be viable without the other?

One benefit of the four basic rights of capitalism is that people are willing to take more risks than they might otherwise. President Franklin Roosevelt believed four additional freedoms were essential to economic success: freedom of speech and expression, freedom to worship in your own way, freedom from want, and freedom from fear. Do you see the benefits of these additional freedoms?

Now let's explore how the free market works. What role do consumers play in the process? How do businesses learn what consumers need and want? These questions and more are answered next.

How Free Markets Work

A free market is one in which decisions about what and how much to produce are made by the market—by buyers and sellers negotiating prices for goods and services. You and I and other consumers send signals to tell producers what to make, how many, in what color, and so on. We do that by choosing to buy (or not to buy) certain products and services.

For example, if all of us decided we wanted T-shirts supporting our favorite baseball team, the clothing industry would respond in certain ways. Manufacturers and retailers would increase the price of those T-shirts, because they know people are willing to pay more for the shirts they want. They would also realize they could make more money by making more of those T-shirts. Thus, they have an incentive to pay workers to start earlier and end later. Further, the number of companies making T-shirts would increase. How many T-shirts they make depends on how many we request or buy in the stores. Prices and quantities will continue to change as the number of T-shirts we buy changes.

The same process occurs with most other products. The *price* tells producers how much to produce. If something is wanted but isn't available, the price tends to go up until someone begins making more of that product, sells the ones already on hand, or makes a substitute. As a consequence, there's rarely a long-term shortage of goods in the United States.

The economic concept of demand measures the quantities of goods and services that people are willing to buy at a given price. All else equal, the lower the price, the higher the demand will be. Do you think there would be this many customers rushing to shop on Black Friday if it wasn't for those low-price/low-quantity deals?

How Prices Are Determined

In a free market, *prices are not determined by sellers;* they are determined by buyers and sellers negotiating in the marketplace. A seller may want to receive $50 for a T-shirt, but the quantity buyers demand at that high price may be quite low. If the seller lowers the price, the quantity demanded is likely to increase. How is a price determined that is acceptable to both buyers and sellers? The answer is found in the microeconomic concepts of supply and demand. We shall explore both next.

 connect

iSee It! Need help understanding supply and demand? Visit your Connect e-book video tab for a brief animated explanation.

The Economic Concept of Supply

Supply refers to the quantities of products manufacturers or owners are willing to sell at different prices at a specific time. Generally speaking, the amount supplied will increase as the price increases, because sellers can make more money with a higher price.

Economists show this relationship between quantity supplied and price on a graph. Figure 2.1 shows a simple supply curve for T-shirts. The price of the shirts in dollars is shown vertically on the left of the graph. The quantity of shirts sellers are willing to supply is shown horizontally at the bottom of the graph. The various points on the curve indicate how many T-shirts sellers would provide at different prices. For example, at a price of $5 a shirt, a T-shirt vendor would provide only 5 shirts, but at $50 a shirt the vendor would supply 50 shirts. The supply curve indicates the relationship between the price and the quantity supplied. All things being equal, the higher the price, the more the vendor will be willing to supply.

supply
The quantity of products that manufacturers or owners are willing to sell at different prices at a specific time.

The Economic Concept of Demand

Demand refers to the quantity of products that people are willing to buy at different prices at a specific time. Generally speaking, the quantity demanded will increase as the price decreases. Again, we can show the relationship between price and quantity demanded in a graph. Figure 2.2 shows a simple demand curve for T-shirts. The various points on the graph indicate the quantity demanded at various prices. For example, at $45, buyers demand just 5 shirts, but at $5, the quantity demanded would increase to 35 shirts. All things being equal, the lower the price, the more buyers are willing to buy.

demand
The quantity of products that people are willing to buy at different prices at a specific time.

The Equilibrium Point, or Market Price

You might realize from Figures 2.1 and 2.2 that the key factor in determining the quantities supplied and demanded is *price.* If you were to lay the two graphs one on top of the other, the supply curve and the demand curve would cross where quantity demanded and quantity supplied are equal. Figure 2.3 illustrates that point. At a price of $15, the quantity of T-shirts demanded and the quantity supplied are equal (25 shirts). That crossing point is known as the *equilibrium point* or *equilibrium price.* In the long run, that price will become the market price. **Market price**, then, is determined by supply and demand. It is the price toward which the market will trend.

Proponents of a free market argue that, because supply and demand interactions determine prices, there is no need for the government to set prices. If quantity supplied exceeds quantity demanded, the resulting surplus

market price
The price determined by supply and demand.

FIGURE 2.1 THE SUPPLY CURVE AT VARIOUS PRICES
The supply curve rises from left to right. Think it through. The higher the price of T-shirts goes (the vertical axis), the more sellers will be willing to supply.

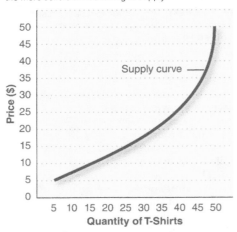

FIGURE 2.2 THE DEMAND CURVE AT VARIOUS PRICES
This is a simple demand curve showing the quantity of T-shirts demanded at different prices. The demand curve falls from left to right. It is easy to understand why. The lower the price of T-shirts, the higher the quantity demanded.

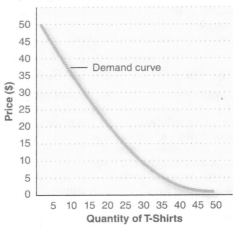

FIGURE 2.3 THE EQUILIBRIUM POINT
The place where quantity demanded and quantity supplied meet is called the equilibrium point. When we put both the supply and demand curves on the same graph, we find that they intersect at a price where the quantity supplied and the quantity demanded are equal. In the long run, the market price will tend toward the equilibrium point.

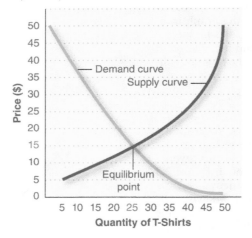

signals sellers to lower the price. If shortages develop because the quantity supplied is less than quantity demanded, it signals sellers to increase the price. Eventually, supply will again equal demand if nothing interferes with market forces. The Spotlight on Small Business box shows how environmental forces can influence supply and demand.

In countries without a free market, there is no mechanism to reveal to businesses (via price) what to produce and in what amounts, so there are often shortages (not enough products) or surpluses (too many products). In such countries, the government decides what to produce and in what quantity, but without price signals it has no way of knowing what the proper quantities are. Furthermore, when the government interferes in otherwise free markets, such as when it subsidizes farm goods, surpluses and shortages may develop. Competition differs in free markets, too. We shall explore that concept next.

Competition within Free Markets

Economists generally agree there are four different degrees of competition: (1) perfect competition, (2) monopolistic competition, (3) oligopoly, and (4) monopoly.

Perfect competition exists when there are many sellers in a market and none is large enough to dictate the price of a product. Sellers' products appear to be identical, such as agricultural products like apples, corn, and potatoes. There are no true examples of perfect competition. Today, government price supports and drastic reductions in the number of farms make it hard to argue that even farming represents perfect competition.

perfect competition
The degree of competition in which there are many sellers in a market and none is large enough to dictate the price of a product.

www.gulfcitrus.org

spotlight on **small business**

Bugs Bug Orange Farmers and Drive Prices Up

Normally, it takes a large force to significantly affect a product's supply and demand. However, in the case of 2013's Florida orange crop, the supply of this commodity experienced a major disruption due to tiny invaders. The state experienced its worst crop since 1990, thanks to an orange-killing disease brought on by gnat-sized insects called Asian citrus psyllids. As a result, orange prices rose by as much as 16 percent throughout 2014.

An unusually dry spell brought the wrath of the gnats swarming on Florida's orange groves. For small farmers throughout the state, the next step to take is unclear. "We're in uncharted territory," says John Ortelle, an expert who's been following the citrus industry for more than 30 years. "Whatever producers have tried to tackle the disease has had a minimal effect so far. Growers took out trees and added extra nutrients. You just don't know when and if the effects will be positive." With immediate solutions to the problem still out of reach, Florida's farmers can only hope that no other circumstances beyond their control harm crops and drive prices up further. In fact, the state's orange growers dodged a bullet during the harsh 2013/2014 winter season as temperatures often hovered around freezing. Thankfully for Florida's citrus farmers (as well as the nation's frugal OJ drinkers), oranges aren't damaged by cold unless the temperature drops below 28 degrees Fahrenheit.

Sources: Marvin G. Perez, "Bug Bites Cut Florida Orange Crop to Lowest in 2 Decades," *Bloomberg*, December 26, 2013; and Claudia Carpenter, Luzi Ann Javier, and Jeff Wilson, "Florida Oranges to U.S. Wheat Seen Escaping Freeze Damage," *Bloomberg*, January 7, 2014.

Under **monopolistic competition** a large number of sellers produce very similar products that buyers nevertheless perceive as different, such as hot dogs, sodas, personal computers, and T-shirts. Product differentiation—the attempt to make buyers think similar products are different in some way—is a key to success. Think about what that means. Through advertising, branding, and packaging, sellers try to convince buyers that their products are different from competitors', though they may be very similar or even interchangeable. The fast-food industry, with its pricing battles among hamburger offerings and the like, offers a good example of monopolistic competition.

An **oligopoly** is a degree of competition in which just a few sellers dominate a market, as we see in tobacco, gasoline, automobiles, aluminum, and aircraft. One reason some industries remain in the hands of a few sellers is that the initial investment required to enter the business often is tremendous. Think, for example, of how much it would cost to start a new airplane manufacturing facility.

In an oligopoly, products from different companies tend to be priced about the same. The reason is simple: Intense price competition would lower profits for everyone, since a price cut by one producer would most likely be matched by the others. As in monopolistic competition, product differentiation, rather than price, is usually the major factor in market success in an oligopoly. Note, for example, that most cereals are priced about the same, as are soft drinks. Thus, advertising is a major factor determining which of the few available brands consumers buy, because often it is advertising that creates the perceived differences.

A **monopoly** occurs when one seller controls the total supply of a product or service, and sets the price. In the United States, laws prohibit the creation of monopolies. Nonetheless, the U.S. legal system has permitted monopolies

monopolistic competition
The degree of competition in which a large number of sellers produce very similar products that buyers nevertheless perceive as different.

oligopoly
A degree of competition in which just a few sellers dominate the market.

monopoly
A degree of competition in which only one seller controls the total supply of a product or service, and sets the price.

in the markets for public utilities that sell natural gas, water, and electric power. These companies' prices and profits are usually controlled by public service commissions to protect the interest of buyers. For example, the Florida Public Service Commission is the administering agency over the Florida Power and Light utility company. Legislation ended the monopoly status of utilities in some areas, letting consumers choose among providers. The intention of such *deregulation* is to increase competition among utility companies and, ultimately, lower prices for consumers.

Benefits and Limitations of Free Markets

One benefit of the free market is that it allows open competition among companies. Businesses must provide customers with high-quality products at fair prices with good service. If they don't, they lose customers to businesses that do. Do government services have the same incentives?

The free market—with its competition and incentives—was a major factor in creating the wealth that industrialized countries now enjoy. Some people even talk of the free market as an economic miracle. Free-market capitalism, more than any other economic system, provides opportunities for poor people to work their way out of poverty. Capitalism also encourages businesses to be more efficient so they can successfully compete on price and quality. Would you say that the United States is increasing or decreasing the emphasis on capitalism? Why?

Yet, even as free-market capitalism has brought prosperity to the United States and to much of the rest of the world, it has brought inequality as well. Business owners and managers usually make more money and have more wealth than lower-level workers. Yet people who are old, disabled, or sick may not be able to start and manage a business, and others may not have the talent or the drive. What should society do about such inequality?[20]

One of the dangers of free markets is that some people let greed dictate how they act. Criminal charges brought against some big businesses in banking, oil, accounting, telecommunications, insurance, and pharmaceuticals indicate the scope of the potential problem. Some businesspeople have deceived the public about their products; others have deceived stockholders about the value of their stock, all in order to increase executives' personal assets.

Clearly, some government laws and regulations are necessary to protect businesses' stakeholders and make sure people who cannot work get the basic care they need. To overcome some of capitalism's limitations, some countries have adopted an economic system called socialism. It, too, has its good and bad points. We explore these after you review the following Test Prep questions.

Use LearnSmart to help retain what you have learned. Access your instructor's Connect course to check out LearnSmart, or go to learnsmartadvantage.com for help.

test prep

- What are the four basic rights that people have under free-market capitalism?
- How do businesspeople know what to produce and in what quantity?
- How are prices determined?
- What are the four degrees of competition, and what are some examples of each?

LO 2–3 Compare socialism and communism.

UNDERSTANDING SOCIALISM

Socialism is an economic system based on the premise that some, if not most, basic businesses (e.g., steel mills, coal mines, and utilities) should be owned by the government so that profits can be more evenly distributed among the people. Entrepreneurs often own and run smaller businesses, and individuals are often taxed relatively steeply to pay for social programs. The top federal personal income tax rate in the United States, for example, was 39.6 percent recently, but in some socialist countries the top proposed rate can be as much as 75 percent.[21] While U.S. shoppers pay sales taxes ranging from over 10 percent in Chicago to zero in Delaware, some socialist countries charge a similar value-added tax of 15 to 20 percent or more. Socialists acknowledge the major benefit of capitalism—wealth creation—but believe that wealth should be more evenly distributed than occurs in free-market capitalism. They believe the government should carry out the distribution and be much more involved in protecting the environment and providing for the poor. Do you see evidence of that happening in the United States today?

socialism
An economic system based on the premise that some, if not most, basic businesses should be owned by the government so that profits can be more evenly distributed among the people.

brain drain
The loss of the best and brightest people to other countries.

The Benefits of Socialism

The major benefit of socialism is supposed to be social equality. Ideally it comes about because the government takes income from wealthier people, in the form of taxes, and redistributes it to poorer people through various government programs. Free education through college, free health care, and free child care are some of the benefits socialist governments, using the money from taxes, may provide to their people. Workers in socialist countries usually get longer vacations, work fewer hours per week, and have more employee benefits (e.g., generous sick leave) than those in countries where free-market capitalism prevails.

Socialism has been more successful in some countries than in others. This photo shows Denmark's clean and modern public transportation system. In Greece, overspending caused a debt crisis that forced the government to impose austerity measures that many Greeks oppose. What other factors might lead to slower growth in socialist countries?

The Negative Consequences of Socialism

Socialism may create more equality than capitalism, but it takes away some of businesspeople's incentives. For example, tax rates in some socialist nations once reached 83 percent. Today, doctors, lawyers, business owners, and others who earn a lot of money pay very high tax rates. As a consequence, many of them leave socialist countries for capitalistic countries with lower taxes, such as the United States. This loss of the best and brightest people to other countries is called a **brain drain**.

Imagine an experiment in socialism in your own class. Imagine that after the first exam, those with grades of 90 and above have to give some of their points to those who make 70 and below so that everyone ends up with grades in the 80s. Would those who got 90s study as hard for the second exam? What about those who got 70s? Can you see why workers may not work as hard or as well if they all get the same benefits regardless of how hard they work?

Socialism also tends to result in fewer inventions and less innovation, because those who come up with new ideas usually don't receive as much reward as they would in a capitalist system. Communism may be considered a more intensive version of socialism. We shall explore that system next.

UNDERSTANDING COMMUNISM

communism
An economic and political system in which the government makes almost all economic decisions and owns almost all the major factors of production.

Communism is an economic and political system in which the government makes almost all economic decisions and owns almost all the major factors of production. It intrudes further into the lives of people than socialism does. For example, some communist countries have not allowed their citizens to practice certain religions, change jobs, or move to the town of their choice.

One problem with communism is that the government has no way of knowing what to produce, because prices don't reflect supply and demand as they do in free markets. The government must guess what the people need. As a result, shortages of many items, including food and clothing, may develop. Another problem is that communism doesn't inspire businesspeople to work hard because the incentives are not there. Therefore, communism is slowly disappearing as an economic form.

Most communist countries today are suffering severe economic depression. In North Korea, many people are starving. In Cuba, people suffer a lack of goods and services readily available in most other countries, and some fear the government.

While some parts of the former Soviet Union remain influenced by communist ideals, Russia itself now has a flat tax of only 13 percent. Yet this low rate increased the government's tax revenues by nearly 30 percent, because more people were willing to pay.

LO 2–4   Analyze the trend toward mixed economies.

THE TREND TOWARD MIXED ECONOMIES

The nations of the world have largely been divided between those that followed the concepts of capitalism and those that adopted the concepts of communism or socialism. We can now contrast the two major economic systems as follows:

free-market economies
Economic systems in which the market largely determines what goods and services get produced, who gets them, and how the economy grows.

1. **Free-market economies** exist when the market largely determines what goods and services get produced, who gets them, and how the economy grows. *Capitalism* is the popular term for this economic system.

command economies
Economic systems in which the government largely decides what goods and services will be produced, who will get them, and how the economy will grow.

2. **Command economies** exist when the government largely decides what goods and services will be produced, who gets them, and how the economy will grow. *Socialism* and *communism* are variations on this economic system.

Although all countries actually have some mix of the two systems, neither free-market nor command economies have resulted in optimal economic conditions. Free-market mechanisms don't seem to respond enough to the needs of those who are poor, elderly, or disabled. Some people also believe that businesses in free-market economies have not done enough to protect the environment. Over time, voters in mostly free-market countries, such as the United States, have elected officials who have adopted many social and environmental programs such as Social Security, welfare, unemployment compensation, and various clean air and water acts. What new or enhanced social policies do you know of that have been enacted or are being considered today?

Russia has been moving away from communism toward a viable market economy. As poverty begins to decline, a middle class is emerging, but many of the country's vast natural resources are difficult to tap. Laws that help promote business are few, and there is an active black market for many goods. Many observers are optimistic that Russia can prosper. What do you think?

Socialism and communism haven't always created enough jobs or wealth to keep economies growing fast enough. Thus, communist governments are disappearing, and some socialist governments have been cutting back on social programs and lowering taxes on businesses and workers to generate more business growth and more revenue.

The trend, then, has been for mostly capitalist countries (like the United States) to move toward socialism (e.g., more government involvement in health care), and for some socialist countries to move toward capitalism (more private businesses, lower taxes). All countries have some mix of the two systems. Thus, the long-term global trend is toward a blend of capitalism and socialism. This trend likely will increase with the opening of global markets made easier by the Internet. The net effect is the emergence throughout the world of mixed economies (see the Reaching Beyond Our Borders box).

Mixed economies exist where some allocation of resources is made by the market and some by the government. Most countries don't have a name for such a system. If free-market mechanisms allocate most resources, the leaders call their system capitalism. If the government allocates most resources, the leaders call it socialism. Figure 2.4 compares the various economic systems.

Like most other nations of the world, the United States has a mixed economy. The U.S. government has now become the largest employer in the country, which means there are more workers in the public sector (government) than in any of the major businesses in the United States. Do you see the government growing or declining in the coming years?

mixed economies
Economic systems in which some allocation of resources is made by the market and some by the government.

www.imf.org

reaching beyond **our borders**

Economic Expansion in Africa

For much of the 20th century, stories about Africa's economy inevitably focused on the continent's rampant poverty. The end of colonial rule in Africa brought military dictatorships and other oppressive forces to power in many countries. Coupled with disease and an almost nonexistent infrastructure, Africa's economy and its people suffered horribly.

Thankfully, so far the 21st century has been brighter for many Africans. A booming commodities market along with expanding manufacturing and service economies are leading to unprecedented growth. Over the last decade, six of the world's 10 fastest-growing countries have been African. In eight of those years, Africa has even outpaced the growth of East Asia, including

Japan. Looking to the future, experts expect the continent's GDP to grow 6 percent annually over the next 10 years.

Many Africans have seen their lives change radically as economies on the continent have expanded. Income per person has shot up 30 percent over the last decade, while life expectancy has increased by 10 percent. Even small, formerly war-torn nations are seeing improvements. For instance, in the 1990s Rwanda suffered a horrific civil war and genocide that claimed the lives of hundreds of thousands of citizens. Subsequent years of peace and a relatively stable government have since turned the country around significantly. Although many on the continent still experience major

hardships, improving economic conditions are allowing more and more people to enter the middle class. Goods and services that used to be scarce are now becoming commonplace. There are now three mobile phones for every four people in Africa, and by 2017 nearly 30 percent of households are expected to own a television. School enrollment has also skyrocketed in the last few years. Experts hope that this younger generation will take advantage of improving educational opportunities and ensure Africa's place on the global economic stage.

Sources: "A Hopeful Continent," *The Economist*, March 2, 2013; "Business in Rwanda: Africa's Singapore?" *The Economist*, February 25, 2012; and John O'Sullivan, "Middle East and Africa: Digging Deeper," *The Economist*, November 18, 2013.

Use LearnSmart to help retain what you have learned. Access your instructor's Connect course to check out LearnSmart, or go to learnsmartadvantage.com for help.

≣LEARNSMART·

Test **prep**

- What led to the emergence of socialism?
- What are the benefits and drawbacks of socialism?
- What countries still practice communism?
- What are the characteristics of a mixed economy?

LO 2–5   Describe the economic system of the United States, including the significance of key economic indicators (especially GDP), productivity, and the business cycle.

UNDERSTANDING THE U.S. ECONOMIC SYSTEM

The following sections will introduce the terms and concepts that you, as an informed citizen, will need to understand in order to grasp the issues facing government and business leaders in the United States.

iSee It! Need help understanding basic economic systems? Visit your Connect e-book video tab for a brief animated explanation.

Key Economic Indicators

Three major indicators of economic conditions are (1) the gross domestic product (GDP), (2) the unemployment rate, and (3) price indexes. Another important statistic is the increase or decrease in productivity. When you read

FIGURE 2.4 COMPARISONS OF KEY ECONOMIC SYSTEMS

	CAPITALISM* (United States)	SOCIALISM (Sweden)	COMMUNISM (North Korea)	MIXED ECONOMY (Germany)
Social and Economic Goals	Private ownership of land and business. Liberty and the pursuit of happiness. Free trade. Emphasis on freedom and the profit motive for economic growth.	Public ownership of major businesses. Some private ownership of smaller businesses and shops. Government control of education, health care, utilities, mining, transportation, and media. Very high taxation. Emphasis on equality.	Public ownership of all businesses. Government-run education and health care. Emphasis on equality. Many limitations on freedom, including freedom to own businesses and to assemble to protest government actions.	Private ownership of land and business with government regulation. Government control of some institutions (e.g., mail). High taxation for defense and the common welfare. Emphasis on a balance between freedom and equality.
Motivation of Workers	Much incentive to work efficiently and hard because profits are retained by owners. Workers are rewarded for high productivity.	Capitalist incentives exist in private businesses. Government control of wages in public institutions limits incentives.	Very little incentive to work hard or to produce quality goods or services.	Incentives are similar to capitalism except in government-owned enterprises, which may have fewer incentives.
Control over Markets	Complete freedom of trade within and among nations. Some government control of markets.	Some markets are controlled by the government and some are free. Trade restrictions among nations vary and include some free-trade agreements.	Total government control over markets except for illegal transactions.	Some government control of trade within and among nations (trade protectionism).
Choices in the Market	A wide variety of goods and services is available. Almost no scarcity or over-supply exists for long because supply and demand control the market.	Variety in the marketplace varies considerably from country to country. Choice is directly related to government involvement in markets.	Very little choice among competing goods.	Similar to capitalism, but scarcity and oversupply may be caused by government involvement in the market (e.g., subsidies for farms).
Social Freedoms	Freedom of speech, press, assembly, religion, job choice, movement, and elections.	Similar to mixed economy. Governments may restrict job choice, movement among countries, and who may attend upper-level schools (i.e., college).	Very limited freedom to protest the government, practice religion, or change houses or jobs.	Some restrictions on freedoms of assembly and speech. Separation of church and state may limit religious practices in schools.

*The United States is a mixed economy based on a foundation of capitalism.

business literature, you'll see these terms used again and again. Let's explore what they mean.

Gross Domestic Product   **Gross domestic product (GDP)**, which we mentioned briefly in Chapter 1, is the total value of final goods and services produced in a country in a given year. Both domestic and foreign-owned companies can produce the goods and services included in GDP, as long as the companies are located within the country's boundaries. For example, production values from Japanese automaker Honda's factory in Ohio are included in U.S. GDP. Revenue generated by Ford's factory in Mexico is included in Mexico's GDP, even though Ford is a U.S. company. Although the country relies on such data, the accuracy of the data (at least in the short run) is questionable.[22]

Starting in the spring of 2014, the United States Bureau of Economic Analysis at the Commerce Department will report a statistic called gross output (GO). **Gross output (GO)** is a measure of total sales volume at all stages of production. GO is almost twice the size of GDP and is considered a better indicator of the business cycle and more consistent with economic growth theory. It shows that consumer spending is the effect, not the cause, of prosperity.[23]

Almost every discussion about a nation's economy is based on GDP. If growth in GDP slows or declines, businesses may feel many negative effects. A major influence on the growth of GDP is the productivity of the workforce—that is, how much output workers create with a given amount of input. The level of U.S. economic activity is actually larger than the GDP figures show, because those figures don't take into account illicit activities such as sales of illegal drugs. The high GDP in the United States is what enables its citizens to enjoy a high standard of living.

The Unemployment Rate   The **unemployment rate** refers to the percentage of civilians at least 16 years old who are unemployed *and tried to find a job within the prior four weeks*. The unemployment rate was over 7 percent in 2013 and went down below 6.5 percent in 2014 (see Figure 2.5). However, many people had given up looking for jobs (people who are not actively looking for work are not included in the unemployment figures).[24] Some people feel that the unemployment statistics don't accurately measure the pain being felt by those who have been unemployed for a long time or those who have

gross domestic product (GDP)
The total value of final goods and services produced in a country in a given year.

gross output (GO)
A measure of total sales volume at all stages of production.

unemployment rate
The number of civilians at least 16 years old who are unemployed and tried to find a job within the prior four weeks.

The overall unemployment rate in the United States fluctuates. Over the last decade, it has been as low as less than 5 percent and as high as more than 10 percent. Unemployment insurance goes only so far to relieve the loss of income caused by losing your job. How high is the unemployment rate in your area today?

FIGURE 2.5 U.S. UNEMPLOYMENT RATE 1989–2014

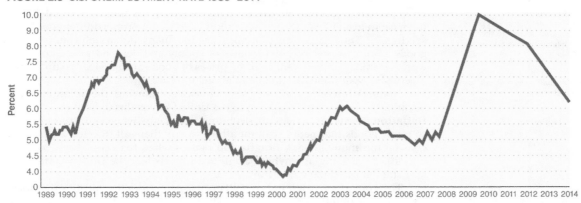

simply given up looking for a job.[25] Some believe that government benefits may lead to more unemployment.[26] Do you agree?

Figure 2.6 describes the four types of unemployment: frictional, structural, cyclical, and seasonal. The United States tries to protect those who are unemployed because of recessions (defined later in the chapter), industry shifts, and other cyclical factors. Nonetheless, the *underemployment* figure in 2014 was about 13.1 percent (this includes those who are working part time and want to work full time and those who have stopped looking for work).[27] Such high numbers raise the question of what the U.S. can do to increase employment.[28]

Inflation and Price Indexes   Price indexes help gauge the health of the economy by measuring the levels of inflation, disinflation, deflation, and stagflation. **Inflation** is a general rise in the prices of goods and services over time.

inflation
A general rise in the prices of goods and services over time.

FIGURE 2.6 FOUR TYPES OF UNEMPLOYMENT

Frictional unemployment

Frictional unemployment refers to those people who have quit work because they didn't like the job, the boss, or the working conditions and who haven't yet found a new job. It also refers to those people who are entering the labor force for the first time (e.g., new graduates) or are returning to the labor force after significant time away (e.g., parents who reared children). There will always be some frictional unemployment because it takes some time to find a first job or a new job.

Structural unemployment

Structural unemployment refers to unemployment caused by the restructuring of firms or by a mismatch between the skills (or location) of job seekers and the requirements (or location) of available jobs (e.g., coal miners in an area where mines have been closed).

Cyclical unemployment

Cyclical unemployment occurs because of a recession or a similar downturn in the business cycle (the ups and downs of business growth and decline over time). This type of unemployment is the most serious.

Seasonal unemployment

Seasonal unemployment occurs where demand for labor varies over the year, as with the harvesting of crops.

disinflation
A situation in which price increases are slowing (the inflation rate is declining).

deflation
A situation in which prices are declining.

stagflation
A situation when the economy is slowing but prices are going up anyhow.

consumer price index (CPI)
Monthly statistics that measure the pace of inflation or deflation.

core inflation
CPI minus food and energy costs.

producer price index (PPI)
An index that measures prices at the wholesale level.

The official definition is "a persistent increase in the level of consumer prices or a persistent decline in the purchasing power of money, caused by an increase in available currency and credit beyond the proportion of goods and services."[29] Thus, it is also described as "too many dollars chasing too few goods." Go back and review the laws of supply and demand to see how that works. Rapid inflation is scary. If the prices of goods and services go up by just 7 percent a year, they will double in about 10 years.

Disinflation occurs when price increases are slowing (the inflation rate is declining). That was the situation in the United States throughout the 1990s.[30] **Deflation** means that prices are declining.[31] It occurs when countries produce so many goods that people cannot afford to buy them all (too few dollars are chasing too many goods). **Stagflation** occurs when the economy is slowing but prices are going up anyhow. Some economists fear the United States may face stagflation in the near future.

The **consumer price index (CPI)** consists of monthly statistics that measure the pace of inflation or deflation. The government can compute the cost of goods and services, including housing, food, apparel, and medical care, to see whether or not they are going up or down. Today, however, the government is relying more on the measure of **core inflation**. That means the CPI minus food and energy costs. Since the costs of food and energy have been going up rapidly, the inflation measures reported (core inflation) are actually lower than real costs. This is important to you because some wages and salaries, rents and leases, tax brackets, government benefits, and interest rates are based on these data.

The **producer price index (PPI)** measures prices at the wholesale level. Other indicators of the economy's condition include housing starts, retail sales, and changes in personal income. You can learn more about such indicators by reading business periodicals, listening to business broadcasts on radio and television, and exploring business sites on the Internet.

Productivity in the United States

An increase in productivity means a worker can produce more goods and services than before in the same time period, usually thanks to machinery or other equipment. Productivity in the United States has risen because computers and other technology have made production faster and easier. The higher productivity is, the lower the costs are of producing goods and services, and the lower prices can be. Therefore, businesspeople are eager to increase productivity. Remember, however, that high productivity can lead to high unemployment. Certainly, that is what the United States in now experiencing.[32]

Now that the U.S. economy is a service economy, productivity is an issue because service firms are so labor-intensive. Spurred by foreign competition, productivity in the manufacturing sector is rising rapidly. In the service sector, productivity is growing more slowly because service workers—like teachers, clerks, lawyers, and barbers—have fewer new technologies available than there are for factory workers.

Productivity in the Service Sector

One problem with the service industry is that an influx of machinery may add to the quality of the service provided but not to the output per worker. For example, you've probably noticed how many computers there are on college campuses. They add to the quality of education but don't necessarily boost professors' productivity. The same is true of some equipment in hospitals, such as CAT scanners, PET scanners, and MRI scanners. They improve patient care but don't necessarily increase the number of patients doctors can see. In other words, today's productivity measures in the service industry fail to capture the increase in quality caused by new technology.

Clearly, the United States and other countries need to develop new measures of productivity for the service economy that include quality as well as quantity of output. Despite productivity improvement, the economy is likely to go through a series of ups and downs, much as it has over the past few years. We'll explore that process next.

The Business Cycle

Business cycles are the periodic rises and falls that occur in economies over time. Economists look at a number of business cycles, from seasonal cycles that occur within a year to cycles that occur every 48–60 years.

Economist Joseph Schumpeter identified the four phases of long-term business cycles as boom–recession–depression–recovery:

1. An *economic boom* is just what it sounds like—business is booming.

2. **Recession** is two or more consecutive quarters of decline in the GDP. In a recession prices fall, people purchase fewer products, and businesses fail. A recession brings high unemployment, increased business failures, and an overall drop in living standards.

3. A **depression** is a severe recession, usually accompanied by deflation. Business cycles rarely go through a depression phase. In fact, while there were many business cycles during the 20th century, there was only one severe depression (1930s).

4. A *recovery* occurs when the economy stabilizes and starts to grow. This eventually leads to an economic boom, starting the cycle all over again.

One goal of some economists is to predict such ups and downs. That is very difficult to do. Business cycles are identified according to facts, but we can explain those facts only by using theories. Therefore, we cannot predict with certainty. But one thing is certain: over time, the economy will rise and fall as it has done lately.

Since dramatic swings up and down in the economy cause all kinds of disruptions to businesses, the government tries to minimize such changes. It uses fiscal policy and monetary policy to try to keep the economy from slowing too much or growing too rapidly.

> *It can be difficult to measure productivity in the service sector. New technology can improve the quality of services without necessarily increasing the number of people served. A doctor can make more-accurate diagnoses with scans, for instance, but still can see only so many patients in a day. How can productivity measures capture improvements in the quality of service?*

business cycles
The periodic rises and falls that occur in economies over time.

recession
Two or more consecutive quarters of decline in the GDP.

depression
A severe recession, usually accompanied by deflation.

LO 2–6   Contrast fiscal policy and monetary policy, and explain how each affects the economy.

Stabilizing the Economy through Fiscal Policy

Fiscal policy refers to the federal government's efforts to keep the economy stable by increasing or decreasing taxes or government spending. The first fiscal policy tool is taxation. Theoretically, high tax rates tend to slow the economy because they draw money away from the private sector and put it into the government. High tax rates may discourage small-business ownership because

fiscal policy
The federal government's efforts to keep the economy stable by increasing or decreasing taxes or government spending.

they decrease the profits businesses can earn and make the effort less reward-ing. It follows, then, that low tax rates will theoretically give the economy a boost. When you count all fees, sales taxes, and more, taxes on the highest-earning U.S. citizens could exceed 50 percent. Is that figure too high or not high enough in your opinion? Why?

The second fiscal policy tool is government spending on highways, social programs, education, infrastructure (e.g., roads and utilities), defense, and so on. The national deficit is the amount of money the federal government spends beyond what it gathers in taxes for a given fiscal year. The deficit is expected to be over $1 trillion for the next several years. Such deficits increase the national debt. The **national debt** is the sum of government deficits over time. Recently, the national debt was over $17 trillion (see Figure 2.7). That is a rather misleading number, however, since the unfunded obligation for Medicare has been estimated to be over $70 trillion (Various sources cite dif-ferent numbers for the unfunded obligations for both Medicare and Social Security, but the number is high enough to be of concern, no matter how high it is.) If the government takes in more revenue than it spends (i.e., tax revenues exceed expenditures), there is a national *surplus*. That is not likely to happen soon.

One way to lessen deficits is to cut government spending. Many presi-dents and those in Congress have promised to make the government "smaller," that is, to reduce government spending—but that doesn't hap-pen very often. There always seems to be a need for more social programs each year, and thus the deficits continue and add to the national debt. Some people believe that government spending helps the economy grow.

national debt
The sum of government deficits over time.

FIGURE 2.7 THE NATIONAL DEBT

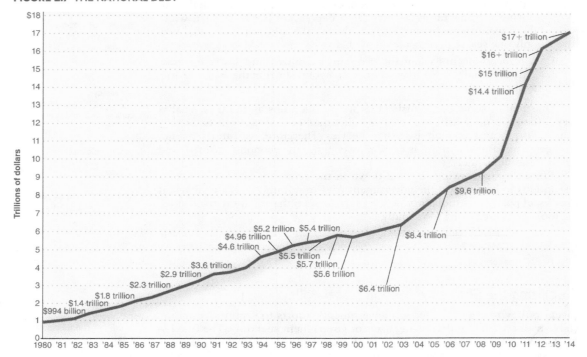

Others believe that the money the government spends comes out of the pockets of consumers and businesspeople, and thus slows growth. What do you think?

Fiscal Policy in Action during an Economic Crisis

During much of the early 2000s, the U.S. federal government followed the basic economic principles of free markets. By 2008, however, the economy was facing a dire economic crisis and the government spent more than $1 trillion of taxpayer money in an effort to revive the failing economy (including helping out banks, the auto industry, and others). ($1 trillion is about $3,272 per person in the United States.) The government was then following the basic economic theory of John Maynard Keynes. **Keynesian economic theory** is the theory that a government policy of increasing spending could stimulate the economy in a recession. The Federal Reserve has continued to pump trillions of dollars into the economy over the last few years. Recently, the Fed cut back on dollar generation from $85 billion to $65 billion per month. What do you expect the result of that cut will be?

The financial crisis beginning in 2008 caused much anguish among Wall Street workers and people in general. How effective was the government's response?

Using Monetary Policy to Keep the Economy Growing

Have you ever wondered what organization adds money to or subtracts money from the economy? As noted above, the answer is the Federal Reserve Bank (the Fed). The Fed is a semiprivate organization that is not under the direct control of the government but does have members appointed by the president. We will discuss the Fed in detail when we look at banking in Chapter 20. Now we simply introduce monetary policy and the role of the Fed in controlling the economy. **Monetary policy** is the management of the money supply and interest rates by the Federal Reserve Bank. The Fed's most visible role is the raising and lowering of interest rates. When the economy is booming, the Fed tends to raise interest rates. This makes money more expensive to borrow. Businesses thus borrow less, and the economy slows as businesspeople spend less money on everything they need to grow, including labor and machinery. The opposite is true when the Fed lowers interest rates. Businesses tend to borrow more, and the economy is expected to grow. Raising and lowering interest rates should help control the rapid ups and downs of the economy. In 2010–2014, the Fed kept interest rates near zero, but the economy remained sluggish. You can imagine the pressure that puts on Janet Yellen, the new head of the Federal Reserve. Again, we shall discuss her later in the text.

The Fed also controls the money supply. A simple explanation of this function is that the more money the Fed makes available to businesspeople and others, the faster the economy is supposed to grow. To slow the economy (and prevent inflation), the Fed lowers the money supply. The Fed poured money into the economy in 2008–2014. What would you expect the result to be?

To sum up, there are two major tools for managing the economy of the United States: fiscal policy (government taxes and spending) and monetary policy (the Fed's control over interest rates and the money supply). The goal is to keep the economy growing so that more people can rise up the economic ladder and enjoy a higher standard of living and quality of life.

Keynesian economic theory
The theory that a government policy of increasing spending could stimulate the economy in a recession.

monetary policy
The management of the money supply and interest rates by the Federal Reserve.

test prep

- Name the three economic indicators and describe how well the United States is doing based on each indicator.
- What's the difference between a recession and a depression?
- How does the government manage the economy using fiscal policy?
- What does the term *monetary policy* mean? What organization is responsible for monetary policy?

Summary

LO 1–1   Explain basic economics.

- **What is economics?**
  Economics is the study of how society chooses to employ resources to produce goods and services and distribute them for consumption among various competing groups and individuals.

- **What are the two branches of economics?**
  There are two major branches of economics: macroeconomics studies the operation of a nation's economy as a whole, and microeconomics studies the behavior of people and organizations in particular markets (e.g., why people buy smaller cars when gas prices go up).

- **How can we be assured of having enough resources?**
  Resource development is the study of how to increase resources and create the conditions that will make better use of them.

- **How does capitalism create a climate for economic growth?**
  Under capitalism, businesspeople don't often deliberately set out to help others; they work mostly for their own prosperity and growth. Yet people's efforts to improve their own situation in life act like an *invisible hand* to help the economy grow and prosper through the production of needed goods, services, and ideas.

LO 1–2   Explain what capitalism is and how free markets work.

- **What is capitalism?**
  Capitalism is an economic system in which all or most of the means of production and distribution are privately owned and operated for profit.

- **Who decides what to produce under capitalism?**
  In capitalist countries, businesspeople decide what to produce, how much to pay workers, and how much to charge for goods and services. They also decide whether to produce certain goods in their own countries, import those goods, or have them made in other countries.

- **What is state capitalism?**
  State capitalism is a combination of freer markets and some government control.

- **What are the basic rights people have under capitalism?**
  The four basic rights under capitalism are (1) the right to own private property, (2) the right to own a business and to keep all of that business's

profits after taxes, (3) the right to freedom of competition, and (4) the right to freedom of choice. President Franklin D. Roosevelt felt that other freedoms were also important: the right to freedom of speech and expression, the right to worship in your own way, and freedom from want and fear.

- **How does the free market work?**
The free market is one in which buyers and sellers negotiating prices for goods and services influence the decisions about what gets produced and in what quantities. Buyers' decisions in the marketplace tell sellers what to produce and in what quantity. When buyers demand more goods, the price goes up, signaling suppliers to produce more. The higher the price, the more goods and services suppliers are willing to produce. Price is the mechanism that allows free markets to work.

LO 1–3   Compare socialism and communism.

- **What is socialism?**
Socialism is an economic system based on the premise that some businesses should be owned by the government.

- **What are the advantages and disadvantages of socialism?**
Socialism intends to create more social equity. Workers in socialist countries usually receive more education, health care, and other benefits and also work fewer hours, with longer vacations. The major disadvantage of socialism is that it lowers the incentive to start a business or to work hard. Socialist economies tend to have a higher unemployment rate and a slower growth rate than capitalist economies.

- **How does socialism differ from communism?**
Under communism, the government owns almost all major production facilities and dictates what gets produced and by whom. Communism is also more restrictive when it comes to personal freedoms, such as religious freedom.

LO 1–4   Analyze the trend toward mixed economies.

- **What is a mixed economy?**
A mixed economy is part capitalist and part socialist. Some businesses are privately owned, but taxes tend to be high to distribute income more evenly among the population.

- **What countries have mixed economies?**
The United States has a mixed economy, as do most other industrialized countries.

- **What are the benefits of mixed economies?**
A mixed economy has most of the benefits of wealth creation that free markets bring plus the benefits of greater social equality and concern for the environment that socialism promises.

LO 1–5   Describe the economic system of the United States, including the significance of key economic indicators (especially GDP), productivity, and the business cycle.

- **What are the key economic indicators in the United States?**
Gross domestic product (GDP) is the total value of final goods and services produced in a country in a given year. The *unemployment rate* refers to the percentage of civilians at least 16 years old who are unemployed and tried

to find a job within the most recent four weeks. The *consumer price index (CPI)* measures changes in the prices of about 400 goods and services that consumers buy.

- **What is gross output?**
  Gross output (GO) is a measure of total sales volume at all stages of production.

- **What are the four phases of business cycles?**
  In an *economic boom*, businesses do well. A *recession* occurs when two or more quarters show declines in the GDP, prices fall, people purchase fewer products, and businesses fail. A *depression* is a severe recession. *Recovery* occurs when the economy stabilizes and starts to grow.

LO 1–6   Contrast fiscal policy and monetary policy, and explain how each affects the economy.

- **What is fiscal policy?**
  Fiscal policy consists of government efforts to keep the economy stable by increasing or decreasing taxes or government spending.

- **What is the importance of monetary policy to the economy?**
  Monetary policy is the management of the money supply and interest rates. When unemployment gets too high, the Federal Reserve Bank (the Fed) may put more money into the economy and lower interest rates. That is supposed to provide a boost to the economy as businesses borrow and spend more money and hire more people.

Access your instructor's Connect course to check out LearnSmart or go to learnsmartadvantage.com for help.

connect

key terms

critical thinking

The U.S. Supreme Court ruled that cities could have school voucher programs that give money directly to parents, who could then choose among competing schools, public or private. The idea was to create competition among schools. Like businesses, schools were expected to improve their services (how effectively they teach) to win students from competitors. The result would be improvement in all schools, private and public, to benefit many students.

1. Do you believe economic principles, like competition, apply in both private and public organizations? Be prepared to defend your answer.

2. Are there other public functions that might benefit from more competition, including competition from private firms?

3. Many people say that businesspeople do not do enough for society. Some students choose to go into the public sector instead of business because they want to help others. However, businesspeople say that they do more to help others than nonprofit groups do because they provide jobs for people rather than giving them charity. Furthermore, they believe businesses create all the wealth that nonprofit groups distribute.

   a. How can you find some middle ground in this debate to show that both businesspeople and those who work for nonprofit organizations contribute to society and need to work together more closely to help people?

   b. How could you use the concepts of Adam Smith to help illustrate your position?

developing **workplace skills**

Key: ● **Team**   ★ **Analytic**   ▲ **Communication**   ▣ **Technology**

1. In teams, develop a list of the advantages of living in a capitalist society. Then develop lists headed "What are the disadvantages?" and "How could such disadvantages be minimized?" Describe why a poor person in a socialist country might reject capitalism and prefer a socialist state.   ●▲★

2. Show your understanding of the principles of supply and demand by looking at the oil market today. Go online and search for a chart of oil prices for the last few years. Why does the price of oil fluctuate so greatly? What will happen as more and more people in China and India decide to buy automobiles? What would happen if most U.S consumers decided to drive electric cars?   ▣★

3. This exercise will help you understand socialism from different perspectives. Form three groups. Each group should adopt a different role in a socialist economy: one group will be the business owners, another group will be workers, and another will be government leaders. Within your group discuss and list the advantages and disadvantages to you of lowering taxes on businesses. Then have each group choose a representative to go to the front of the class and debate the tax issue with the representatives from the other groups.   ●▲★

4. Draw a line and mark one end "Free-Market Capitalism" and the other end "Central Planning." Mark where on the line the United States is now. Explain why you marked the spot you chose. Students from other countries may want to do this exercise for their own countries and explain the differences to the class.   ▲★

5. Break into small groups. In your group discuss how the following changes have affected people's purchasing behavior and attitudes toward the United States and its economy: the wars in Iraq and Afghanistan, the increased amount spent on homeland security, the government involvement in banking and other industries, and the growth of the Internet. Have a group member prepare a short summary for the class.   ●▲★

taking it to the **net**

PURPOSE

To familiarize you with the sources of economic information that are important to business decision makers.

EXERCISE

Imagine that your boss asked you to help her to prepare the company's sales forecast for the coming two years. In the past, she felt that trends in the nation's GDP, U.S. manufacturing, and manufacturing in Illinois were especially helpful in forecasting sales. She would like you to do the following:

1. Go to the Bureau of Economic Analysis's website (www.bea.gov) and locate the gross domestic product data. Compare the annual figure for the last four years. What do the figures indicate for the next couple of years?

2. At the Bureau of Labor Statistics' website (www.bls.gov) under Industries, click on Industries at a Glance to find the information about the manufacturing industry. What is the employment trend in manufacturing over the last four years (percentage change from preceding period)?

3. Return to the Bureau of Labor Statistics' home page and use the Search feature to find trends in employment for the state of Illinois. Look around the website to see what other information is available. Plot the trend in manufacturing employment in Illinois over the last four years. On your own, discuss what economic changes may have influenced that trend.

4. Based on the information you have gathered, write a brief summary of what may happen to company sales over the next couple of years.

video case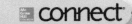

OPPORTUNITY INTERNATIONAL: GIVING THE POOR A WORKING CHANCE

Billions of people in the world make $2 a day or less. In fact, a billion people make less than $1 a day. In such places, a loan of $100 or $200 makes a huge difference. That's where microloans from organizations such as Opportunity International come in.

Opportunity International is an organization that grants microloans to people, mostly women, in developing countries so they can invest in a business. Those investments often lead to community growth and employment, and help the owners themselves to prosper on a moderate scale. The borrowers must pay back the money with interest—when they do, they can borrow more and keep growing. Opportunity International, unlike some other microlending organizations, also provides a banking function where entrepreneurs can safely

put their money. They can also buy some insurance to protect themselves against loss.

Opportunity International helps over a million people in over 28 countries, giving them the opportunity to change their lives for the better. This video introduces you to some of those people, but primarily explains how freedom and a little money can combine to create huge differences in people's lives.

Adam Smith was one of the first people to point out that wealth comes from freedom, the ability to own land, and the ability to keep the profits from what you do on that land. When people try to maximize profits, they have to hire other people to help them do the work. This provides jobs for others and wealth for the entrepreneur. And, like an invisible hand, the whole community benefits from the entrepreneurs' desire to earn a profit. In the video, you can see a woman in Uganda who has applied those principles to benefit her family, provide employment, and help her community.

Free-market capitalism is the system where people can own their own land and businesses and keep the profits they earn. Such a system demands that people can (1) own their own property (not a reality in many developing nations); (2) keep the profits from any business they start; (3) compete with other businesses (it is difficult to compete with the government); and (4) work wherever and whenever they want. The key word in capitalism is *freedom*—freedom of religion, freedom to own land, and freedom to prosper and grow. Opportunity International is making an attempt to show people how freedom plus a few dollars can make a huge difference in an economy.

In a free-market economy, price is determined by buyers and sellers negotiating over the price of a good or service. The equilibrium point is the place where buyers and sellers agree to an exchange; it is also called the market price. Without free markets, there is no way of knowing what buyers need and what sellers need to produce. Thus, in command economies, where there is no supply-and-demand mechanism in operation, there can be shortages or surpluses in food, clothing, and other necessities.

Socialism and communism are alternatives to a free-market economy. Under such systems, people are more likely to have a bit of equality, but there are fewer incentives to work hard, and entrepreneurs are often lured to countries where they can make more money by working harder. The result is called a brain drain, where the best and the brightest often move to free-market countries. There are advantages to socialism and communism, such as free schools, free health care, free day care, etc. But the taxes are higher, and there is usually less innovation and higher unemployment.

The trend in the world is toward mixed economies, where most of the economy is based on free-market principles, but the government gets involved in things such as education, health care, and welfare. The United States has been basically a free-market economy, but it is clear that there is a movement toward more government involvement. On the other hand, some countries are reducing the role of government in society and moving toward freer markets. Thus the world is moving toward mixed economies.

The United States government tries to control the money supply through the Federal Reserve and fiscal policy. Fiscal policy has to do with taxes and spending. The less the government spends, the more that is available for businesses to invest. And the lower the tax rates on entrepreneurs, the more they will invest in businesses and the faster the economy will grow.

Opportunity International shows the poorest of the poor how important entrepreneurs, freedom, opportunity, and a little bit of money are to economic growth and prosperity. You are encouraged in this video to participate in helping poor people around the world. You can do this by contributing time and money to organizations like Opportunity International. You can join the Peace Corps or other groups designed to assist less-developed countries.

THINKING IT OVER

1. Why is there a need for organizations like Opportunity International? Can't poor people get loans from banks and other sources?

2. Identify the four major requirements necessary for a free-market system to operate.

3. What is the main difference between capitalism and a mixed economy? Which model is used in the United States?

notes

1. Terry Miller, "America's Dwindling Economic Freedom," *The Wall Street Journal*, January 14, 2014.
2. Randall Stephenson, "A Business Short List for Growth," *The Wall Street Journal*, January 15, 2014.
3. Romain Hatchuel, "The Coming Global Wealth Tax," *The Wall Street Journal*, December 4, 2013.
4. Roger Lowenstein, "Macro Master," *The Wall Street Journal*, January 18–19, 2014.
5. Janet Hook and Kristina Peterson, "Congress Passes a Debt Bill," *The Wall Street Journal*, October 13, 2013.
6. Robert J. Samuelson, "Macroeconomics Loses Its Magic," *The Washington Post*, April 22, 2013.
7. Nidaa Bakhsh, "Shale Goes Global," *Bloomberg Businessweek*, November 18, 2013–January 2, 2014.
8. Nicholas Eberstadt, "China's Coming One-Child Crisis," *The Wall Street Journal*, November 27, 2013.
9. Charles Kenny, "The Reproductive Recession," *Bloomberg Businessweek*, February 11–February 17, 2013.
10. Stephenson, "A Business Short List for Growth."
11. Ed Feulner, "The Slow Fade of Economic Freedom," *The Washington Times*, January 14, 2014.
12. Donald Lambro, "Dickensian Poverty in 2013," *The Washington Times*, December 25, 2013.
13. Charles Lane, "The Politics of Inequality," *The Washington Post*, December 10, 2013.

14. "The Philanthropic," special feature, *Forbes,* December 2, 2013.
15. Steve Matthews, "For Many, the Age of Entrepreneurship Starts at 55," *The Washington Post,* January 12, 2014.
16. John Mackey and Raj Sisodia, *Conscious Capitalism* (Boston, MA: Harvard Business Review Press, 2013).
17. Ibid., p. 11.
18. "What Kind of Capitalism?" editorial, *The Economist,* October 12, 2013.
19. Charles Wolf Jr., "A Truly Great Leap Forward: How China Became Capitalist," *The Wall Street Journal,* May 1, 2013.
20. Peter Coy, "The Sting of Long-Term Unemployment," *Bloomberg Businessweek,* February 11–February 17, 2013.
21. Romain Hatchuel, "What's French for Economic Nonsense?" *The Wall Street Journal,* March 29, 2013.
22. Samuel Rines, "Monthly Economic Data Aren't Reliable," *The Wall Street Journal,* June 28, 2013.
23. Mark Skousen, "A New Way to Measure the Economy," *Forbes,* December 16, 2013.
24. John Cassidy, "Meet the 'Missing Millions' Who've Vanished from the Economy," *Fortune,* April 8, 2013.
25. Peter Coy, "The Sting of Long-Term Unemployment," *Bloomberg Businessweek,* February 11–February 17, 2013.
26. Richard Vedder, "The Wages of Unemployment," *The Wall Street Journal,* January 16, 2013; Brenda Cronin, "Jobless Benefits Set to Expire," *The Wall Street Journal,* December 28–29, 2013; and Arthur Laffer, "Work Disincentives, Still Crazy after All These Years," *The Wall Street Journal,* February 9–10, 2013.
27. "The Latest Jobs Miss," editorial, *The Wall Street Journal,* January 11–12, 2014.
28. Brenda Cronin and Jonathan House, "Hiring Slowdown Blurs Growth View," *The Wall Street Journal,* January 11–12, 2014.
29. www.thefreedictionary.com, accessed September 2014.
30. Gene Epstein, "More Disinflation Lies Ahead," *Barron's,* January 20, 2014.
31. Paul Hannon, "Economist Warns Europe on Deflation," *The Wall Street Journal,* January 18–19, 2014.
32. "Does More Work Lead to a Healthier Economy?" HBR Reprint, *Harvard Business Review,* December 2013.

photo credits

Chapter 2

Strategic Leadership: Managing the Strategy Process

Learning Objectives

After studying this chapter, you should be able to:

LO 2-1   Describe the roles of vision, mission, and values in the strategic management process.

LO 2-2   Evaluate the strategic implications of product-oriented and customer-oriented vision statements.

LO 2-3   Explain why anchoring a firm in ethical values is essential for long-term success.

LO 2-4   Outline how managers become strategic leaders.

LO 2-5   Describe the roles of corporate, business, and functional managers in strategy formulation and implementation.

LO 2-6   Evaluate top-down strategic planning, scenario planning, and strategy as planned emergence.

CHAPTER**CASE 2**

PepsiCo's Indra Nooyi: "Performance with a Purpose"

AS CHIEF EXECUTIVE Officer (CEO) of PepsiCo, Indra Nooyi is one of the world's most powerful business leaders. A native of Chennai, India, Ms. Nooyi holds multiple degrees: a bachelor's degree in physics, chemistry, and mathematics from Madras Christian College, an MBA from the Indian Institute of Management, and a master's degree from Yale University. Prior to joining PepsiCo in 1994, Ms. Nooyi worked for Johnson & Johnson, Boston Consulting Group, Motorola, and ABB. Ms. Nooyi is not your typical Fortune 500 CEO, though: She is well known for walking around the office barefoot and singing—a remnant from her lead role in an all-girls rock band in high school.

It should come as no surprise, therefore, that Ms. Nooyi has been shaking things up at PepsiCo, a company with roughly $70 billion in annual revenues and some 300,000 employees worldwide. She took the lead role in spinning off Taco Bell, Pizza Hut, and KFC in 1997. Later, she masterminded the acquisitions of Tropicana in 1998 and Quaker Oats (including Gatorade) in 2001. As CEO, Ms. Nooyi declared PepsiCo's vision to be "Performance with a Purpose," as defined by three dimensions:

1. *Human sustainability.* PepsiCo's strategic intent is to make its product portfolio healthier to combat obesity. It wants to reduce the salt and fat in its "fun foods" such as Frito-Lay and Doritos, and to include healthy choices such as Quaker Oats products and Tropicana fruit juices in its lineup. Ms. Nooyi is convinced that if food and beverage companies do not make their products healthier, they will face stricter regulation and lawsuits, as tobacco companies did. Ms. Nooyi's goal is to increase PepsiCo's revenues for nutritious foods from $10 billion today to $30 billion by 2020.

2. *Environmental sustainability.* PepsiCo has instituted various initiatives to ensure that its operations don't harm the natural environment. The company has programs in place to reduce water and energy use, increase recycling, and promote sustainable agriculture. The goal is to transform PepsiCo into a company with a net-zero impact on the environment. Ms. Nooyi believes that young people today will not patronize a company that does not have a strategy that also addresses ecological sustainability.

3. *The whole person at work.* PepsiCo wants to create a corporate culture in which employees do not "just make a living, but also have a life." Ms. Nooyi argues that this type of culture allows employees to unleash both their mental and emotional energies.

PepsiCo's vision of performance with a purpose acknowledges the importance of corporate social responsibility and stakeholder strategy. Ms. Nooyi is convinced that companies have a duty to society to "do better by doing better." She subscribes to a triple-bottom-line approach to competitive advantage, which considers not only economic but also social and environmental performance. Ms. Nooyi declares that the true profits of an enterprise are not just "revenues *minus* costs" but "revenues *minus* costs *minus* costs to society." Problems such as pollution or the increased cost of health care to combat obesity impose costs on society (externalities) that companies typically do not bear. As Indra Nooyi sees it, the time when corporations can just pass on their externalities to society is nearing an end.[1]

After reading this chapter, you will find more about this case, along with related questions, on page 48.

HOW DO STRATEGIC LEADERS like Indra Nooyi develop and implement a vision for their company to achieve strategic goals? How do they use vision, mission, and values to guide and motivate employees? In Chapter 2, we move from thinking about why strategy is important to considering how firms and other organizations define their vision, mission, and values, and how strategic leaders manage the strategy process.

An effective strategy process can lay the foundation on which to build a sustainable competitive advantage. The first step in the strategy process is to define an organization's vision, mission, and values. With those guiding principles in place, we then consider how strategic leaders formulate strategy across different levels: corporate, business, and functional. Next, we introduce three complementary frameworks of the strategy-creation process: strategic planning, scenario planning, and strategy as planned emergence. Finally, we conclude with practical *Implications for the Strategist.*

2.1 Vision, Mission, and Values

LO 2-1

Describe the roles of vision, mission, and values in the strategic management process.

The first steps in the strategic management process are to define a firm's vision, mission, and values. An effective **strategic management process** is the method put in place by strategic leaders to conceive and implement a strategy. It can lay the foundation for a sustainable competitive advantage. **Strategic leadership** pertains to executives' use of power and influence to direct the activities of others when pursuing an organization's goals.[2] As described in ChapterCase 2, Indra Nooyi is demonstrating strategic leadership when defining goals and putting systems, structures, and incentives in place to achieve the vision of "performance with a purpose."

To begin the strategic management process, strategic leaders ask the following questions:

- What do we want to accomplish ultimately? What is our *vision?*
- How do we accomplish our goals? What is our *mission?*
- What guardrails do we put in place to act ethically and legally as we pursue our vision and mission? What are our *values?*

VISION AND MISSION

To answer questions about vision, mission, and values, strategic leaders *need to* begin with the end in mind. Think of building a house. The future owner must communicate her vision to the architect, who draws up a blueprint of the home. The process is iterated a couple of times until all the homeowner's ideas have been translated into the blueprint. Only then does the building of the house begin. The same holds for strategic success. Indra Nooyi has a clear picture in mind of what PepsiCo will look like in the future:

> *Performance with a purpose means delivering sustainable growth by investing in a healthier future for people and our planet. . . . We will continue to build a portfolio of enjoyable and healthier foods and beverages, find innovative ways to reduce the use of energy, water and packaging, and provide a great workplace for our associates. . . . Because a healthier future for all people and our planet means a more successful future for PepsiCo. This is our promise.[3]*

Such a statement about what an organization ultimately wants to accomplish is its **vision.** It captures the company's aspiration. An effective vision pervades the organization with a sense of winning and motivates employees at all levels to aim for the same target, while leaving room for individual and team contributions. Employees in visionary companies tend to feel like part of something bigger than themselves. An inspiring vision helps employees find meaning in their work, beyond monetary rewards. It allows employees to experience a greater sense of purpose and taps into people's intrinsic motivations to make the world a better place through their work activities.[4] This greater individual purpose can in turn lead to higher organizational performance.[5] Basing actions on its vision, a firm will build the necessary resources and capabilities through continuous organizational learning, including learning from failure, to translate into reality what begins as a stretch goal.[6]

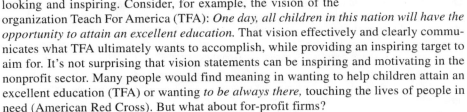

To provide meaning for employees in pursuit of the organization's ultimate goals, vision statements should be forward-looking and inspiring. Consider, for example, the vision of the organization Teach For America (TFA): *One day, all children in this nation will have the opportunity to attain an excellent education.* That vision effectively and clearly communicates what TFA ultimately wants to accomplish, while providing an inspiring target to aim for. It's not surprising that vision statements can be inspiring and motivating in the nonprofit sector. Many people would find meaning in wanting to help children attain an excellent education (TFA) or wanting *to be always there,* touching the lives of people in need (American Red Cross). But what about for-profit firms?

The main difference in the visions of for-profit firms is the metric by which the organization assesses successful performance. TFA measures its organizational success by the impact its teachers have on student performance. In the for-profit sector, many companies measure success primarily by financial performance. Other visionary companies, including 3M, General Electric, Merck, Nordstrom, Procter & Gamble (P&G), and Walmart, provide more aspirational ideas that are not exclusively financial.[7] Visionary companies often are able not only to gain a competitive advantage, but also to outperform their competitors over the long run. Tracking the stock market performance of companies over many decades, strategy scholars found that these visionary companies outperformed their peers by a wide margin. This goes to show that a truly meaningful and inspiring vision makes employees feel they are part of something bigger. In turn, this is highly motivating and can improve financial performance.

Building on the vision, organizations establish a **mission,** which describes what an organization actually does—that is, the products and services it plans to provide, and the markets in which it will compete. Although the terms *vision* and *mission* are often used interchangeably, they are different: Vision defines what an organization wants to accomplish ultimately, and thus the goal can be described by the verb "*to.*" For instance, TFA's vision is *to attain an excellent education for all children.* In contrast, mission describes what an organization does; it defines the means "*by*" which vision is accomplished. Accordingly, TFA's mission is achieved *by enlisting our nation's most promising future leaders in the effort (we will be able to attain an excellent education for all children).* Exhibit 2.1 presents TFA's vision, mission, and values. (See MiniCase 4 for a detailed discussion on how Teach For America inspires future leaders.)

---

strategic management process Method put in place by strategic leaders to conceive and implement a strategy, which can lay the foundation for a sustainable competitive advantage.

strategic leadership Executives' use of power and influence to direct the activities of others when pursuing an organization's goals.

vision A statement about what an organization ultimately wants to accomplish; it captures the company's aspiration.

mission Description of what an organization actually does—the products and services it plans to provide, and the markets in which it will compete.

EXHIBIT 2.1 / Teach For America: Vision, Mission, and Values

VISION	One day, all children in this nation will have the opportunity to attain an excellent education.
MISSION	Teach For America is growing the movement of leaders who work to ensure that kids growing up in poverty get an excellent education.
CORE VALUES	**Transformational Change:** We seek to expand educational opportunity in ways that are life-changing for children and transforming for our country. Given our deep belief in children and communities, the magnitude of educational inequity and its consequences, and our optimism about the solvability of the problem, we act with high standards, urgency, and a long-term view.
	Leadership: We strive to develop and become the leaders necessary to realize educational excellence and equity. We establish bold visions and invest others in working towards them. We work in purposeful, strategic, and resourceful ways, define broadly what is within our control to solve, and learn and improve constantly. We operate with a sense of possibility, persevere in the face of challenges, ensure alignment between our actions and beliefs, and assume personal responsibility for results.
	Team: We value and care about each other, operate with a generosity of spirit, and have fun in the process of working together. To maximize our collective impact, we inspire, challenge, and support each other to be our best and sustain our effort.
	Diversity: We act on our belief that the movement to ensure educational equity will succeed only if it is diverse in every respect. In particular, we value the perspective and credibility that individuals who share the racial and economic backgrounds of the students with whom we work can bring to our organization, classrooms, and the long-term effort for change.
	Respect & Humility: We value the strengths, experiences, and perspectives of others, and we recognize our own limitations. We are committed to partnering effectively with families, schools, and communities to ensure that our work advances the broader good for all children.

SOURCE: www.teachforamerica.org.

strategic commitments
Actions that are costly, long-term–oriented, and difficult to reverse.

To be effective, firms need to back up their visions and missions with **strategic commitments,** actions that are costly, long-term–oriented, and difficult to reverse.[8] For instance, the vision of EADS, the parent company of Airbus, is *to be the world's leading aerospace company.* Airbus translates this ultimate goal into its mission *by manufacturing the world's best aircraft, with passengers at heart and airlines in mind.* Airbus spent 10 years and $15 billion to develop the A380 super jumbo, which can accommodate over 850 passengers and fly almost 10,000 miles (a sufficient range to fly non-stop from New York to Singapore). The company's vision is backed up by a powerful strategic commitment. Without such commitments, a firm's vision and mission statements are just words. However noble the mission statement, companies will not achieve competitive advantage without strategic actions to back it up.

So, we must ask, do vision statements help firms gain and sustain competitive advantage? The effectiveness of vision statements differs based on whether they are *customer-oriented* or *product-oriented.* Customer-oriented vision statements allow companies to adapt to changing environments, while product-oriented vision statements often do not. Given that our environments are ever-changing, increased strategic flexibility is often a necessary condition to achieve competitive advantage.[9] Let's look at both types of vision statements.

LO 2-2

Evaluate the strategic implications of product-oriented and customer-oriented vision statements.

PRODUCT-ORIENTED VISION STATEMENTS. A product-oriented vision defines a business in terms of a good or service provided. Product-oriented visions tend to force managers to take a more myopic view of the competitive landscape. As an example, let's consider the strategic decisions of U.S. railroad companies. Railroads are in the business of moving goods and people from point A to point B by rail. When they started, their short-distance competition was the horse or horse-drawn carriage. There was little long-distance competition (e.g., ship canals and good roads) to cover the U.S. from coast to coast. Due to their monopoly, especially in long-distance travel, these companies were initially extremely profitable. Not surprisingly, the early U.S. railroad companies saw their vision as being in the railroad business, clearly a product-based definition.

However, the railroad companies' monopoly did not last, as technological innovations changed the transportation business dramatically. After the introduction of the automobile and the commercial jet, consumers had a wider range of choices to meet their long-distance transportation needs. Rail companies were slow to respond; they did not redefine their business in terms of services provided to the consumer. Had they envisioned themselves as serving the full range of transportation needs of people across America (a customer-oriented vision), they might have become successful forerunners of modern logistics companies like FedEx or UPS.

Recently, the railroad companies seem to be learning some lessons: CSX Railroad is now redefining itself as a green-transportation alternative. It claims it can move one ton of freight 423 miles on one gallon of fuel. However, its vision remains product-oriented: *to be the safest, most progressive North American railroad.*

CUSTOMER-ORIENTED VISION STATEMENTS. *A customer-oriented vision* defines a business in terms of providing solutions to customer needs. For example, "We are in the business of providing solutions to professional communication needs." Companies that have customer-oriented visions tend to be more flexible when adapting to changing environments. In contrast, companies that define themselves based on product-oriented statements (e.g., "We are in the typewriter business") tend to be less flexible and thus more likely to fail. The lack of an inspiring need-based vision can cause the long-range problem of failing to adapt to a changing environment.

It is important not to confuse customer-oriented vision statements with listening to your customer. They are not the same thing. Customer-oriented visions identify a critical need but leave open the means of how to meet that need. It is critical not to define *how* a customer need will be met. The future is unknowable, and innovation may provide new ways to meet needs that we cannot fathom today. Even if customer needs are unchanging, the *means* of meeting those needs can certainly change over time. An organization's vision should be flexible, to allow for change and adaptation.

Think about the customer need for personal mobility. A little over 100 years ago, this need was met by horse-drawn buggies, horseback riding, or by trains for long distances. But Henry Ford had a different idea. In fact, he is famous for saying, "If I had listened to my customers, I would have built a better horse and buggy."[10] Instead, Henry Ford's original vision was *to make the automobile accessible to every American.* He succeeded, and the automobile dramatically changed how mobility was achieved.

Fast-forward to today: Ford Motor Company's vision is *to provide personal mobility for people around the world.* Note that it does not even mention the automobile. By focusing on the consumer need for personal mobility, Ford is leaving the door open for exactly how it will fulfill that need. Today, it's mostly with traditional cars and trucks propelled by gas-powered internal combustion engines, with some hybrid electric vehicles in its lineup. In the near future, Ford is likely to provide vehicles powered by alternative energy sources such as electric power or hydrogen. In the far-reaching future, perhaps Ford will get into the business of individual flying devices. Throughout all of this, its vision would still be relevant and compel its managers to engage in future markets. In contrast, a product-oriented vision would have greatly constrained Ford's degree of strategic flexibility.

Sometimes, effective vision statements work through metaphors (implied comparisons). Metaphors can help employees make appropriate decisions when faced with day-to-day situations that can sometimes be novel or stressful. Let's look at Disney's customer-oriented vision—*to make people happy.*[11] Disney translates this vision through the metaphor that its theme parks are like stage performances. Employees are not simply employees, but cast members of a

EXHIBIT 2.2

Companies with
Customer-Oriented
Vision Statements

Amazon: To be earth's most customer centric company; to build a place where people can come to find and discover anything they might want to buy online.

eBay: To provide a global trading platform where practically anyone can trade practically anything.

GE: To turn imaginative ideas into leading products and services that help solve some of the world's toughest problems.

Google: To organize the world's information and make it universally accessible and useful.

IBM: To be the best service organization in the world.

Microsoft: To enable people and businesses throughout the world to realize their full potential.

Nike: To bring inspiration and innovation to every athlete in the world.

Walmart: To give ordinary folk the chance to buy the same thing as rich people.

show. Similarly, visitors to the park are not customers, but audience members. Disney's metaphor has implications for employee behavior. Rather than interviewing for a job, for instance, candidates audition for a role. Any time a Disney park employee is in uniform, he or she is "on stage," delivering a performance. Even street sweepers (often college students on break) are part of the cast. Because they have the closest contact with guests, street sweepers are trained in great detail. They are evaluated not only on street-sweeping performance, but also on their knowledge about rides, parades, and restaurant and restroom locations. Like cast members in a theater company, Disney employees pull off daily performances with a "the show must go on" attitude that allows them to fulfill Disney's vision to make people happy. Exhibit 2.2 provides additional examples of companies with customer-oriented vision statements.

MOVING FROM PRODUCT-ORIENTED TO CUSTOMER-ORIENTED VISION STATEMENTS. In some cases, product-oriented vision statements do not interfere with the firm's success in achieving superior performance and competitive advantage. Consider Intel Corporation, one of the world's leading silicon innovators. Intel's early vision was *to be the preeminent building-block supplier of the PC industry.* Intel designed the first commercial microprocessor chip in 1971 and set the standard for microprocessors in 1978. During the personal computer (PC) revolution in the 1980s, microprocessors became Intel's main line of business. Intel's customers were original equipment manufacturers that produced consumer end-products, such as computer manufacturers HP, IBM, Dell, and Compaq.

In the Internet age, though, the standalone PC as the end-product has become less important. Customers want to stream video and share photos online. These activities consume a tremendous amount of computing power. To reflect this shift, Intel in 1999 changed its vision to focus on being *the preeminent building-block supplier to the Internet economy.* Although its product-oriented vision statements did not impede performance or competitive advantage, in 2008 Intel fully made the shift to a customer-oriented vision: to *delight our customers, employees, and shareholders by relentlessly delivering the platform and technology advancements that become essential to the way we work and live.* Part of this shift was reflected by the hugely successful "Intel Inside" advertising campaign in the 1990s that made Intel a household name worldwide.

Intel accomplished superior firm performance over decades through continuous adaptations to changing market realities. Its formal vision statement lagged behind the firm's strategic transformations. Intel regularly changed its vision statement *after* it had accomplished each successful transformation.[12] In such a case, vision statements and firm performance are clearly not related to one another.

Taken together, empirical research shows that sometimes vision statements and firm performance are *associated* with one another. A positive relationship between vision statements and firm performance is more likely to exist under certain circumstances: if the visions are customer-oriented; if internal stakeholders are invested in defining and revising the visions; and if organizational structures such as compensation systems are aligned with the firm's vision statement.[13] The upshot is that an effective vision statement can lay the foundation upon which to craft a strategy that creates competitive advantage.

LIVING THE VALUES

Organizational values are the ethical standards and norms that govern the behavior of individuals within a firm or organization. Strong ethical values have two important functions. First, they form a solid foundation on which a firm can build its vision and mission, and thus lay the groundwork for long-term success. Second, values serve as the guardrails put in place to keep the company on track when pursuing its vision and mission in its quest for competitive advantage.

The values espoused by a company provide answers to the question, *how do we accomplish our goals?* They help individuals make choices that are both ethical and effective in advancing the company's goals. As discussed in Strategy Highlight 2.1 (next page), the pharmaceutical company Merck provides an example of how values can drive strategic decision making, and what can happen if a company deviates from its core values.

There's one last point to make about organizational values. Without commitment and involvement from top managers, any statement of values remains merely a public relations exercise. Employees tend to follow values practiced by strategic leaders. They observe the day-to-day decisions of top managers and quickly decide whether managers are merely paying lip service to the company's stated values. True values must be lived with integrity, especially by the top management team. Unethical behavior by top managers is like a virus that spreads quickly throughout an entire organization. It is imperative that strategic leaders set an example of ethical behavior by living the values. Since strategic leaders have such a strong influence in setting an organization's vision, mission, and values, we next discuss strategic leadership.

> **LO 2-3**
>
> Explain why anchoring a firm in ethical values is essential for long-term success.
>
> **organizational values** Ethical standards and norms that govern the behavior of individuals within a firm or organization.

2.2 Strategic Leadership

Executives whose vision and actions enable their organizations to achieve competitive advantage demonstrate **strategic leadership**—the behaviors and styles of executives that influence others to achieve the organization's vision and mission.[14] Merck's then-CEO Raymond Gilmartin, for example, demonstrated strategic leadership in reconfirming the company's core value that patients come before profits by voluntarily withdrawing Vioxx from the market. Strategic leadership typically resides in executives who have overall profit-and-loss responsibility for an entire organization. These executives may be the CEO, or other members of the top-management team.

Although the effect of strategic leaders varies across industries and time, they do matter to firm performance.[15] Just think of great business founders and their impact on the organizations they built: Jack Ma at Alibaba, Jeff Bezos at Amazon, Robin Li at Baidu, Mark Zuckerberg at Facebook, Sergei Brin and Larry Page at Google, Bill Gates at Microsoft, Richard Branson at Virgin Group, and John Mackey at Whole Foods, among many others. There are also strategic leaders who have shaped and revitalized existing businesses: Allan Mulally at Ford, Chung Mong-Koo at Hyundai, Irene Rosenfelt at Kraft Foods, Sheryl Sandberg at Facebook, Don Thompson at McDonald's, Yun Jong-Yong at Samsung, Howard Schultz at Starbucks, Ratan Tata at the Tata Group, and Marissa Mayer at Yahoo.[16]

At the other end of the spectrum, unfortunately, are CEOs whose decisions have led to a massive destruction of shareholder value: Brian Dunn at Best Buy, Charles Prince at Citigroup, Richard Wagoner at GM, Robert Nardelli at The Home Depot (and later Chrysler), Ron Johnson at JCPenney, Richard Fuld at Lehman Brothers, Ed Zander at Motorola, and Gerald Levin at Time Warner.

> **LO 2-4**
>
> Outline how managers become strategic leaders.
>
> **strategic leadership** The behaviors and styles of executives that influence others to achieve the organization's vision and mission.

Strategy Highlight 2.1

Merck: Reconfirming Its Core Values

Merck's vision is *to preserve and improve human life.* The words of founder George W. Merck still form the basis of the company's values today: *We try to never forget that medicine is for the people. It is not for profits. The profits follow, and if we have remembered that, they have never failed to appear. The better we have remembered it, the larger they have been.*[17]

Guided by these ethical principles, Merck's strategic leaders decided to help end river blindness in Africa. For centuries, river blindness—a parasitic disease that leads to loss of eyesight—plagued remote communities in Africa and other parts of the world, with no cure. In 1987, Ray Vagelos, a former Merck scientist turned CEO, announced that the company would donate its recently discovered drug Mectizan, without charge, to treat river blindness. Merck's executives formed a novel private-public partnership called the Mectizan Donation Program (MDP), set up to distribute the drug in remote areas, where health services are often not available.

By 2012, Merck had donated more than one billion treatments to about 120,000 communities, primarily in Africa but also in Latin America and the Middle East. As a result, no new cases of river blindness have been reported, and the disease has effectively been eradicated. Merck's current CEO Kenneth Frazier summarizes the effect of the company's value-driven actions as follows: "We are humbled by the great work of the alliance of partners to protect future generations from a disease that carries devastating implications for people, families, healthcare systems and local economies."[18]

In the case of Vioxx, though, Merck's values were brought into question. Vioxx was a painkiller developed to produce fewer gastrointestinal side-effects than traditional products like aspirin or Advil. The Food and Drug Administration (FDA) approved the new drug in 1999 to treat rheumatoid arthritis and other acute pain conditions. Merck engaged in heavy direct-to-consumer advertising via TV ads and other media outlets. Moreover, it is common industry practice for pharma companies to induce doctors to heavily prescribe newly launched drugs by offering consulting contracts and other perks such as attending seminars at exotic resort destinations. Merck applied these industry practices when marketing Vioxx. Merck's new drug was a blockbuster, generating revenues of $2.5 billion a year by 2002 and growing fast.

Merck CEO Kenneth Frazier

Allegations began to appear, however, that Vioxx caused heart attacks and strokes. Critics alleged that Merck had suppressed evidence about Vioxx's dangerous side-effects from clinical trials before it was approved. Merck's CEO at the time, Raymond Gilmartin, described the situation:

> . . . a telephone call from our head of research started a chain of events that put to test the conviction in our core beliefs. He told me that our long-term safety study of Vioxx was showing an increased risk of cardiovascular events compared to placebo, and the trial was being discontinued. We agreed that whatever course of action we decided to take would be based on what we believed the science said about what was in the best interests of patients.
>
> After analyzing the data further and consulting with outside experts, the Merck scientists recommended that we voluntarily withdraw the drug. They said that it might be possible to go to the FDA, add warnings to the label, and keep Vioxx on the market, but they believed that the most responsible course of action in the interests of the patient was to voluntarily withdraw the drug. I, along with the rest of my management team and the board, agreed with the recommendation, and the drug was withdrawn.[19]

Reconfirming its core value that patients come before profits, Merck announced the voluntary withdrawal of Vioxx from the market. The September 30, 2004, recall had a dramatic impact on Merck's stock price and adversely affected the sales of Merck's other drugs. Shares fell 27 percent to $33, eradicating $27 billion in market value almost overnight. That loss in shareholder value was much greater than the estimated net present value of the profits that Merck would have obtained from continued sales of Vioxx. Merck has been burdened by lawsuits ever since, and legal liabilities have cost the company up to $30 billion thus far. Some corporate social responsibility experts argue that Merck should have never put Vioxx on the market in the first place, or that it should have at least provided up-front, clear assessments of the risks associated with Vioxx, including increased risks of heart attack and strokes.[20]

Why do some leaders create great companies or manage them to greatness, while others destroy them? To answer that question, let's first consider what strategic leaders actually do.

WHAT DO STRATEGIC LEADERS DO?

What do strategic leaders do, and what makes some strategic leaders more effective than others? In a recent study of over 350 CEOs, strategy scholars found that they spend, on average, 67 percent of their time in meetings, 13 percent working alone, 7 percent on e-mail, 6 percent on phone calls, 5 percent on business meals, and 2 percent on public events such as ribbon-cutting for a new factory (see Exhibit 2.3).[21] Other studies have also found that most managers prefer oral communication: CEOs spend most of their time "interacting—talking, cajoling, soothing, selling, listening, and nodding—with a wide array of parties inside and outside the organization." Surprisingly given the advances in information technology, CEOs today spend most of their time in face-to-face meetings. They consider face-to-face meetings most effective in getting their message across and obtaining the information they need. Not only do meetings present data through presentations and verbal communications, but they enable CEOs to pick up on rich nonverbal cues such as facial expressions, body language, and mood, that are not apparent to them if they use e-mail or Skype, for example.[22]

HOW DO YOU BECOME AN EFFECTIVE AND ETHICAL STRATEGIC LEADER?

How do you become an ethical and effective strategic leader? Is it innate? Can it be learned? According to the **upper-echelons theory,**[23] organizational outcomes including strategic choices and performance levels reflect the values of the top management team (the individuals at the upper echelons, or levels, of an organization). The theory states that executives interpret situations through the lens of their unique perspectives, shaped by personal circumstances, values, and experiences. Their leadership actions reflect characteristics of age, education, and career experiences, filtered through personal interpretations of the situations they face. The upper-echelons theory favors the idea that strong leadership is the result of both innate abilities *and* learning.

upper-echelons theory A conceptual framework that views organizational outcomes—strategic choices and performance levels—as reflections of the values of the members of the top management team, who interpret situations through the lens of their unique perspectives.

EXHIBIT 2.3

How CEOs Spend Their Days

SOURCE: Author's depiction of data from O. Bandiera, A. Prat, and R. Sadun (2012), "Managerial capital at the top: Evidence from the time use of CEOs," *London School of Economics and Harvard Business School Working Paper.*

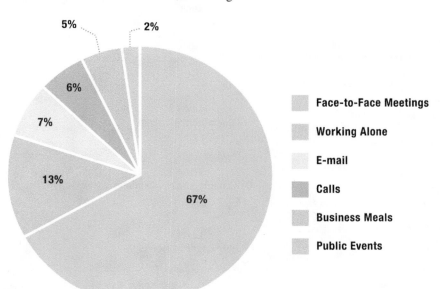

- Face-to-Face Meetings
- Working Alone
- E-mail
- Calls
- Business Meals
- Public Events

In the bestseller *Good to Great*, Jim Collins identified *great companies* as those that transitioned from average performance to sustained competitive advantage. He measured that transition as "cumulative stock returns of 6.9 times the general market in the fifteen years following their transition points."[24] Examples of companies having made the transition from good to great include health care company Abbott Laboratories, personal care products company Kimberly-Clark, Gillette (now a subsidiary of Procter & Gamble), grocery chain Kroger, steel maker Nucor, tobacco company Philip Morris, and drug retailing chain Walgreens. Collins found consistent patterns of leadership among the companies he studied, as pictured in the **Level-5 leadership pyramid** in Exhibit 2.4.[25] The pyramid is a conceptual framework that shows leadership progression through five distinct, sequential levels. Collins found that all the companies he identified as *great* were led by Level-5 executives.

Level-5 leadership pyramid A conceptual framework of leadership progression with five distinct, sequential levels.

According to the Level-5 leadership pyramid, effective strategic leaders go through a natural progression of five different levels. Each level builds upon the previous one; the manager can move on to the next level of leadership only when the current level has been mastered. Characteristics of the five levels are:

- The *Level-1* manager is a highly capable individual who makes productive contributions through motivation, talent, knowledge, and skills.
- The *Level-2* manager masters the skills required at Level 1, but is also a contributing team member who works effectively with others to achieve synergies and team objectives.
- The *Level-3* manager is a well-rounded and highly capable manager, who "does things right." He or she is an effective team player and organizes resources effectively to achieve predetermined goals.

EXHIBIT 2.4 / Strategic Leaders: The Level-5 Pyramid

Builds enduring greatness through a combination of willpower and humility.

Level 5: Executive

Presents compelling vision and mission to guide groups toward superior performance. Does the right things.

Level 4: Effective Leader

Is efficient and effective in organizing resources to accomplish stated goals and objectives. Does things right.

Level 3: Competent Manager

Uses high level of individual capability to work effectively with others in order to achieve team objectives.

Level 2: Contributing Team Member

Makes productive contributions through motivation, talent, knowledge, and skills.

Level 1: Highly Capable Individual

SOURCE: Adapted from J. Collins (2001), *Good to Great: Why Some Companies Make the Leap . . . And Others Don't* (New York: HarperCollins), p. 20.

- At Level 4, the effective Level-3 manager becomes a leader who determines what the right decisions are. The *Level-4* manager effectively communicates a compelling vision and mission to guide the firm toward superior performance. He or she "does the right things."

- Finally, the *Level-5* manager reaches a leadership pinnacle, turning into a strategic leader. An effective strategic leader is an executive that builds enduring greatness into the organizations he or she leads. Indeed, Collins goes so far as to argue that the greatness of a strategic leader can truly be judged only if the organizations are able to sustain a competitive advantage in the years *after* the successful executive has departed from the organization.

FORMULATING STRATEGY ACROSS LEVELS: CORPORATE, BUSINESS, AND FUNCTIONAL MANAGERS

According to the upper-echelons theory, it is the top management team that primarily determines whether a firm is able to gain and sustain a competitive advantage through the strategies they pursue. Given their importance, we need to gain a deeper understanding of how strategies are formed.

Strategy formulation concerns the choice of strategy in terms of *where and how to compete*. It is helpful to break down strategy formulation into three distinct areas—corporate, business, and functional:

- *Corporate strategy* concerns questions relating to where to compete (industry, markets, and geography).

- *Business strategy* concerns the question of how to compete (cost leadership, differentiation, or integration).

- *Functional strategy* concerns the question of how to implement business strategy.

Exhibit 2.5 shows the three areas of strategy formulation.

Although we generally speak of the firm in an abstract form, it is individuals who make strategic decisions—whether at the corporate, business, or functional level. *Corporate*

LO 2-5

Describe the roles of corporate, business, and functional managers in strategy formulation and implementation.

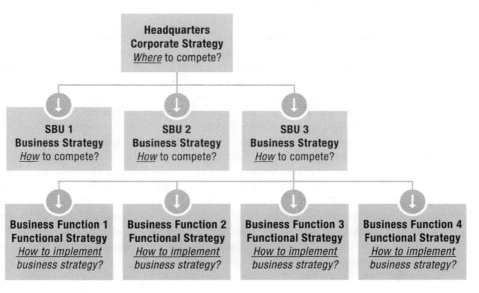

EXHIBIT 2.5 /

Strategy Formulation and Implementation Across Levels: Corporate, Business, and Functional Strategy

executives at headquarters formulate corporate strategy. Examples of corporate executives are Mukesh Ambani (Reliance Industries), Maria das Graças Silva Foster (Petrobras-Petróleo Brasil), Jeffrey Immelt (GE), Virginia Rometty (IBM), and Ursula Burns (Xerox). Corporate executives need to decide in which industries, markets, and geographies their companies should compete. They need to formulate a strategy that can create synergies across business units that may be quite different, and determine the boundaries of the firm by deciding whether to enter certain industries and markets and whether to sell certain divisions. They are responsible for setting overarching strategic objectives and allocating scarce resources among different business divisions, monitoring performance, and making adjustments to the overall portfolio of businesses as needed. The objective of corporate-level strategy is to increase overall corporate value so that it is higher than the sum of the individual business units.

strategic business unit (SBU)
A standalone division of a larger conglomerate, with its own profit-and-loss responsibility.

Business strategy occurs within **strategic business units,** or **SBUs,** the standalone divisions of a larger conglomerate, each with its own profit-and-loss responsibility. General managers in SBUs must answer business strategy questions relating to how to compete in order to achieve superior performance. Within the guidelines received from corporate headquarters, they formulate an appropriate generic business strategy (cost leadership, differentiation, or integration) in their quest for competitive advantage.

Within each strategic business unit are various business *functions:* accounting, finance, human resources, product development, operations, manufacturing, marketing, and customer service. Each *functional manager* is responsible for decisions and actions within a single functional area. These decisions aid in the implementation of the business-level strategy, made at the level above.

In ChapterCase 2, we saw how Indra Nooyi determined PepsiCo's corporate strategy. She wants to reposition PepsiCo toward a more sustainable future by focusing not only on economic but also social and environmental contributions. As chief executive officer, Ms. Nooyi is the corporate executive responsible for the performance of the entire organization. She makes a wide range of corporate strategy decisions:

- What types of products PepsiCo offers
- Where in the value chain (ranging from raw materials to retailing of the final product) to participate
- What industries (e.g., beverages and foods) to compete in
- Where in the world to compete

For the time being, Ms. Nooyi has decided that PepsiCo creates more value when both the beverage and snack foods division are together in one corporation, rather than split up into two companies. In contrast, PepsiCo's archrival, Coca-Cola, focuses on only the nonalcoholic beverages line of business.

As a company, PepsiCo is organized on both a geographic and a product basis. Along the *geographic* dimension, PepsiCo consists of a number of standalone business divisions in the Americas, Europe, Africa, and the Middle East.[26] PepsiCo's revenues are split roughly 50–50 between the U.S. and international sales. Along the *product* dimension, PepsiCo's Americas division is split into two product units, Americas beverages and Americas foods. A general manager leads each geographic and product division. He or she has profit-and-loss (P&L) responsibility for his or her region and product line. These SBU managers in turn report to PepsiCo's CEO.

To implement specific business strategies, PepsiCo's regional and product leaders rely on functional managers, who are responsible for a particular business function such as bottling, supply chain management, marketing, retail, or customer service. The functional managers receive strategic directives from their respective regional and product leaders, and implement these directives within the business activities they are responsible for.

2.3 The Strategic Management Process

We have gained some insight into the corporate, business, and functional levels into which strategy is broken down. Next, we turn to the process or method by which strategic leaders formulate and implement strategy. When strategizing for competitive advantage, managers rely on three different approaches: (1) strategic planning, (2) scenario planning, and (3) strategy as planned emergence. This order also indicates how these approaches were developed over time. Strategic planning was the first framework, before scenario planning was introduced, and strategy as planned emergence is the most recent addition. As you'll see, the first two are relatively formal, "rational" top-down planning approaches. Although the third approach also begins with a strategic plan, it is a less formal and less stylized approach to the development of strategy.

LO 2-6

Evaluate top-down strategic planning, scenario planning, and strategy as planned emergence.

TOP-DOWN STRATEGIC PLANNING

The prosperous decades after World War II resulted in the tremendous growth of corporations. As company executives needed a way to manage ever more complex firms more effectively, they began to use strategic planning. **Top-down strategic planning** is a rational, top-down process through which executives attempt to program future success.[27] In this approach, all strategic intelligence and decision-making responsibilities are concentrated in the office of the CEO. The CEO, much like a military general, leads the company strategically through competitive battles.

Exhibit 2.6 shows the three steps of analysis, formulation, and implementation in a traditional top-down strategic planning process. Strategic planners provide careful analyses of internal and external data and apply it to all quantifiable areas: prices, costs, margins, market demand, head count, and production runs. Five-year plans, revisited regularly, predict future sales based on anticipated future growth. Top executives tie the allocation of the annual corporate budget to the strategic plan and monitor ongoing performance accordingly. Based on a careful analysis of these data, top managers reconfirm or adjust the company's vision, mission, and values before formulating corporate, business, and functional strategies. Appropriate organizational structures and controls as well as governance mechanisms aid in effective implementation.

Top-down strategic planning A rational, top-down process through which management can program future success; typically concentrates strategic intelligence and decision-making responsibilities in the office of the CEO.

In this process, the formulation of strategy is separate from implementation, and thinking about strategy is separate from doing it. Information flows one way only: top-down.

At times, strategic leaders impose their visions onto a company's strategy, structure, and culture from the top down in order to create and enact a desired future state. Under its co-founder and longtime CEO, Steve Jobs, Apple was one of the few successful tech companies using a top-down strategic planning process.[28] Jobs felt that he knew best what the next big thing should be. Under his top-down, autocratic leadership, Apple did not engage in market research, because Jobs firmly believed that "people don't know what they want until you show it to them."[29] Since Jobs' death, Apple's strategy process has become more

EXHIBIT 2.6 / Top-Down Strategic Planning in the AFI Framework

*A*nalysis
- Vision, Mission, and Values
- External Analysis
- Internal Analysis

*F*ormulation
- Corporate Strategy
- Business Strategy
- Functional Strategy

*I*mplementation
- Structure, Culture, & Control
- Corporate Governance & Business Ethics

flexible under its new CEO Tim Cook, and the company is now trying to incorporate the possibilities of different future scenarios and bottom-up strategic initiatives.[30]

Top-down strategic planning rests on the assumption that we can predict the future from the past. The approach works reasonably well when the environment does not change much. One major shortcoming of the strategic planning approach is that we simply cannot know the future. Strategic leaders' visions of the future can be downright wrong; unforeseen events can make even the most scientifically developed and formalized plans obsolete. Thus, many companies are now using a more flexible approach in their strategic management process.

SCENARIO PLANNING

Given that the only constant is change, should managers even try to strategically plan for the future? The answer is yes—but they also need to expect that unpredictable events will happen. We can compare strategic planning in a fast-changing environment to a fire department operation.[31] There is no way to know where and when the next emergency will arise, nor can we know its magnitude beforehand. Nonetheless, fire chiefs put contingency plans in place to address a wide range of emergencies along different dimensions.

scenario planning
Strategy-planning activity in which managers envision different what-if scenarios to anticipate plausible futures.

In the same way, **scenario planning** asks those "what if" questions. Similar to top-down strategic planning, scenario planning also uses a rational, scientific approach to the strategy process. In addition, in scenario planning managers envision different scenarios, to anticipate plausible futures. For example, new laws might restrict carbon emissions or expand employee health care. Demographic shifts may alter the ethnic diversity of a nation; changing tastes or economic conditions will affect consumer behavior. How would any of these changes affect a firm, and how should it respond? Scenario planning takes place at both the corporate and business levels of strategy.

Typical scenario planning addresses both optimistic and pessimistic futures. For instance, strategy executives at UPS recently identified six issues as critical to shaping its future competitive scenarios: (1) the price of oil; (2) climate change; (3) trade barriers (such as "buy American" or "buy Chinese" clauses in new laws around the world); (4) the emerging BRIC (Brazil, Russia, India, and China) economies; (5) political instability; and (6) online commerce worldwide.[32] Managers then formulated strategies they could activate and implement should the envisioned optimistic or pessimistic scenarios begin to appear.

Exhibit 2.7 shows the use of scenario planning with the AFI strategy framework. The goal is to create strategic plans that are more flexible, and thus more effective, than those created through the more static strategic planning approach. In the *analysis stage,* managers brainstorm to identify possible future scenarios. Input from several different hierarchies within the organization and from different functional areas such as R&D, manufacturing, and marketing and sales is critical. UPS executives considered how they would compete if the price of a barrel of oil was $45, or $125, or even $200. Managers may also attach probabilities (highly likely versus unlikely, or 85 percent likely versus 2 percent likely) to different future states.

Although managers often tend to overlook pessimistic future scenarios, it is imperative to consider negative scenarios more carefully. An exporter such as Boeing, Harley-Davidson, or John Deere would want to analyze the impact of shifts in exchange rates on sales and production costs: What if the euro depreciated to $1 per euro, or the Chinese yuan depreciated rather than appreciated? How would Disney and other theme park operators compete if the dollar were to appreciate so much as to make visits by foreign tourists to its California and Florida theme parks prohibitively expensive? Other problems to consider could include how to maintain liquidity when credit and equity markets are tight. Managers might also consider how black swan events (discussed in Chapter 1) might affect their strategic planning. The BP oil spill was such a black swan for many businesses on the Gulf Coast, including the tourism, fishing, and energy industries.

EXHIBIT 2.7 /

Scenario Planning
Within the AFI
Strategy Framework

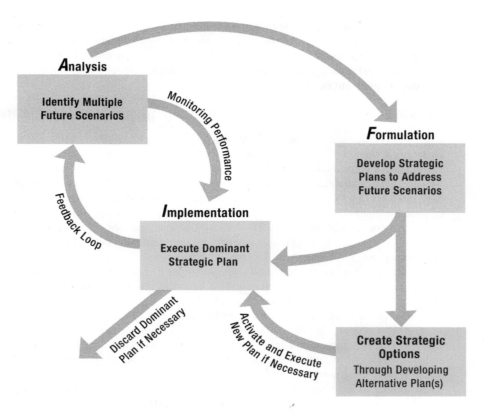

In the *formulation stage* in scenario planning, management teams develop different strategic plans to address possible future scenarios. This kind of what-if exercise forces managers to consider contingency plans before events occur. Each plan relies on an entire set of analytical tools (which will be introduced in upcoming chapters). They capture the firm's internal and external environments and answer several key questions:

- What resources and capabilities do we need to compete successfully in with each future scenario?
- What strategic initiatives should we put in place to respond to each respective scenario?
- How can we shape our expected future environment?

By formulating responses to the varying scenarios, managers build a portfolio of future options. Managers continue to integrate additional information over time, which in turn influences future decisions. Finally, they transform the most viable options into full-fledged, detailed strategic plans that can be activated and executed as needed. The scenarios and planned responses promote strategic flexibility for the organization.

In the *implementation stage,* managers execute the **dominant strategic plan,** the option that top managers decide most closely matches the current reality. If the situation changes, managers can quickly retrieve and implement any of the alternate plans developed in the formulation stage. The firm's subsequent performance in the marketplace gives managers real-time feedback about the effectiveness of the dominant strategic plan. If performance feedback is positive, managers continue to pursue the dominant strategic plan, fine-tuning it in the process. If performance feedback is negative, or if reality changes, managers consider whether to modify further the dominant strategic plan in order to enhance firm performance, or to activate an alternative strategic plan.

dominant strategic plan The strategic option that top managers decide most closely matches the current reality and which is then executed.

The circular nature of the scenario-planning model in Exhibit 2.7 highlights the continuous interaction among analysis, formulation, and implementation. Through this interactive process, managers can adjust and modify their actions as new realities emerge. The interdependence among analysis, formulation, and implementation also enhances organizational learning and flexibility.

STRATEGY AS PLANNED EMERGENCE: TOP-DOWN *AND* BOTTOM-UP

Critics of top-down and scenario planning argue that *strategic planning* is not the same as *strategic thinking*.[33] In fact, they argue the strategic planning processes are often too regimented and confining. As such, they do not allow for the necessary strategic thinking. Managers doing strategic planning may also fall prey to an *illusion of control*—that is, the hard numbers in a strategic plan can convey a false sense of security. According to critics of strategic planning, in order to be successful, a strategy should be based on an inspiring vision and not on hard data alone. They advise that managers should focus on all types of information sources, including soft sources that can generate new insights, such as personal experience or the experience of front-line employees. The important work, according to this viewpoint, is to synthesize *all available input* from different internal and external sources into an overall strategic vision. This vision in turn should then guide the firm's strategy (as discussed earlier in this chapter).

These critics, most notably Henry Mintzberg, propose a third approach to the strategic management process. In contrast to the two rational planning approaches just discussed, this one is a less formal and less stylized approach to the development of strategy. To reflect the reality that strategy can be planned *or* emerge from the bottom up, Exhibit 2.8 shows a more integrative approach to strategy-making.

According to this more holistic model, the strategy process also begins with a top-down strategic plan. Top-level executives design an **intended strategy**—the outcome of a rational and structured, top-down strategic plan. In today's complex and uncertain world, however, unpredictable events can have tremendous effects. In 1990, online retailing was nonexistent. Today, almost all Internet users have engaged in online retailing. As a total of all sales, online retailing was almost 10 percent (in 2012), and continues to grow fast.[34] Given the dramatic success of Amazon as the world's leading online retailer and eBay as the world's

EXHIBIT 2.8

Realized Strategy Is a Combination of Top-Down Intended Strategy and Bottom-Up Emergent Strategy

SOURCE: Adapted from H. Mintzberg and A. McHugh (1985), "Strategy formation in an adhocracy," *Administrative Science Quarterly* 30: 162.

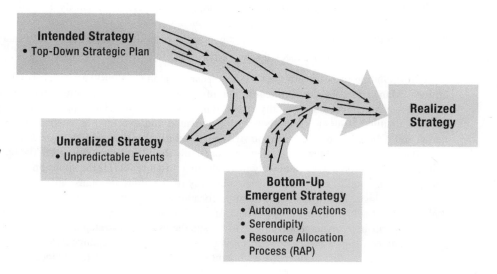

largest online marketplace, brick-and-mortar companies such as Best Buy, Radio Shack, JCPenney, and Sears have all been forced to respond and adjust their strategies in order to avoid bankruptcy. Exhibit 2.8 illustrates how parts of a firm's *intended strategy* fall by the wayside due to unpredictable events and thus turn into *unrealized strategy*.

A firm's **realized strategy** is generally a combination of its top-down strategic intentions and bottom-up emergent strategy. An **emergent strategy** describes any unplanned strategic initiative undertaken by mid-level employees of their own volition. If successful, emergent strategies have the potential to influence and shape a firm's strategy.

The strategic initiative is a key feature in the strategy as a planned emergence model. A **strategic initiative** is any activity a firm pursues to explore and develop new products and processes, new markets, or new ventures. Strategic initiatives can come from anywhere. They could be the result of a response to external trends (such as online retailing) or come from internal sources. As such, strategic initiatives can be the result of top-down planning by executives, or they can also emerge through a *bottom-up process*. (The black arrows in Exhibit 2.8 represent different strategic initiatives.) In particular, strategic initiatives can bubble up from deep within a firm through:

- *Autonomous actions* by lower-level employees
- *Serendipity* (random events, pleasant surprises, accidental happenstances)
- The *resource allocation process (RAP)*[35]

Strategy Highlight 2.2 illustrates that successful emergent strategies are sometimes the result of *serendipity* combined with *autonomous actions* of lower-level employees. (See MiniCase 4, which describes the serendipitous discovery of Viagra.)

Functional managers (such as Diana, the Starbucks store manager featured in Strategy Highlight 2.2) are much closer to the final products, services, and customers than corporate- or business-level managers. As a result, functional managers may initiate strategic initiatives based on autonomous actions that can influence the direction of the company. To be successful, however, top-level executives need to support emergent strategies that they believe fit with the firm's vision and mission. Diana's autonomous actions might not have succeeded (or even got her in trouble) if she did not garner the support of a senior Starbucks executive (Howard Behar). This executive championed her initiative and helped persuade other top executives. Consider the following examples, in which the impetus for strategic initiatives all emerged from the bottom up through *autonomous actions:*

- The Internet company Google organizes the work of its engineers according to a 70-20-10 rule. The majority of the engineers' work time (70 percent) is focused on its main business (search and ads).[36] Google also allows its engineers to spend one day a week (20 percent) on ideas of their own choosing, and the remainder (10 percent) on total wild cards (such as a driverless car). Google reports that half of its new products came from the *20 percent rule.* Examples of innovations that resulted from the 20 percent rule include Gmail, Google Maps, Google News, and Orkut.[37]
- In 2001, a mid-level engineer at General Electric proposed buying Enron Wind, a division that was up for sale as part of Enron's bankruptcy proceedings. Then-CEO Jack Welch didn't want anything with the name Enron on it, given Enron's large-scale

---

intended strategy The outcome of a rational and structured top-down strategic plan.

realized strategy Combination of intended and emergent strategy.

emergent strategy Any unplanned strategic initiative undertaken by mid-level employees of their own volition.

strategic initiative Any activity a firm pursues to explore and develop new products and processes, new markets, or new ventures.

Strategy Highlight 2.2

Starbucks' CEO: "It's Not What We Do"

Diana, a Starbucks store manager in southern California, received several requests a day for an iced beverage offered by a local competitor. After receiving more than 30 requests one day, she tried the beverage herself. Thinking it might be a good idea for Starbucks to offer a similar iced beverage, she requested that headquarters consider adding it to the product lineup. Diana had an internal champion in Howard Behar, then one of Starbucks' top executives. Mr. Behar presented this strategic initiative to the Starbucks executive committee. The committee voted down the idea in a 7:1 vote. Starbucks' CEO Howard Schultz commented, "We do coffee, we don't do iced drinks."

Diana, however, was undeterred. She experimented until she created the iced drink, and then began to offer it in her store. When Howard Behar visited Diana's store, he was shocked to see this new drink on the menu—all

Starbucks stores were supposed to offer only company-approved drinks. But Diana told him the new drink was selling well.

Howard Behar flew Diana's team to Starbucks headquarters in Seattle to serve the iced-coffee drink to the executive committee. They liked its taste, but still said no. Then Behar pulled out the sales numbers that Diana had carefully kept. The drink was selling like crazy: 40 drinks a day the first week, 50 drinks a day the next week, and then 70 drinks a day in the third week after introduction. They had never seen such growth numbers. These results persuaded the executive team to give reluctant approval to introduce the drink in all Starbucks stores.

You've probably guessed by now that we're talking about Starbucks' Frappuccino. Frappuccino is now a billion-dollar business for Starbucks. At one point, this iced-drink brought in more than 20 percent of Starbucks' total revenues (which were $13 billion in 2012).[38]

accounting fraud. When the mid-level engineer kept insisting, even after being rejected several times, GE's leadership relented and bought Enron Wind for $200 million. It turned out to be a huge success, generating revenues over $10 billion in 2012, and opening up other significant opportunities for GE in the alternative-energy industry, including its *ecomagination* initiative. GE's shift from a product-oriented company ("*We bring good things to life*") to a more consumer-oriented one ("*Imagination at work*") was part of the leadership change from Jack Welch to Jeffrey Immelt, who approved the investment in Enron Wind.[39]

Although emergent strategies can arise in the most unusual circumstances, it is important to emphasize the role that top management teams play in this type of strategy process. In the strategy-as-planned-emergence approach, executives need to decide which of the bottom-up initiatives to pursue and which to shut down. This critical decision is made on the basis of whether the strategic initiative fits with the company's vision and mission, and whether it provides an opportunity worth exploiting. In the GE wind energy example, Jeffrey Immelt decided to support this strategic initiative and provided appropriate resources and structures to grow this emergent strategy into a major strategic initiative that's now worth billions of dollars.

In contrast, Google fumbled its social networking opportunity presented by Orkut.[40] In 2002, some two years before Facebook was started (equating to eons in Internet time), Google engineer Orkut Buyukkokten had developed a social network using his 20 percent discretionary time. Marissa Mayer, Google's vice president in charge of this project, liked what she saw and provided initial support. After adding more engineers to further Orkut's development, Google was astonished at the early success of the social network: within the first month alone after release, hundreds of thousands of people signed up. Today, it has a mere 30 million users (mostly in Brazil and India), which pales in comparison to Facebook's over 1 billion users worldwide.

Why did Google fumble its lead over Facebook? Google had a huge opportunity to become the leader in social networking because MySpace imploded after it was acquired by News Corp. Despite initial support, Google's top executives felt that social networking did not fit its vision *to organize the world's information and make it universally accessible and useful.* Google relied on highly complex and proprietary algorithms to organize the knowledge available on the Internet and serve up targeted search ads. Social networking software, in comparison, is fairly pedestrian. Google's co-founders, Sergey Brin and Larry Page, both exceptional computer scientists, looked down on social networking. They felt their PageRank algorithm that accounts for hundreds of variables and considers all available websites was far superior in providing *objective* recommendations to users' search queries than *subjective* endorsements by someone's (online) friends. As a consequence, they snubbed social networking. Moreover, given the many different projects Google was pursuing at that time, Orkut was ranked as a low priority by Google's top executives. Starved of further resources, the social networking site withered, making Facebook the undisputed leader.

In 2011, Google launched Google Plus, its newest social networking service. By integrating all its services such as Gmail, YouTube, Chrome, and others into one user interface (and requiring users of even just one Google product to sign in to its portal), the company hopes to catch up with Facebook. Not being able to access Facebook users' activities limits Google's ability to serve targeted ads, and thus cuts into its main line of business. AdWords is Google's main online advertising product and garners some 85 percent of Google's total revenues of $50 billion (in 2012).[41]

Finally, bottom-up strategies can also emerge as a consequence of the firm's resource allocation process (RAP).[42] The way a firm allocates its resources can be critical in shaping its realized strategy.[43] Intel Corp. illustrates this concept.[44] Intel was founded in 1968 to produce DRAM (dynamic random-access memory) chips. From the start, producing these chips was the firm's top-down strategic plan, and initially it worked well. In the 1980s, Japanese competitors brought better-quality chips to the market at lower cost, threatening Intel's position and strategic plan. However, Intel was able to pursue a strategic transformation due to the way it set up its resource allocation process. In a sense, Intel was using functional-level managers to drive business and corporate strategies in a bottom-up fashion. In particular, during this time Intel had only a few "fabs" (fabrication plants to produce silicon-based products). It would have taken several years and billions of dollars to build additional capacity by bringing new fabs online.

With constrained production capacity, Intel had implemented the production-decision rule *to maximize margin-per-wafer-start.* Each time functional managers initiated a new production run, they were to consider the profit margins for DRAM chips and for semiconductors (the "brains" of personal computers); they then could produce *whichever product* delivered the higher margin. By following this simple rule, front-line managers shifted Intel's production capacity away from the lower-margin DRAM business to the higher-margin semiconductor business. The firm's focus on semiconductors emerged from the bottom up, based on resource allocation. Indeed, by the time top management finally approved the de facto strategic switch, the company's market share in DRAM had dwindled to less than 3 percent.[45]

Taken together, a firm's realized strategy is frequently a combination of top-down strategic intent and bottom-up emergent strategies, as Exhibit 2.8 shows. This type of strategy process is called **planned emergence**. In that process, organizational structure and systems allow bottom-up strategic initiatives to emerge and be evaluated and coordinated by top management.[46]

planned emergence
Strategy process in which organizational structure and systems allow bottom-up strategic initiatives to emerge and be evaluated and coordinated by top management.

2.4 ◄► Implications for the Strategist

Two ingredients are needed to create a powerful foundation upon which to formulate and implement a strategy in order to gain and sustain a competitive advantage: First, the firm needs an inspiring vision and mission backed up by ethical values. Second, the firm needs an effective strategic management process.

Each of the three strategy processes introduced in this chapter has its strengths and weaknesses. The effectiveness of the chosen strategy process is *contingent* upon the rate of change in the internal and external environments of the firm. In a slow-moving environment, top-down strategic planning might be the most effective approach. Besides the rate of change, a second dimension is firm size. Larger firms tend to use either a top-down strategic planning process or scenario planning. For a nuclear power provider such as Areva in France that provides over 75 percent of the country's energy and has the long-term backing of the state, for instance, using a top-down strategy approach might work well. Given that nuclear accidents are rare, but when they occur they have a tremendous impact (such as in Chernobyl, Russia, and Fukushima, Japan), Areva might use scenario planning to prepare for black swan events. In fast-moving environments, in contrast, Internet companies such as Alibaba, eBay, Facebook, Google, Dropbox, Pinterest, or Twitter tend to use the strategy-as-planned-emergence process.

Another important implication of our discussion is that all employees should be involved in setting an inspiring vision and mission to create more meaningful work. Belief in a company's vision and mission motivates its employees. Moreover, every employee plays a strategic role. Lower-level employees focus mainly on strategy implementation when a firm is using top-down or scenario planning. As the examples, however, have shown, *any employee* (even at the entry level) can have great ideas that might become *strategic initiatives* with the potential to transform companies.

Here we conclude our discussion of the strategic management process, which marks the end of the "getting started" portion of the AFI framework. The next chapter moves us into the analysis part of the framework, where we begin by studying external and internal analyses.

CHAPTER**CASE 2** / Consider This . . .

MANY OBSERVERS APPLAUD Indra Nooyi for taking a stakeholder strategy approach by making PepsiCo's strategic vision *Performance with a Purpose*. Although Ms. Nooyi has defined an inspiring vision for PepsiCo, financial performance seems to be lagging, especially in comparison with its archrival Coca-Cola, which has done well by continuing to concentrate on its core business in soda and other non-alcoholic beverages. In particular, critics allege that Ms. Nooyi has not paid enough attention to the company's flagship beverage business: Pepsi-Cola fell to No. 3 in U.S. soda sales, behind Coke and Diet Coke. As a result, PepsiCo's stock has underperformed archrival Coca-Cola in recent years.

Some critics even go so far as to call for the replacement of Ms. Nooyi. They also propose splitting PepsiCo into two standalone companies. One would focus on beverages (Pepsi, Gatorade, Tropicana); the other would focus on snack foods (Frito-Lay, Doritos). This move would unlock additional profit potential, the argument goes, because well-performing snack foods would no longer need to subsidize underperforming beverages.

Questions

Thinking about ChapterCase 2, answer the following questions.

1. What "grade" would you give Ms. Nooyi for her job performance as a strategic leader? What are her strengths and weaknesses? Where would you place Ms. Nooyi on the Level-5 pyramid of strategic leadership (see Exhibit 2.4), and why? Support your answers.

2. What should a strategic leader like Ms. Nooyi do if his or her vision does not seem to lead to an immediate (financial) competitive advantage? What would be your top-three recommendations? Support your arguments.

3. If you were a member of PepsiCo's board of directors, would you be concerned with Ms. Nooyi's and/or PepsiCo's performance? If you were concerned, what course of action would you recommend? Would you go so far as to endorse Ms. Nooyi's replacement with a new CEO who would focus more on PepsiCo's stock market performance? Why or why not?

4. Do you agree with Ms. Nooyi's critics that PepsiCo should be split up into two companies—one focusing on beverages, and one focusing on snack foods? What would be the advantages and disadvantages of such a move?

TAKE-AWAY CONCEPTS

This chapter explained the role of vision, mission, and values in the strategic management process. It provided an overview of strategic leadership and explained different processes to create strategy, as summarized by the following learning objectives and related take-away concepts.

LO 2-1 / Describe the roles of vision, mission, and values in the strategic management process.

■ A vision captures an organization's aspirations. An effective vision inspires and motivates members of the organization.

■ A mission statement describes what an organization actually does—what its business is—and why and how it does it.

■ Values define the ethical standards and norms that should govern the behavior of individuals within the firm.

LO 2-2 / Evaluate the strategic implications of product-oriented and customer-oriented vision statements.

■ Product-oriented vision statements define a business in terms of a good or service provided.

■ Customer-oriented vision statements define business in terms of providing solutions to customer needs.

■ Customer-oriented vision statements provide managers with more strategic flexibility than product-oriented missions.

■ To be effective, visions and missions need to be backed up by hard-to-reverse strategic commitments.

LO 2-3 / Explain why anchoring a firm in ethical values is essential for long-term success.

■ Employees tend to follow values practiced by strategic leaders. Without commitment from top managers, statements of values remain merely public relations exercises.

■ Ethical values are the guardrails that help keep the company on track when pursuing its mission and its quest for competitive advantage.

LO 2-4 / Outline how managers become strategic leaders.

■ To become an effective strategic leader, a manager needs to develop skills to move sequentially through five different leadership levels: highly capable individual, contributing team member, competent manager, effective leader, and executive.

LO 2-5 / Describe the roles of corporate, business, and functional managers in strategy formulation and implementation.

- Corporate executives must provide answers to the question of *where* to compete (in industries, markets, and geographies), and *how to create synergies* among different business units.

- General managers in strategic business units must answer the strategic question of *how to compete* in order to achieve superior performance. They must manage and align the firm's different functional areas for competitive advantage.

- Functional managers are responsible for *implementing business strategy* within a single functional area.

LO 2-6 / Evaluate top-down strategic planning, scenario planning, and strategy as planned emergence.

- Top-down strategic planning is a sequential, linear process that works reasonably well when the environment does not change much.

- In scenario planning, managers envision what-if scenarios and prepare contingency plans that can be called upon when necessary.

- Strategic initiatives can be the result of top-down planning or can emerge through a bottom-up process from deep within the organization. They have the potential to shape a firm's strategy.

- A firm's realized strategy is generally a combination of its top-down intended strategy and bottom-up emergent strategy, resulting in planned emergence.

KEY TERMS

Dominant strategic plan	Planned emergence	Strategic leadership
Emergent strategy	Realized strategy	Strategic management process
Intended strategy	Scenario planning	Top-down strategic planning
Level-5 leadership pyramid	Strategic business unit (SBU)	Upper-echelons theory
Mission	Strategic commitments	Vision
Organizational values	Strategic initiative	

DISCUSSION QUESTIONS

1. What characteristics does an effective mission statement have?

2. In what situations is top-down planning likely to be superior to bottom-up emergent strategy development?

3. This chapter introduces three different levels appropriate for strategic considerations (see Exhibit 2.5). In what situations would some of these levels be more important than others? For example, what issues might be considered by the corporate level? What do you see as the primary responsibilities of corporate-level executives? When might the business-level managers bear more responsibility for considering how to respond to an issue? In what situations might the functional-level managers have a primary responsibility for considering an issue? How should the organization ensure the proper attention to each level of strategy as needed?

4. Identify an industry that is undergoing intense competition or is being featured in the business press. Discuss how scenario planning might be used by competitors to prepare for future events. Can some industries benefit more than others from this type of process? Explain why.

ETHICAL/SOCIAL ISSUES

1. Over 50,000 people lost their jobs and many their life savings in the Enron debacle. Some of those at Enron who were closely involved in the scandal, such as Jeffrey Skilling (CEO) and Andrew Fastow (CFO), are serving significant prison sentences. Why do you think only one employee initially came forward to report the irregularities and help with the investigation? What responsibility do lower-level executives bear for not reporting such questionable practices by the firm's leadership?

2. The list below shows a sample of various vision/mission statements. Guess the company, and identify whether the statements are customer-oriented, product-oriented, or a combination.

	Vision/Mission Statement	Company	Type of Statement
a.	To be earth's most customer centric company; to build a place where people can come to find and discover anything they might want to buy online.		
b.	To be the most respected global financial services company.		
c.	To provide personal vehicle owners and enthusiasts with the vehicle related products and knowledge that fulfill their wants and needs at the right price.		
d.	To provide technology advancing every company, products enhancing every home, and innovation improving every life.		
e.	To become the Beauty company most women turn to worldwide.		
f.	To provide a global trading platform where practically anyone can trade practically anything.		
g.	To operate the best specialty retail business in America, regardless of the product we sell.		
h.	To combine aggressive strategic marketing with quality products and services at competitive prices to provide the best insurance value for consumers.		
i.	To be the most respected global financial services company.		
j.	To nourish and delight everyone we serve.		
k.	To help our clients make distinctive, lasting, and substantial improvements in their performance and to build a great firm that attracts, develops, excites, and retains exceptional people.		
l.	To be America's best run, most profitable automotive retailer.		
m.	[To] use our pioneering spirit to responsibly deliver energy to the world.		
n.	[To] provide high-quality [chocolate] products while conducting our business in a socially responsible and environmentally sustainable manner.		
o.	Bringing the best to everyone we touch		
p.	[To provide] high value-added supply chain, transportation, business and related information services through focused operating companies.		
q.	[To provide] convenience and low prices.		
r.	To become the first platform of choice for sharing data, to be an enterprise that has the happiest employees, and to last at least 102 years.		
s.	To organize the world's information and make it universally accessible and useful.		
t.	To give ordinary folk the chance to buy the same thing as rich people.		
u.	To give the people the power to share and make the world more open and connected.		

SMALL-GROUP EXERCISES

//// Small-Group Exercise 1

A popular topic in education and public policy is the need to support the STEM disciplines (Science, Technology, Engineering, Mathematics) as the key to U.S. competitiveness. These disciplines generate innovative ideas and build new companies—and perhaps new industries. As you have learned in this chapter, innovative ideas can help sustain competitive advantage. Many American businesses, however, are concerned about whether there will be an adequate supply of STEM workers in the future because the growth in job opportunities for STEM occupations is expected to be nearly three times as fast as for non-STEM occupations. A key advocate for federal support for funding STEM education is the STEM Education Coalition, which expresses its mission as "to ensure that STEM education is recognized as a national policy priority."

The skills and expertise of the STEM occupations will be critical in dealing with the National Intelligence Council's Global Trends 2030 initiatives, which will confront the global community over the next 15 years. In particular, the key trends include a need for new communication and manufacturing technologies, cyber-security, health care advances and preparations to manage pandemic threats, innovative and sustainable designs for infrastructure improvements, and improvements in the production and management of food, water, and energy that will meet the needs of a growing population. Business organizations may find opportunities to build sustainable competitive advantages by responding to these trends, but they will need adequate STEM expertise in order to create innovative and appropriate responses to these challenges. With innovation and cooperation, these trends can be confronted peacefully in order to benefit geopolitical stability.

1. Discuss within your group methods that the STEM Education Coalition might use to gain partners, particularly business organizations, that will help them make sure STEM education is a national policy priority. Given the budget crisis, how can they persuade congressional representatives to support funding?

2. How does funding for STEM education affect job opportunities for business majors?

3. Although group members may not be STEM majors, brainstorm ideas about how you might advise businesses to modify their operations or to expand/transform their operations in order to find opportunities in the Global Trends over the next 15 years. Choose a business of interest to the group. Then consider scenarios in which the business may thrive as one of the five trends develop. For example, the majority of businesses might want to ask, "What if threats to cyber-security increase?" Or, "What if water resources become more scarce? How would this affect production or demand for the goods produced?" Your group may also consider businesses or industries that may decline as a result of the trends.

4. What additional developmental opportunities might prepare business majors for playing key roles in facing the Global Trends 2030? What skills will you need in order to manage effectively the STEM employees who are central to innovation?

//// Small-Group Exercise 2

In many situations, promising ideas emerge from the lower levels of an organization, only to be discarded before they can be implemented. It was only extraordinary tenacity (and indeed, disregard) for the policy of selling only corporate-approved drinks that permitted the Frappuccino to "bloom" within Starbucks (see Strategy Highlight 2.2).

Some scholars have suggested that companies set aside up to 2 percent of their budgets for *any* manager with budget control to be able to invest in new ideas within the company.[47] Thus, someone with a $100,000 annual budget to manage would be able to invest $2,000 in cash or staff time toward such a project. Multiple managers could go in together for somewhat larger funds or time amounts. Through such a process, the organization could generate a network of "angel investors." Small funds or staff time could be invested into a variety of projects. Approval mechanisms would be easier for these small "seed-stock" ideas, to give them a chance to develop before going for bigger funding at the top levels of the organization.

What would be some problems that would need to be addressed to introduce this angel-network idea into a firm? Use a firm someone in your group has worked for or knows well to discuss possible issues of widely distributing small funding level approvals across the firm.

STRATEGY TERM PROJECT

//// Module 2: Mission, Goals, and the Strategic Management Process

1. Search for a vision, mission statement, and statement of values for your chosen firm. Note that not all organizations publish these statements specifically, so you may need to make inferences from the available information. Relevant information is often available at the firm's website (though it may take some searching) or is contained in its annual reports. You may also interview a manager of the firm or contact Investor Relations. You may also be able to compare the official statement with the business press coverage of the firm.

2. Identify the major goals of the company. What are its short-term versus long-term goals? What resources must the firm acquire to achieve its long-term goals?

3. Trace any changes in strategy that you can identify over time. Try to determine whether the strategic changes of your selected firm are a result of intended strategies, emergent strategies, or some combination of both.

my STRATEGY

How Much Are Your Values Worth to You?

How much are you willing to pay for the job you want? This may sound like a strange question, since your employer will pay you to work, but think again. Consider how much you value a specific type of work, or how much you would want to work for a specific organization because of its values.

A recent study shows scientists who want to continue engaging in research will accept some $14,000 less in annual salary to work at an organization that permits them to publish their findings in academic journals, implying that some scientists will "pay to be scientists." This finding appears to hold in the general business world, too. In a recent survey, 97 percent of Stanford MBA students indicated they would forgo some 14 percent of their expected salary, or about $11,480 a year, to work for a company that matches their own values with concern for stakeholders and sustainability. According to Monster.com, an online career service, about 92 percent of all undergraduates want to work for a "green" company. These diverse examples demonstrate that people put a real dollar amount on pursuing careers in sync with their values.

On the other hand, certain high-powered jobs such as management consulting or investment banking pay very well, but their high salaries come with strings attached. Professionals in these jobs work very long hours, including weekends, and often take little or no vacation time. These workers "pay for pay" in that they are often unable to form stable relationships, have little or no leisure time, and sometimes even sacrifice their health. People "pay for"—make certain sacrifices for—what they value, because strategic decisions require important trade-offs.[48]

1. Identify your personal values. How do you expect these values to affect your work life or your career choice?

2. How much less salary would (did) you accept to find employment with a company that is aligned with your values?

3. How much are you willing to "pay for pay" if your dream job is in management consulting or investment banking?

ENDNOTES

1. This ChapterCase is based on: "PepsiCo shakes it up," *BusinessWeek,* August 14, 2006; "The Pepsi challenge," *The Economist,* August 17, 2006; "Keeping cool in hot water," *BusinessWeek,* June 11, 2007; "Pepsi gets a makeover," *The Economist,* March 25, 2010; "Indra Nooyi on Performance with Purpose 2009," PepsiCo Video, http://bit.ly/Ubhvs8; "Conversation with Indra Nooyi Yale SOM '80"; "PepsiCo wakes up and smells the cola," *The Wall Street Journal,* June 28, 2011; "Should Pepsi break up? *The Economist,* October 11, 2011; "As Pepsi struggles to regain market share, Indra Nooyi's job is on the line," *The Economist,* May 17, 2012; and www.wolframalpha.com.

2. Finkelstein, S., D. C. Hambrick, and A. A. Cannella (2008), *Strategic Leadership: Theory and Research on Executives, Top Management Teams, and Boards* (Oxford, UK: Oxford University Press); and Yulk, G. (1998), *Leadership in Organizations,* 4th ed. (Englewood Cliff, NJ: Prentice-Hall).

3. http://www.pepsico.com/Purpose/Overview.html.

4. Frankl, V. E. (1984), *Man's Search for Meaning.*

5. Pink, D. H. (2011). *The Surprising Truth About What Motivates Us* (New York: Riverhead Books).

6. Hamel, G., and C. K. Prahalad (1989), "Strategic intent," *Harvard Business Review* (May–June): 64–65; Hamel, G., and C. K. Prahalad (1994), *Competing for the Future* (Boston, MA: Harvard Business School Press); and Collins, J. C., and J. I. Porras (1994), *Built to Last: Successful Habits of Visionary Companies* (New York: Harper Collins).

7. Collins, J. C., and J. I. Porras (1994), *Built to Last: Successful Habits of Visionary Companies.*

8. Dixit, A., and B. Nalebuff (1991), *Thinking Strategically: The Competitive Edge in Business, Politics, and Everyday Life* (New York: Norton); and Brandenburger, A. M., and B. J. Nalebuff (1996), *Co-opetition* (New York: Currency Doubleday).

9. Germain, R., and M. B. Cooper (1990), "How a customer mission statement affects company performance," *Industrial Marketing Management* 19(2), 47–54; Bart, C. K. (1997), "Industrial firms and the power of mission," *Industrial Marketing Management* 26 (4): 371–383; and Bart, C. K. (2001), "Measuring the mission effect in human intellectual capital," *Journal of Intellectual Capital* 2(3): 320–330.

10. "The three habits . . . of highly irritating management gurus," *The Economist,* October 22, 2009.

11. The Disney and Subway discussion is based on: Heath, C., and D. Heath (2007), *Made to Stick,* pp. 60–61.

12. Burgelman, R. A., and A. S. Grove (1996), "Strategic dissonance," *California Management Review* 38: 8–28; and Grove, A. S. (1996), *Only the Paranoid Survive: How to Exploit the Crisis Points that Challenge Every Company* (New York: Currency Doubleday).

13. Bart, C. K., and M. C. Baetz (1998), "The relationship between mission statements and firm performance: An exploratory study," *Journal of Management Studies* 35: 823–853.

14. Finkelstein, S., D. C. Hambrick, and A. A. Cannella (2008), *Strategic Leadership,* p. 4.

15. Hambrick, D. C., and E. Abrahamson (1995), "Assessing managerial discretion across industries: A multimethod approach," *Academy of Management Journal* 38: 1427–1441.

16. "The 100 best performing CEOs in the World," *Harvard Business Review,* January–February 2013.

17. As quoted in: Collins, J. (2009), *How the Mighty Fall. And Why Some Companies Never Give In* (New York: Harper Collins), p. 53.

18. http://www.merck.com/about/featured-stories/mectizan1.html.

19. Gilmartin, R. V. (2011), "The Vioxx recall tested our leadership," *Harvard Business Review Blog Network,* October 6.

20. The Merck River Blindness case and the quote by CEO Kenneth Frazier are drawn from: http://www.merck.com/about/featured-stories/mectizan1.html. This Vioxx example is drawn from: "Jury finds Merck liable in Vioxx death and awards $253 million," *The New York Times,* August 19, 2005; Heal, G. (2008), *When Principles Pay: Corporate Social Responsibility and the Bottom Line* (New York: Columbia Business School); and Collins, J. (2009), *How the Mighty Fall: And Why Some Companies Never Give In* (New York: Harper Collins).

21. Bandiera, O., A. Prat, and R. Sadun (2012), "Managerial capital at the top: Evidence from the time use of CEOs," *London School of Economics and Harvard Business School Working Paper;* and "In defense of the CEO," *The Wall Street Journal,* January 15, 2013. The patterns of how CEOs spend their time have held in a number of different studies across the world.

22. Finkelstein, S., D. C. Hambrick, and A. A. Cannella (2008), *Strategic Leadership,* p. 17.

23. Hambrick, D. C. (2007), "Upper echelons theory: An update," *Academy of Management Review* 32: 334–343; and Hambrick, D. C., and P. A. Mason (1984), "Upper echelons: The organization as a reflection of its top managers," *Academy of Management Review* 9: 193–206.

24. Collins, J. (2001), *Good to Great: Why Some Companies Make the Leap . . . And Others Don't* (New York: HarperCollins), p. 3.

25. Ibid.

26. PepsiCo, Inc. 2011 Annual Report.

27. This discussion is based on: Mintzberg, H. (1993), *The Rise and Fall of Strategic Planning: Reconceiving Roles for Planning, Plans, and Planners* (New York: Simon & Schuster); and Mintzberg, H. (1994), "The fall and rise of strategic planning," *Harvard Business Review* (January–February): 107–114.

28. Isaacson, W. (2011), *Steve Jobs* (New York: Simon & Schuster). See also: Isaacson, W. (2012), "The real leadership lessons of Steve Jobs," *Harvard Business Review* (April).

29. Jobs, S. (1998), "There is sanity returning," *BusinessWeek,* May 25.

30. "CEO Tim Cook pushes employee-friendly benefits long shunned by Steve Jobs," *The Wall Street Journal,* November 12, 2012.

31. Grove, A. S. (1996), *Only the Paranoid Survive.*

32. Personal communication with UPS strategy executives during onsite visit in corporate headquarters, June 17, 2009.

33. Mintzberg, H. (1993), *The Rise and Fall of Strategic Planning;* and Mintzberg, H. (1994), "The fall and rise of strategic planning."

34. Data from the U.S. census bureau, reported in "E-commerce," *The Economist,* April 6, 2013.

35. Arthur, B. W. (1989), "Competing technologies, increasing returns, and lock-in by historical events," *Economic Journal* 99: 116–131; and Brown, S. L., and K. M. Eisenhardt (1998), *Competing on the Edge: Strategy as Structured Chaos* (Boston, MA: Harvard Business School Press); Bower, J. L. (1970), *Managing the Resource Allocation Process* (Boston, MA: Harvard Business School Press); Bower, J. L., and C. G. Gilbert (2005), *From Resource Allocation to Strategy* (Oxford, UK: Oxford University Press); Burgelman, R. A. (1983), "A model of the interaction of strategic behavior, corporate context, and the concept of strategy," *Academy* *of Management Review* 8: 61–71; and Burgelman, R. A. (1983), "A process model of internal corporate venturing in a major diversified firm," *Administrative Science Quarterly* 28: 223–244.

36. Levy, S. (2011), *In the Plex: How Google Thinks, Works, and Shapes Our Lives* (New York: Simon & Schuster).

37. Mayer, M. (2006), "Nine lessons learned about creativity at Google," presentation at Stanford Technology Ventures Program, May 17.

38. Based on Howard Behar (retired President, Starbucks North America and Starbucks International) (2009), Impact Speaker Series Presentation, College of Management, Georgia Institute of Technology, October 14. See also Behar, H. (2007), *It's Not About the Coffee: Leadership Principles from a Life at Starbucks* (New York: Portfolio).

39. John Rice (GE Vice Chairman, President, and CEO, GE Technology Infrastructure) (2009), presentation at Georgia Institute of Technology, May 11.

40. This case vignette is drawn from: Levy, S. (2011), *In the Plex: How Google Thinks, Works, and Shapes Our Lives* (New York: Simon & Schuster).

41. Google's 10-K report. U.S. Securities and Exchange Commission (SEC), Washington, D.C., December 31, 2012.

42. Bower, J. L. (1970), *Managing the Resource Allocation Process* (Boston, MA: Harvard Business School Press); Bower, J. L., and C. G. Gilbert (2005), *From Resource Allocation to Strategy* (Oxford, UK: Oxford University Press); Burgelman, R. A. (1983), "A model of the interaction of strategic behavior, corporate context, and the concept of strategy," *Academy of Management Review* 8: 61–71; and Burgelman, R. A. (1983), "A process model of internal corporate venturing in a major diversified firm," *Administrative Science Quarterly* 28: 223–244.

43. Bower, J. L., and C. G. Gilbert (2005), *From Resource Allocation to Strategy.*

44. Burgelman, R. A. (1994), "Fading memories: A process theory of strategic business exit in dynamic environments," *Administrative Science Quarterly* 39: 24–56.

45. Burgelman, R. A., and A. S. Grove (1996), "Strategic dissonance," *California Management Review* 38: 8–28.

46. Grant, R. M. (2003), "Strategic planning in a turbulent environment: Evidence from the oil majors," *Strategic Management Journal* 24: 491–517; Brown, S. L., and K. M. Eisenhardt (1997), "The art of continuous change: Linking complexity theory and time-based evolution in relentlessly shifting organizations," *Administrative Science Quarterly* 42: 1–34; Farjourn, M. (2002), "Towards an organic perspective on strategy," *Strategic Management Journal* 23: 561–594; Mahoney, J. (2005), *Economic Foundation of Strategy* (Thousand Oaks, CA: Sage); and Burgelman, R. A., and A. S. Grove (2007), "Let chaos reign, then rein in chaos – repeatedly: Managing strategic dynamics for corporate longevity," *Strategic Management Journal* 28: 965–979.

47. Hamel, G. (2007), *The Future of Management* (Boston, MA: Harvard Business School Publishing).

48. This *my*Strategy module is based on: Stern, S. (2004), "Do scientists pay to be scientists?" *Management Science* 50(6): 835–853; and Esty, D. C., and A. S. Winston (2009), *Green to Gold: How Smart Companies Use Environmental Strategy to Innovate, Create Value, and Build Competitive Advantage,* revised and updated (Hoboken, NJ: John Wiley).

13 Marketing: Helping Buyers Buy

Learning Objectives

AFTER YOU HAVE READ AND STUDIED THIS CHAPTER, YOU SHOULD BE ABLE TO

LO 13-1 Define *marketing*, and apply the marketing concept to both for-profit and nonprofit organizations.

LO 13-2 Describe the four Ps of marketing.

LO 13-3 Summarize the marketing research process.

LO 13-4 Show how marketers use environmental scanning to learn about the changing marketing environment.

LO 13-5 Explain how marketers apply the tools of market segmentation, relationship marketing, and the study of consumer behavior.

LO 13-6 Compare the business-to-business market and the consumer market.

Getting to Know **Daymond John**

I n the business world, you don't necessarily have to be the first person to think of a good idea in order for it to become successful. Oftentimes, the entrepreneurs who uniquely market an existing product or service enjoy big returns on their investments.

Daymond John set off on his path to prosperity in 1989 when he began sewing wool hats in his Queens, New York, apartment. For the previous few weeks he had noticed young men in the neighborhood sporting short snowcaps with the tops cut off and cinched together with string. John couldn't believe that department stores were selling the hats for as much as $20. So, with the help of a neighbor, he sewed dozens of hats and sold them for $10 in front of the New York Coliseum. John was astounded when he ended up with $800 after his first day. Knowing he had a great concept on his hands, John threw himself into his new apparel business. As a nod to the do-it-yourself origins of the venture, he named the company FUBU—"For Us By Us."

To go along with his distinctive brand name, John designed a graffiti-inspired logo and sewed it onto sweatshirts, tees, and other sportswear. Despite a strong start, John soon ran into problems. "Like most entrepreneurs, the initial struggle was to go past the point of imagination and make it a point of conception, where I was actually putting together a product and producing it," said John. "Everyone has an idea, but it's taking those first steps toward turning that idea into a reality that are always the toughest." Finding the time to accomplish all this proved difficult. After a day of calling distributors and sewing, John would then trudge off to his night job as a server at Red Lobster. FUBU ended up running out of money three times, causing John to consider abandoning the idea altogether.

But in 1992 he relaunched the brand with the help of three partners and a new business strategy. John knew he certainly wasn't the only talented individual living in Hollis, Queens. The neighborhood had been home to hip-hop legends like Run-DMC, Salt-N-Pepa, and LL Cool J. In order to get FUBU into the public eye, John worked hard to put his clothes into the hands of his famous friends. "I'd give them a shirt to wear on stage, sneak in their trailer, steal it and give it to another rapper," said John. The company's big break came in 1993 when LL Cool J wore a FUBU hat in a commercial for Gap. The retailer pulled the commercial a month later when executives realized they had been unknowingly promoting another brand, but by then the spot had done wonders to raise FUBU's profile. Still, the company wasn't solvent enough to receive approval for a small-business loan. As a result, John and his mother mortgaged their house for $100,000 and bet their future on FUBU's success.

It turned out to be a good decision. John achieved another professional coup when he took the brand to a famous industry trade show in Las Vegas. Despite not having enough money to buy a booth at the event, John and his partners managed to negotiate more than $300,000 worth of orders out of a hotel room. Meanwhile, the brand continued to gain traction with many in the hip-hop community. In 1996 FUBU secured LL Cool J's services as an official celebrity spokesman. "I'm a firm believer in utilizing celebrities because they tap into people on an emotional basis," said John. "When you get behind a celebrity, he'll get behind you." By the end of the 1990s, FUBU was bringing in more than $350 million in annual revenue. Since then, John has used his position as a millionaire mogul to invest in tech start-ups and advise other entrepreneurs, especially in his role as a judge on the TV show *Shark Tank*.

In this chapter you'll learn how master marketers like Daymond John identify their audience and figure out how to reach them. Whether through distribution, advertising, or publicity, successful marketing makes a connection with a customer that they won't soon forget.

Daymond John
- Founder of FUBU
- Started by sewing wool hats in his apartment
- Turned FUBU into a multimillion-dollar lifestyle brand

www.fubu.com

@fubuapparel

Sources: Emily Inverso, "Shark Tank's Daymond John on the Business of Being Broke—And More," *Forbes*, March 6, 2014; Harley Finkelstein, "Daymond John Answers Your Questions," *Huffington Post*, February 10, 2014; and Teri Evans, "Shark Tank's Daymond John on Thinking Big," *Entrepreneur*, October 31, 2012.

name that **company**

This company studies population growth and regional trends as it expands its product line for specific regions of the country. Its research led to the creation of Creole flavors targeted primarily to the South and spicy nacho cheese flavors made especially for Texas and California. Name that company. (The answer can be found in this chapter.)

LO 13–1 Define *marketing*, and apply the marketing concept to both for-profit and nonprofit organizations.

WHAT IS MARKETING?

marketing
The activity, set of institutions, and processes for creating, communicating, delivering, and exchanging offerings that have value for customers, clients, partners, and society at large.

The term *marketing* means different things to different people. Many think of marketing as simply "selling" or "advertising." Yes, selling and advertising are part of marketing, but it's much more. The American Marketing Association has defined **marketing** as the activity, set of institutions, and processes for creating, communicating, delivering, and exchanging offerings that have value for customers, clients, partners, and society at large. We can also think of marketing, more simply, as the activities buyers and sellers perform to facilitate mutually satisfying exchanges.

In the past marketing focused almost entirely on helping the seller sell. That's why many people still think of it as mostly selling, advertising, and distribution from the seller to the buyer. Today, much of marketing is instead about helping the buyer buy.[1] Let's examine a couple of examples.

Today, when people want to buy a new or used car, they often go online first. They go to a website like Cars.com to search for the vehicle they want. At other websites they compare prices and features. By the time they go to the dealer, they may know exactly which car they want and the best price available.

The websites have helped the buyer buy. Not only are customers spared searching one dealership after another to find the best price, but manufacturers and dealers are eager to participate so that they don't lose customers. The future of marketing is doing everything you can to help the buyer buy. The easier a marketer makes the purchase decision process, the more that marketer will sell.[2]

Let's look at another case. In the past, one of the few ways students and parents could find the college with the right "fit" was to travel from campus to campus, a grueling and expensive process. Today, colleges use podcasts, virtual tours, live chats, and other interactive technologies to make on-campus visits less necessary. Such virtual tours help students and their parents buy.

Of course, helping the buyer buy also helps the seller sell. Think about that for a minute. In the vacation market, many people find the trip they want themselves. They go online to find the right spot, and then make choices, sometimes questioning potential sellers. In industries like this, the role of marketing is to make sure that a company's products or services are easily found online, and that the company responds effectively to potential customers. Websites like Expedia, Travelocity, and Priceline allow customers to find the best price or set their own.

These are only a few examples of the marketing trend toward helping buyers buy. Consumers today spend hours searching the Internet for good deals.

Wise marketers provide a wealth of information online and even cultivate customer relationships using blogs and social networking sites such as Facebook and Twitter.[3]

Online communities provide an opportunity to observe people (customers and others) interacting with one another, expressing their own opinions, forming relationships, and commenting on various goods and services. It is important for marketers to track what relevant bloggers are writing by doing blog searches using key terms that define their market. Vendors who have text-mining tools can help companies measure conversations about their products and their personnel. Much of the future of marketing lies in mining such online conversations and responding appropriately. For example, marketers are learning why people shop online, put the goods into a shopping cart, but then end the sale before they give their credit card information.[4] Retailers and other marketers who rely solely on traditional advertising and selling are losing out to new ways of marketing.[5]

The Evolution of Marketing

What marketers do at any particular time depends on what they need to do to fill customers' needs and wants, which continually change. Let's take a brief look at how those changes have influenced the evolution of marketing. Marketing in the United States has passed through four eras: (1) production, (2) selling, (3) marketing concept, and (4) customer relationship. Today, a new era is emerging: mobile/on-demand marketing (see Figure 13.1).

The Production Era   From the time the first European settlers began their struggle to survive in America until the early 1900s, the general philosophy of business was "Produce as much as you can, because there is a limitless market for it." Given the limited production capability and vast demand for products in those days, that production philosophy was both logical and profitable. Business owners were mostly farmers, carpenters, and trade workers. They needed to produce more and more, so their goals centered on production.

The Selling Era   By the 1920s, businesses had developed mass-production techniques (such as automobile assembly lines), and production capacity often exceeded the immediate market demand. Therefore, the business philosophy

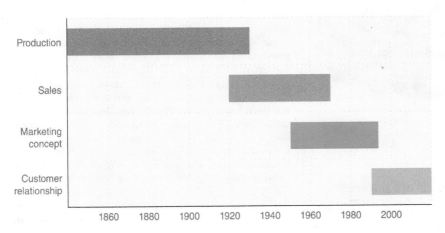

FIGURE 13.1 MARKETING ERAS

The evolution of marketing in the United States involved four eras: (1) production, (2) selling, (3) marketing concept, and (4) customer relationship. Today a new era is emerging: mobile/on-demand marketing.

turned from producing to selling. Most companies emphasized selling and advertising in an effort to persuade consumers to buy existing products; few offered extensive service after the sale.

The Marketing Concept Era   After World War II ended in 1945, returning soldiers starting new careers and beginning families sparked a tremendous demand for goods and services. The postwar years launched the sudden increase in the birthrate that we now call the baby boom, and also a boom in consumer spending. Competition for the consumer's dollar was fierce. Businesses recognized that they needed to be responsive to consumers if they wanted to get their business, and a philosophy emerged in the 1950s called the marketing concept.

The **marketing concept** had three parts:

1. *A customer orientation.* Find out what consumers want and provide it for them. (Note the emphasis on meeting consumer needs rather than on promotion or sales.)

2. *A service orientation.* Make sure everyone in the organization has the same objective: customer satisfaction. This should be a total and integrated organizational effort. That is, everyone from the president of the firm to the delivery people should be customer-oriented. Does that seem to be the norm today?

3. *A profit orientation.* Focus on those goods and services that will earn the most profit and enable the organization to survive and expand to serve more consumer wants and needs.

It took awhile for businesses to implement the marketing concept. The process went slowly during the 1960s and 1970s. During the 1980s, businesses began to apply the marketing concept more aggressively than they had done over the preceding 30 years. That led to a focus on customer relationship management (CRM) that has become very important today. We explore that concept next.

The Customer Relationship Era   In the 1990s and early 2000s, some managers extended the marketing concept by adopting the practice of customer relationship management. **Customer relationship management (CRM)** is the process of learning as much as possible about present customers and doing everything you can over time to satisfy them—or even to exceed their expectations—with goods and services.[6] The idea is to enhance customer satisfaction and stimulate long-term customer loyalty. For example, most airlines offer frequent-flier programs that reward loyal customers with free flights. The newest in customer relationship building, as mentioned earlier, involves social networks, online communities, tweets, and blogs. Relationship building is important in global markets as well. For example, it's important to build good relationships with partners in China.[7]

Clearly, the degree of consumer dissatisfaction that exists, especially with services such as airlines and phone companies, shows that marketers have

marketing concept
A three-part business philosophy: (1) a customer orientation, (2) a service orientation, and (3) a profit orientation.

customer relationship management (CRM)
The process of learning as much as possible about customers and doing everything you can to satisfy them—or even exceed their expectations—with goods and services.

In the selling era, the focus of marketing was on selling, with little service afterward and less customization. What economic and social factors made this approach appropriate for the time?

www.campbellsoupcompany.com

seeking **sustainability**

Making Sustainability Just Peachy

We probably all remember enjoying a piping hot bowl of Campbell's soup on a blustery day. As the company slogan said, it was "mmm mmm" good. What you may not know is Campbell Soup is one of only 18 U.S. companies named to the Global 100 Most Sustainable Corporations in the World list. Through its corporate social responsibility program, the company strives to make a positive impact in the markets it serves. Its work with the Food Bank of South New Jersey is a great example of being responsible and promoting sustainability.

The Food Bank of South Jersey learned that local farmers were discarding almost 1 million peaches a year in landfills. The peaches were perfectly fine to

eat, but had bruises and other imperfections that made them unacceptable to grocery store produce managers. When the food bank asked if it could have the peaches, the farmers agreed to donate them at no cost. The question of what to do with the peaches was challenging until the Food Bank and Campbell's teamed up and "Just Peachy Salsa" was born.

Campbell's agreed to manufacture the salsa at no cost. In fact,

employees donated their time and agreed to label 42,000 jars of "Just Peachy Salsa" by hand. Because of the collaboration, South Jersey farmers did not have the expense of dumping peaches or the negative environmental impact of clogging landfills. The local Food Bank was able to generate close to $100,000 per year to provide additional food products to people in need, and consumers can enjoy a healthy product. When it comes to seeking sustainability, Campbell's really is "mmm mmm" good.

Sources: Kurt Kuehn and Lynnette McIntire, "Sustainability a CFO Can Love," *Harvard Business Review*, April 2014; "Campbell Soup Company Named to Global 100 Sustainability Index," *Reuters*, January 22, 2014; and Campbell Soup Company, www.campbellsoupcompany.com (accessed April 2014).

a long way to go to create customer satisfaction and loyalty. Since many consumers today are interested in green products and protecting the environment, relationship building also means responding to that desire. The Seeking Sustainability box explores sustainability in the food industry.

The Emerging Mobile/On-Demand Marketing Era The digital age is increasing consumers' power and pushing marketing toward being on demand, not just always "on." Consumers are demanding relevant information exactly when they want it, without all the noise of unwanted messages. Search technologies have made product information pervasive. Consumers share, compare, and rate experiences through social media; and mobile devices make it all available 24/7.

Developments such as inexpensive microtransmitters embedded in products will allow consumers to search by image, voice, or gestures. For example, if your friend has a product you like, you will be able to just tap it with your phone and instantly get product reviews, prices, and so on. If you can't decide what color to buy, you can just send the photo to your Facebook friends who can vote for their favorite. After you buy it, you will get special offers from the manufacturer or its partners for similar products or services.

As digital technology continues to grow, consumer demands are likely to rise in four areas:[8]

1. *Now.* Consumers want to interact anywhere, anytime.
2. *Can I?* They want to do new things with different kinds of information in ways that create value for them. For example, a couple wanting to know if they can afford to buy a house they walk by could simply snap a photo and instantly see the sale price and other property information; while at

Kids will spend 11 minutes dressing Spike up like a princess.

How about two minutes to brush their teeth?

Brushing for two minutes now can save your child from severe tooth pain later. Two minutes, twice a day. They have the time. For fun, 2-minute videos to watch while brushing, go to 2min2x.org.

Ad Council

PARTNERSHIP FOR
Healthy Mouths
Healthy Lives

©2013 Healthy Mouths, Healthy Lives

The Ad Council sponsors many public service ads like this one. The idea is to make the public more aware of various needs that only nonprofit organizations are meeting. The ads then encourage the public to get engaged in the issue somehow, if only by donating money. Have you responded to any Ad Council advertisements?

 connect

▶ **iSee It!** Need help understanding the marketing mix? Visit your Connect e-book video tab for a brief animated explanation.

marketing mix
The ingredients that go into a marketing program: product, price, place, and promotion.

the same time the device automatically accesses their financial information, contacts mortgagers, and obtains loan preapproval.

3. *For me.* Consumers expect all data stored about them to be used to personalize what they experience.

4. *Simple.* Consumers expect all interactions to be easy.

Companies will be looking for employees who can improve the business's handling of social media, big data, and customer experiences. Maybe you will be one of them.

Nonprofit Organizations and Marketing

Even though the marketing concept emphasizes a profit orientation, marketing is a critical part of almost all organizations, including nonprofits.[9] Charities use marketing to raise funds for combating world hunger, for instance, or to obtain other resources. The Red Cross uses promotion to encourage people to donate blood when local or national supplies run low. Greenpeace uses marketing to promote ecologically safe technologies. Environmental groups use marketing to try to cut carbon emissions. Churches use marketing to attract new members and raise funds. Politicians use marketing to get votes.

States use marketing to attract new businesses and tourists. Many states, for example, have competed to get automobile companies from other countries to locate plants in their area. Schools use marketing to attract new students. Other organizations, such as arts groups, unions, and social groups, also use marketing. The Ad Council, for example, uses public service ads to create awareness and change attitudes on such issues as drunk driving and fire prevention.

Organizations use marketing, in fact, to promote everything from environmentalism and crime prevention ("Take A Bite Out Of Crime") to social issues ("Friends Don't Let Friends Drive Drunk").

LO 13–2   Describe the four Ps of marketing.

THE MARKETING MIX

We can divide much of what marketing people do into four factors, called the four Ps to make them easy to remember. They are:

1. Product
2. Price
3. Place
4. Promotion

Managing the controllable parts of the marketing process means (1) designing a want-satisfying product, (2) setting a price for the product, (3) putting the product in a place where people will buy it, and (4) promoting the product. These four factors are called the **marketing mix** because businesses blend them together in a well-designed marketing program (see Figure 13.2).

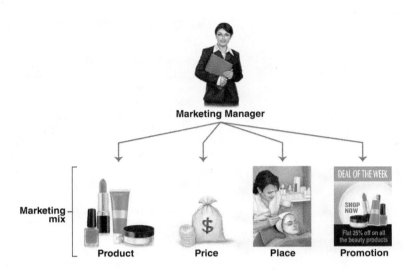

FIGURE 13.2 MARKETING MANAGERS AND THE MARKETING MIX
Marketing managers must choose how to implement the four Ps of the marketing mix: product, price, place, and promotion. The goals are to please customers and make a profit.

Applying the Marketing Process

The four Ps are a convenient way to remember the basics of marketing, but they don't necessarily include everything that goes into the marketing process for all products. One of the best ways to understand the entire marketing process is to take a product or a group of products and follow the process that led to their development and sale (see Figure 13.3).

Imagine, for example, that you and your friends want to start a money-making business near your college. You've noticed a lot of vegetarians among your acquaintances. You do a quick survey in a few dorms, sororities, and fraternities and find many vegetarians—and other students who like to eat vegetarian meals once in a while. Your preliminary research indicates some demand for a vegetarian restaurant nearby. You check the fast-food stores in the area and find that none offer more than one or two vegetarian meals. In fact, most don't have any, except salads and some soups.

You note that haute-vegetarian menus are big in Europe.[10] Why not in the United States? You also note that McDonald's went vegetarian in India in 2013.[11] You find that KFC Canada offers a vegan version of its chicken sandwich in 500 of its 750 outlets. Further research identifies a number of different kinds of vegetarians. Vegans eat neither eggs nor dairy products. Vegan diets took off when Beyonce's 22-day vegan diet was announced. Bill Clinton says he's been vegan since 2009.[12] Such publicity led to the announcement that 2014 was "the year of the vegan."[13]

You conclude that a vegetarian restaurant would have to appeal to all kinds of vegetarians to be a success. Your research identifies vegan farmers who don't use any synthetic chemical fertilizers, pesticides, herbicides, or genetically modified ingredients. You also find that there is a company that is making an egg-like product from vegetables. That would appeal to those vegetarians who don't eat eggs.[14]

You've just performed the first few steps in the marketing process. You noticed an opportunity (a need for vegetarian food, perhaps near campus). You conducted some preliminary research to see whether your idea had any merit. And then you identified groups of people who might be interested in your product. They will be your *target market* (the people you will try to persuade to come to your restaurant).

FIGURE 13.3 THE MARKETING PROCESS WITH THE FOUR PS

product
Any physical good, service, or idea that satisfies a want or need plus anything that would enhance the product in the eyes of consumers, such as the brand.

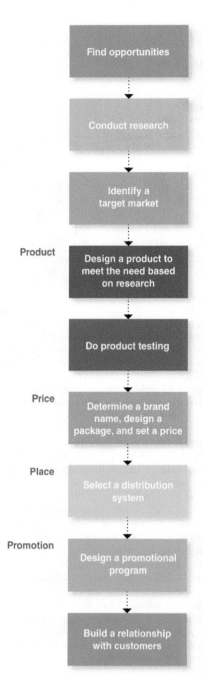

Find opportunities

Conduct research

Identify a target market

Product
Design a product to meet the need based on research

Do product testing

Price
Determine a brand name, design a package, and set a price

Place
Select a distribution system

Promotion
Design a promotional program

Build a relationship with customers

test marketing
The process of testing products among potential users.

brand name
A word, letter, or group of words or letters that differentiates one seller's goods and services from those of competitors.

Designing a Product to Meet Consumer Needs

Once you've researched consumer needs and found a target market (which we'll discuss in more detail later) for your product, the four Ps of marketing come into play. You start by developing a product or products. A **product** is any physical good, service, or idea that satisfies a want or need, plus anything that would enhance the product in the eyes of consumers, such as the brand name. In this case, your proposed product is a restaurant that would serve different kinds of vegetarian meals. You keep up your research, and find that a restaurant called Freshii is bringing quinoa and kale to the masses.[15] You are getting a better idea of what your products should be.

It's a good idea at this point to do concept testing. That is, you develop an accurate description of your restaurant and ask people, in person or online, whether the idea of the restaurant and the kind of meals you intend to offer appeals to them. If it does, you might go to a supplier that offers vegetarian products to get the ingredients to prepare samples that you can take to consumers to test their reactions. The process of testing products among potential users is called **test marketing**. For example, you can test market your vegetarian burgers and learn how best to prepare them.[16]

If consumers like the products and agree they would buy them, you have the information you need to find investors and look for a convenient location to open a restaurant. You'll have to think of a catchy name. (For practice, stop for a minute and try to think of one.) We'll use Very Vegetarian in this text, although we're sure you can think of a better name. Meanwhile, let's continue with the discussion of product development.

You may want to offer some well-known brand names to attract people right away. A **brand name** is a word, letter, or group of words or letters that differentiates one seller's goods and services from those of competitors. Brand names of vegetarian products include Tofurky, Mori-Nu, and Yves Veggie Cuisine. We'll discuss the product development process in detail in Chapter 14, and follow the Very Vegetarian case to show you how all marketing and other business decisions tie together. For now, we're simply sketching the whole marketing process to give you an overall picture. So far, we've covered the first P of the marketing mix: product. Next comes price.

Setting an Appropriate Price

After you've decided what products and services you want to offer consumers, you have to set appropriate prices. Those prices depend on a number of factors. In the restaurant business, the price could be close to what other restaurants charge to stay competitive. Or you might charge less to attract business, especially at the beginning. Or you may offer high-quality products for which customers are willing to pay a little more (as Starbucks does). You also have to consider the costs of producing, distributing, and promoting the product, which all influence your price. We'll discuss pricing issues in more detail in Chapter 14.

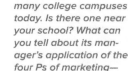

A vegetarian restaurant might fill a popular need in the neighborhood of many college campuses today. Is there one near your school? What can you tell about its manager's application of the four Ps of marketing—product, price, place, and promotion?

Getting the Product to the Right Place

There are several ways you can serve the market for vegetarian meals. You can have people come in, sit down, and eat at the restaurant, but that's not the only alternative—think of pizza. You could deliver the food to customers' dorms, apartments, and student unions. You may want to sell your products in supermarkets or health-food stores, or through organizations that specialize in distributing food products. Such intermediaries are the middle links in a series of organizations that distribute goods from producers to consumers. (The more traditional word for them is *middlemen.*) Getting the product to consumers when and where they want it is critical to market success. Don't forget to consider the Internet as a way to reach consumers. We'll discuss the importance of marketing intermediaries and distribution in detail in Chapter 15.

Developing an Effective Promotional Strategy

The last of the four Ps of marketing is promotion. **Promotion** consists of all the techniques sellers use to inform people about and motivate them to buy their products or services. Promotion includes advertising; personal selling; public relations; publicity; word of mouth (viral marketing); and various sales promotion efforts, such as coupons, rebates, samples, and cents-off deals. We'll discuss promotion in detail in Chapter 16.

Promotion often includes relationship building with customers. Among other activities, that means responding to suggestions consumers make to improve the products or their marketing, including price and packaging. For Very Vegetarian, postpurchase, or after-sale, service may include refusing payment for meals that weren't satisfactory and stocking additional vegetarian products customers say they would like. Listening to customers and responding to their needs is the key to the ongoing process that is marketing.

promotion
All the techniques sellers use to inform people about and motivate them to buy their products or services.

Use LearnSmart to help retain what you have learned. Access your instructor's Connect course to check out LearnSmart, or go to learnsmartadvantage.com for help.

LEARNSMART

test prep

- What does it mean to "help the buyer buy"?
- What are the three parts of the marketing concept?
- What are the four Ps of the marketing mix?

LO 13-3 Summarize the marketing research process.

PROVIDING MARKETERS WITH INFORMATION

Every decision in the marketing process depends on information. When they conduct **marketing research**, marketers analyze markets to determine opportunities and challenges, and to find the information they need to make good decisions.

Marketing research helps identify what products customers have purchased in the past, and what changes have occurred to alter what they want now and what they're likely to want in the future. Marketers also conduct research on business trends, the ecological impact of their decisions, global trends, and more. Businesses need information to compete effectively, and marketing research is the activity that gathers it. You have learned, for example, how important research is to a person contemplating starting a vegetarian restaurant. Besides listening to customers, marketing researchers also pay attention to what employees, shareholders, dealers, consumer advocates, media representatives, and other stakeholders have to say. As noted earlier, much of that research is now being gathered online through social media. Despite all that research, however, marketers still have difficulty understanding their customers as well as they should.[17]

The Marketing Research Process

A simplified marketing research process consists of at least four key steps:

1. Defining the question (the problem or opportunity) and determining the present situation.
2. Collecting research data.
3. Analyzing the research data.
4. Choosing the best solution and implementing it.

The following sections look at each of these steps.

Defining the Question and Determining the Present Situation Marketing researchers need the freedom to discover what the present situation is, what the problems or opportunities are, what the alternatives are, what information they need, and how to go about gathering and analyzing data.

Collecting Data Usable information is vital to the marketing research process. Research can become quite expensive, however, so marketers must often make a trade-off between the need for information and the cost of obtaining it. Normally the least expensive method is to gather information already compiled by others and published in journals and books or made available online.

Such existing data are called **secondary data**, since you aren't the first one to gather them. Figure 13.4 lists the principal sources of secondary marketing research information. Despite its name, *secondary* data is what marketers should gather *first* to avoid incurring unnecessary expense. To find secondary data about vegetarians, go to the website for *Vegetarian Times* (www.vegetariantimes.com) or search other websites on vegetarianism.

marketing research
The analysis of markets to determine opportunities and challenges, and to find the information needed to make good decisions.

secondary data
Information that has already been compiled by others and published in journals and books or made available online.

Personal interviews are one way of collecting primary research data about customers' needs, wants, and buying habits. Perhaps someone has stopped you in a shopping mall recently to ask you some questions about a product or product category you use. What might contribute to the difficulty of collecting information through such interviews, and how can marketers improve the process?

FIGURE 13.4 SELECTED SOURCES OF PRIMARY AND SECONDARY INFORMATION

PRIMARY SOURCES	SECONDARY SOURCES		
Interviews	**Government Publications**		
Surveys	*Statistical Abstract of the United States*		*Census of Transportation*
Observation	*Survey of Current Business*		*Annual Survey of Manufacturers*
Focus groups	*Census of Retail Trade*		
Online surveys			
Questionnaires	**Commercial Publications**		
Customer comments	ACNielsen Company studies on retailing and media		
Letters from	Marketing Research Corporation of America studies on consumer purchases		
customers	Selling Areas—Marketing Inc. reports on food sales		

Magazines

Entrepreneur	*Journal of Retailing*	*Journal of Advertising Research*
Bloomberg Businessweek	*Journal of Consumer Research*	Trade magazines
Fortune	*Journal of Advertising*	appropriate to your
Inc.	*Journal of Marketing Research*	industry such as
Advertising Age	*Marketing News*	*Progressive Grocer*
Forbes	*Hispanic Business*	Reports from various
Harvard Business Review	*Black Enterprise*	chambers of commerce
Journal of Marketing		

Newspapers

The Wall Street Journal, Barron's, your local newspapers

Internal Sources

Company records	Income statements
Balance sheets	Prior research reports

General Sources

Internet searches	Commercial databases
Google-type searches	

Often, secondary data don't provide all the information managers need for important business decisions. To gather additional in-depth information, marketers must do their own research. The results of such *new studies* are called **primary data**. One way to gather primary data is to conduct a survey.

Telephone surveys, online surveys, mail surveys, and personal interviews are the most common forms of primary data collection. Focus groups (defined below) are another popular method of surveying individuals. What do you think would be the best way to survey students about your potential new restaurant? Would you do a different kind of survey after it had been open a few months? How could you help vegetarians find your restaurant? That is, how could you help your buyers buy? One question researchers pay close attention to is: "Would you recommend this product to a friend?"

A **focus group** is a group of people who meet under the direction of a discussion leader to communicate their opinions about an organization, its products, or other given issues. This textbook is updated periodically using many focus groups made up of faculty and students. They tell us, the authors, what subjects and examples they like and dislike, and the authors follow their suggestions for changes.

Marketers can now gather both secondary and primary data online. The authors of this text, for example, do much research online, but they also gather data from books, articles, interviews, and other sources.

primary data
Data that you gather yourself (not from secondary sources such as books and magazines).

focus group
A small group of people who meet under the direction of a discussion leader to communicate their opinions about an organization, its products, or other given issues.

The authors of this text enjoy the benefits of using focus groups. College faculty and students come to these meetings and tell us how to improve this book and its support material. We listen carefully and make as many changes as we can in response. Suggestions have included adding more descriptive captions to the photos in the book and making the text as user-friendly as possible. How are we doing so far?

Analyzing the Research Data   Marketers must turn the data they collect in the research process into useful information. Careful, honest interpretation of the data can help a company find useful alternatives to specific marketing challenges. For example, by doing primary research, Fresh Italy, a small Italian pizzeria, found that its pizza's taste was rated superior to that of the larger pizza chains. However, the company's sales lagged behind the competition. Secondary research on the industry revealed that free delivery (which Fresh Italy did not offer) was more important to customers than taste. Fresh Italy now delivers—and has increased its market share.

Choosing the Best Solution and Implementing It   After collecting and analyzing data, market researchers determine alternative strategies and make recommendations about which may be best and why. This final step in a research effort also includes following up on actions taken to see whether the results were what was expected. If not, the company can take corrective action and conduct new studies in its ongoing attempt to provide consumer satisfaction at the lowest cost. You can see, then, that marketing research is a continuous process of responding to changes in the marketplace and in consumer preferences.

LO 13–4   Show how marketers use environmental scanning to learn about the changing marketing environment.

THE MARKETING ENVIRONMENT

environmental scanning
The process of identifying the factors that can affect marketing success.

Marketing managers must be aware of the surrounding environment when making marketing mix decisions. **Environmental scanning** is the process of identifying factors that can affect marketing success. As you can see in Figure 13.5, they include global, technological, sociocultural, competitive, and economic influences. We discussed these factors in some detail in Chapter 1, but now let's review them from a strictly marketing perspective.

FIGURE 13.5 THE MARKETING ENVIRONMENT

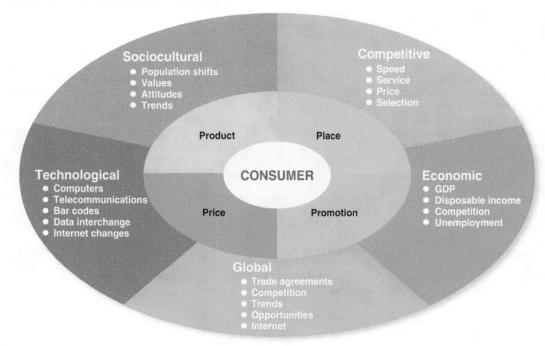

Global Factors

Using the Internet, businesses can reach many of the world's consumers relatively easily and carry on a dialogue with them about the goods and services they want (see the Reaching Beyond Our Borders box). The globalization process puts more pressure on those whose responsibility it is to deliver products to these global customers.

Technological Factors

The most important technological changes also relate to the Internet. Using consumer databases, blogs, social networking, and the like, companies can develop products and services that closely match consumers' needs. As you read in Chapter 9, firms can now produce customized goods and services for about the same price as mass-produced goods. Thus flexible manufacturing and mass customization are also major influences on marketers. You can imagine, for example, using databases to help you devise custom-made fruit mixes and various salads for your customers at Very Vegetarian.

Sociocultural Factors

Marketers must monitor social trends to maintain their close relationship with customers, since population growth and changing demographics can have an effect on sales. One of the fastest-growing segments of the U.S. population in the 21st century is people over 65. The increase in the number of older adults creates growing demand for retirement communities, health care, prescription drugs, recreation, continuing education, and more. Do you see any evidence that older people would enjoy having more vegetarian meals?

www.lego.com

reaching beyond **our borders**

Two Is Better Than One

After more than 35 years of a strict one-child policy, China agreed to change the infamous regulation. The new law allows married couples to have two children if one of the spouses is an only child. Besides affecting countless families, the new reform promises to have a big impact on businesses as the policy switch could mean 9.5 million additional babies coming into the Chinese market in the next five years. Producers of everything from baby formula and diapers, to violins and *guzhengs* (a Chinese string instrument) predict a future sales windfall with the new policy.

While many businesses can expect added growth due to the policy shift, one the greatest long-term beneficiaries of the change may be Lego, the world's second largest toymaker. Since the company has little room to

grow in the U.S. (where Lego controls 85 percent of the construction toy market), China is now one of its key target markets. In 2013, Lego enjoyed sales growth in China of 70 percent as parents sought educational toys for their children. Chinese parents are particularly attracted to Lego because they feel the toy helps develop their children's creativity.

Lego, however, faces a price obstacle in China because its

sets cost twice as much as they do in the United States due to import and distribution costs. To reduce the high cost of Legos in China, the company has committed to build a factory in Jiaxing, an industrial town near Shanghai. The cost of building a factory may be a relatively small price to pay since the Asia-Pacific region is predicted to overtake North America as the largest regional toy market sometime in the next few years. With the expected number of Chinese children expected to grow significantly, Lego feels this is a market it can clearly "build on."

Sources: Isabella Steger and Laurie Burkitt, "Chinese Couples—and Investors—Are Pregnant with Anticipation," *The Wall Street Journal*, November 19, 2013; Ted Trautman, "The Year of the Lego," *The New Yorker*, November 11, 2013; and Susan Scutti, "One-Child Policy Is One Big Problem for China," *Newsweek*, January 23, 2014.

Other shifts in the U.S. population are creating new challenges for marketers as they adjust their products to meet the tastes and preferences of Hispanic, Asian, and other growing ethnic groups. To appeal to diverse groups, marketers must listen better and be more responsive to unique ethnic needs. What might you do to appeal to specific ethnic groups with Very Vegetarian?

Competitive Factors

Of course, marketers must pay attention to the dynamic competitive environment. Many brick-and-mortar companies must be aware of new competition from the Internet, including firms that sell automobiles, insurance, music, and clothes. In the book business, Barnes & Noble is still adjusting to the new reality of Amazon.com's huge selection of books at good prices. Borders Books went out of business. What will the challenge from Kindle and other eReaders provide? Now that consumers can literally search the world for the best buys online, marketers must adjust their pricing, delivery, and services accordingly. Can you see any opportunities for Very Vegetarian to make use of the Internet and social media?

Economic Factors

Marketers must pay close attention to the economic environment. As we began the new millennium, the United States was experiencing slow growth, and few customers were eager to buy the most expensive automobiles, watches, and vacations. As the economy slowed, marketers had to adapt by offering products that were less expensive and more tailored to consumers with modest incomes.

What economic changes are occurring around your school that might affect a new vegetarian restaurant? How has the economic crisis or natural disasters, such as floods and drought, affected your area?

TWO DIFFERENT MARKETS: CONSUMER AND BUSINESS-TO-BUSINESS (B2B)

Marketers must know as much as possible about the market they wish to serve. As we defined it in Chapter 6, a market consists of people with unsatisfied wants and needs who have both the resources and the willingness to buy. There are two major markets in business: the *consumer market* and the *business-to-business market*. The **consumer market** consists of all the individuals or households that want goods and services for personal consumption or use and have the resources to buy them.

The **business-to-business (B2B) market** consists of all the individuals and organizations that want goods and services to use in producing other goods and services or to sell, rent, or supply goods to others.[18] Oil-drilling bits, cash registers, display cases, office desks, public accounting audits, and business software are B2B goods and services. Traditionally, they have been known as *industrial* goods and services because they are used in industry.

The important thing to remember is that the buyer's reason for buying—that is, the end use of the product—determines whether a product is a consumer product or a B2B product. A cup of yogurt that a student buys for breakfast is a consumer product. However, when Very Vegetarian purchases the same cup of yogurt to sell to its breakfast customers, it has purchased a B2B product. The following sections outline consumer and B2B markets.

The business-to-business (B2B) market consists of individuals and organizations that sell goods and services to other businesses. A manufacturer, for instance, buys its parts and supplies in the B2B market.

consumer market
All the individuals or households that want goods and services for personal consumption or use.

business-to-business (B2B) market
All the individuals and organizations that want goods and services to use in producing other goods and services or to sell, rent, or supply goods to others.

- What are the four steps in the marketing research process?
- What is environmental scanning?
- What factors are included in environmental scanning?

LO 13–5   Explain how marketers apply the tools of market segmentation, relationship marketing, and the study of consumer behavior.

THE CONSUMER MARKET

The total potential consumer market consists of the billions of people in global markets. Because consumer groups differ greatly by age, education level, income, and taste, a business usually can't fill the needs of every group. It must decide which groups to serve, and then develop products and services specially tailored to their needs.

Take the Campbell Soup Company, for example. You know Campbell for its traditional soups such as chicken noodle and tomato. You may also have

market segmentation
The process of dividing the total market into groups whose members have similar characteristics.

target marketing
Marketing directed toward those groups (market segments) an organization decides it can serve profitably.

FIGURE 13.6 MARKET SEGMENTATION
This table shows some of the methods marketers use to divide the market. The aim of segmentation is to break the market into smaller units.

noticed that Campbell has expanded its U.S. product line to appeal to a number of different tastes. Aware of population growth in the South and in Latino communities in cities across the nation, it introduced a Creole soup for the southern market and a red bean soup for the Latino market. In Texas and California, where people like their food with a bit of kick, Campbell makes its nacho cheese soup spicier than in other parts of the country. It's just one company that has had some success studying the consumer market, breaking it down into categories, and developing products for separate groups.

The process of dividing the total market into groups with similar characteristics is called **market segmentation**. Selecting which groups or segments an organization can serve profitably is **target marketing**. For example, a shoe store may choose to sell only women's shoes, only children's shoes, or only athletic shoes. The issue is finding the right *target market*—the most profitable segment—to serve.

Segmenting the Consumer Market

A firm can segment the consumer market several ways (see Figure 13.6). Rather than selling your product throughout the United States, you might focus on just

Main Dimension	Sample Variables	Typical Segments
Geographic segmentation	Region	Northeast, Midwest, South, West
	City or county size	Under 5,000; 5,000–10,999; 11,000–19,999; 20,000–49,000; 50,000 and up
	Density	Urban, suburban, rural
Demographic segmentation	Gender	Male, female
	Age	Under 5; 5–10; 11–18; 19–34; 35–49; 50–64; 65 and over
	Education	Some high school or less, high school graduate, some college, college graduate, postgraduate
	Race	Caucasian, African American, Indian, Asian, Hispanic
	Nationality	American, Asian, Eastern European, Japanese
	Life stage	Infant, preschool, child, teenager, collegiate, adult, senior
	Income	Under $15,000; $15,000–$24,999; $25,000–$44,999; $45,000–$74,999; $75,000 and over
	Household size	1; 2; 3–4; 5 or more
	Occupation	Professional, technical, clerical, sales supervisors, farmers, students, home-based business owners, retired, unemployed
Psychographic segmentation	Personality	Gregarious, compulsive, extroverted, aggressive, ambitious
	Values	Actualizers, fulfillers, achievers, experiencers, believers, strivers, makers, strugglers
	Lifestyle	Upscale, moderate
Benefit segmentation	Comfort Convenience Durability Economy Health Luxury Safety Status	(Benefit segmentation divides an already established market into smaller, more homogeneous segments. Those people who desire economy in a car would be an example. The benefit desired varies by product.)
Volume segmentation	Usage	Heavy users, light users, nonusers
	Loyalty status	None, medium, strong

one or two regions where you can be most successful, say, southern states such as Florida, Texas, and South Carolina. Dividing a market by cities, counties, states, or regions is **geographic segmentation**.

Alternatively, you could aim your product's promotions toward people ages 25 to 45 who have some college education and above-average incomes. Automobiles such as Lexus are often targeted to this audience. Age, income, and education level are criteria for **demographic segmentation**. So are religion, race, and occupation. Demographics are the most widely used segmentation variable, but not necessarily the best.

Bass Pro Shops offers a vast array of products for the wide range of outdoor enthusiasts who visit its stores. Dividing its market into identifiable segments is crucial to the success of the company. What different market segments do you think the company targets?

You may want your ads to portray a target group's lifestyle. To do that, you would study the group's values, attitudes, and interests in a strategy called **psychographic segmentation**. If you decide to target Generation Y, you would do an in-depth study of members' values and interests, like which TV shows they watch and which personalities they like best. With that information you would develop advertisements for those TV shows using those stars. Some marketers talk about ethnographic segmentation. Basically, such segmentation is like psychographic segmentation in that the idea is to talk with consumers and develop stories about the product from their perspective. Often customers have an entirely different view of your product than you do.[19]

In marketing for Very Vegetarian, what benefits of vegetarianism might you talk about? Should you emphasize freshness, heart-healthiness, taste, or something else? Determining which product benefits your target market prefers and using those benefits to promote a product is **benefit segmentation**.

You can also determine who are the big eaters of vegetarian food. Does your restaurant seem to attract more men or more women? More students or more faculty members? Are your repeat customers from the local community or are they commuters? Separating the market by volume of product use is called **volume (or usage) segmentation**. Once you know who your customer base is, you can design your promotions to better appeal to that specific group or groups.

The best segmentation strategy is to use all the variables to come up with a consumer profile that represents a sizable, reachable, and profitable target market. That may mean not segmenting the market at all and instead going after the total market (everyone). Or it may mean going after ever-smaller segments. We'll discuss that strategy next.

Reaching Smaller Market Segments

Niche marketing is identifying small but profitable market segments and designing or finding products for them. Because it so easily offers an unlimited choice of goods, the Internet is transforming a consumer culture once based on big hits and best-sellers into one that supports more specialized

geographic segmentation
Dividing a market by cities, counties, states, or regions.

demographic segmentation
Dividing the market by age, income, and education level.

psychographic segmentation
Dividing the market using groups' values, attitudes, and interests.

benefit segmentation
Dividing the market by determining which benefits of the product to talk about.

volume (or usage) segmentation
Dividing the market by usage (volume of use).

niche marketing
The process of finding small but profitable market segments and designing or finding products for them.

niche products. With only 5 percent of Americans identifying themselves as vegetarians, what types of vegetarian products do you think Very Vegetarian might sell online to this niche market?

One-to-one marketing means developing a unique mix of goods and services for each individual customer. Travel agencies often develop such packages, including airline reservations, hotel reservations, rental cars, restaurants, and admission to museums and other attractions for individual customers. This is relatively easy to do in B2B markets where each customer may buy in huge volume. But one-to-one marketing is possible in consumer markets as well. Computer companies like Dell and Apple can produce a unique computer system for each customer. Can you envision designing special Very Vegetarian menu items for individual customers?

Building Marketing Relationships

In the world of mass production following the Industrial Revolution, marketers responded by practicing mass marketing. **Mass marketing** means developing products and promotions to please large groups of people. That is, there is little market segmentation. The mass marketer tries to sell the same products to as many people as possible. That means using mass media such as TV, radio, and newspapers to reach them. Although mass marketing led many firms to success, marketing managers often got so caught up with their products and competition that they became less responsive to the market. Airlines, for example, are so intent on meeting competition that they often annoy their customers.

Relationship marketing tends to lead away from mass production and toward custom-made goods and services. The goal is to keep individual customers over time by offering them new products that exactly meet their requirements. Technology enables sellers to work with individual buyers to determine their wants and needs and to develop goods and services specifically designed for them, like hand-tailored shirts and unique vacations.

Understanding consumers is so important to marketing that a whole area of marketing has emerged called the study of *consumer behavior*.[20] We explore that area next.

The Consumer Decision-Making Process

The first step in the consumer decision-making process is *problem recognition,* which may occur when your washing machine breaks down and you realize you need a new one. This leads to an *information search*—you look for ads and brochures about washing machines. You may consult a secondary data source like *Consumer Reports* or other information online. And you'll likely seek advice from other people who have purchased washing machines. The Adapting to Change box discusses how online reviews influence consumer decision making.

After compiling all this information, you *evaluate alternatives* and make a *purchase decision.* But your buying process doesn't end there. After the purchase, you may ask the people you spoke to previously how their machines perform and then do other comparisons to your new washer.

Marketing researchers investigate these consumer thought processes and behavior at each stage in a purchase to determine the best way to help the buyer buy. As we mentioned, this area of study is called *consumer behavior.* Factors that affect consumer behavior include the following.

- *Learning* creates changes in an individual's behavior resulting from previous experiences and information. If you've tried a particular brand of shampoo and don't like it, you've learned not to buy it again.

one-to-one marketing
Developing a unique mix of goods and services for each individual customer.

connect

iSee It! Need help understanding how marketers segment target market? Visit your Connect e-book video tab for a brief animated explanation.

mass marketing
Developing products and promotions to please large groups of people.

relationship marketing
Marketing strategy with the goal of keeping individual customers over time by offering them products that exactly meet their requirements.

Turning Negatives to Positive

When Amazon invited customers to start posting reviews of products 20 years ago, many thought the online retailer had lost its good sense. Today, market researchers admit that Amazon's move created a monumental change in the consumer decision-making process. A recent Nielsen research report helped confirm this shift. The company surveyed 28,000 Internet users in 56 countries and found that online reviews from sites like Amazon are the second most trusted source of a brand's reliability (second only to the recommendations of friends and family). It's no wonder then that in this digital age, we are overwhelmed with the opinions of others about products, opinions we tend to treat as trustworthy and factual. But exactly how reliable are the ratings assigned by reviewers? Is the trust we place in these ratings misplaced? The best answer might be "maybe."

As human beings we have a "herding" tendency that often causes us to think and act in the same way as people around us. Therefore, if reviewers read other product reviews that lean positively toward a product, there's a good chance they may rate the product favorably even if that was not their original impression. Such behavior may be a major reason why extremely high ratings easily outnumber negative ratings on Amazon. Researchers also believe that online reviewers are more positively predisposed to a product because they voluntarily bought the product and are less likely to criticize it. This is generally referred to as a *selection bias*.

Another problem with the validity of online reviews is that reviewers will sometimes rate products negatively when there are shipping or other ordering problems that have nothing to do with the quality of the products

themselves. Amazon has tried to correct these inherent challenges through the creation of Amazon Vine, an invitation-only program that involves the site's top reviewers. These elite reviewers are sent free merchandise to review. Amazon believes working with the site's most trusted reviewers provides more useful reviews for customers to consider. Still, critics contend that giving products for free might create a bias toward a positive rather than negative rating. However, research has shown that the Vine reviewers actually bestow fewer stars than regular reviewers. Strangely, research has also shown that even a product with only negative reviews sells better than a product with no reviews at all. Go figure.

Sources: Lisa Chow, "Top Reviewers on Amazon Get Tons of Free Stuff," *NPR*, October 30, 2013; Joe Queenan, "Why I'm Hating All That Online Rating," *The Wall Street Journal*, February 21, 2014; and Sinan Aral, "The Problem with Online Ratings," *MIT Sloan Management Review*, Winter 2014.

- *Reference group* is the group an individual uses as a reference point in forming beliefs, attitudes, values, or behavior. A college student who carries a briefcase instead of a backpack may see businesspeople as his or her reference group.

- *Culture* is the set of values, attitudes, and ways of doing things transmitted from one generation to another in a given society. The U.S. culture emphasizes and transmits the values of education, freedom, and diversity.

- *Subculture* is the set of values, attitudes, and ways of doing things that results from belonging to a certain ethnic group, racial group, or other group with which one closely identifies (e.g., teenagers).

- *Cognitive dissonance* is a type of psychological conflict that can occur after a purchase. Consumers who make a major purchase may have doubts about whether they got the best product at the best price. Marketers must reassure such consumers after the sale that they made a good decision. An auto dealer, for example, may send positive press articles about the particular car a consumer purchased, offer product guarantees, and provide certain free services.

Many universities have expanded the marketing curriculum to include courses in business-to-business marketing. As you'll learn below, that market is huge.

LO 13–6   Compare the business-to-business market and the consumer market.

THE BUSINESS-TO-BUSINESS MARKET

Business-to-business (B2B) marketers include manufacturers; intermediaries such as retailers; institutions like hospitals, schools, and charities; and the government. The B2B market is larger than the consumer market because items are often sold and resold several times in the B2B process before they reach the final consumer. B2B marketing strategies also differ from consumer marketing because business buyers have their own decision-making process. Several factors make B2B marketing different, including these:

1. Customers in the B2B market are relatively few; there are just a few large construction firms or mining operations compared to the 80 million or so households in the U.S. consumer market.[21]

2. Business customers are relatively large; that is, big organizations account for most of the employment in the production of various goods and services. Nonetheless, there are many small- to medium-sized firms in the United States that together make an attractive market.

3. B2B markets tend to be geographically concentrated. For example, oilfields are found in the Southwest and Canada. Thus B2B marketers can concentrate their efforts on a particular area and minimize distribution problems by locating warehouses near industrial centers.

4. Business buyers are generally more rational and less emotional than ultimate consumers; they use product specifications to guide buying choices and often more carefully weigh the total product offer, including quality, price, and service.

5. B2B sales tend to be direct, but not always. Tire manufacturers sell directly to auto manufacturers but use intermediaries, such as wholesalers and retailers, to sell to ultimate consumers.

6. Whereas consumer promotions are based more on *advertising*, B2B sales are based on *personal selling*. There are fewer customers and they usually demand more personal service.

Figure 13.7 shows some of the differences between buying behavior in the B2B and consumer markets. B2B buyers also use the Internet to make purchases. You'll learn more about the business-to-business market in advanced marketing courses.

YOUR PROSPECTS IN MARKETING

There is a wider variety of careers in marketing than in most business disciplines. If you major in marketing, an array of career options will be available to you. You could become a manager in a retail store like Saks or Target. You could do marketing research or work in product management. You could go into selling, advertising, sales promotion, or public relations. You could work in transportation, storage, or international distribution. You could design interactive websites. These are just a few of the possibilities. Think, for

FIGURE 13.7 COMPARING BUSINESS-TO-BUSINESS AND CONSUMER BUYING BEHAVIOR

	Business-to-business Market	Consumer Market
Market Structure	Relatively few potential customers	Many potential customers
	Larger purchases	Smaller purchases
	Geographically concentrated	Geographically dispersed
Products	Require technical, complex products	Require less technical products
	Frequently require customization	Sometimes require customization
	Frequently require technical advice, delivery, and after-sale service	Sometimes require technical advice, delivery, and after-sale service
	Buyers are trained	No special training
Buying Procedures	Negotiate details of most purchases	Accept standard terms for most purchases
	Follow objective standards	Use personal judgment
	Formal process involving specific employees	Informal process involving household members
	Closer relationships between marketers and buyers	Impersonal relationships between marketers and consumers
	Often buy from multiple sources	Rarely buy from multiple sources

example, of the many ways to use Facebook, Google, and other new technologies in marketing. As you read through the following marketing chapters, consider whether a marketing career would interest you.

test prep

- Can you define the terms *consumer market* and *business-to-business market*?
- Can you name and describe five ways to segment the consumer market?
- What is niche marketing, and how does it differ from one-to-one marketing?
- What are four key factors that make B2B markets different from consumer markets?

Use LearnSmart to help retain what you have learned. Access your instructor's Connect course to check out LearnSmart, or go to learnsmartadvantage.com for help.

LEARNSMART

summary

LO 13–1 Define *marketing*, and apply the marketing concept to both for-profit and nonprofit organizations.

- **What is marketing?**
Marketing is the activity, set of institutions, and processes for creating, communicating, delivering, and exchanging offerings that have value for customers, clients, partners, and society at large.

Access your instructor's Connect course to check out LearnSmart or go to learnsmartadvantage.com for help.

connect

- **How has marketing changed over time?**
  During the *production era,* marketing was largely a distribution function. Emphasis was on producing as many goods as possible and getting them to markets. By the early 1920s, during the *selling era,* the emphasis turned to selling and advertising to persuade customers to buy the existing goods produced by mass production. After World War II, the tremendous demand for goods and services led to the *marketing concept era,* when businesses recognized the need to be responsive to customers' needs. During the 1990s, marketing entered the *customer relationship era,* focusing on enhancing customer satisfaction and stimulating long-term customer loyalty. Today marketers are using mobile/on-demand marketing to engage customers.

- **What are the three parts of the marketing concept?**
  The three parts of the marketing concept are (1) a customer orientation, (2) a service orientation, and (3) a profit orientation (that is, marketing goods and services that will earn a profit and enable the firm to survive and expand).

- **What kinds of organizations are involved in marketing?**
  All kinds of organizations use marketing, including for-profit and nonprofit organizations like states, charities, churches, politicians, and schools.

LO 13–2   Describe the four Ps of marketing.

- **How do marketers implement the four Ps?**
  The idea behind the four Ps is to design a *product* people want, *price* it competitively, *place* it where consumers can find it easily, and *promote* it so consumers know it exists.

LO 13–3   Summarize the marketing research process.

- **What are the steps in conducting marketing research?**
  (1) Define the problem or opportunity and determine the present situation, (2) collect data, (3) analyze the data, and (4) choose the best solution.

LO 13–4   Show how marketers use environmental scanning to learn about the changing marketing environment.

- **What is environmental scanning?**
  Environmental scanning is the process of identifying factors that can affect marketing success. Marketers pay attention to all the environmental factors that create opportunities and threats.

- **What are some of the more important environmental trends in marketing?**
  The most important global and technological change is probably the growth of the Internet and mobile marketing. Another is the growth of consumer databases, with which companies can develop products and services that closely match consumers' needs. Marketers must monitor social trends like population growth and shifts to maintain their close relationship with customers. They must also monitor the dynamic competitive and economic environments.

LO 13–5   Explain how marketers apply the tools of market segmentation, relationship marketing, and the study of consumer behavior.

- **What are some of the ways marketers segment the consumer market?**
  Geographic segmentation means dividing the market into different regions. Segmentation by age, income, and education level is *demographic*

segmentation. We study a group's values, attitudes, and interests using *psychographic segmentation*. Determining which benefits customers prefer and using them to promote a product is *benefit segmentation*. Separating the market by usage is called *volume segmentation*. The best segmentation strategy is to use all the variables to come up with a consumer profile for a target market that's sizable, reachable, and profitable.

- **What is the difference between mass marketing and relationship marketing?**
  Mass marketing means developing products and promotions to please large groups of people. Relationship marketing tends to lead away from mass production and toward custom-made goods and services. Its goal is to keep individual customers over time by offering them products or services that meet their needs.

- **What are some of the factors that influence the consumer decision-making process?**
  Factors that influence the consumer decision-making process include learning, reference group, culture, subculture, and cognitive dissonance.

LO 13–6   Compare the business-to-business market and the consumer market.

- **What makes the business-to-business market different from the consumer market?**
  Customers in the B2B market are relatively few and large. B2B markets tend to be geographically concentrated, and industrial buyers generally are more rational than ultimate consumers in their selection of goods and services. B2B sales tend to be direct, and there is much more emphasis on personal selling than in consumer markets.

key terms

benefit segmentation 377
brand name 368
business-to-business (B2B) market 375
consumer market 375
customer relationship management (CRM) 364
demographic segmentation 377
environmental scanning 372
focus group 371

geographic segmentation 377
marketing 362
marketing concept 364
marketing mix 366
marketing research 370
market segmentation 376
mass marketing 378
niche marketing 377
one-to-one marketing 378
primary data 371

product 368
promotion 369
psychographic segmentation 377
relationship marketing 378
secondary data 370
target marketing 376
test marketing 368
volume (or usage) segmentation 377

critical thinking

1. When businesses buy goods and services from other businesses, they usually buy in large volume. Salespeople in the business-to-business market usually are paid on a commission basis; that is, they earn a certain percentage of each sale they make. Why might B2B sales be a more financially rewarding career area than consumer sales?

2. Industrial companies sell goods such as steel, lumber, computers, engines, parts, and supplies. Name three such companies.

3. What environmental changes are occurring in your community? What was the impact of the recent economic crisis? What environmental changes in marketing are most likely to change your career prospects in the future? How can you learn more about those changes? What might you do to prepare for them?

4. Which of your needs are not being met by businesses and/or nonprofit organizations in your area? Are there enough people with similar needs to attract an organization that would meet those needs? How would you find out?

developing **workplace skills**

Key: ● Team   ★ Analytic   ▲ Communication   ▣ Technology

★▲ 1. Think of an effective marketing mix for a new electric car or a brushless car wash for your neighborhood. Be prepared to discuss your ideas in class.

●★▲ 2. Working in teams of five, think of a product or service your friends want but cannot get on or near campus. You might ask your friends at other schools what's available there. What kind of product would fill that need? Discuss your results in class and how you might go about marketing that new product or service.

★ 3. Business has fallen off greatly at your upscale restaurant because of the slow economy. List four things you can do to win back the loyalty of your past customers.

●★▲ 4. Working in teams of four or five, list as many brand names of pizza as you can, including from pizza shops, restaurants, supermarkets, and so on. Merge your list with the lists from other groups or classmates. Then try to identify the target market for each brand. Do they all seem to be after the same market, or are there different brands for different markets? What are the separate appeals?

★▲ 5. Take a little time to review the concepts in this chapter as they apply to Very Vegetarian, the restaurant we used as an example throughout. Have an open discussion in class about (a) a different name for the restaurant, (b) a location for the restaurant, (c) a promotional program, and (d) a way to establish a long-term relationship with customers.

taking it to the **net**

PURPOSE

To demonstrate how the Internet can be used to enhance marketing relationships.

EXERCISE

Nike wants to help its customers add soul to their soles and express their individuality by customizing their own shoes. See for yourself at www.nike.com. Enter "customize" in the search box and build a shoe that fits your style.

1. What if you're in the middle of your shoe design and have questions about what to do next? Where can you go for help?

2. How does Nike's website help the company strengthen its relationships with its stakeholders? Give examples to support your answer.

3. How do the elements of the website reflect Nike's target market?

4. Does Nike invite comments from visitors to its website? If so, how does this affect its attempt to build positive relationships with its customers?

video case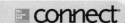

USING THE 4 Ps AT ENERGIZER

The Energizer Bunny is a marketing icon. How many people are not familiar with this marketing campaign? The precursor to the company known today as Energizer was founded by two inventors: the inventor of the battery and the inventor of the flashlight. The synergy should be obvious. This partnership grew into the leading manufacturer and seller of batteries in the world today. Energizer is truly a global company—operating across the globe. Energizer has developed and implemented an outstanding marketing approach to its product lines. In fact, Energizer demonstrates the full range of marketing concepts, including the use of social media and market research in successfully promoting and sustaining a brand.

Advertising Age magazine ranks the brand icon Energizer Bunny as the number five brand icon of the twentieth century. This provides Energizer a competitive advantage in many of its markets. The company is continually involved in new product development through the identification and understanding of consumer needs, including how a person intends to use a battery, in what devices, and the types of users for various products where Energizer batteries can be used.

Energizer has a well-developed and highly effective marketing division that is responsible for helping to ensure the success of current and new products. The video walks the viewer through the four Ps of marketing—product, price, place, and promotion—and shows how Energizer utilizes marketing concepts effectively.

The company views its approach to marketing and selling its product lines as one that is focused on developing, cultivating, and expanding customer relationships. Energizer is a company that has been significantly impacted by the growth of technology and uses this and the growth of the Internet as parts of its overall marketing communications approach to develop strong and lasting relationships with its customers.

The video demonstrates the importance of relationship marketing as a key to Energizer's success. The complexities involved in the marketing mix, marketing research, and new product development are highlighted through specific examples in the video, such as the new product introduced by the company each summer. We see how the company uses qualitative data such as focus groups and secondary data to test market its product, elicit customer feedback, collect demographic and other data, and match its marketing strategy to be consistent with the appropriate segmentation factors.

THINKING IT OVER

1. Identify the elements that must be considered in the marketing environment.

2. Briefly discuss the evolution of marketing at Energizer as described in the video.

3. The Energizer Bunny is considered a marketing icon. What does this mean?

notes

1. Brent Adamson, Matthew Dixon, and Nicholas Toman, "A New Guide to Selling," *Harvard Business Review,* August 2012.
2. Patrick Spenner and Karen Freeman, "To Keep Your Customers, Keep It Simple," *Harvard Business Review,* May 2012.
3. Barbara Giamanco and Kent Gregoire, "Tweet Me, Friend Me, Make Me Buy," *Harvard Business Review,* July–August 2012.
4. Kasey Wehrum, "Their Carts Are Full, So Why Won't They Buy?" *Inc.,* December 2013.
5. J. J. Martin, "The Shopping Social Networks," *The Wall Street Journal,* October 27–28, 2012.
6. Jason Fried, "Marketing Without Marketing," *Inc.,* January 2014.
7. Roy J. Chua, "Building Effective Relationships in China," *Sloan Management Review,* Summer 2012.

8. Peter Dahlström and David Edelman, "The Coming Era of 'On-Demand' Marketing," *McKinsey Quarterly,* April 2013.

9. Vanessa Small, "LinkedIn Connects Members with Volunteer Options," *The Washington Post,* January 21, 2014.

10. Alexander Lobrano, "La Nouvelle Veg," *The Wall Street Journal,* April 20–21, 2013.

11. Annie Gasparro and Juoie Jargon, "McDonald's to Go Vegetarian in India," *The Wall Street Journal,* September 5, 2012.

12. Jenn Harris, "Al Gore Is Now Vegan, Just Like Bill Clinton," *Los Angeles Times,* November 26, 2013.

13. Trupti Rami, "Veganism in Seven Decades," *New York,* January 20–27, 2014.

14. Terence Chea, "San Francisco Startup Seeks Egg Alternatives," *The Washington Times,* December 9, 2013.

15. Dinah Eng, "A Fresh Take on Food," *Fortune,* April 29, 2013.

16. Tim Kraft, "The Trick to Getting NoBull on More Grills," *The Washington Post,* January 20, 2013.

17. Susan Dumenco, "Data, Data Everywhere, and Not an Insight in Sight," *Advertising Age,* March 18, 2013.

18. Mark Henricks, "B2B," *Inc.,* February 2014.

19. Julien Cayla, Robin Beers, and Eric Arnould, "Stories That Deliver Business Insights," *Sloan Management Review,* Winter 2014.

20. Julie Liesse, "How Understanding Consumers' Purchase Cycle Can Help Brands Grow," *Advertising Age,* September 30, 2013.

21. U.S. Census Bureau, www.census.gov, accessed April 2014.

photo credits

18

Financial Management

Learning Objectives

AFTER YOU HAVE READ AND STUDIED THIS CHAPTER, YOU SHOULD BE ABLE TO

LO 18-1 Explain the role and responsibilities of financial managers.

LO 18-2 Outline the financial planning process, and explain the three key budgets in the financial plan.

LO 18-3 Explain why firms need operating funds.

LO 18-4 Identify and describe different sources of short-term financing.

LO 18-5 Identify and describe different sources of long-term financing.

Getting to know **Sabrina Simmons**

As chief financial officer (CFO) of Gap, Sabrina Simmons knows a thing or two about keeping current with trends. Fashion is a volatile industry that can shift suddenly on the whims of consumers. Companies that lose their "cool" factor can quickly disappear from the market if they fail to rebuild their brand. Gap was in the middle of a crisis of this scale when Simmons joined as treasurer in 2001. Besides being stuck in a creative rut, a series of poor capital market investments had hurt the company's finances. In her first act on the job, Simmons balanced the books and made executives swear that the company would never rely on risky investments to drive revenue again. It's an accomplishment that she remains proud of to this day. "Nobody is coming through this recession unscathed, but it feels great to sleep at night knowing our balance sheet is rock solid," said Simmons.

Before making a splash at Gap, Simmons earned her bachelor's degree in finance from University of California, Berkeley, and her MBA from UCLA. A certified public accountant, Simmons spent her post-grad years in various bookkeeping jobs at companies like Hewlett-Packard and Ford subsidiary USL Capital. She took her first foray into fashion as an assistant treasurer at Levi Strauss. Her performance at the iconic blue jean maker caught the eye of British genetics firm Sygen International, which hired Simmons as its CFO in the late 1990s. However, the slow world of science made Simmons miss the apparel business. When a treasurer position at Gap opened up, she seized the opportunity to get back into fashion.

While her handling of the company's early-2000s identity crisis put her in the spotlight, Simmons didn't have time to celebrate. Soon Gap began investing millions in an offshoot store called Forth & Towne. Unlike the company's collection of youthful brands, like Old Navy and Banana Republic, Forth & Towne was meant to appeal to older shoppers who had lost touch with

Gap over the years. Unfortunately, the retailer's heavily hyped launch did little to generate interest among its target market. "After investing tens of millions of dollars, we made the difficult decision to cut our losses and shut it down after two years," said Simmons. "The silver lining is we learned many tough lessons. And this failure, though very public, didn't stop us from taking those lessons learned and investing in other good ideas."

One of those good ideas was Piperlime.com, an accessories brand that launched a year after Forth & Towne's failure. The online boutique quickly developed a customer base and continues to grow. In recognition of her accomplishments with the company, Gap appointed Simmons CFO in 2008. She's had to put out a number of fires since then, including the closing of hundreds of stores in 2012. Nevertheless, Simmons is steadfast in her commitment to never accept defeat. "Take intelligent risks and accept sensible failures," said Simmons. "Tenacity and persistence are great traits. And don't be afraid to fail. It's a great way to learn."

Risk and uncertainty clearly define the role of financial management. In this chapter, you'll explore the role of finance in business. We'll discuss the challenges and the tools top managers like Sabrina Simmons use to attain financial stability and growth.

Sources: Paul Quintaro, "Gap Offers Details on Advances in Omni-Channel Retailing, Global Growth," *Benzinga*, April 16, 2014; Sabrina Simmons, "Commencement Address 2010: Berkeley-Haas Undergraduate Program," www.Haas.Berkeley.edu, May 19 2010; and Susan Berfield, "Can Rebekka Bay Fix the Gap?" *Bloomberg Businessweek*, March 20, 2014.

Sabrina Simmons

- CFO of Gap
- Balanced the company's books
- Accepted and learned from failures

www.gap.com

@Gap

name that **company**

This company spends over $6 billion a year on research to develop new products even though it may take as long as 10 years before the products are approved and introduced to the market. Since long-term funding is critical in our business, high-level managers are very involved in the finance decisions. What is the name of this company? (Find the answer in the chapter.)

LO 18–1   Explain the role and responsibilities of financial managers.

THE ROLE OF FINANCE AND FINANCIAL MANAGERS

finance
The function in a business that acquires funds for the firm and manages those funds within the firm.

financial management
The job of managing a firm's resources so it can meet its goals and objectives.

financial managers
Managers who examine financial data prepared by accountants and recommend strategies for improving the financial performance of the firm.

The goal of this chapter is to answer two major questions: "What is finance?" and "What do financial managers do?" **Finance** is the function in a business that acquires funds for the firm and manages them within the firm. Finance activities include preparing budgets; doing cash flow analysis; and planning for the expenditure of funds on such assets as plant, equipment, and machinery. **Financial management** is the job of managing a firm's resources to meet its goals and objectives. Without a carefully calculated financial plan and sound financial management, a firm has little chance for survival, regardless of its product or marketing effectiveness. Let's briefly review the roles of accountants and financial managers.

We can compare an accountant to a skilled laboratory technician who takes blood samples and other measures of a person's health and writes the findings on a health report (in business, this process is the preparation of financial statements). A financial manager is like the doctor who interprets the report and makes recommendations that will improve the patient's health. In short, **financial managers** examine financial data prepared by accountants and recommend strategies for improving the financial performance of the firm.

Clearly financial managers can make sound financial decisions only if they understand accounting information. That's why we examined accounting in Chapter 17. Similarly, a good accountant needs to understand finance. Accounting and finance go together like peanut butter and jelly. In large and medium-sized organizations, both the accounting and finance functions are generally under the control of a chief financial officer (CFO). A CFO is generally the second highest paid person in an organization and CFOs often advance to the top job of CEO.[1] However, financial management could also be in the hands of a person who serves as company treasurer or vice president of finance. A comptroller is the chief *accounting* officer.

Figure 18.1 highlights a financial manager's tasks. As you can see, two key responsibilities are to obtain funds and to effectively control the use of those funds. Controlling funds includes managing the firm's cash, credit accounts (accounts receivable), and inventory. Finance is a critical activity in both profit-seeking and nonprofit organizations.[2]

Finance is important, no matter what the firm's size. As you may remember from Chapter 6, financing a small business is essential if the firm expects to survive its important first five years. But the need for careful financial management remains a challenge that any business, large or small, must face throughout its existence. This is a lesson many U.S. businesses learned the hard way when the recent financial crisis threatened the economy.[3]

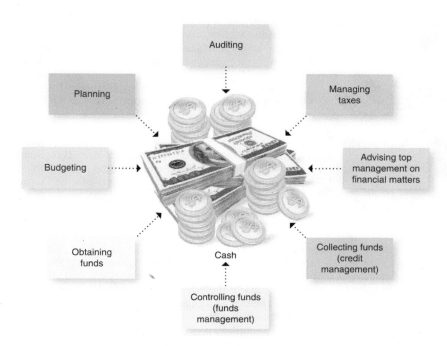

FIGURE 18.1 WHAT FINANCIAL MANAGERS DO

General Motors (GM), once the world's dominant automaker, faced extinction in 2009 because of severe financial problems. The company survived due to a direct government loan of $7 billion and an additional $43 billion in bailout funds from the U.S. Treasury.[4] The $43 billion in bailout funds gave the government 60 percent ownership in the company. (The government sold its last share of GM in 2013 for a total loss of about $10 billion.)[5] The government also approved an $85 billion loan to save insurance giant American International Group (AIG) from collapse and passed the $700 billion Troubled Assets Relief Program (TARP) to help restore confidence and stability in the U.S. financial system. Today, many small banks are still struggling to repay the TARP funds.[6]

The Value of Understanding Finance

Three of the most common reasons a firm fails financially are:

1. Undercapitalization (insufficient funds to start the business).
2. Poor control over cash flow.
3. Inadequate expense control.

You can see all three in the following classic story:

Two friends, Elizabeth Bertani and Pat Sherwood, started a company called Parsley Patch on what can best be described as a shoestring budget. It began when Bertani prepared salt-free seasonings for her husband, who was on a no-salt diet. Her friend Sherwood

Michael Miller overhauled the underperforming Goodwill Industries operation in Portland, Oregon, by treating the nonprofit like a for-profit business. He trimmed operating expenses comparing sales by store, closing weak outlets and opening new ones in better locations, and cutting distribution costs. Sales soared from $4 million to over $135 million, eliminating the need for outside funding.

Most businesses have predictable day-to-day needs, like the need to buy supplies, pay for fuel and utilities, and pay employees. Financial management is the function that helps ensure firms have the funds they need when they need them. What would happen to the company providing the work in this photo if it couldn't buy fuel for its trucks?

thought the seasonings were good enough to sell. Bertani agreed, and Parsley Patch Inc. was born. The business began with an investment of $5,000 that was rapidly depleted on a logo and label design. Bertani and Sherwood quickly learned about the need for capital in getting a business going. Eventually, they invested more than $100,000 of their own money to keep the business from being undercapitalized.

Everything started well, and hundreds of gourmet shops adopted the product line. But when sales failed to meet expectations, the women decided the health-food market offered more potential because salt-free seasonings were a natural for people with restricted diets. The choice was a good one. Sales soared, approaching $30,000 a month. Still, the company earned no profits.

Bertani and Sherwood weren't trained in monitoring cash flow or in controlling expenses. In fact, they were told not to worry about costs, and they hadn't. They eventually hired a certified public accountant (CPA) and an experienced financial manager, who taught them how to compute the costs of their products, and how to control expenses as well as cash moving in and out of the company (cash flow). Soon Parsley Patch was earning a comfortable margin on operations that ran close to $1 million a year. Luckily, the owners were able to turn things around before it was too late. Eventually, they sold the firm to spice and seasonings giant McCormick.[7]

If Bertani and Sherwood had understood finance before starting their business, they might have been able to avoid the problems they encountered. The key word here is *understood*. You do not have to pursue finance as a career to understand it. Financial understanding is important to anyone who wants to start a small business, invest in stocks and bonds, or plan a retirement fund. In short, finance and accounting are two areas everyone in business should study. Since we discussed accounting in Chapter 17, let's look more closely at what financial management is all about.

What Is Financial Management?

Financial managers are responsible for paying the company's bills at the appropriate time, and for collecting overdue payments to make sure the company does not lose too much money to bad debts (people or firms that don't pay their bills). Therefore, finance functions, such as buying merchandise on credit (accounts payable) and collecting payment from customers (accounts receivable), are key components of the financial manager's job. While these functions are vital to all types of businesses, they are particularly critical to small and medium-sized businesses, which typically have smaller cash or credit cushions than large corporations.[8]

It's also essential that financial managers stay abreast of changes or opportunities in finance, such as changes in tax law, since taxes represent an outflow of cash from the business.[9] Financial managers must also analyze the tax implications of managerial decisions to minimize the taxes the business must pay. Usually a member of the firm's finance department, the internal auditor, also checks the journals, ledgers, and financial statements the accounting department prepares, to make sure all transactions are in accordance with generally accepted accounting principles (GAAP). Without such audits, accounting statements would be less reliable.[10] Therefore, it is important that internal auditors be objective and critical of any improprieties or deficiencies noted in their evaluation.[11] Thorough internal audits assist the firm in financial planning, which we'll look at next.

LO 18–2   Outline the financial planning process, and explain the three key budgets in the financial plan.

FINANCIAL PLANNING

Financial planning means analyzing short-term and long-term money flows to and from the firm. Its overall objective is to optimize the firm's profitability and make the best use of its money. It has three steps: (1) forecasting the firm's short-term and long-term financial needs, (2) developing budgets to meet those needs, and (3) establishing financial controls to see whether the company is achieving its goals (see Figure 18.2). Let's look at each step and the role it plays in improving the organization's financial health.

Forecasting Financial Needs

Forecasting is an important part of any firm's financial plan. A **short-term forecast** predicts revenues, costs, and expenses for a period of one year or less. Part of the short-term forecast may be a **cash flow forecast**, which predicts the cash inflows and outflows in future periods, usually months or quarters. The inflows and outflows of cash recorded in the cash flow forecast are based on expected sales revenues and various costs and expenses incurred, as well as when they are due for payment. The company's sales forecast estimates projected sales for a particular period. A business often uses its past financial statements as a basis for projecting expected sales and various costs and expenses.

A **long-term forecast** predicts revenues, costs, and expenses for a period longer than 1 year, sometimes as long as 5 or 10 years. This forecast plays a

short-term forecast
Forecast that predicts revenues, costs, and expenses for a period of one year or less.

cash flow forecast
Forecast that predicts the cash inflows and outflows in future periods, usually months or quarters.

long-term forecast
Forecast that predicts revenues, costs, and expenses for a period longer than 1 year, and sometimes as far as 5 or 10 years into the future.

FIGURE 18.2 FINANCIAL PLANNING
Note the close link between financial planning and budgeting.

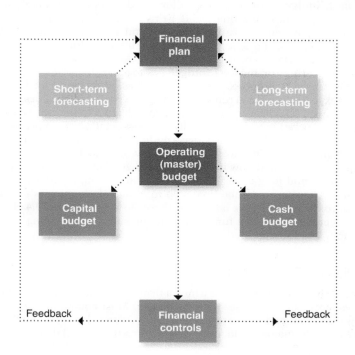

508   **PART 6   Managing Financial Resources**

crucial part in the company's long-term strategic plan, which asks questions such as: What business are we in? Should we be in it five years from now? How much money should we invest in technology and new plant and equipment over the next decade? Will we have cash available to meet long-term obligations? Innovations in web-based software help financial managers address these long-term forecasting questions.

The long-term financial forecast gives top management, as well as operations managers, some sense of the income or profit potential of different strategic plans.[12] It also helps in preparing company budgets.

Working with the Budget Process

budget
A financial plan that sets forth management's expectations and, on the basis of those expectations, allocates the use of specific resources throughout the firm.

A **budget** sets forth management's expectations for revenues and, on the basis of those expectations, allocates the use of specific resources throughout the firm. As a financial plan, it depends heavily on the accuracy of the firm's balance sheet, income statement, statement of cash flows, and short-term and long-term financial forecasts, which all need to be as accurate as possible. To effectively prepare budgets, financial managers must take their forecasting responsibilities seriously.[13] A budget becomes the primary guide for the firm's financial operations and expected financial needs.

There are usually several types of budgets in a firm's financial plan:

- A capital budget.
- A cash budget.
- An operating or master budget.

Let's look at each.

capital budget
A budget that highlights a firm's spending plans for major asset purchases that often require large sums of money.

A **capital budget** highlights a firm's spending plans for major asset purchases that often require large sums of money, like property, buildings, and equipment.

cash budget
A budget that estimates cash inflows and outflows during a particular period like a month or a quarter.

A **cash budget** estimates cash inflows and outflows during a particular period, like a month or a quarter. It helps managers anticipate borrowing needs, debt repayment, operating expenses, and short-term investments, and is often the last budget prepared. A sample cash budget for our example company, Very Vegetarian, is provided in Figure 18.3.

operating (or master) budget
The budget that ties together the firm's other budgets and summarizes its proposed financial activities.

The **operating (or master) budget** ties together the firm's other budgets and summarizes its proposed financial activities. More formally, it estimates costs and expenses needed to run a business, given projected revenues. The firm's spending on supplies, travel, rent, technology, advertising, and salaries is determined in the operating budget, generally the most detailed a firm prepares.

Financial planning obviously plays an important role in the firm's operations and often determines what long-term investments it makes, when it will need specific funds, and how it will generate them. Once a company forecasts its short-term and long-term financial needs and compiles budgets to show how it will allocate funds, the final step in financial planning is to establish financial controls. Before we talk about those, however, Figure 18.4 challenges you to check your personal financial planning skill by developing a monthly budget for "You Incorporated."

Establishing Financial Controls

financial control
A process in which a firm periodically compares its actual revenues, costs, and expenses with its budget.

Financial control is a process in which a firm periodically compares its actual revenues, costs, and expenses with its budget. Most companies hold at least monthly financial reviews as a way to ensure financial control. Such control procedures help managers identify variances to the financial plan and allow

VERY VEGETARIAN Monthly Cash Budget	JANUARY	FEBRUARY	MARCH
Sales forecast	$50,000	$45,000	$40,000
Collections			
Cash sales (20%)		$ 9,000	$ 8,000
Credit sales (80% of past month)		$40,000	$36,000
Monthly cash collection		$49,000	$44,000
Payments schedule			
Supplies and material		$ 11,000	$ 10,000
Salaries		12,000	12,000
Direct labor		9,000	9,000
Taxes		3,000	3,000
Other expenses		7,000	5,000
Monthly cash payments		$42,000	$39,000
Cash budget			
Cash flow		$ 7,000	$ 5,000
Beginning cash		−1,000	6,000
Total cash		$ 6,000	$ 11,000
Less minimum cash balance		−6,000	−6,000
Excess cash to market securities		$ 0	$ 5,000
Loans needed for minimum balance		0	0

FIGURE 18.3 A SAMPLE CASH BUDGET FOR VERY VEGETARIAN

them to take corrective action if necessary. Financial controls also help reveal which specific accounts, departments, and people are varying from the financial plan. Finance managers can judge whether these variances are legitimate and thereby merit adjustments to the plan. Shifts in the economy or unexpected global events can also alter financial plans. For example, currency problems in emerging markets or a slowdown in the Chinese economy can cause many companies to consider adjusting their financial plans.[14] After the Test Prep, we'll see why firms need readily available funds.

test prep

- Name three finance functions important to the firm's overall operations and performance.
- What three primary financial problems cause firms to fail?
- How do short-term and long-term financial forecasts differ?
- What is the purpose of preparing budgets in an organization? Can you identify three different types of budgets?

FIGURE 18.4 YOU INCORPORATED MONTHLY BUDGET
In Chapter 17, you compiled a sample balance sheet for You Inc. Now, let's develop a monthly budget for You Inc. Be honest and think of everything that needs to be included for an accurate monthly budget for You!

	EXPECTED	ACTUAL	DIFFERENCE
Monthly income			
Wages (net pay after taxes)	_____	_____	_____
Savings account withdrawal	_____	_____	_____
Family support	_____	_____	_____
Loans	_____	_____	_____
Other sources	_____	_____	_____
Total monthly income	_____	_____	_____
Monthly expenses			
Fixed expenses	_____	_____	_____
Rent or mortgage	_____	_____	_____
Car payment	_____	_____	_____
Health insurance	_____	_____	_____
Life insurance	_____	_____	_____
Tuition or fees	_____	_____	_____
Other fixed expenses	_____	_____	_____
Subtotal of fixed expenses	_____	_____	_____
Variable expenses	_____	_____	_____
Food	_____	_____	_____
Clothing	_____	_____	_____
Entertainment	_____	_____	_____
Transportation	_____	_____	_____
Phone	_____	_____	_____
Utilities	_____	_____	_____
Publications	_____	_____	_____
Internet connection	_____	_____	_____
Cable television	_____	_____	_____
Other expenses	_____	_____	_____
Subtotal of variable expenses	_____	_____	_____
Total expenses	_____	_____	_____
Total income − Total expenses = Cash on hand/(Cash deficit)	_____	_____	_____

LO 18–3   Explain why firms need operating funds.

THE NEED FOR OPERATING FUNDS

In business, the need for operating funds never seems to end. That's why sound financial management is essential to all businesses. And like our personal financial needs, the capital needs of a business change over time. Remember the example of Parsley Patch to see why a small business's financial requirements can shift considerably. The same is true for large corporations such as Apple, Johnson & Johnson, and Nike when they venture into new-product areas or new markets. Virtually all organizations have operational needs for which they need funds. Key areas include:

- Managing day-by-day needs of the business.
- Controlling credit operations.
- Acquiring needed inventory.
- Making capital expenditures.

Let's look carefully at the financial needs of these key areas, which affect both the smallest and the largest of businesses.

Managing Day-by-Day Needs of the Business

If workers expect to be paid on Friday, they don't want to wait until Monday for their paychecks. If tax payments are due on the 15th of the month, the government expects the money on time. If the interest payment on a business loan is due on the 30th of this month, the lender doesn't mean the 1st of next month. As you can see, funds have to be available to meet the daily operational costs of the business.

Financial managers must ensure that funds are available to meet daily cash needs without compromising the firm's opportunities to invest money for its future. Money has a *time value*.[15] In other words, if someone offered to give you $200 either today or one year from today, you would benefit by taking the $200 today. Why? It's very simple. You could invest the $200 you receive today and over a year's time it would grow. The same is true in business; the interest a firm gains on its investments is important in maximizing the profit it will gain. That's why financial managers often try to minimize cash expenditures to free up funds for investment in interest-bearing accounts. They suggest the company pay its bills as late as possible (unless a cash discount is available for early payment). They also advise companies to try to collect what's owed them as fast as possible, to maximize the investment potential of the firm's funds. Unfortunately, collecting funds as fast as possible can be particularly challenging. This was especially true during the Great Recession.[16] Efficient cash management is particularly important to small firms since their access to capital is much more limited than larger businesses.[17]

Controlling Credit Operations

Financial managers know that in today's highly competitive business environment, making credit available helps keep current customers happy and helps attract new ones. Credit for customers can be especially important during tough financial times like the recession that began in 2008 when lenders were hesitant to make loans.

The problem with selling on credit is that as much as 25 percent of the business's assets could be tied up in its credit accounts (accounts receivable). This forces the firm to use its own funds to pay for goods or services sold to customers who bought on credit. Financial managers in such firms often develop efficient collection procedures, like offering cash or quantity discounts to buyers who pay their accounts by a certain time. They also scrutinize old and new credit customers to see whether they have a history of meeting credit obligations on time.

It's difficult to think of a business that doesn't make credit available to its customers. However, collecting accounts receivable can be time-consuming and expensive. Accepting credit cards such as Visa, MasterCard, and American Express can simplify transactions for sellers and guarantee payment. What types of products do you regularly purchase with a credit card?

making **ethical decisions**

Good Finance or Bad Medicine?

Imagine that you have just earned your business degree and have been hired as a hospital administrator at a small hospital that, like many others, is experiencing financial problems. Having studied finance, you know that efficient cash management is important to all firms in all industries to meet the day-by-day operations of the firm. One way to ensure such efficiency is to use a carefully planned and managed inventory control system that can reduce the amount of cash an organization has tied up in inventory. Being familiar with just-in-time inventory, you know it is a proven system that helps reduce the costs of managing inventory.

At a meeting of the hospital's executive committee, you recommend that the hospital save money by using a just-in-time inventory system to manage its drug supply. You suggest discontinuing the hospital's large stockpile of drugs, especially expensive cancer treatment drugs that tie up a great deal of the hospital's cash, and shift to ordering them just when they are needed. Several members seem to like the idea, but the doctors in charge of practicing medicine and oncology are outraged, claiming you are sacrificing patients' well-being for cash. After debate, the committee says the decision is up to you. What will you do? What could result from your decision?

One convenient way to decrease the time and expense of collecting accounts receivable is to accept bank credit cards such as MasterCard or Visa. The banks that issue these cards have already established the customer's creditworthiness, which reduces the business's risk. Businesses must pay a fee to accept credit cards, but the costs are usually offset by the benefits.[18] In an effort to reduce those credit card costs as well as speed up the transaction process, many businesses today accept mobile payments through services like Square and Level Up.[19] For example, Chipotle, Starbucks, and Dunkin Donuts have invested in mobile payment systems.[20] Mobile payment systems not only make transactions quick and simple, the processors usually charge lower fees than traditional credit card companies.[21]

Acquiring Needed Inventory

As we saw in Chapter 13, effective marketing requires focusing on the customer and providing high-quality service and readily available goods. A carefully constructed inventory policy helps manage the firm's available funds and maximize profitability. Doozle's, an ice cream parlor in St. Louis, Missouri, deliberately ties up fewer funds in its inventory of ice cream in winter. It's obvious why: demand for ice cream is lower in winter.

Just-in-time inventory control (see Chapter 9) and other such methods can reduce the funds a firm must tie up in inventory. Carefully evaluating its inventory turnover ratio (see Chapter 17) can also help a firm control the outflow of cash for inventory. A business of any size must understand that poorly managed inventory can seriously affect cash flow and drain its finances dry. The nearby Making Ethical Decisions box raises an interesting question about sound financial management and inventory control in a critical industry.

Making Capital Expenditures

capital expenditures
Major investments in either tangible long-term assets such as land, buildings, and equipment or intangible assets such as patents, trademarks, and copyrights.

Capital expenditures are major investments in either tangible long-term assets such as land, buildings, and equipment, or intangible assets such as patents, trademarks, and copyrights. In many organizations the purchase of major assets—such as land for future expansion, manufacturing plants to increase production capabilities, research to develop new-product ideas, and

Financial Management   CHAPTER 18   513

FIGURE 18.5 WHY FIRMS NEED FUNDS

SHORT-TERM FUNDS	LONG-TERM FUNDS
Monthly expenses	New-product development
Unanticipated emergencies	Replacement of capital equipment
Cash flow problems	Mergers or acquisitions
Expansion of current inventory	Expansion into new markets (domestic or global)
Temporary promotional programs	New facilities

equipment to maintain or exceed current levels of output—is essential. Expanding into new markets can be expensive with no guarantee of success. Therefore, it's critical that companies weigh all possible options before committing a large portion of available resources.

Consider a firm that needs to expand its production capabilities due to increased customer demand. It could buy land and build a new plant, purchase an existing plant, or rent space. Can you think of financial and accounting considerations at play in this decision?

The need for operating funds raises several questions for financial managers: How does the firm obtain funds to finance operations and other business needs? Will it require specific funds in the long or the short term? How much will it cost (i.e., interest) to obtain these funds? Will they come from internal or external sources? We address these questions next.

Alternative Sources of Funds

We described finance earlier as the function in a business responsible for acquiring and managing funds. Sound financial management determines the amount of money needed and the most appropriate sources from which to obtain it. A firm can raise needed capital by borrowing money (debt), selling ownership (equity), or earning profits (retained earnings). **Debt financing** refers to funds raised through various forms of borrowing that must be repaid. **Equity financing** is money raised from within the firm, from operations or through the sale of ownership in the firm (stock). Firms can borrow funds either short-term or long-term. **Short-term financing** refers to funds needed for a year or less. **Long-term financing** covers funds needed for more than a year (usually 2 to 10 years). Figure 18.5 highlights reasons why firms may need short-term and long-term funds.

We'll explore the different sources of short- and long-term financing next. Let's first pause to check your understanding by doing the Test Prep.

connect

► **iSee It!** Need help understanding equity financing and debt financing? Visit your Connect e-book video tab for a brief animated explanation.

debt financing
Funds raised through various forms of borrowing that must be repaid.

equity financing
Money raised from within the firm, from operations or through the sale of ownership in the firm (stock or venture capital).

short-term financing
Funds needed for a year or less.

long-term financing
Funds needed for more than a year (usually 2 to 10 years).

test prep

- Money has time value. What does this mean?
- Why is accounts receivable a financial concern to the firm?
- What's the primary reason an organization spends a good deal of its available funds on inventory and capital expenditures?
- What's the difference between debt and equity financing?

Use LearnSmart to help retain what you have learned. Access your instructor's Connect course to check out LearnSmart, or go to learnsmartadvantage.com for help.

LEARNSMART

LO 18–4   Identify and describe different sources of short-term financing.

OBTAINING SHORT-TERM FINANCING

The bulk of a finance manager's job does not relate to obtaining long-term funds. In small businesses, for example, long-term financing is often out of the question.[22] Instead, day-to-day operations call for the careful management of *short-term* financial needs. Firms may need to borrow short-term funds for purchasing additional inventory or for meeting bills that come due unexpectedly. Like an individual, a business, especially a small business, sometimes needs to secure short-term funds when its cash reserves are low. Let's see how it does so.

Trade Credit

trade credit
The practice of buying goods and services now and paying for them later.

promissory note
A written contract with a promise to pay a supplier a specific sum of money at a definite time.

One thing you can never have too much of is cash. Financial managers must make certain there is enough cash available to meet daily financial needs and still have funds to invest in its future. What does it mean when we say cash has a time value?

Trade credit is the practice of buying goods or services now and paying for them later. It is the most widely used source of short-term funding, the least expensive, and the most convenient. Small businesses rely heavily on trade credit from firms such as United Parcel Service, as do large firms such as Kmart or Macy's. When a firm buys merchandise, it receives an invoice (a bill) much like the one you receive when you buy something with a credit card. As you'll see, however, the terms businesses receive are often different from those on your monthly statement.

Business invoices often contain terms such as *2/10, net 30*. This means the buyer can take a 2 percent discount for paying the invoice within 10 days. Otherwise the total bill (net) is due in 30 days. Finance managers pay close attention to such discounts because they create opportunities to reduce the firm's costs. Think about it for a moment: If the terms are 2/10, net 30, the customer will pay 2 percent more by waiting an extra 20 days to pay the invoice. If the firm *can* pay its bill within 10 days, it is needlessly increasing its costs by not doing so.

Some suppliers hesitate to give trade credit to an organization with a poor credit rating, no credit history, or a history of slow payment. They may insist the customer sign a **promissory note**, a written contract with a promise to pay a supplier a specific sum of money at a definite time. Promissory notes are negotiable. The supplier can sell them to a bank at a discount (the amount of the promissory note less a fee for the bank's services in collecting the amount due), and the business is then responsible for paying the bank.

Family and Friends

As we discussed in Chapter 17, firms often have several bills coming due at the same time with no sources of funds to pay them. Many small firms obtain short-term funds by borrowing money from family and friends. Such loans can create problems, however, if all parties do not understand cash flow. That's why it's sometimes better, when possible, to go to a commercial bank that fully understands the business's risk and can help analyze its future financial needs rather than borrow from friends or relatives.[23]

Entrepreneurs appear to be listening to this advice. According to the National Federation of Independent Business, entrepreneurs today are relying less on family and friends as a source of borrowed funds than they have in the past.[24] If an entrepreneur decides to ask

family or friends for financial assistance, it's important that both parties (1) agree to specific loan terms, (2) put the agreement in writing, and (3) arrange for repayment in the same way they would for a bank loan. Such actions help keep family relationships and friendships intact.

Commercial Banks

Banks, being sensitive to risk, generally prefer to lend short-term money to larger, established businesses. Imagine the different types of businesspeople who go to banks for a loan, and you'll get a better idea of the requests bankers evaluate. Picture, for example, a farmer going to the bank in spring to borrow funds for seed, fertilizer, equipment, and other needs that will be repaid after the fall harvest. Or consider a local toy store buying merchandise for Christmas sales. The store borrows the money for such purchases in the summer and plans to pay it back after Christmas. Restaurants often borrow funds at the beginning of the month and pay at the end of the month.

How much a business borrows and for how long depends on the kind of business it is, and how quickly it can resell the merchandise it purchases with a bank loan or use it to generate funds. In a large business, specialists in a company's finance and accounting departments do a cash flow forecast. Small-business owners generally lack such specialists and must monitor cash flow themselves.

The Great Recession severely curtailed bank lending to small businesses. It was difficult for even a promising and well-organized small business to obtain a bank loan. Fortunately, the situation seems to be changing as the economy is improving. The Consumer Finance Protection Bureau is even said to be considering investigating loans to small businesses as part of its job.[25] What's important for a small firm to remember is if it gets a bank loan, the owner or person in charge of finance should keep in close touch with the bank and send regular financial statements to keep the bank up-to-date on its operations. The bank may spot cash flow problems early or be more willing to lend money in a crisis if the business has established a strong relationship built on trust and sound management. The Adapting to Change box discusses how changing its strategy helped one business attract investors.

Did you ever wonder how retail stores get the money to buy all the treasures we splurge on during the holidays? Department stores and other large retailers make extensive use of commercial banks and other lenders to borrow the funds they need to buy merchandise and stock their shelves. How do the stores benefit from using this type of financing?

adapting to **change**

Threading the Financial Needle

Coming up with a great idea is only the first step in starting a business. Entrepreneurs need money to turn their ideas into reality. Luckily, a number of potential investors are willing to open their wallets for what they think is going to be the next big thing. But to attract these "angel investors," entrepreneurs must be sure their business concepts have been carefully planned. James Reinhart, CEO of the clothing exchange website thredUP, knows this about as well as anyone.

While attending college, Reinhart and his roommate realized that they owned too many clothes. After gathering start-up funds of $70,000 from family, friends, and personal savings, Reinhart and his partners launched thredUP, a website where people could buy and sell used clothing cheaply. Within three months the site drew in more than 10,000 members.

Reinhart soon discovered that the market for used children's

clothes was much larger than the adult market since children grow out of their clothes every three to six months. So the site changed its focus to targeting parents looking to "trade up" their kids' wardrobes. Parents send in clothes that are assessed by professional buyers to judge quality and the firm's ability to resell them. The higher the quality, the more money the company pays the sender. The company then resells the clothing on its website.

Reinhart was able to improve the site thanks to a $250,000 angel investor who loved thredUP's new strategy. Soon thredUP attracted $1.4 million more in investment, which it used to phase out the site's original service entirely to focus solely on the children's clothing. The next year, the company secured a round of venture capital funding, this time topping out at a whopping $50 million. With the new investment, Reinhart could have expanded thredUP into other areas. Instead he focused on spending the money to improve the current business model. "As an entrepreneur, you're always thinking about the adjacent things to do, but we have the opportunity to build a really big, important business in the market," Reinhart said. "That's what we're going to do."

Sources: thredUP, www.thredUP.com, accessed April 2014; Philip Levinson, "thredUP's HBS Founders Master the Art of the Pivot," *The Harbus*, March 7, 2012; and "thredUP.com Releases Second Annual Clothing Resale Report," *The Providence Journal*, February 26, 2014.

Different Forms of Short-Term Loans

secured loan
A loan backed by collateral, something valuable such as property.

Commercial banks offer different types of short-term loans. A **secured loan** is backed by *collateral*, something valuable such as property. If the borrower fails to pay the loan, the lender may take possession of the collateral. An automobile loan is a secured loan. If the borrower doesn't repay it, the lender will repossess the car. Inventory of raw materials like coal, copper, and steel often serve as collateral for business loans. Collateral removes some of the bank's risk in lending the money.

Accounts receivable are company assets often used as collateral for a loan; this process is called *pledging* and works as follows: A percentage of the value of a firm's accounts receivable pledged (usually about 75 percent) is advanced to the borrowing firm. As customers pay off their accounts, the funds received are forwarded to the lender in repayment of the funds that were advanced.

unsecured loan
A loan that doesn't require any collateral.

An **unsecured loan** is more difficult to obtain because it doesn't require any collateral. Normally, lenders give unsecured loans only to highly regarded customers—long-standing businesses or those considered financially stable.

line of credit
A given amount of unsecured short-term funds a bank will lend to a business, provided the funds are readily available.

If a business develops a strong relationship with a bank, the bank may open a **line of credit** for the firm, a given amount of unsecured short-term

A secured loan is backed by collateral, a tangible item of value. A car loan, for instance, is a secured loan in which the car itself is the collateral. What is the collateral in a mortgage loan?

funds a bank will lend to a business, provided the funds are readily available. A line of credit is *not* guaranteed to a business. However, it speeds up the borrowing process since a firm does not have to apply for a new loan every time it needs funds.[26] As a business matures and becomes more financially secure, banks will often increase its line of credit. Some even offer a **revolving credit agreement**, a line of credit that's guaranteed but usually comes with a fee. Both lines of credit and revolving credit agreements are particularly good sources of funds for unexpected cash needs.

    If a business is unable to secure a short-term loan from a bank, the financial manager may seek short-term funds from **commercial finance companies**. These non-deposit-type organizations make short-term loans to borrowers who offer tangible assets like property, plant, and equipment as collateral. Commercial finance companies will often make loans to businesses that cannot get short-term funds elsewhere. Since commercial finance companies assume higher degrees of risk than commercial banks, they usually charge higher interest rates. General Electric Capital is one of the world's largest commercial finance companies, with $584 billion in assets and operations in over 50 countries around the world.[27]

revolving credit agreement
A line of credit that's guaranteed but usually comes with a fee.

commercial finance companies
Organizations that make short-term loans to borrowers who offer tangible assets as collateral.

Factoring Accounts Receivable

One relatively expensive source of short-term funds for a firm is **factoring**, the process of selling accounts receivable for cash. Factoring dates as far back as 4,000 years, during the days of ancient Babylon. Here's how it works: Let's say a firm sells many of its products on credit to consumers and other businesses, creating a number of accounts receivable. Some buyers may be slow in paying their bills, so a large amount of money is due the firm. A *factor* is a market intermediary (usually a financial institution or a commercial bank) that agrees to buy the firm's accounts receivable, at a discount, for cash. The discount depends on the age of the accounts receivable, the nature of the business, and the condition of the economy. When it collects the accounts receivable that were originally owed to the firm, the factor keeps them.

factoring
The process of selling accounts receivable for cash.

While factors charge more than banks' loan rates, remember many small businesses cannot qualify for a loan. So even though factoring is an expensive way of raising short-term funds, it is popular among small businesses. A company can often reduce its factoring cost if it agrees to reimburse the factor for slow-paying accounts, or to assume the risk for customers who don't pay at all. Remember, factoring is not a loan; it is the sale of a firm's asset (accounts receivable). Factoring is common in the textile and furniture businesses, and in growing numbers of global trade ventures.

Commercial Paper

commercial paper
Unsecured promissory notes of $100,000 and up that mature (come due) in 270 days or less.

Often a corporation needs funds for just a few months and prefers not to have to negotiate with a commercial bank. One strategy available to larger firms is to sell commercial paper. **Commercial paper** consists of *unsecured* promissory notes, in amounts of $100,000 and up, that mature or come due in 270 days or less. Commercial paper states a fixed amount of money the business agrees to repay to the lender (investor) on a specific date at a specified rate of interest.

Because commercial paper is unsecured, only financially stable firms (mainly large corporations with excellent credit reputations) are able to sell it. Commercial paper can be a quick path to short-term funds at lower interest than charged by commercial banks. Even very stable firms like General Electric, however, had trouble selling commercial paper during the Great Recession. The Federal Reserve had to step in and assist many companies with their short-term financing by purchasing their short-term commercial paper. Since most commercial paper matures in 30 to 90 days, it can be an investment opportunity for buyers who can afford to put up cash for short periods to earn some interest on their money.[28]

Credit Cards

According to the National Small Business Association (NSBA), nearly one-third of all small firms now use credit cards to finance their businesses.[29] Even though more businesses are turning to credit cards for financing, two-thirds believe the terms of their cards are getting worse and it's very likely they are correct. The Credit Card Responsibility Accountability and Disclosure Act reduced consumer interest rates and approved many protections for consumers against card-company abuses. Unfortunately rates for small-business and corporate credit cards did not fall under the protection of the law. Still, with many traditional financing options closed to them, entrepreneurs are often forced to finance their firms with credit cards.

Credit cards provide a readily available line of credit that can save time and the likely embarrassment of being rejected for a bank loan. Of course, in contrast to the convenience they offer, credit cards are extremely risky and costly. Interest rates can be exorbitant, and there can be considerable penalties if users fail to make their payments on time. Savvy businesspersons study the perks that are offered with many cards and determine which might be the most beneficial to their companies. Joe Speiser, of pet-food distributor Petflow.com, found a cash-back card that helped put additional dollars back into his business.[30] Still, when dealing with credit cards, remember it's an expensive way to borrow money and credit cards are probably best used as a last resort.

After the Test Prep questions, we'll look into long-term financing options.

test prep

- What does an invoice containing the terms *2/10, net 30* mean?
- What's the difference between trade credit and a line of credit?
- What's the key difference between a secured and an unsecured loan?
- What is factoring? What are some of the considerations factors consider in establishing their discount rate?

> Use LearnSmart to help retain what you have learned. Access your instructor's Connect course to check out LearnSmart, or go to learnsmartadvantage.com for help.
>
> ▦ LEARNSMART

LO 18–5 Identify and describe different sources of long-term financing.

OBTAINING LONG-TERM FINANCING

In a financial plan, forecasting determines the amount of funding the firm will need over various periods and the most appropriate sources for obtaining those funds. In setting long-term financing objectives, financial managers generally ask three questions:

1. What are our organization's long-term goals and objectives?
2. What funds do we need to achieve the firm's long-term goals and objectives?
3. What sources of long-term funding (capital) are available, and which will best fit our needs?

Firms need long-term capital to purchase expensive assets such as plant and equipment, to develop new products, or perhaps finance their expansion. In major corporations, the board of directors and top management usually make decisions about long-term financing, along with finance and accounting executives. Pfizer, one of the world's largest research-based biomedical and pharmaceutical companies, spends over $6 billion a year researching and developing new products.[31] The development of a single new drug could take 10 years and cost the firm over $1 billion before it brings in any profit. Plus the company loses its patent protection on a drug after 20 years.[32] It's easy to see why high-level managers make the long-term financing decisions at Pfizer. Owners of small and medium-sized businesses are almost always actively engaged in analyzing their long-term financing decisions.

As we noted earlier, long-term funding comes from two major sources, debt financing and equity financing. Let's look at these sources next. But first check out the Reaching Beyond Our Borders box to learn why a source of long-term funding is raising eyebrows in the financial community.

Debt Financing

Debt financing is borrowing money the company has a legal obligation to repay. Firms can borrow by either getting a loan from a lending institution or issuing bonds.

Debt Financing by Borrowing from Lending Institutions Long-term loans are usually due within 3 to 7 years but may extend to 15 or 20 years. A **term-loan agreement** is a promissory note that requires the borrower to repay the loan

term-loan agreement
A promissory note that requires the borrower to repay the loan in specified installments.

www.adia.ae

reaching beyond **our borders**

Are They Heroes or Hustlers?

Sovereign wealth funds (SWFs) are large investment companies that are owned by governments. They have been a part of global financial markets for decades and today are currently valued at over $6 trillion. The largest SWFs are operated by Norway, United Arab Emirates, Saudi Arabia, China, Kuwait, and Singapore. During the recent financial crisis, SWFs were hailed as heroes and saviors in the U.S. financial community because of the billions of dollars they invested in U.S. companies that were struggling to survive. Although SWFs provide distressed companies with much-needed capital when it is needed, the presence of foreign governments in the U.S. business world makes some people nervous. This is especially true with SWFs controlled by nations that the United States sometimes has shaky relationships with in global affairs.

Time Warner's Manhattan headquarters found ready buyers from the SWFs of Abu Dhabi and Singapore. New foreign investors from China's SWF are making their debut in the U. S. economy. Such activity has caused some politicians and business executives to question the motives and intentions of these government-operated investment funds.

Fortunately, the facts don't seem to support the suspicions about SWFs. Although purchases like Time Warner's headquarters raise questions about U.S. real estate being taken over by foreign governments, in reality foreign investment in the United States accounted for only 10 percent of the total real estate purchases in 2013. SWFs also face significant investigation by the U.S. government if they attempt to purchase more than 10 percent of a U.S.-based company. It seems that SWFs provide more advantages for the U.S. economy than serious threats. However, it's always safe to be prudent when inviting investments from foreign governments. For the moment, though, foreign governments seem more focused on addressing their own problems rather than causing a stir here.

Sources: Eliot Brown, "Time Warner Nears Deal to Sell Headquarters," *The Wall Street Journal*, January 15, 2014; Ashley Stahl, "The Promise and Perils of Sovereign Wealth Funds," *Forbes*, December 19, 2013; and John Aziz, "Does the United States Need a Sovereign Wealth Fund?" *The Week*, January 20, 2014.

with interest in specified monthly or annual installments. A major advantage is that the loan interest is tax-deductible.

Long-term loans are both larger and more expensive to the firm than short-term loans. Since the repayment period can be quite long, lenders assume more risk and usually require collateral, which may be real estate, machinery, equipment, company stock, or other items of value. Lenders may also require certain restrictions to force the firm to act responsibly. The interest rate is based on the adequacy of collateral, the firm's credit rating, and the general level of market interest rates. The greater the risk a lender takes in making a loan, the higher the rate of interest. This principle is known as the **risk/return trade-off**.

risk/return trade-off
The principle that the greater the risk a lender takes in making a loan, the higher the interest rate required.

Debt Financing by Issuing Bonds   If an organization is unable to obtain its long-term financing needs by getting a loan from a lending institution such as a bank, it may try to issue bonds. To put it simply, a bond is like an IOU with a promise to repay the amount borrowed, with interest, on a certain date. The terms of the agreement in a bond issue are the **indenture terms**. The types of organizations that can issue bonds include federal, state, and local governments; federal government agencies; foreign governments; and corporations.

indenture terms
The terms of agreement in a bond issue.

You may already be familiar with bonds. You may own investments like U.S. government savings bonds, or perhaps you volunteered your time to help a local school district pass a bond issue. If your community is building a new stadium or cultural center, it may sell bonds to finance the project. Businesses and governments compete when issuing bonds. Potential investors (individuals and institutions) measure the risk of purchasing a bond against the return the bond promises to pay—the interest—and the issuer's ability to repay when promised.

Major League Baseball is a big business, and building a new stadium requires big dollars. When the St. Louis Cardinals needed financing to replace their old stadium with a new state-of-the-art facility, St. Louis County issued bonds that helped finance the construction of the Cardinals' new home. What organizations in your community have issued bonds, and for what purpose?

Like other forms of long-term debt, bonds can be secured or unsecured. A **secured bond** is issued with some form of collateral, such as real estate, equipment, or other pledged assets. If the bond's indenture terms are violated (e.g., not paying interest payments), the bondholder can issue a claim on the collateral. An **unsecured bond**, called a debenture bond, is backed only by the reputation of the issuer. Investors in such bonds simply trust that the organization issuing the bond will make good on its financial commitments.

Bonds are a key means of long-term financing for many organizations. They can also be valuable investments for private individuals or institutions. Given this importance, we will discuss bonds in depth in Chapter 19.

secured bond
A bond issued with some form of collateral.

unsecured bond
A bond backed only by the reputation of the issuer; also called a debenture bond.

Equity Financing

If a firm cannot obtain a long-term loan from a lending institution or is unable to sell bonds to investors, it may seek equity financing. Equity financing makes funds available when the owners of the firm sell shares of ownership to outside investors in the form of stock, when they reinvest company earnings in the business, or when they obtain funds from venture capitalists.

Equity Financing by Selling Stock   The key thing to remember about stock is that stockholders become owners in the organization. Generally, the corporation's board of directors decides the number of shares of stock that will be offered to investors for purchase. The first time a company offers to sell its stock to the general public is called an *initial public offering (IPO)*. Selling stock to the public to obtain funds is by no means easy or automatic. U.S. companies can issue stock for public purchase only if they meet requirements set by the U.S. Securities and Exchange Commission (SEC) and various state agencies.[33] They can offer different types of stock such as common and preferred. We'll discuss IPOs and common and preferred stock in depth in Chapter 19.

Equity Financing from Retained Earnings   You probably remember from Chapter 17 that the profits the company keeps and reinvests in the firm are called *retained earnings*. Retained earnings often are a major source of

522   PART 6   Managing Financial Resources

When credit grew tight in the recent financial crisis, John Mickey, who makes promotional items with corporate logos, tapped his retirement funds to obtain start-up money for his new venture. Why is this financing strategy considered risky?

long-term funds, especially for small businesses since they often have fewer financing alternatives, such as selling stock or bonds, than large businesses do. However, large corporations also depend on retained earnings for needed long-term funding. In fact, retained earnings are usually the most favored source of meeting long-term capital needs. A company that uses them saves interest payments, dividends (payments for investing in stock), and any possible underwriting fees for issuing bonds or stock. Retained earnings also create no new ownership in the firm, as stock does.

Suppose you wanted to buy an expensive personal asset such as a new car. Ideally you would go to your personal savings account and take out the necessary cash. No hassle! No interest! Unfortunately, few people have such large amounts of cash available. Most businesses are no different. Even though they would like to finance long-term needs from operations (retained earnings), few have the resources available to accomplish this.

Equity Financing from Venture Capital   The hardest time for a business to raise money is when it is starting up or just beginning to expand.[34] A start-up business typically has few assets and no market track record, so the chances of borrowing significant amounts of money from a bank are slim. **Venture capital** is money invested in new or emerging companies that some investors—venture capitalists—believe have great profit potential. Venture capital helped firms like Intel, Apple, and Cisco Systems get started and helped Facebook and Google expand and grow. Venture capitalists invest in a company in return for part ownership of the business. They expect higher-than-average returns and competent management performance for their investment.

The venture capital industry originally began as an alternative investment vehicle for wealthy families. The Rockefeller family, for example (whose vast fortune came from John D. Rockefeller's Standard Oil Company, started in the 19th century), financed Sanford McDonnell when he was operating his company from an airplane hangar. That small venture eventually grew into McDonnell Douglas, a large aerospace and defense contractor that merged with Boeing Corporation in 1997. The venture capital industry grew significantly in

venture capital
Money that is invested in new or emerging companies that are perceived as having great profit potential.

the 1990s, especially in high-tech centers like California's Silicon Valley, where venture capitalists concentrated on Internet-related companies. Problems in the technology industry and a slowdown in the economy in the early 2000s reduced venture capital expenditures. The Great Recession caused venture capital spending to drop to new lows. Today, as the economy recovers from the recession, venture capital is slowly rising again.

Comparing Debt and Equity Financing

Figure 18.6 compares debt and equity financing options. Raising funds through borrowing to increase the firm's rate of return is referred to as **leverage**. Though debt increases risk because it creates a financial obligation that must be repaid, it also enhances the firm's ability to increase profits. Recall that two key jobs of the financial manager or CFO are forecasting the firm's need for borrowed funds and planning how to manage these funds once they are obtained.

leverage
Raising needed funds through borrowing to increase a firm's rate of return.

Firms are very concerned with the cost of capital. **Cost of capital** is the rate of return a company must earn in order to meet the demands of its lenders and expectations of its equity holders (stockholders or venture capitalists). If the firm's earnings are larger than the interest payments on borrowed funds, business owners can realize a higher rate of return than if they used equity financing. Figure 18.7 describes an example, again involving our vegetarian restaurant, Very Vegetarian (introduced in Chapter 13). If Very Vegetarian needed $200,000 in new financing, it could consider debt by selling bonds or equity through offering stock. Comparing the two options in this situation, you can see that Very Vegetarian would benefit by selling bonds since the company's earnings are greater than the interest paid on borrowed funds (bonds). However, if the firm's earnings were less than the interest paid on borrowed funds (bonds), Very Vegetarian could lose money. It's also important to remember that bonds, like all debt, have to be repaid at a specific time.

cost of capital
The rate of return a company must earn in order to meet the demands of its lenders and expectations of its equity holders.

Individual firms must determine exactly how to balance debt and equity financing by comparing the costs and benefits of each. Leverage ratios (discussed in Chapter 17) can also give companies an industry standard for this balance, to which they can compare themselves. Still debt varies considerably among major companies and industries. Tech leader Apple, for example, has modest long-term debt of $16 billion even though it has more than $140 billion in cash available. Automaker Ford Motor Company has almost $110

FIGURE 18.6 DIFFERENCES BETWEEN DEBT AND EQUITY FINANCING

Conditions	Type of Financing	
	Debt	**Equity**
Management influence	There's usually none unless special conditions have been agreed on.	Common stockholders have voting rights.
Repayment	Debt has a maturity date.	Stock has no maturity date.
	Principal must be repaid.	The company is never required to repay equity.
Yearly obligations	Payment of interest is a contractual obligation.	The firm isn't legally liable to pay dividends.
Tax benefits	Interest is tax-deductible.	Dividends are paid from after-tax income and aren't deductible.

FIGURE 18.7 USING
LEVERAGE (DEBT)
VERSUS EQUITY
FINANCING
Very Vegetarian wants to
raise $200,000 in new capital.
Compare the firm's debt and
equity options.

Additional Debt		Additional Equity	
Stockholders' equity	$500,000	Stockholders' equity	$500,000
Additional equity	—	Additional equity	$200,000
Total equity	$500,000	Total equity	$700,000
Bond @ 8% interest	200,000	Bond interest	—
Total shareholder equity	$500,000	Total shareholder equity	$700,000
Year-End Earnings			
Gross profit	$100,000	Gross profit	$100,000
Less bond interest	−16,000	Less interest	—
Operating profit	$ 84,000	Operating profit	$100,000
Return on equity	16.8%	Return on equity	14.3%
($84,000 ÷ $500,000 = 16.8%)		($100,000 ÷ $700,000 = 14.3%)	

billion of debt on its balance sheet, mild compared to General Electric, which has over $360 billion of debt on its balance sheet. According to Standard & Poor's and Moody's Investors Service (firms that provide corporate and financial research), the debt of large industrial corporations and utilities typically ranges between 30 and 35 percent of its total assets. The amount of small-business debt obviously varies considerably from firm to firm.

Lessons Learned from the Recent Financial Crisis

The financial crisis that started in 2008 caused financial markets to suffer their worst fall since the Great Depression of the 1920s and 1930s. The collapse of financial markets could be laid at the feet of financial managers for failing to do their job effectively. Poor investment decisions and risky financial dealings (especially in real estate) caused long-standing financial firms such as Lehman Brothers to close their doors. The multibillion-dollar Ponzi scheme of once-respected "financial manager" Bernie Madoff further caused the public's trust in financial managers to disappear. Unfortunately, it also caused many investors' funds to disappear as well.

The financial meltdown led the U.S. Congress to pass sweeping financial regulatory reform. The Dodd-Frank Wall Street Reform and Consumer Protection Act affects almost every aspect of the U.S. financial services industry. As the government increases its involvement and intervention in financial markets, the requirements of financial institutions and financial managers have become more stringent.[35] This means that the job of the financial manager promises to become even more challenging. The events in the late 2000s questioned the integrity and good judgment of financial managers much like events in the early 2000s questioned the integrity and judgment of the accounting industry (see Chapter 17). Without a doubt, financial managers have a long road back to earning the trust of the public.

Chapter 19 takes a close look at securities markets as a source of securing long-term financing for businesses and as a base for investment options for private investors. You will learn how securities exchanges work, how firms issue stocks and bonds, how to choose the right investment strategy, how to buy and sell stock, where to find up-to-date information about stocks and bonds, and more. Finance takes on a new dimension when you see how you can participate in financial markets yourself.

test prep

- What are the two major forms of debt financing available to a firm?
- How does debt financing differ from equity financing?
- What are the three major forms of equity financing available to a firm?
- What is leverage, and why do firms choose to use it?

Use LearnSmart to help retain what you have learned. Access your instructor's Connect course to check out LearnSmart, or go to learnsmartadvantage.com for help.

LEARNSMART

summary

LO 18–1 Explain the role and responsibilities of financial managers.

Access your instructor's Connect course to check out LearnSmart or go to learnsmartadvantage.com for help.

- **What are the most common ways firms fail financially?**
  The most common financial problems are (1) undercapitalization, (2) poor control over cash flow, and (3) inadequate expense control.
- **What do financial managers do?**
  Financial managers plan, budget, control funds, obtain funds, collect funds, conduct audits, manage taxes, and advise top management on financial matters.

LO 18–2 Outline the financial planning process, and explain the three key budgets in the financial plan.

- **What are the three budgets in a financial plan?**
  The capital budget is the spending plan for expensive assets such as property, plant, and equipment. The cash budget is the projected cash balance at the end of a given period. The operating (master) budget summarizes the information in the other two budgets. It projects dollar allocations to various costs and expenses given various revenues.

LO 18–3 Explain why firms need operating funds.

- **What are firms' major financial needs?**
  Businesses need financing for four major tasks: (1) managing day-by-day operations, (2) controlling credit operations, (3) acquiring needed inventory, and (4) making capital expenditures.
- **What's the difference between debt financing and equity financing?**
  Debt financing raises funds by borrowing. Equity financing raises funds from within the firm through investment of retained earnings, sale of stock to investors, or sale of part ownership to venture capitalists.
- **What's the difference between short-term and long-term financing?**
  Short-term financing raises funds to be repaid in less than a year, whereas long-term financing raises funds to be repaid over a longer period.

LO 18–4 Identify and describe different sources of short-term financing.

- **Why should businesses use trade credit?**
  Trade credit is the least expensive and most convenient form of short-term financing. Businesses can buy goods today and pay for them sometime in the future.

- **What is meant by a line of credit and a revolving credit agreement?**
  A line of credit is an agreement by a bank to lend a specified amount of money to the business at any time, if the money is available. A revolving credit agreement is a line of credit that guarantees a loan will be available—for a fee.

- **What's the difference between a secured loan and an unsecured loan?**
  An unsecured loan has no collateral backing it. Secured loans have collateral backed by assets such as accounts receivable, inventory, or other property of value.

- **Is factoring a form of secured loan?**
  No, factoring means selling accounts receivable at a discounted rate to a factor (an intermediary that pays cash for those accounts and keeps the funds it collects on them).

- **What's commercial paper?**
  Commercial paper is a corporation's unsecured promissory note maturing in 270 days or less.

LO 18–5   Identify and describe different sources of long-term financing.

- **What are the major sources of long-term financing?**
  Debt financing is the sale of bonds to investors and long-term loans from banks and other financial institutions. Equity financing is obtained through the sale of company stock, from the firm's retained earnings, or from venture capital firms.

- **What are the two major forms of debt financing?**
  Debt financing comes from two sources: selling bonds and borrowing from individuals, banks, and other financial institutions. Bonds can be secured by some form of collateral or unsecured. The same is true of loans.

- **What's leverage, and how do firms use it?**
  Leverage is borrowing funds to invest in expansion, major asset purchases, or research and development. Firms measure the risk of borrowing against the potential for higher profits.

key terms

budget 508	**finance** 504	**revolving credit** **agreement** 517
capital budget 508	**financial control** 508	**risk/return trade-off** 520
capital expenditures 512	**financial management** 504	**secured bond** 521
cash budget 508	**financial managers** 504	**secured loan** 516
cash flow forecast 507	**indenture terms** 520	**short-term financing** 513
commercial finance **companies** 517	**leverage** 523	**short-term forecast** 507
commercial paper 518	**line of credit** 516	**term-loan agreement** 519
cost of capital 523	**long-term financing** 513	**trade credit** 514
debt financing 513	**long-term forecast** 507	**unsecured bond** 521
equity financing 513	**operating (or master)** **budget** 508	**unsecured loan** 516
factoring 517	**promissory note** 514	**venture capital** 522

critical thinking

1. What are the primary sources of short-term funds for new business owners? What are their major sources of long-term funds?

2. Why does a finance manager need to understand accounting information if the firm has a trained accountant on its staff?

3. Why do firms generally prefer to borrow funds to obtain long-term financing rather than issue shares of stock?

developing **workplace skills**

Key: ● **Team**   ★ **Analytic**   ▲ **Communication**   ◙ **Technology**

1. Go to your college's website and see whether its operating budget is online.   ◙ ★
   If not, go to the campus library and see whether the reference librarian
   has a copy of your college's operating budget for the current year. Try to
   identify major capital expenditures your college has planned for the future.

2. One of the most difficult concepts to get across to small-business owners   ★ ▲ ●
   is the need to take all the trade credit they can get. For example, the credit
   terms 2/10, net 30 can save businesses money if they pay their bills in the
   first 10 days. Work with a group of classmates to build a convincing financial argument for using trade credit.

3. Go online and check the capitalization required to open a franchise of   ◙ ★
   your choice, like Subway or McDonald's. Does the franchisor offer financial assistance to prospective franchisees? Evaluate the cost of the franchise versus its business potential using the risk/return trade-off discussed
   in the chapter.

4. Contact a lending officer at a local bank in your community, or visit the   ◙ ★
   bank's website, to check the bank's policies on providing a business a line
   of credit and a revolving line of credit. Evaluate the chances that this bank
   will give a small business either form of short-term loan.

5. Factoring accounts receivable is a form of financing used since the days of   ◙ ★ ▲
   Babylonian King Hammurabi 4,000 years ago. Today it's still a source of
   short-term funds used by small businesses. Visit www.21stfinancialsolutions.
   com to get more in-depth information about factoring and be prepared to
   discuss the pros and cons of factoring to the class.

taking it to the **net**

PURPOSE

To identify which types of companies qualify for financing through the Small
Business Administration.

EXERCISE

Many small-business owners have a difficult time finding financing to start or
expand their business. The Small Business Administration is one potential
source of financing for many types of small businesses, but there are also

some businesses that do not qualify for SBA loans. Go to www.sba.gov/content/businesses-eligible-ineligible-sba-assistance and see whether the following businesses are eligible to apply for SBA financing:

1. Growing Like a Weed is a lawn care business that needs funding to buy additional equipment in order to expand. Does it meet SBA criteria? Why or why not?

2. Glamour Galore is a cosmetic company that pays sales commissions based on a system that depends upon salespeople recruiting additional salespeople. It needs funding to build a marketing campaign. Does it meet SBA criteria? Why or why not?

3. Glory Days is an old-time pinball and jukebox refurbishing company. Its founding partners need funding to buy inventory. Do they meet SBA criteria? Why or why not?

4. Lettuce Entertain U is a company needing funding to remodel an old warehouse to house its latest vegan restaurant. Does it meet SBA criteria? Why or why not?

video case · connect

STARTING UP: TOM AND EDDIE'S

This video features the start-up company called Tom and Eddie's, an upscale hamburger restaurant in the Chicago area. Started in 2009 at the height of the great recession, the partners had a difficult time securing bank financing. As a result, they financed the operation themselves with the help of a third partner, Vince Nocarando. The partners both had long and successful careers as executives with McDonald's. Tom was executive vice president for new locations and Eddie was the president and CEO of North American operations.

Both partners, as a result of their experience at McDonald's, are well suited for the restaurant business. One of the most challenging and important elements of a successful start-up, like Tom and Eddie's, is a talented financial manager. Recognizing the importance of the financial function, they hired another former McDonald's executive, Brian Gordon, as CFO. Gordon explains that cash flow is the most important element in starting up a restaurant. In fact, cash flow is more important than profits in the first and perhaps second year of operation. Second to cash flow in terms of importance for sustainability is the management and control of inventory.

Cash flow is important, according to the CFO, because of the "known" costs, such as rent, payroll, inventory, taxes, and utilities. These are "known" costs because they are recurring and the relative costs are known on a weekly or monthly basis. CFO Gordon explains that cash flow is important in managing these known costs because of the significant "unknown" factor, which is sales.

Tom and Eddie's uses a very technology-intensive inventory management and control system because of the perishable nature of foodstuffs associated with the restaurant business. According to CFO Gordon, the restaurant has "net 14" terms with its food vendors. This means that the invoice is paid 14 days after the receipt of the goods. This is a form of financing, according to the CFO, that allows the company to turn that inventory once or twice during the 14-day period.

At the time of the video, Tom and Eddie's was in its fifteenth month of operation with three restaurants in the Chicago area. According to one of the partners, Eddie, the goal is to grow to 10 stores and then look at franchising the operation. When considering where to open a new operation, Eddie indicates that careful consideration is given to the demographics of the area, including the average income level of those working and living in the area to be served, the age of the population, the square footage of the surrounding commercial space, and ease of access to the location. Equipment is purchased rather than financed by the partners.

According to the partners, entrepreneurs think in terms of opportunities, not in terms of potential failure. With 15 months of successful operation, capital will be easier to raise from traditional sources of financing, such as banks, to expand the operation. Who knows, maybe a franchised Tom and Eddie's will be opening soon in a location near you.

THINKING IT OVER

1. What are the three factors associated with operating funds, according to the video?

2. What is meant by the term "front of the house"?

3. Why, according to the video, was bank financing unavailable for Tom and Eddie's start-up?

notes

1. Karen Weise, "Big Paydays for CFOs," *Bloomberg Businessweek*, May 19, 2013; and Emily Coyle, "Meet the Five Highest Paid CFOs in the S&P 500," *The Week*, July 8, 2013.
2. Mariella Segarra and David M. Katz, "What's It Like to Be a Nonprofit CFO?" *CFO.com*, November 27, 2013.
3. Jake Grouvm, "2008 Financial Crisis Impact Still Hurting States," *USA Today*, September 15, 2013.
4. Tim Higgins, Ian Katz, and Kasia Kimasinaska, "GM Bailout Ends as U.S. Sells Last of 'Government Motors,'" *Bloomberg Personal Finance*, December 9, 2013; and Bill Vlasic and Anne Lowery, "U.S. Ends Bailout of G.M., Selling Last Shares of Stock," *The New York Times*, December 9, 2013.
5. Ibid.
6. Saabria Chaudhuri, Michael Rapoport, and Alan Zibel, "Small Banks Face TARP Hit," *The Wall Street Journal*, February 7, 2014.
7. McCormick, www.mccormick.com, accessed February 2014.
8. Amy Haimerl, "15 Costly Mistakes Startups Make," *Crain's Detroit Business*, February 10, 2014.
9. Glenn Kessler, "Senator Scott's Claim That the Medical Device Tax Will Cost Small Business $29 Billion," *The Washington Post*, February 4, 2014.
10. Kathy Hoffelder, "Poor Internal Control Tests Hurt Financial Statement Audits," *CFO*, October 13, 2013.
11. Kathy Hoffelder, "Internal Audit Shines Brighter with Boards," *CFO*, March 22, 2013.
12. Bill Conerly, "Long-Term Economic Forecast: Key Issues and Business Strategy Implications," *Forbes*, January 12, 2014.
13. Russ Banham, "May the Field Be with You," *CFO*, October 9, 2013.
14. Keith Bradsher, "As China's Economy Slows, the Pain Hits Home," *The New York Times*, January 29, 2014; and Steve Shafer, "Why Panic-Prone Emerging Markets Are Breaking Down in 2014," *Forbes*, February 3, 2014.
15. Khan Academy, www.khanacademy.org, accessed February 2014.
16. Edward Teach, "Calm, Cool, and Collecting," *CFO*, October 15, 2013; and Jennifer Smith, "Law Firms Press to Get Bill Paid by Year End," *The Wall Street Journal*, December 22, 2013.
17. Scott Liebs, "4 Money Mistakes That Entrepreneurs Must Avoid," *Inc.*, February 2014.
18. T. J. McCue, "Why Don't More Small Businesses Accept Credit Cards?" *Forbes*, August 8, 2013; and "What You May Not Know about Your Credit Card Processor," *Milwaukee Journal Sentinal*, February 3, 2014.
19. Scott Kirsner, "Startups Offer Tech to Change the Way You Pay," *The Boston Globe*, February 9, 2014.
20. Venessa Wong, "Chipotle Wants to Speed Up with Mobile Payments," *Bloomberg Businessweek*, February 3, 2014.
21. J. J. Colao, "Interchange Fees Are for Suckers: LevelUp Hints at the Future of Mobile Payments," *Forbes*, March 21, 2013.
22. Ty Kisel, "Small Business Financing Is Available, Just Not Where You're Looking," *Forbes*, September 24, 2013.
23. Karen Haywood Queen, "Borrowing from Friends and Family," *MSN Money*, September 3, 2013.
24. National Federation of Independent Business, www.nfib.com, accessed February 2014.
25. "Consumer Finance Protection Bureau," *The Economist*, February 1, 2014.
26. Stephen D. Simpson, CFA, "The Basics of Lines of Credit," *Forbes.com*, August 6, 2013.
27. www.gecapital.com, accessed February 2014; and Chanella Bessette, "At GE, a Push for Innovation Through Partnerships," *Fortune*, February 7, 2014.
28. John Parry, "U.S. Commercial Paper Contracts to Lowest Level Since September," *Bloomberg Businessweek*, January 23, 2014.
29. Catherine Clifford, "Best Credit Cards for Small Business Owners in 2013," *Entrepreneur*, June 7, 2013; and National Small Business Advocate, www.nsba.biz, accessed February 2014.
30. Annamaria Andriotis, "The Return of Small-Business Credit Cards," *The Wall Street Journal*, January 16, 2012; "American Express OPEN Revamps Simple Cash (R) Business Credit Card by Giving Small Business Owners the Ability to Customize Their Cash Back Rewards," *The Wall Street Journal*, January 28, 2014; and "Petflow.com Continues Dominant Rise to Become Highest-Trafficked Online Pet Property in North America," *Business Wire*, February 13, 2014.
31. Jonathan D. Rockoff and Tess Stynes, "Pfizer Is Upbeat about Breast Cancer Drug, Pneumonia Vaccine," *The Wall Street Journal*, January 28, 2014.
32. Dan Carroll, "Pfizer Beats Falling Profit as the Dow Bounces Back from Recent Lows," *The Motley Fool*, January 28, 2014; and Johanna Bennett, "Pfizer's Finally a Buy," *Barron's*, February 12, 2014.
33. Ryan C. Fuhrman, "The Road to Creating an IPO," *Forbes*, August 28, 2013; and David Gelles and Michael J. de la Merced, "New IPO Rules Promise a Lot Less Information," *Boston Globe*, February 10, 2014.
34. Sam Hogg, "Why So Many Startups Never Reach Their Second Funding Round," *Entrepreneur*, February 8, 2014.
35. Abha Bhattarai and Catherine Ho, "Four Years into Dodd-Frank, Local Banks Say This Is the Year They'll Feel the Most Impact," *The Washington Post*, February 7, 2014.

photo credits

11 Human Resource Management:

Finding and Keeping the Best Employees

Learning Objectives

AFTER YOU HAVE READ AND STUDIED THIS CHAPTER, YOU SHOULD BE ABLE TO

LO 11-1 Explain the importance of human resource management, and describe current issues in managing human resources.

LO 11-2 Illustrate the effects of legislation on human resource management.

LO 11-3 Summarize the five steps in human resource planning.

LO 11-4 Describe methods that companies use to recruit new employees, and explain some of the issues that make recruitment challenging.

LO 11-5 Outline the six steps in selecting employees.

LO 11-6 Illustrate employee training and development methods.

LO 11-7 Trace the six steps in appraising employee performance.

LO 11-8 Summarize the objectives of employee compensation programs, and evaluate pay systems and fringe benefits.

LO 11-9 Demonstrate how managers use scheduling plans to adapt to workers' needs.

LO 11-10 Describe how employees can move through a company: promotion, reassignment, termination, and retirement.

Getting to know **Tony Hsieh**

Although online shopping sites are becoming the dominant force in the retail world, they often fall short of their brick-and-mortar rivals in terms of customer service. At the online shoe vendor Zappos, however, a unique company culture ensures customers don't have to sacrifice quality service for convenience.

When Tony Hsieh joined Zappos as CEO, he wanted to change the corporate work environment for the better. After selling his first company to Microsoft for a whopping $265 million, Hsieh didn't want a job in a gray, cubicle-filled office. "For me, I didn't want to be part of a company where I dreaded going into the office," said Hsieh. To set Zappos apart from other online retailers, he wanted his service representatives to wow customers with their energy and expertise. To do that Hsieh needed upbeat employees who were motivated by the love of their work. He gave his call center staffers remarkable freedom, allowing them to talk to customers for hours at a time or send flowers and thank-you notes on the company's dime.

Not only does this strategy do wonders for customer satisfaction, it also keeps employee morale sky high. In order to succeed at this job, Zappos's service reps must be creative, energetic, generous, and understanding. But this commitment to excellence doesn't end with the company's spirited call center employees. When candidates for departments like marketing or management reach the interview stage, Hsieh starts testing them before they even set foot in the company's Las Vegas headquarters. "A lot of our job candidates are from out of town, and we'll pick them up from the airport in a Zappos shuttle, give them a tour, and then they'll spend the rest of the day interviewing," said Hsieh. "At the end of the day of interviews, the recruiter will circle back to the shuttle driver and ask how he or she was treated. It doesn't matter how well the day of interviews went, if our shuttle driver wasn't treated well, then we won't hire that person." The examination doesn't end once the person lands the job. Regardless of their position, new hires must spend their first month helping customers in the call center. If they can't thrive, they're gone.

Along with creating open and accessible work environments, Hsieh also tries to break down as many barriers between employees and management as possible. Zappos executives are affectionately referred to as "monkeys," and the best view from the company's 10-story Vegas high-rise is reserved for the call center workers. In fact, Hsieh puts so much faith in his staff that in 2014 he announced Zappos would be eliminating most of its traditional managers, corporate titles, and hierarchy entirely. Instead, the company will be replacing its standard chain of command with a "holacracy." This new company structure splits employees into overlapping but mostly self-ruling "circles" that allow them to have a greater voice in how the company is run. Although time will tell whether or not this radical system works, Tony Hsieh's commitment to an offbeat but efficient workplace has already grown Zappos into a $2 billion company. If anybody can pull off such an unorthodox office structure, it's Hsieh.

In this chapter, you'll learn how businesses that succeed like Zappos recruit, manage, and make the most of their employees.

Tony Hsieh
- CEO of Zappos
- Created an offbeat but efficient workplace
- Empowers staffers to wow customers

www.zappos.com

@zappos

Sources: Jena McGregor, "Zappos Says Goodbye to Bosses," *The Washington Post*, January 3, 2014; Edward Lewine, "Tony Hsieh's Office: Welcome to the Rain Forest," *The New York Times*, December 28, 2013; Max Nisen, "Tony Hsieh's Brilliant Strategy for Hiring Kind People," *Business Insider*, November 22, 2013; Kim Bhasin, "Tony Hsieh: Here's Why I Don't Want My Employees to Work From Home," *Business Insider*, March 6, 2013; and Adam Bryant, "On a Scale of 1 to 10, How Weird Are You?" *The New York Times*, January 9, 2010.

name that **company**

This company manages its global workforce of about 100,000 employees and 100,000 subcontractors with a database that matches employee skills, experiences, schedules, and references with jobs available. For example, if a client in Quebec has a monthlong project that needs a consultant who speaks English and French, and has an advanced degree in engineering and experience with Linux programming, the system can quickly find the best-suited person available. Name that company. (Find the answer in the chapter.)

LO 11–1 Explain the importance of human resource management, and describe current issues in managing human resources.

WORKING WITH PEOPLE IS JUST THE BEGINNING

Students often say they want to go into human resource management because they want to "work with people." Human resource managers do work with people, but they are also deeply involved in planning, record keeping, and other administrative duties. To begin a career in human resource management, you need a better reason than "I want to work with people." This chapter will tell you what else human resource management is all about.

Human resource management (HRM) is the process of determining human resource needs and then recruiting, selecting, developing, motivating, evaluating, compensating, and scheduling employees to achieve organizational goals (see Figure 11.1). For many years, human resource management was called "personnel" and involved clerical functions such as screening applications, keeping records, processing the payroll, and finding new employees when necessary. The roles and responsibilities of HRM have evolved primarily because of two key factors: (1) organizations' recognition of employees as their ultimate resource and (2) changes in the law that rewrote many traditional practices. Let's explore both.

Developing the Ultimate Resource

One reason human resource management is receiving increased attention now is that the U.S. economy has experienced a major shift—from traditional manufacturing industries to service and high-tech manufacturing industries that require highly technical job skills. This shift means that many workers must be retrained for new, more challenging jobs. They truly are the ultimate resource. People develop the ideas that eventually become products to satisfy consumers' wants and needs. Take away their creative minds, and leading firms such as Disney, Apple, Procter & Gamble, Google, Facebook, and General Electric would be nothing.

In the past, human resources were plentiful, so there was little need to nurture and develop them. If you needed qualified people, you simply hired them. If they didn't work out, you fired them and found others. Most firms assigned the job of recruiting, selecting, training, evaluating, compensating, motivating, and, yes, firing people to the functional departments that employed them, like accounting, manufacturing, and marketing. Today the job of human

human resource management (HRM)
The process of determining human resource needs and then recruiting, selecting, developing, motivating, evaluating, compensating, and scheduling employees to achieve organizational goals.

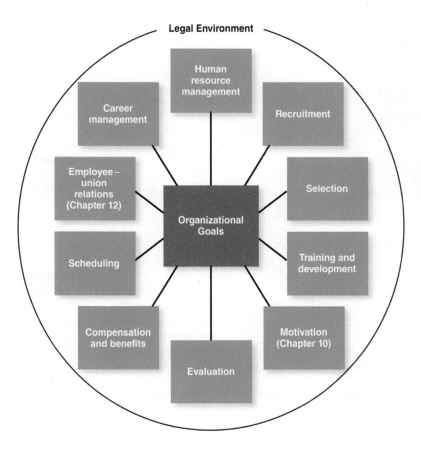

FIGURE 11.1 HUMAN RESOURCE MANAGEMENT

As this figure shows, human resource management is more than hiring and firing personnel. All activities are designed to achieve organizational goals within the laws that affect human resource management. (Note that human resource management includes motivation, as discussed in Chapter 10, and employee–union relations, as discussed in Chapter 12.)

resource management has taken on an increased role in the firm since *qualified* employees are much scarcer, which makes recruiting and retaining people more important and more difficult.[1]

In the future, human resource management may become the firm's most critical function, responsible for dealing with all aspects of a business's most critical resource—people. In fact, the human resource function has become so important that it's no longer the job of just one department; it's a responsibility of *all* managers. What human resource challenges do all managers face? We'll outline a few next.

The Human Resource Challenge

Many of the changes that have had the most dramatic impact on U.S. business are those in the labor force.[2] The ability to compete in global markets depends on new ideas, new products, and new levels of productivity—in other words, on people with good ideas. These are some of the challenges and opportunities in human resources:

- Shortages of trained workers in growth areas, such as computer technology, biotechnology, robotics, green technology, and the sciences.
- Large numbers of skilled and unskilled workers from declining industries, such as steel and automobiles, who are unemployed or underemployed and need retraining. *Underemployed workers* are those who have more

302   PART 4   Management of Human Resources: Motivating Employees to Produce Quality Goods and Services

U.S. firms face a shortage of workers skilled in areas like science, green technology, and the development of clean energy sources like these solar panels. What other job markets do you think will grow as companies focus more on environmentally friendly policies? Which ones appeal to you?

skills or knowledge than their current jobs require or those with part-time jobs who want to work full-time.

- A growing percentage of new workers who are undereducated and unprepared for jobs in the contemporary business environment.

- A shortage of workers in skilled trades due to the retirement of aging baby boomers.[3]

- An increasing number of baby boomers who, due to the recession, delay retirement (preventing the promotion of younger workers) or move to lower-level jobs (increasing the supply of workers for such jobs).

- An increasing number of both single-parent and two-income families, resulting in a demand for job sharing, maternity leave, and special career advancement programs for women.

- A shift in employee attitudes toward work. Leisure time has become a much higher priority, as have flextime and a shorter workweek.

- A severe recession that took a toll on employee morale and increased the demand for temporary and part-time workers.[4]

- A challenge from overseas labor pools whose members work for lower wages and are subject to fewer laws and regulations than U.S. workers. This results in many jobs being outsourced overseas.

- An increased demand for benefits tailored to the individual yet cost-effective to the company.

- Growing concerns over health care, elder care, child care, drug testing, workplace violence (all discussed in Chapter 12), and opportunities for people with disabilities.

- Changes through the Affordable Care Act that have added a large number of new regulations that employers must read, interpret, implement, and track.[5]

- A decreased sense of employee loyalty, which increases employee turnover and the cost of replacing lost workers.

Given these issues, you can see why human resource management has taken a central place in management thinking. However, significant changes in laws covering hiring, safety, unionization, equal pay, and affirmative action have also had a major influence. Let's look at their impact on human resource management.

LO 11–2   Illustrate the effects of legislation on human resource management.

LAWS AFFECTING HUMAN RESOURCE MANAGEMENT

Until the 1930s, the U.S. government had little to do with human resource decisions. Since then, legislation and legal decisions have greatly affected all areas of human resource management, from hiring to training to monitoring working conditions (see Figure 11.2). These laws were passed because many businesses did not exercise fair labor practices voluntarily.

One of the more important pieces of social legislation passed by Congress was the Civil Rights Act of 1964. This act generated much debate and was amended 97 times before final passage. Title VII of that act brought the

FIGURE 11.2 GOVERNMENT LEGISLATION AFFECTING HUMAN RESOURCE MANAGEMENT

National Labor Relations Act of 1935. Established collective bargaining in labor–management relations and limited management interference in the right of employees to have a collective bargaining agent.

Fair Labor Standards Act of 1938. Established a minimum wage and overtime pay for employees working more than 40 hours a week. Amendments expanded the classes of workers covered, raised the minimum wage, redefined regular-time work, raised overtime payments, and equalized pay scales for men and women.

Manpower Development and Training Act of 1962. Provided for the training and retraining of unemployed workers.

Equal Pay Act of 1963. Specified that men and women doing equal jobs must be paid the same wage.

Civil Rights Act of 1964. For firms with 15 or more employees, outlawed discrimination in employment based on sex, race, color, religion, or national origin.

Age Discrimination in Employment Act of 1967. Outlawed employment practices that discriminate against people 40 and older. An amendment outlaws requiring retirement by a specific age.

Occupational Safety and Health Act of 1970. Regulated the degree to which employees can be exposed to hazardous substances and specified the safety equipment the employer must provide.

Equal Employment Opportunity Act of 1972. Strengthened the Equal Employment Opportunity Commission (EEOC) and authorized the EEOC to set guidelines for human resource management.

Comprehensive Employment and Training Act of 1973 (CETA). Provided funds for training unemployed workers.

Vocational Rehabilitation Act of 1973. Extended protection to people with any physical or mental disability.

Employee Retirement Income Security Act of 1974 (ERISA). Regulated and insured company retirement plans.

Immigration Reform and Control Act of 1986. Required employers to verify employment eligibility of all new hires including U.S. citizens.

Supreme Court ruling against set-aside programs (affirmative action), 1989. Declared that setting aside 30 percent of contracting jobs for minority businesses was reverse discrimination and unconstitutional.

Older Workers Benefit Protection Act, 1990. Protects older people from signing away their rights to pensions and protection from illegal age discrimination.

Civil Rights Act of 1991. For firms with over 15 employees, extends the right to a jury trial and punitive damages to victims of intentional job discrimination.

Americans with Disabilities Act of 1990 (1992 implementation). Prohibits employers from discriminating against qualified individuals with disabilities in hiring, advancement, or compensation and requires them to adapt the workplace if necessary.

Family and Medical Leave Act of 1993. Businesses with 50 or more employees must provide up to 12 weeks of unpaid leave per year upon birth or adoption of an employee's child or upon serious illness of a parent, spouse, or child.

Americans with Disabilities Amendments Act of 2008 (ADA). Provides broader protection for disabled workers and reverses Supreme Court decisions deemed too restrictive. Adds disabilities such as epilepsy and cancer to ADA coverage.

Lilly Ledbetter Fair Pay Act of 2009. Amends the Civil Rights Act of 1964 by changing the start of the 180-day statute of limitations for filing a discrimination suit from the date of the first discriminatory paycheck to the date of the most recent discriminatory paycheck.

government directly into the operations of human resource management. Title VII prohibits discrimination in hiring, firing, compensation, apprenticeships, training, terms, conditions, or privileges of employment based on race, religion, creed, sex, or national origin. Age was later added to the conditions of the act. The Civil Rights Act of 1964 was expected to stamp out discrimination in the workplace, but specific language in it made enforcement quite difficult. Congress took on the task of amending the law.

In 1972, the Equal Employment Opportunity Act (EEOA) was added as an amendment to Title VII. It strengthened the Equal Employment Opportunity Commission (EEOC), which was created by the Civil Rights Act, by giving it

affirmative action
Employment activities designed to "right past wrongs" by increasing opportunities for minorities and women.

reverse discrimination
Discrimination against members of a dominant or majority group (e.g., whites or males) usually as a result of policies designed to correct previous discrimination against minority or disadvantaged groups.

The Americans with Disabilities Act guarantees that all U.S. workers have equal opportunity in employment. This legislation requires businesses to make "reasonable accommodations" on the job for people with disabilities. What required accommodations do you think would be reasonable?

rather broad powers. For example, it permitted the EEOC to issue guidelines for acceptable employer conduct in administering equal employment opportunity. The EEOC also mandated specific record-keeping procedures, and Congress vested it with the power of enforcement to ensure these mandates were carried out. The EEOC became a formidable regulatory force in the administration of human resource management.[6]

Perhaps the most controversial policy enforced by the EEOC involved **affirmative action**, designed to "right past wrongs" by increasing opportunities for minorities and women. Interpretation of the affirmative action law led employers to actively recruit, and in some cases give preference to, women and minority group members. Questions persist about the legality of affirmative action and the effect it may have in creating a sort of reverse discrimination in the workplace. **Reverse discrimination** has been defined as discriminating against members of a dominant or majority group (e.g., whites or males) usually as a result of policies designed to correct previous discrimination. The issue has generated heated debate as well as many lawsuits.

The Civil Rights Act of 1991 expanded the remedies available to victims of discrimination by amending Title VII of the Civil Rights Act of 1964. Now victims of discrimination have the right to a jury trial and punitive damages. Human resource managers must follow court decisions closely to see how the law is enforced.

The Office of Federal Contract Compliance Programs (OFCCP) ensures that employers comply with nondiscrimination and affirmative action laws and regulations when doing business with the federal government.

Laws Protecting Employees with Disabilities and Older Employees

As you read above, laws prohibit discrimination related to race, sex, or age in hiring, firing, and training. The Vocational Rehabilitation Act of 1973 extended protection to people with any physical or mental disability.

The Americans with Disabilities Act of 1990 (ADA) requires employers to give applicants with physical or mental disabilities the same consideration for employment as people without disabilities. The ADA also protects individuals with disabilities from discrimination in public accommodations, transportation, and telecommunications.

The ADA requires making "reasonable accommodations" for employees with disabilities, such as modifying equipment or widening doorways. Most companies have no trouble making structural changes to be accommodating. However, at times such changes can be difficult for some small businesses.[7] Employers used to think that being fair meant treating everyone the same, but *accommodation* in fact means treating people *according to their specific needs*. That can include putting up barriers to isolate people readily distracted by noise, reassigning workers to new tasks, and making changes in supervisors' management styles. Accommodations are not always expensive; an inexpensive headset can allow someone with cerebral palsy to talk on the phone.

In 2008, Congress passed the Americans with Disabilities Amendments Act, which overturned Supreme Court decisions that had reduced protections for certain people with disabilities such as diabetes, epilepsy, heart disease, autism, major depression, and cancer.[8] In 2011, the EEOC issued regulations that widened the range of disabilities covered by the ADA and shifted the burden of proof of disability in labor disputes from employees to business owners. Enforcement of this law promises to be a continuing issue for human resource management.

The Age Discrimination in Employment Act of 1967 (ADEA) protects individuals 40 or older from employment and workplace discrimination in hiring, firing, promotion, layoff, compensation, benefits, job assignments, and training. The ADEA is enforced by the EEOC, applies to employers with 20 or more employees, and protects both employees and job applicants.[9] It also outlaws mandatory retirement in most organizations. It does, however, allow age restrictions for certain job categories such as airline pilot or bus driver if evidence shows that the ability to perform significantly diminishes with age or that age imposes a danger to society.

Effects of Legislation

Clearly, laws ranging from the Social Security Act of 1935 to the 2008 Americans with Disabilities Amendments Act require human resource managers to keep abreast of laws and court decisions to effectively perform their jobs. Choosing a career in human resource management offers a challenge to anyone willing to put forth the effort. Remember:

- Employers must know and act in accordance with the legal rights of their employees or risk costly court cases.

- Legislation affects all areas of human resource management, from hiring and training to compensation.

- Court cases demonstrate that it is sometimes legal to provide special employment (affirmative action) and training to correct discrimination in the past.

- New court cases and legislation change human resource management almost daily; the only way to keep current is to read the business literature and stay familiar with emerging issues.

test prep

- What is human resource management?
- What did Title VII of the Civil Rights Act of 1964 achieve?
- What is the EEOC, and what was the intention of affirmative action?
- What does *accommodations* mean in the Americans with Disabilities Act of 1990?

Use LearnSmart to help retain what you have learned. Access your instructor's Connect course to check out LearnSmart or go to learnsmartadvantage.com for help.

LEARNSMART

LO 11-3   Summarize the five steps in human resource planning.

DETERMINING A FIRM'S HUMAN RESOURCE NEEDS

All management, including human resource management, begins with planning. The five steps in the human resource planning process are:

1. *Preparing a human resource inventory of the organization's employees.* This inventory should include ages, names, education, capabilities, training, specialized skills, and other relevant information (such as

languages spoken). It reveals whether the labor force is technically up-to-date and thoroughly trained.[10]

job analysis
A study of what employees do who hold various job titles.

job description
A summary of the objectives of a job, the type of work to be done, the responsibilities and duties, the working conditions, and the relationship of the job to other functions.

job specifications
A written summary of the minimum qualifications required of workers to do a particular job.

2. *Preparing a job analysis.* A **job analysis** is a study of what employees do who hold various job titles. It's necessary in order to recruit and train employees with the necessary skills to do the job. The results of job analysis are two written statements: job descriptions and job specifications. A **job description** specifies the objectives of the job, the type of work, the responsibilities and duties, working conditions, and the job's relationship to other functions. **Job specifications** are a written summary of the minimal education and skills to do a particular job. In short, job descriptions are about the job, and job specifications are about the person who does the job. Visit the Occupational Information Network (O*NET) at www.onetcenter.org for detailed information about job analyses and job descriptions. See Figure 11.3 for a hypothetical job description and job specifications.

3. *Assessing future human resource demand.* Because technology changes rapidly, effective human resource managers are proactive; that is, they forecast the organization's requirements and train people ahead of time or ensure trained people are available when needed.

4. *Assessing future labor supply.* The labor force is constantly shifting: getting older, becoming more technically oriented, becoming more diverse. Some workers will be scarcer in the future, like biomedical engineers and robotic repair workers, and others will be oversupplied, like assembly-line workers.

5. *Establishing a strategic plan.* The human resource strategic plan must address recruiting, selecting, training, developing, appraising, compensating, and scheduling the labor force. Because the first four steps lead up to this one, we'll focus on them in the rest of the chapter.

FIGURE 11.3 JOB ANALYSIS
A job analysis yields two important statements: job descriptions and job specifications. Here you have a job description and job specifications for a sales representative.

JOB ANALYSIS
Observe current sales representatives doing the job. Discuss job with sales managers. Have current sales reps keep a diary of their activities.

JOB DESCRIPTION	JOB SPECIFICATIONS
Primary objective is to sell company's products to stores in Territory Z. Duties include servicing accounts and maintaining positive relationships with clients. Responsibilities include: • Introducing the new products to store managers in the area. • Helping the store managers estimate the volume to order. • Negotiating prime shelf space. • Explaining sales promotion activities to store managers. • Stocking and maintaining shelves in stores that wish such service.	Characteristics of the person qualifying for this job include: • Two years' sales experience. • Positive attitude. • Well-groomed appearance. • Good communication skills. • High school diploma and two years of college credit.

Some companies use advanced technology to perform the human resource planning process more efficiently. IBM manages its global workforce of about 100,000 employees and 100,000 subcontractors with a database that matches employee skills, experiences, schedules, and references with jobs available. The company also created a cloud-hosted software suite that's designed for automating and improving human resource tasks.[11] For example, if a client in Quebec, Canada, has a monthlong project requiring a consultant who speaks English and French, has an advanced degree in engineering, and experience with Linux programming, IBM can find the best-suited consultant available and put him or her in touch with the client.

LO 11–4   Describe methods that companies use to recruit new employees, and explain some of the issues that make recruitment challenging.

RECRUITING EMPLOYEES FROM A DIVERSE POPULATION

Recruitment is the set of activities for obtaining the right number of qualified people at the right time. Its purpose is to select those who best meet the needs of the organization. You might think a continuous flow of new people into the workforce makes recruiting easy. On the contrary, it's become very challenging for several reasons:

- Some organizations have policies that demand promotions from within, operate under union regulations, or offer low wages, which makes recruiting and keeping employees difficult or subject to outside influence and restrictions.

- An emphasis on corporate culture, teamwork, and participative management makes it important to hire people who not only are skilled but also fit in with the culture and leadership style of the company. Wegmans Food Markets (a member of *Fortune* magazine's list of best companies to work for 17 straight years) encourages employees to do whatever they think is necessary to make a customer happy. The company is currently experimenting with a personal

connect

 iSee It! Need help understanding the five steps of human resource planning? Visit your Connect e-book video tab for a brief animated explanation.

recruitment
The set of activities used to obtain a sufficient number of the right employees at the right time.

Human resource managers today have the opportunity to recruit people from a wide range of cultural and ethnic backgrounds. What are some of the advantages of a diverse workforce?

shopper service. This service allows customers to create a shopping list on Wegman's website or smartphone app; employees will gather the order and then deliver it to the customer's car when they come to the store.[12]

- Sometimes people with the necessary skills are not available; then workers must be hired and trained internally.[13]

Human resource managers can turn to many sources for recruiting assistance (see Figure 11.4). *Internal sources* include current employees who can be transferred or promoted or who can recommend others to hire. Using internal sources is less expensive than recruiting from outside and helps maintain employee morale. However, it isn't always possible to find qualified workers within the company, so human resource managers also use *external sources* such as advertisements, public and private employment agencies, college placement bureaus, management consultants, Internet sites, professional organizations, referrals, and online and walk-in applications. Management consulting firm McKinsey uses a database of 27,000 former consultants who left the firm in good standing as brand ambassadors and recruiters for the firm.[14]

Recruiting qualified workers may be particularly difficult for small businesses with few staff members and less-than-competitive compensation to attract external sources.[15] CareerBuilder.com, Monster.com, and Indeed.com have helped such firms by attracting more than 80 million visitors per month. The Spotlight on Small Business box offers additional ways small businesses can recruit.

FIGURE 11.4 EMPLOYEE SOURCES
Internal sources are often given first consideration, so it's useful to get a recommendation from a current employee of the firm for which you want to work. College placement offices are also an important source. Be sure to learn about such facilities early so that you can plan a strategy throughout your college career.

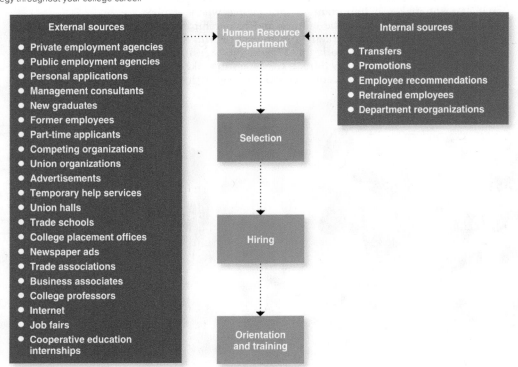

www.monster.com

spotlight on **small business**

Competing for the Cream of the Crop

Most small-business owners would agree that attracting top-quality employees is one of their major challenges. Unfortunately, competing for the cream of the crop is difficult when you can't afford expensive recruiters or pay gold-plated benefits to lure qualified workers. Despite these hurdles, small businesses can compete if they follow certain recruiting recommendations. Here are a few helpful tips:

- *Define who you are as a company.* Instead of describing what skills and experience are required of a prospective employee, start off by explaining what your company does and what its vision is all about. Quite often top-quality candidates will not agree to an interview until they know what the job is all about.
- *Build a strong staff referral program.* The more your current staff is engaged in the search and interview process, the better the chance to find recruits with

the right personality and skills. Remember, no recruiter or website knows the organization's culture better than its employees.
- *Have future employees audition for the job.* Hiring workers first on a temporary basis or an internship allows you to test candidates before deciding whether to make an offer of permanent employment.
- *Look at your customers.* Loyal and informed customers can often be a source of potential employees. Build-A-Bear Workshop, for example, often hires customers who come into its stores and exhibit a real interest in the company and its products.
- *Become involved with community organizations.* Many community organizations have top-notch volunteers or employees who may be looking for a new opportunity. Also, don't forget nonprofit organizations or agencies that welcome immigrants new to a region or people in need of a job who may be excellent candidates you can train.

- *Actively seek publicity and word of mouth to create a "buzz" for your company.* Publicity is more believable than advertising; word of mouth is a very effective recruiting tool. Building an image of a dynamic workplace with eager and energetic workers will attract others.
- *Make use of Internet services, social media, and local government agencies.* Recruiting on an online service like Monster.com is very cost-efficient. Government employment services are free and social media creates opportunities to target key employee groups. While not as potent as staff referrals, all provide a source of reaching potential prize employees.

Sources: Raj Sheth, "Small Business Advice: How to Establish a Recruiting Process and Develop a Culture," *The Washington Post,* January 29, 2014; Ritika Puri, "Four Ways Small Businesses Can Recruit Top Talent," *Forbes,* February 18, 2014; and Marc Wayshak, "5 Things You Should Not Do When Hiring for Your Organization," *Entrepreneur,* April 1, 2014.

LO 11–5   Outline the six steps in selecting employees.

SELECTING EMPLOYEES WHO WILL BE PRODUCTIVE

Selection is the process of gathering information and deciding who should be hired, under legal guidelines, to serve the best interests of the individual and the organization. Selecting and training employees are extremely expensive processes in some firms. Just think what's involved: advertising or recruiting agency fees, interview time, medical exams, training costs, unproductive time spent learning the job, possible travel and moving expenses, and more. It can cost one and a half times the employee's annual salary to recruit, process, and train even an entry-level worker, and over six figures for a top manager.[16]

A typical selection process has six steps:

1. *Obtaining complete application forms.* Although equal employment laws limit the kinds of questions that can appear, applications help reveal the applicant's educational background, work experience, career objectives, and other qualifications directly related to the job.

selection
The process of gathering information and deciding who should be hired, under legal guidelines, to serve the best interests of the individual and the organization.

Large retail employers like Winn-Dixie and Finish Line make the application process more efficient by using an automated program called Workforce Talent Acquisition.[17] An applicant sits at a computer and answers questions about job experience, time available to work, and personality. The software e-mails a report to the hiring manager recommending whether to interview the applicant and, if so, suggesting questions to ask. Mike Marchetti, executive vice president of store operations for Finish Line, says his company processed 330,000 applications, eliminating 60,000 interview hours and reducing turnover 24 percent.[18]

2. *Conducting initial and follow-up interviews.* A staff member from the human resource department often screens applicants in a first interview. If the interviewer considers the applicant a potential hire, the manager who will supervise the new employee may interview the applicant as well. It's important that managers prepare adequately for the interview to avoid selection decisions they may regret.[19] No matter how innocent the intention, missteps such as asking about pregnancy or child care could later be evidence if the applicant files discrimination charges.

3. *Giving employment tests.* Organizations often use tests to measure basic competency in specific job skills like welding or firefighting, and to help evaluate applicants' personalities and interests. The tests should always be directly related to the job. Employment tests have been legally challenged as potential means of discrimination. Many companies test potential employees in assessment centers where they perform actual job tasks. Such testing can make the selection process more efficient and will generally satisfy legal requirements.

4. *Conducting background investigations.* Most organizations now investigate a candidate's work record, school record, credit history, and references more carefully than in the past to help identify those most likely to succeed. It is simply too costly to hire, train, and motivate people only to lose them and have to start the process over. Services such as LexisNexis allow prospective employers not only to conduct speedy background checks of criminal records, driving records, and credit histories but also to verify work experience and professional and educational credentials.[20] The Adapting to Change box discusses how companies use Facebook and other social media to screen job applicants and weed out those with undesirable traits.

5. *Obtaining results from physical exams.* There are obvious benefits to hiring physically and mentally healthy people. However, according to the Americans with Disabilities Act, medical tests cannot be given just to screen out individuals. In some states, physical exams can be given only after an offer of employment has been accepted. In states that allow pre-employment physical exams, they must be given to everyone applying for the same position. Pre-employment testing to detect drug or alcohol abuse has been controversial, as has screening to detect carriers of HIV, the virus that causes AIDS.

6. *Establishing trial (probationary) periods.* Often an organization will hire an employee conditionally to let the person prove his or her value on the job. After a specified probationary period (perhaps six months or a year), the firm can either permanently hire or discharge that employee on the basis of supervisors' evaluations. Although such systems make it easier to fire inefficient or problem employees, they do not eliminate the high cost of turnover.

www.shrm.org

adapting to **change**

Keeping the Right Face on Facebook

Today, the Internet offers companies a gold mine of information concerning potential employees. Estimates are that three out of five organizations use social networking sites such as LinkedIn, Twitter, and of course Facebook to screen prospective hires and evaluate a person's fit with a company's culture. What this means to you is that your social media footprint could be a selling tool in your job search—or could end up costing you a job.

What you do online goes into the virtual world and stays there. The online personality you project reflects to employers who you really are. The growing use of social media background checks has created a new set of candidate disqualifiers. Some of the most flagrant violations that will put you in a company's reject pile include posting:

- Provocative or inappropriate photos
- Information about excessive drinking or using drugs
- Negative comments about a previous employer
- Discriminatory comments related to race, gender, religion, etc.

It's best to use social media to your advantage. Many companies admit to hiring a candidate because of the professional image they conveyed on social media. If you have reservations about posting something on Facebook, the best advice is, don't.

Sources: Kerry Hannon, "Social Media Can Cost You a Job: 6 Solutions," *Forbes*, June 30, 2013; Leslie Kwoh, "Beware: Potential Employers Are Watching You," *The Wall Street Journal*, October 29, 2012; and Ed Zitron, "Social Media Habits of Highly Annoying People," *Inc.*, February 7, 2014.

The selection process is often long and difficult, but it is worth the effort to select new employees carefully because of the high cost of replacing them.[21] Care helps ensure that new employees meet all requirements, including communication skills, education, technical skills, experience, personality, and health.

Hiring Contingent Workers

A company with employment needs that vary—from hour to hour, day to day, week to week, or season to season—may find it cost-effective to hire contingent workers. **Contingent workers** include part-time workers (anyone who works 1 to 34 hours per week), temporary workers (workers paid by temporary employment agencies), seasonal workers, independent contractors, interns, and co-op students.

Companies may also hire contingent workers when full-timers are on some type of leave (such as maternity leave), when there is a peak demand for labor or products (like the holiday shopping season), or when quick service to customers is a priority. Companies also tend to hire more contingent workers in an uncertain economy, particularly when they are available and qualified, and when the jobs require minimal training.

Contingent workers receive few benefits; they are rarely offered health insurance, vacation time, or company pensions. They also tend to earn less than permanent workers do. On the positive side, many on temporary assignments are eventually offered full-time positions. Managers see using temporary workers as a way of weeding out poor workers and finding good hires. Although exact numbers are difficult to gather, the Bureau of Labor Statistics estimates there are approximately 5.7 million contingent workers in the United States, with the majority under age 25.[22] Experts say temps are filling openings in an increasingly broad range of jobs, from unskilled manufacturing and distribution positions to middle management. Increasing numbers of contingent workers are educated professionals such as accountants, attorneys, and engineers.

Many companies include college students in their contingent workforce plan. Working with temporary staffing agencies, companies have easier access

contingent workers
Employees that include part-time workers, temporary workers, seasonal workers, independent contractors, interns, and co-op students.

to workers who have already been screened. Of course, temp agencies benefit college students as well. Once the agencies have assessed the workers, their information is entered into their databases. Then when students are coming back in town for vacations or whatever, they can call the agency and ask them to put their names into the system for work assignments. There is no need to spend time searching for openings or running around town for interviews. Companies such as Randstad USA, a global staffing services giant with over 1,000 branches in the United States, welcomes college students primarily because of their computer skills and familiarity with many of the popular software programs that companies use.[23]

College interns can be considered temporary workers. However, when these internships are unpaid, ethical questions could arise (see the Making Ethical Decisions box).

In an era of rapid change and economic uncertainty, some contingent workers have even found that temping can be more secure than full-time employment.

Seasonal businesses, such as Halloween stores and haunted houses, depend on hiring contingent (temporary) workers to help them through the limited times they are operational. What are the advantages and disadvantages of hiring contingent workers? What are the advantages and disadvantages of being a contingent worker?

 test **prep**

- What are the five steps in human resource planning?
- What factors make it difficult to recruit qualified employees?
- What are the six steps in the selection process?
- Who is considered a contingent worker, and why do companies hire such workers?

Use LearnSmart to help retain what you have learned. Access your instructor's Connect course to check out LearnSmart, or go to learnsmartadvantage.com for help.

■LEARNSMART

LO 11–6   Illustrate employee training and development methods.

TRAINING AND DEVELOPING EMPLOYEES FOR OPTIMUM PERFORMANCE

As technology and other innovations change the workplace, companies must offer training programs that often are quite sophisticated. The term **training and development** includes all attempts to improve productivity by increasing an employee's ability to perform. A well-designed training program often leads to higher retention rates, increased productivity, and greater job satisfaction. Employers in the United States generally find that money for training is well spent. *Training* focuses on short-term skills, whereas *development* focuses on long-term abilities. Both include three steps: (1) assessing organization needs

college.monster.com/education

making **ethical decisions**

Intern or Indentured Servant?

Traditionally, unpaid internships have been a great way for young people to transition from college to the workforce. The sacrifice of financial benefits usually pays off in practical experience the interns otherwise would not get in a classroom. Businesses in turn risk nothing financially, but could end up benefiting in the long run if an intern eventually becomes a key paid employee. However, with entry-level positions scarce in today's job market, interns can end up in an unpaid position for as long as six months with no chance of advancement. At that point, interns may wonder if they are improving their chances for a rewarding career or simply performing free services for the company.

In order to distinguish a quality internship from a dead end, simply look at the tasks you're asked to do every day. If your central duties include keeping the coffee pot full or running errands, chances are that those jobs will not translate into

valuable experience down the line. Interns should be taught about the day-to-day duties of a business, not how to be professional gofers. Management must also be sure to outline an intern's responsibilities explicitly and provide regular feedback. Even without a regular paycheck, internships can be beneficial as long as the person is compensated in experience.

Some businesses are quite willing to give interns plenty of professional responsibility. For example, one Toronto newspaper fired all of its paid staff writers and replaced them with unpaid interns.

Is it ethical for companies to use unpaid interns if they know they will not have any jobs to offer at the end of the internships or if the unpaid internships replace paid jobs? Why or why not?

Sources: Knight Kiplinger, "Are Unpaid Interns Exploited by Employers?" *Kiplinger*, April 2011; Bruce Weinstein, "Dos and Don'ts of Unpaid Internships," *Bloomberg Businessweek*, May 28, 2010; and Cathy Vandewater, "Are Unpaid Internships Fair?" Vault Careers, www.vault.com, February 3, 2012.

---

and employee skills to determine training needs; (2) designing training activities to meet identified needs; and (3) evaluating the training's effectiveness. Some common training and development activities are employee orientation, on-the-job training, apprenticeships, off-the-job training, vestibule training, job simulation, and management training.

- **Orientation** is the activity that initiates new employees into the organization; to fellow employees; to their immediate supervisors; and to the policies, practices, and objectives of the firm. Orientation programs range from informal talks to formal activities that last a day or more and often include scheduled visits to various departments and required reading of handbooks. For example, at Zappos every new employee in the online retailer's Henderson, Nevada, headquarters must spend two weeks answering customer calls, two weeks learning in a classroom, and a week shipping boxes in the company's Kentucky fulfillment center.[24]

- **On-the-job training** lets the employee learn by doing, or by watching others for a while and then imitating them, right at the workplace. Salespeople, for example, are often trained by watching experienced salespeople perform (often called *shadowing*). Naturally, this can be either quite effective or disastrous, depending on the skills and habits of the person being observed. On-the-job training is the easiest kind of training to implement when the job is relatively simple (such as clerking in a store) or repetitive (such as collecting refuse, cleaning

training and development
All attempts to improve productivity by increasing an employee's ability to perform. Training focuses on short-term skills, whereas development focuses on long-term abilities.

orientation
The activity that introduces new employees to the organization; to fellow employees; to their immediate supervisors; and to the policies, practices, and objectives of the firm.

on-the-job training
Training at the workplace that lets the employee learn by doing or by watching others for a while and then imitating them.

apprentice programs
Training programs during which a learner works alongside an experienced employee to master the skills and procedures of a craft.

off-the-job training
Internal or external training programs away from the workplace that develop any of a variety of skills or foster personal development.

online training
Training programs in which employees complete classes via the Internet.

vestibule training
Training done in schools where employees are taught on equipment similar to that used on the job.

At FedEx, time is money. That's why the company spends six times more on employee training than the average firm. Does the added expense pay off? You bet. FedEx enjoys a remarkably low 4 percent employee turnover rate. Should other companies follow FedEx's financial commitment to training? Why?

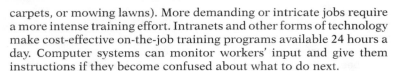

carpets, or mowing lawns). More demanding or intricate jobs require a more intense training effort. Intranets and other forms of technology make cost-effective on-the-job training programs available 24 hours a day. Computer systems can monitor workers' input and give them instructions if they become confused about what to do next.

- In **apprentice programs** a trainee works alongside an experienced employee to master the skills and procedures of a craft. Some apprentice programs include classroom training. Trade unions in skilled crafts, such as bricklaying and plumbing, require a new worker to serve as an apprentice for several years to ensure excellence as well as to limit entry to the union. Workers who successfully complete an apprenticeship earn the classification *journeyman*. As baby boomers retire from skilled trades such as pipefitting, welding, and carpentry, shortages of trained workers are developing. Apprentice programs may be shortened to prepare people for skilled jobs in changing industries such as auto repair and aircraft maintenance that require increased knowledge of computer technology. About 375,000 apprentices are registered with the U.S. Department of Labor.[25]

- **Off-the-job training** occurs away from the workplace and consists of internal or external programs to develop any of a variety of skills or to foster personal development. Training is becoming more sophisticated as jobs become more sophisticated. Furthermore, training is expanding to include education (through the PhD) and personal development. Subjects may include time management, stress management, health and wellness, physical education, nutrition, and even art and languages.

- **Online training** demonstrates how technology is improving the efficiency of many off-the-job training programs. Most colleges and universities now offer a wide variety of online classes, sometimes called *distance learning*, including introductory business courses. Both nonprofit and profit-seeking businesses make extensive use of online training. The Red Cross offers an online tutorial called "Be Red Cross Ready" to help citizens prepare for disasters such as floods, tornadoes, or hurricanes. Technology giants like EMC and large manufacturers like Timken use the online training tool GlobeSmart to teach employees how to operate in different cultures.[26] Online training's key advantage is the ability to provide a large number of employees with consistent content tailored to specific training needs at convenient times.

- **Vestibule training** (or near-the-job training) is done in classrooms with equipment similar to that used on the job so that employees learn proper methods and safety procedures before assuming a specific job assignment. Computer and robotics training is often completed in a vestibule classroom.

- **Job simulation** is the use of equipment that duplicates job conditions and tasks so that trainees can learn skills before attempting them on the job. It differs from vestibule training in that it duplicates the *exact* combination of conditions that occur on the job. This is the kind of training given to astronauts, airline pilots, army tank operators, ship captains, and others who must learn difficult procedures off the job.

Management Development

Managers often need special training. To be good communicators, they need to learn listening skills and empathy. They also need time management, planning, and human relations skills.

Management development, then, is the process of training and educating employees to become good managers, and then monitoring the progress of their managerial skills over time. Management development programs are widespread, especially at colleges, universities, and private management development firms. Managers may participate in role-playing exercises, solve various management cases, and attend films and lectures to improve their skills.

Management development is increasingly being used as a tool to accomplish business objectives. General Electric's and Procter & Gamble's management teams were built with significant investment in their development. Most management training programs include several of the following:

NASA's KC-135 aircraft helped astronauts like these train for space missions. After the plane makes a fast and steep ascent, it suddenly free-falls for 20 to 30 seconds enabling the passengers to experience "apparent weightlessness." (For obvious reasons the plane is also known as the Vomit Comet.) Do you think simulation training is effective for jobs like this? Why or why not?

- *On-the-job coaching.* A senior manager assists a lower-level manager by teaching needed skills and providing direction, advice, and helpful feedback. E-coaching is being developed to coach managers electronically, though it will take time and experimentation before firms figure out how to make coaches come to life online.

- *Understudy positions.* Job titles such as *undersecretary* and *assistant* are part of a relatively successful way of developing managers. Selected employees work as assistants to higher-level managers and participate in planning and other managerial functions until they are ready to assume such positions themselves.

- *Job rotation.* So that they can learn about different functions of the organization, managers are often given assignments in a variety of departments. Such job rotation gives them the broad picture of the organization they need to succeed.

- *Off-the-job courses and training.* Managers periodically go to classes or seminars for a week or more to hone technical and human relations skills. Major universities like the University of Michigan, MIT, and the University of Chicago offer specialized short courses to assist managers in performing their jobs more efficiently. McDonald's Corporation has its own Hamburger University. Managers and potential franchisees attend six days of classes and complete a course of study equivalent to 36 hours of college business-school credit.[27]

Networking

Networking is the process of establishing and maintaining contacts with key managers in your own and other organizations, and using those contacts to weave strong relationships that serve as informal development systems. Of equal or greater importance may be a **mentor**, a corporate manager who supervises, coaches, and guides selected lower-level employees by introducing them to the right people and generally acting as their organizational sponsor.[28] In most organizations informal mentoring occurs as experienced employees assist less experienced workers. However, many organizations formally assign mentors to employees considered to have strong potential.[29]

It's also important to remember that networking and mentoring go beyond the business environment. For example, college is a perfect place to begin networking. Associations you nurture with professors, with local businesspeople through internships, and especially with your classmates can provide a valuable network to turn to for the rest of your career.

job simulation
The use of equipment that duplicates job conditions and tasks so trainees can learn skills before attempting them on the job.

management development
The process of training and educating employees to become good managers, and then monitoring the progress of their managerial skills over time.

networking
The process of establishing and maintaining contacts with key managers in and outside the organization and using those contacts to weave strong relationships that serve as informal development systems.

mentor
An experienced employee who supervises, coaches, and guides lower-level employees by introducing them to the right people and generally being their organizational sponsor.

Informal marketing gatherings like this help professionals make new connections with people in their fields. Why do you think younger workers prefer such informal gatherings?

Diversity in Management Development

As more women moved into management, they learned the importance of networking and of having mentors. Unfortunately, women often have more difficulty than men in networking or finding mentors, since most senior managers are male. In 1988, women won a major legal victory when the U.S. Supreme Court ruled it illegal to bar women from certain clubs, long open to men only, where business activity flows and contacts are made. This decision allowed more women to enter established networking systems or, in some instances, create their own. Today, women are members of such prestigious clubs such as the Augusta National Golf Club.

Similarly, African American and Hispanic managers learned the value of networking. Both groups are forming pools of capital and new opportunities helping many individuals overcome traditional barriers to success. *Black Enterprise* magazine sponsors several networking forums each year for African American professionals. The Hispanic Alliance for Career Enhancement (HACE) is committed to building career opportunities and career advancement for Hispanics. Monte Jade is an association that helps Taiwanese and Chinese professionals assimilate into U.S. business. Sulekha is an Indian networking group that unites Indians in the United States and around the world.

Companies that take the initiative to develop female and minority managers understand three crucial principles: (1) grooming women and minorities for management positions isn't about legality, morality, or even morale but rather about bringing more talent in the door, the key to long-term profitability; (2) the best women and minorities will become harder to attract and retain, so companies that commit to development early have an edge; and (3) having more women and minorities at all levels lets businesses serve their increasingly female and minority customers better. If you don't have a diversity of people working in the back room, how are you going to satisfy the diversity of people coming in the front door?

LO 11–7   Trace the six steps in appraising employee performance.

APPRAISING EMPLOYEE PERFORMANCE TO GET OPTIMUM RESULTS

Managers must be able to determine whether their workers are doing an effective and efficient job, with a minimum of errors and disruptions. They do so by using a **performance appraisal**, an evaluation that measures employee performance against established standards in order to make decisions about promotions, compensation, training, or termination. Performance appraisals have six steps:

1. *Establishing performance standards.* This step is crucial. Standards must be understandable, subject to measurement, and reasonable. Both manager and subordinate must accept them.

2. *Communicating those standards.* It's dangerous to assume that employees know what is expected of them. They must be told clearly and precisely what the standards and expectations are, and how to meet them.

performance appraisal
An evaluation that measures employee performance against established standards in order to make decisions about promotions, compensation, training, or termination.

3. *Evaluating performance.* If the first two steps are done correctly, performance evaluation is relatively easy. It is a matter of evaluating the employee's behavior to see whether it matches standards.

4. *Discussing results with employees.* Employees often make mistakes and fail to meet expectations at first. It takes time to learn a job and do it well. Discussing an employee's successes and areas that need improvement can provide managers an opportunity to be understanding and helpful and guide the employee to better performance. The performance appraisal can also allow employees to suggest how a task could be done better.

5. *Taking corrective action.* As part of performance appraisal, a manager can take corrective action or provide feedback to help the employee perform better. The key word here is *perform.* The primary purpose of an appraisal is to improve employee performance if possible.[30]

6. *Using the results to make decisions.* Decisions about promotions, compensation, additional training, or firing are all based on performance evaluations. An effective performance appraisal system is also a way of satisfying legal requirements about such decisions.

Managing effectively means getting results through top performance. That's what performance appraisals are for at all levels of the organization, including at the top where managers benefit from reviews by their subordinates and peers.

In the *360-degree review,* management gathers opinions from all around the employee, including those under, above, and on the same level, to get an accurate, comprehensive idea of the worker's abilities. Figure 11.5 illustrates how managers can make performance appraisals more meaningful.

DO	DON'T
• **DO** allow sufficient time, without distractions, for appraisal. (Turn off the phone or close the office door.)	• **DON'T** attack the employee personally. Critically evaluate his or her work.
• **DO** include the employee in the process as much as possible. (Let the employee prepare a self-improvement program.)	• **DON'T** make the employee feel uncomfortable or uneasy. Never conduct an appraisal where other employees are present (such as on the shop floor).
• **DO** end the appraisal with positive suggestions for employee improvement.	• **DON'T** wait until the appraisal to address problems with the employee's work that have been developing for some time.

FIGURE 11.5 CONDUCTING EFFECTIVE APPRAISALS AND REVIEWS

test prep

- Name and describe four training techniques.
- What is the primary purpose of a performance appraisal?
- What are the six steps in a performance appraisal?

LO 11—8 Summarize the objectives of employee compensation programs, and evaluate pay systems and fringe benefits.

COMPENSATING EMPLOYEES: ATTRACTING AND KEEPING THE BEST

Companies don't just compete for customers; they also compete for employees. Compensation is one of the main tools companies use to attract qualified employees, and one of their largest operating costs. The long-term success of a firm—perhaps even its survival—may depend on how well it can control employee costs and optimize employee efficiency. Service organizations like hospitals, hotels, and airlines struggle with high employee costs since these firms are *labor-intensive* (the primary cost of operations is the cost of labor). Manufacturing firms in the auto and steel industries have asked employees to take reductions in wages (called givebacks) to make the firms more competitive. (We discuss this in Chapter 12.) Those are just a few reasons compensation and benefit packages require special attention.[31] In fact, some experts believe determining how best to compensate employees is today's greatest human resources challenge.

A carefully managed and competitive compensation and benefit program can accomplish several objectives:

- Attracting the kinds of people the organization needs, and in sufficient numbers.
- Providing employees with the incentive to work efficiently and productively.
- Keeping valued employees from going to competitors or starting competing firms.
- Maintaining a competitive position in the marketplace by keeping costs low through high productivity from a satisfied workforce.
- Providing employees with some sense of financial security through fringe benefits such as insurance and retirement benefits.

Competitive compensation and benefit programs can have a tremendous impact on employee efficiency and productivity. Sometimes businesses reward exceptional performance by awarding bonuses. Does your instructor ever award bonuses for exceptional performance in class?

Pay Systems

The way an organization chooses to pay its employees can have a dramatic effect on efficiency and productivity. Managers thus look for a system that compensates employees fairly.

Many companies still use the pay system known as the Hay system, devised by Edward Hay. This plan is based on job tiers, each of which has a strict pay range. The system is set up on a point basis with three key factors considered: know-how, problem solving, and accountability.

Firms like San Francisco–based Skyline Construction let workers pick their own pay system. They can earn a fixed salary or collect a lower salary with potential for a bonus. John Whitney, author of *The Trust Factor*, believes that companies should set pay at the market level or better and then award all employees the same percentage merit raise. Doing so, he says, sends the message that everyone in the company is important. Figure 11.6 outlines some of the most common pay systems. Which do you think is the fairest?

FIGURE 11.6 PAY SYSTEMS

Salary

Fixed compensation computed on weekly, biweekly, or monthly pay periods (e.g., $1,600 per month or $400 per week). Salaried employees do not receive additional pay for any extra hours worked.

Hourly wage or daywork

Wage based on number of hours or days worked, used for most blue-collar and clerical workers. Often employees must punch a time clock when they arrive at work and when they leave. Hourly wages vary greatly. The federal minimum wage is $7.25, and top wages go as high as $40 per hour or more for skilled craftspeople. This does not include benefits such as retirement systems, which may add 30 percent or more to the total package.

Piecework system

Wage based on the number of items produced rather than by the hour or day. This type of system creates powerful incentives to work efficiently and productively.

Commission plans

Pay based on some percentage of sales. Often used to compensate salespeople, commission plans resemble piecework systems.

Bonus plans

Extra pay for accomplishing or surpassing certain objectives. There are two types of bonuses: monetary and cashless. Money is always a welcome bonus. Cashless rewards include written thank-you notes, appreciation notes sent to the employee's family, movie tickets, flowers, time off, gift certificates, shopping sprees, and other types of recognition.

Profit-sharing plans

Annual bonuses paid to employees based on the company's profits. The amount paid to each employee is based on a predetermined percentage. Profit sharing is one of the most common forms of performance-based pay.

Gain-sharing plans

Annual bonuses paid to employees based on achieving specific goals such as quality measures, customer satisfaction measures, and production targets.

Stock options

Right to purchase stock in the company at a specific price over a specific period. Often this gives employees the right to buy stock cheaply despite huge increases in the price of the stock. For example, if over the course of his employment a worker received options to buy 10,000 shares of the company stock at $10 each and the price of the stock eventually grows to $100, he can use those options to buy the 10,000 shares (now worth $1 million) for $100,000.

Compensating Teams

Thus far, we've talked about compensating individuals. What about teams? Since you want your teams to be more than simply a group of individuals, would you compensate them like individuals? If you can't answer that question immediately, you're not alone. Most managers believe in using teams, but fewer are sure about how to pay them. Team-based pay programs are not as effective or as fully developed as managers would hope. Measuring and rewarding individual performance on teams, while at the same time rewarding team performance, is tricky—but it can be done. Professional football players, for example, are rewarded as a team when they go to the playoffs and to the Super Bowl, but they are paid individually as well. Companies are now experimenting with and developing similar incentive systems.

Jim Fox, founder and senior partner of compensation and human resource specialist firm Fox Lawson & Associates, insists that setting up the team right in the first place is the key element to designing an appropriate team compensation plan. He believes the pay model to enhance performance will be a natural outcome of the team's development process. Jay Schuster, coauthor of a study of team pay, found that when pay is based strictly on individual performance, it erodes team cohesiveness and makes the team less likely meet its goals as a collaborative effort. Workplace studies indicate over 50 percent of team compensation plans are based on team goals. Skill-based pay and gain-sharing systems are the two most common compensation methods for teams.

Skill-based pay rewards the growth of both the individual and the team. Base pay is raised when team members learn and apply new skills. Baldrige Award winner Eastman Chemical Company rewards its teams for proficiency in technical, social, and business knowledge skills. A cross-functional compensation policy team defines the skills. The drawbacks of skill-based pay are twofold: the system is complex, and it is difficult to relate the acquisition of skills directly to profit gains.

Most *gain-sharing systems* base bonuses on improvements over previous performance.[32] Nucor Steel, one of the largest U.S. steel producers, calculates bonuses on quality—tons of steel that go out the door with no defects. There are no limits on bonuses a team can earn; they usually average around $20,000 per employee each year.[33]

It is important to reward individual team players also. Outstanding team players—who go beyond what is required and make an outstanding individual contribution—should be separately recognized, with cash or noncash rewards. A good way to compensate for uneven team participation is to let the team decide which members get what type of individual award. After all, if you really support the team process, you need to give teams freedom to reward themselves.

Fringe Benefits

fringe benefits
Benefits such as sick-leave pay, vacation pay, pension plans, and health plans that represent additional compensation beyond base wages.

Fringe benefits include sick-leave pay, vacation pay, pension plans, and health plans that provide additional compensation to employees beyond base wages. Benefits in recent years grew faster than wages and can't really be considered fringe anymore. In 1929, such benefits accounted for less than 2 percent of payroll; today they can account for about 30 percent. Health care costs have been one of the key reasons for the increase, forcing employees to pay a larger share of their own health insurance bill. Furthermore, it's still unclear exactly what the cost of the Affordable Care Act will be for businesses.[34] Employees often will request more fringe benefits instead of salary, in order to avoid higher taxes. This has resulted in increased debate and government investigation.

Fringe benefits can include recreation facilities, company cars, country club memberships, discounted massages, special home-mortgage rates, paid and unpaid sabbaticals, day care services, and executive dining rooms. Increasingly, employees often want dental care, mental health care, elder care, legal counseling, eye care, and even short workweeks.

The workers at DreamWorks Studios who helped create Shrek enjoy perks like free breakfast and lunch, afternoon yoga classes, free movie screenings, on-campus art classes, and monthly parties. How might fringe benefits like these affect employee performance?

www.shrm.org

reaching beyond **our borders**

Cultural Challenges without Conflict

Human resource management of a global workforce begins with an understanding of the customs, laws, and local business needs of every country in which the organization operates. Country-specific cultural and legal standards can affect a variety of human resource functions:

- *Compensation.* Salaries must be converted to and from foreign currencies. Often employees with international assignments receive special allowances for relocation, children's education, housing, travel, and other business-related expenses.
- *Health and pension standards.* There are different social contexts for benefits in other countries. In the Netherlands, the government provides retirement income and health care.

- *Paid time off.* Four weeks of paid vacation is the standard of many European employers. But many other countries lack the short-term and long-term absence policies offered in the

United States, including sick leave, personal leave, and family and medical leave. Global companies need a standard definition of *time off.*
- *Taxation.* Each country has different taxation rules, and the

payroll department must work within each country's regulations.
- *Communication.* When employees leave to work in another country, they often feel disconnected from their home country. Wise companies use their intranet and the Internet to help these faraway employees keep in direct contact.

Human resource policies at home are influenced more and more by conditions and practices in other countries and cultures. Human resource managers need to sensitize themselves and their organizations to overseas cultural and business practices.

Sources: Roy Mauer, "SHRM Identifies Global HR Trends for 2014," *Society for Human Resource Management,* February 3, 2014; and Will Yakowicz, "The Fine Art of Negotiating in Different Cultures," *Inc.,* December 6, 2013.

Understanding that it takes many incentives to attract and retain the best employees, dozens of firms among *Fortune* magazine's "100 Best Companies to Work For" list offer so-called soft benefits. *Soft benefits* help workers maintain the balance between work and family life that is often as important to hardworking employees as the nature of the job itself. These perks include on-site haircuts and shoe repair, concierge services, and free breakfasts. Freeing employees from errands and chores gives them more time for family—and work. Biotechnology firm Genentech even offers doggie day care and Netflix offers employees unlimited vacation days.[35]

At one time, most employees sought benefits that were similar. Today, however, some may seek child care benefits while others prefer attractive pension plans.[36] To address such growing demands, over half of all large firms offer **cafeteria-style fringe benefits**, in which employees can choose the benefits they want up to a certain dollar amount. Such plans let human resource managers equitably and cost-effectively meet employees' individual needs by allowing them choice.

As the cost of administering benefits programs has accelerated, many companies have chosen to outsource this function. Managing benefits can be especially complicated when employees are located in other countries. The Reaching Beyond Our Borders box discusses the human resource challenges faced by global businesses. To put it simply, benefits are often as important to recruiting top talent as salary and may even become more important in the future.

cafeteria-style fringe benefits
Fringe benefits plan that allows employees to choose the benefits they want up to a certain dollar amount.

LO 11–9   Demonstrate how managers use scheduling plans to adapt to workers' needs.

SCHEDULING EMPLOYEES TO MEET ORGANIZATIONAL AND EMPLOYEE NEEDS

Workplace trends and the increasing costs of transportation have led employees to look for scheduling flexibility. Flextime, in-home employment, and job sharing are important benefits employees seek.

Flextime Plans

flextime plan
Work schedule that gives employees some freedom to choose when to work, as long as they work the required number of hours or complete their assigned tasks.

core time
In a flextime plan, the period when all employees are expected to be at their job stations.

A **flextime plan** gives employees some freedom to choose which hours to work, as long as they work the required number of hours or complete their assigned tasks. The most popular plans allow employees to arrive between 7:00 and 9:00 a.m. and leave between 4:00 and 6:00 p.m. Flextime plans generally incorporate core time. **Core time** is the period when all employees are expected to be at their job stations. An organization may designate core time as 9:00 to 11:00 a.m. and 2:00 to 4:00 p.m. During these hours all employees are required to be at work (see Figure 11.7). Flextime allows employees to adjust to work-life demands. Two-income families find them especially helpful. Companies that use flextime say that it boosts employee productivity and morale.[37]

Flextime is not for all organizations, however. It doesn't suit shift work like fast-food or assembly processes like manufacturing, where everyone on a given shift must be at work at the same time. Another disadvantage is that managers often have to work longer days to assist and supervise in organizations that may operate from 6:00 a.m. to 6:00 p.m. Flextime also makes communication more difficult since certain employees may not be there when others need to talk to them. Furthermore, if not carefully supervised, some employees could abuse the system, causing resentment among others.

compressed workweek
Work schedule that allows an employee to work a full number of hours per week but in fewer days.

Another option that about one in four companies uses is a **compressed workweek**. An employee works the full number of hours, but in fewer than the standard number of days. For example, an employee may work four 10-hour days and then enjoy a long weekend, instead of working five 8-hour days with a traditional weekend. There are obvious advantages of compressed

FIGURE 11.7 A FLEXTIME CHART
At this company, employees can start work anytime between 6:30 and 9:30 a.m. They take a half hour for lunch anytime between 11:00 a.m. and 1:30 p.m. and can leave between 3:00 and 6:30 p.m. Everyone works an eight-hour day. The blue arrows show a typical employee's flextime day.

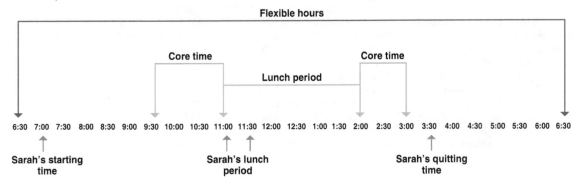

workweeks, but some employees get tired working such long hours, and productivity can decline. Others find the system a great benefit, however, and are enthusiastic about it.[38] Nurses often work compressed weeks.

Home-Based Work

Nearly 13 million U.S. workers now work from home at least once per week.[39] Approximately 12 percent of businesses use some home-based work. Home-based workers can choose their own hours, interrupt work for child care or other tasks, and take time out for personal reasons. Working at home isn't for everyone. It requires discipline to stay focused on the job and not be easily distracted.[40]

Home-based work can also be a cost saver for employers. Estimates are a company can reduce operating costs by almost $6,500 per year for every employee who telecommutes just one day a week.[41] However, home-based work is not for every company either. In 2013, Yahoo! announced that employees would no longer be allowed to work from home. Bank of America also made significant cuts to its popular My Work program that permits employees to work remotely about 60 percent of the time.

Many large companies also offer "hot-desking," or sharing a desk with other employees who work at different times. Companies such as Office Depot have shifted to U.S. home-based call agents and saved 30 or 40 percent on the cost of each call by not providing workspace (or benefits) for its home-based call center workers. Figure 11.8 outlines the benefits and challenges of home-based work to organizations, individuals, and society.

Job-Sharing Plans

Job sharing lets two or more part-time employees share one full-time job. Students and parents with small children, for instance, may work only during school hours, and older workers can work part-time before fully retiring or after retiring. Benefits of job sharing include:

- Employment opportunities for those who cannot or prefer not to work full-time.

job sharing
An arrangement whereby two part-time employees share one full-time job.

FIGURE 11.8 BENEFITS AND CHALLENGES OF HOME-BASED WORK
Home-based work (also known as telecommuting) offers many benefits and challenges to organizations, individuals, and society as a whole.

	BENEFITS	CHALLENGES
To Organization	• Increases productivity due to fewer sick days, fewer absences, higher job satisfaction, and higher work performance ratings • Broadens available talent pool • Reduces costs of providing on-site office space	• Makes it more difficult to appraise job performance • Can negatively affect the social network of the workplace and can make it difficult to promote team cohesiveness • Complicates distribution of tasks (should office files, contact lists, and such be allowed to leave the office?)
To Individual	• Makes more time available for work and family by reducing or eliminating commute time • Reduces expenses of buying and maintaining office clothes • Avoids office politics • Helps balance work and family • Expands employment opportunities for individuals with disabilities	• Can cause feeling of isolation from social network • Can raise concerns regarding promotions and other rewards due to being out of sight, out of mind • May diminish individual's influence within company due to limited opportunity to learn the corporate culture
To Society	• Decreases traffic congestion • Discourages community crime that might otherwise occur in bedroom communities • Increases time available to build community ties	• Increases need to resolve zoning regulations forbidding business deliveries in residential neighborhoods • May reduce ability to interact with other people in a personal, intimate manner

- An enthusiastic and productive workforce.
- Reduced absenteeism and tardiness.
- Ability to schedule part-time workers into peak demand periods (e.g., banks on payday).
- Retention of experienced employees who might otherwise have retired.

Disadvantages include the need to hire, train, motivate, and supervise at least twice as many people and perhaps prorate some fringe benefits. But firms are finding that the advantages generally outweigh the disadvantages.

Lo 11–10   Describe how employees can move through a company: promotion, reassignment, termination, and retirement.

MOVING EMPLOYEES UP, OVER, AND OUT

Employees don't always stay in the position they were hired to fill. They may excel and move up the corporate ladder or fail and move out the door. Employees can also be reassigned or retire. Of course, some choose to move themselves by going to another company.

Promoting and Reassigning Employees

Many companies find that promotion from within the company improves employee morale. It's also cost-effective in that the promoted employees are already familiar with the corporate culture and procedures and don't need to spend valuable time on basic orientation.

In the new, flatter corporate structures (see Chapter 8), there are fewer levels for employees to reach than in the past. Thus they often move *over* to a new position rather than *up*. Such lateral transfers allow employees to develop and display new skills and learn more about the company overall. Reassignment is one way of motivating experienced employees to remain in a company with few advancement opportunities.

During the economic crisis, managers had to terminate a great number of employees. As the economy slowly recovered, have employers rehired full-time workers? Why or why not? What alternatives do employers have?

Terminating Employees

We've seen that the relentless pressure of global competition, shifts in technology, increasing customer demands for greater value, and uncertain economic conditions have human resource managers struggling to manage layoffs and firings. Even if the economy is booming, many companies are hesitant to hire or rehire workers full-time. Why is that the case? One reason is that the cost of terminating employees is prohibitively high in terms of lost training costs and possible damages and legal fees for wrongful discharge suits. That's why many companies are either using temporary employees or outsourcing certain functions.

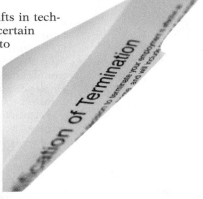

At one time the prevailing employment doctrine in the United States was "employment at will." This meant managers had as much freedom to fire workers as workers had to leave voluntarily. Most states now limit the at-will doctrine to protect employees from wrongful firing. An employer can no longer fire someone for exposing the company's illegal actions or refusing to violate a law. Employees who are members of a minority or other protected group also may have protections under equal employment law. In some cases, workers fired for using illegal drugs have sued on the grounds that they have an illness (addiction) and are therefore protected by laws barring discrimination under the Americans with Disabilities Act (**ADA**). Well-intended legislation has in some ways restricted management's ability to terminate employees as it increased workers' rights to their jobs. See Figure 11.9 for advice about how to minimize the chance of wrongful discharge lawsuits.

FIGURE 11.9 HOW TO AVOID WRONGFUL DISCHARGE LAWSUITS

Sources: "In Economics Old and New, Treatment of Workers Is Paramount," *The Washington Post*, February 11, 2001, p. L1; and U.S. Law, www.uslaw.com.

Consultants offer this advice to minimize the chance of a lawsuit for wrongful discharge:

- Prepare before hiring by requiring recruits to sign a statement that retains management's freedom to terminate at will.
- Don't make unintentional promises by using such terms as *permanent employment*.
- Document reasons before firing and make sure you have an unquestionable business reason for the firing.
- Fire the worst first and be consistent in discipline.
- Buy out bad risk by offering severance pay in exchange for a signed release from any claims.
- Be sure to give employees the true reasons they are being fired. If you do not, you cannot reveal it to a recruiter asking for a reference without risking a defamation lawsuit.
- Disclose the reasons for an employee's dismissal to that person's potential new employers. For example, if you fired an employee for dangerous behavior and you withhold that information from your references, you can be sued if the employee commits a violent act at his or her next job.

Retiring Employees

Companies looking to downsize sometimes offer early retirement benefits to entice older (and more expensive) workers to retire. Such benefits can include one-time cash payments, known in some companies as *golden handshakes*. The advantage early retirement benefits have over layoffs or firing is the increased morale of surviving employees. Retiring senior workers earlier also increases promotion opportunities for younger employees.

Losing Valued Employees

In spite of a company's efforts to retain them, some talented employees will choose to pursue opportunities elsewhere. Knowing their reasons for leaving can be invaluable in preventing the loss of other good people in the future. One way to learn the reasons is to have an outside expert conduct an *exit interview*. Outsiders can provide confidentiality and anonymity that earns more honest feedback than employees are comfortable giving in face-to-face interviews with their bosses. Web-based systems can capture, track, and statistically analyze employee exit interview data to generate reports that identify trouble areas. Such programs can also coordinate exit interview data with employee satisfaction surveys to predict which departments should expect turnover to occur.

Attracting and retaining the best employees is the key to success in the competitive global business environment. Dealing with controversial issues employees have on the job is challenging and never-ending. Chapter 12 discusses such issues.

Use LearnSmart to help retain what you have learned. Access your instructor's Connect course to check out LearnSmart, or go to learnsmartadvantage.com for help.

LEARNSMART

test prep

- Can you name and describe five alternative compensation techniques?
- What advantages do compensation plans such as profit sharing offer an organization?
- What are the benefits and challenges of flextime? Telecommuting? Job sharing?

summary

LO 11–1   Explain the importance of human resource management, and describe current issues in managing human resources.

- **What are current challenges and opportunities in the human resource area?** Many current challenges and opportunities arise from changing demographics: more women, minorities, immigrants, and older workers in the workforce. Others include a shortage of trained workers and an abundance of unskilled workers, skilled workers in declining industries requiring retraining, changing employee work attitudes, and complex laws and regulations.

LO 11–2   Illustrate the effects of legislation on human resource management.

- **What are some of the key laws?**
  See Figure 11.2 and review the text section on laws.

LO 11–3   Summarize the five steps in human resource planning.

- **What are the steps in human resource planning?**
  The five steps are (1) preparing a human resource inventory of the organization's employees; (2) preparing a job analysis; (3) assessing future demand; (4) assessing future supply; and (5) establishing a plan for recruiting, hiring, educating, appraising, compensating, and scheduling employees.

LO 11–4   Describe methods that companies use to recruit new employees, and explain some of the issues that make recruitment challenging.

- **What methods do human resource managers use to recruit new employees?**
  Recruiting sources are classified as either internal or external. Internal sources include those hired from within (transfers, promotions, reassignments) and employees who recommend others to hire. External recruitment sources include advertisements, public and private employment agencies, college placement bureaus, management consultants, professional organizations, referrals, walk-in applications, and the Internet.

- **Why has recruitment become more difficult?**
  Legal restrictions complicate hiring and firing practices. Finding suitable employees can be more difficult if companies are considered unattractive workplaces.

LO 11–5   Outline the six steps in selecting employees.

- **What are the six steps in the selection process?**
  The steps are (1) obtaining complete application forms, (2) conducting initial and follow-up interviews, (3) giving employment tests, (4) conducting background investigations, (5) obtaining results from physical exams, and (6) establishing a trial period of employment.

LO 11–6   Illustrate employee training and development methods.

- **What are some training activities?**
  Training activities include employee orientation, on- and off-the-job training, apprentice programs, online training, vestibule training, and job simulation.

- **What methods help develop managerial skills?**
  Management development methods include on-the-job coaching, understudy positions, job rotation, and off-the-job courses and training.

- **How does networking fit in this process?**
  Networking is the process of establishing contacts with key managers within and outside the organization to get additional development assistance.

LO 11–7   Trace the six steps in appraising employee performance.

- **How do managers evaluate performance?**
  The steps are (1) establish performance standards; (2) communicate those standards; (3) compare performance to standards; (4) discuss results;

(5) take corrective action when needed; and (6) use the results for decisions about promotions, compensation, additional training, or firing.

LO 11–8 Summarize the objectives of employee compensation programs, and describe various pay systems and fringe benefits.

- **What are common types of compensation systems?**
  They include salary systems, hourly wages, piecework, commission plans, bonus plans, profit-sharing plans, and stock options.
- **What types of compensation are appropriate for teams?**
  The most common are gain-sharing and skill-based compensation programs. Managers also reward outstanding individual performance within teams.
- **What are fringe benefits?**
  Fringe benefits include sick leave, vacation pay, company cars, pension plans, and health plans that provide additional compensation to employees beyond base wages. Cafeteria-style fringe benefits plans let employees choose the benefits they want, up to a certain dollar amount.

LO 11–9 Demonstrate how managers use scheduling plans to adapt to workers' needs.

- **What scheduling plans can adjust work to employees' need for flexibility?**
  Such plans include job sharing, flextime, compressed workweeks, and home-based work.

LO 11–10 Describe how employees can move through a company: promotion, reassignment, termination, and retirement.

- **How can employees move within a company?**
  Employees can be moved up (promotion), over (reassignment), or out (termination or retirement) of a company. They can also choose to leave a company to pursue opportunities elsewhere.

Access your instructor's Connect course to check out LearnSmart or go to learnsmartadvantage.com for help.

connect

key terms

critical thinking

1. Does human resource management interest you as a career? What are your experiences working with human resource professionals?

2. What effects have dual-career families had on the human resource function?

3. What problems can arise when family members work together in the same firm?

4. If you were a human resource manager, how would you address the brain drain that occurs as knowledgeable workers retire?

5. Imagine you must fire an employee. What effect might the dismissal have on remaining employees? Explain how you would tell the employee and your other subordinates.

developing **workplace skills**

Key: ● **Team**   ★ **Analytic**   ▲ **Communication**   ▣ **Technology**

1. Look for job listings online or in your local newspaper and find at least two positions you might like to have when you graduate. List the qualifications specified in each of the ads and identify methods the companies might use to determine how well applicants meet them.   ▣ ★

2. Read several current business periodicals or search online to find information about the latest court rulings on benefits, affirmative action, and other human resource issues. Summarize your findings. Is there a trend in these decisions? If so, what is it, and what will it mean for tomorrow's college graduates?   ▣ ★

3. Recall any on-the-job and off-the-job training sessions you've experienced. Write a brief critique of each. How would you improve them? Share your ideas with the class.   ★ ▲

4. Consider the following occupations: doctor, computer salesperson, computer software developer, teacher, and assembly worker. Identify the method of compensation you think is appropriate for each. Explain your answer.   ★ ▲

5. Choose one of these positions: a human resource manager notifying employees of mandatory drug testing or an employee representative protesting such testing. Write a memorandum supporting your position.   ★ ▲

taking it to the **net**

PURPOSE

The two purposes here are to illustrate the types of questions managers typically ask during interviews and to practice answering such questions in a safe environment.

EXERCISE

Go to Monster.com and search for the article "100 Potential Interview Questions." This article lists some of the more common questions asked during an interview. Click on the questions for advice about how to best answer the questions. This will give you the opportunity to test your answers so that when you do go on an actual interview you are less likely to fumble for an answer.

video case   ■■ connect

TEACH FOR AMERICA

There are many critical problems affecting America's public education system, especially the lack of qualified teachers willing to work at troubled inner city schools. The teaching profession's human resource management process may be breaking down in its ability to find and retain the best teachers possible.

The government service program Teach for America tries to solve this problem by training young, highly qualified college grads to teach at underperforming schools. For a two-year period, Teach for America recruits work with students who are dealing with crises like poverty, insufficient nutrition, and low self-esteem. Although most participants use the program as a first step into an education career, others apply the lessons they learn from the program to many different professions.

Ultimately, though, Teach for America's mission is to place more quality teachers into the schools that need them. Many Professional teachers avoid the challenges of inner-city schools, leaving these institutions understaffed. To the human resource managers of many public school systems, Teach for America recruits are an irreplaceable resource. That's because applicants are evaluated rigorously through a lengthy recruitment process. After applicants are interviewed by phone, they must then develop a prospective lesson plan. If they pass that stage, they do an in-person interview, take a written test, and participate in a monitored group discussion with other applicants. In the end, only about 1 applicant in 10 makes it into the popular program.

Once selected, Teach for America recruits go through a structured orientation and off-the-job training program that ends in job simulation exercises. The intensive five-week summer course prepares volunteers for the challenges and needs of the inner-city classroom. They are then assigned to a school, where they receive additional support and training. Since the job can be extremely challenging, Teach for America's relatively generous compensation package serves as a major motivator. As teachers, recruits earn salaries comparable to other colleagues at their grade level.

Teach for America closely evaluates the performance of its teachers to judge the overall effectiveness of the program. Teach for America alumni perform better than many of their counterparts, including some career teachers with more training and education. And even when performance is about the same, recruits may be filling positions that were otherwise impossible to fill because of lack of candidates and resources.

Despite all the good work it's done so far, Teach for America knows that the American public school system still has a lot to learn about educating disadvantaged children. But with the more than 10,000 recruits it trains each year, Teach for America continues to provide challenged students with a fighting chance to fulfill their untapped potential.

THINKING IT OVER

1. What seems to be the primary reason why Teach for America teachers perform better than many other teachers?

2. What types of training do Teach for America recruits undergo before they are placed in the classroom?

3. Why is a rigorous performance appraisal program a key part of the Teach for America program?

notes

1. "Coming to an Office Near You," *The Economist,* January 18, 2014; and "The Onrushing Wave," *The Economist,* January 18, 2014.
2. Floyd Norris, "Changes in the Labor Force Mask Gains in the Jobs Situation," *The New York Times,* November 1, 2013; Brad Plumer, "Three Reasons the U.S. Labor Force Keeps Shrinking," *The Washington Post,* September 6, 2013; and Victoria Stilwell, "Boomers Turn On, Tune In, Drop Out of U.S. Labor Force, *Bloomberg Businessweek,* February 10, 2014.
3. Joshua Wright, "America's Skilled Trades Dilemma: Shortages Loom as Most-in-Demand Group of Workers Ages," *Forbes,* March 7, 2013.
4. Brad Plumer, "CBO: Expect Slower Growth This Decade—and as a Result Higher Deficits," *The Washington Post,* February 4, 2014.
5. Louise Radnofsky and Damien Paletta, "Health Law to Cut into Labor Force," *The Wall Street Journal,* February 4, 2014.
6. Douglas Ernst, "Some Member of Civil-Rights Panel Accuse EEOC of Overreach on Racism," *The Washington Times,* February 20, 2014; and Jacob Gershman, "EEOC Sues Less, but Tactics Draw Flak," *The Wall Street Journal,* February 9, 2014.
7. Patrick May, "Disabled 'Serial Plaintiffs' Do Legal Battle with Small Businesses over Access Issues," *San Jose Mercury News,* February 18, 2014.
8. Equal Employment Opportunity Commission, www.eeoc.gov, accessed March 2014.
9. Penelope Lemov, "What It Takes to Win an Age Discrimination Case," *Forbes,* April 30, 2013.
10. Julian L. Alssid, "A New Gallup Survey Says Colleges and Employers Disagree about How Workforce-Ready Graduates Are . . . Who's Right?" *Huffington Post,* February 27, 2014.
11. Juan Carlos Perez, "IBM Preps Talent Suite for Human Resources Tasks," *PC World,* January 27, 2014.
12. Bennett J. Louden, "Rochester Grocers Wary of Tech, Adapt Slowly," *Rochester Democrat and Chronicle,* February 28, 2014.
13. Patricia Stilwell, "Report: Economy Will Face Shortage of 20 Million Workers in 2020," *US News & World Report,* July 8, 2013.
14. "Gone But Not Forgotten," *The Economist,* March 1, 2014.
15. Mark Cohen, "Online Hiring Tools Are Changing Recruiting Techniques," *The New York Times,* May 15, 2013; and Raj Sheth, "How to Establish a Recruiting Process and Develop a Culture," *The Washington Post,* January 29, 2014.
16. John Brandon, "The Real Cost of Hiring the Wrong Employee," *Inc.,* September 2013.
17. Kronos, www.kronos.com/hiring-software/hiring.aspx, accessed March 2014.
18. Kronos, www.kronos.ca/Case-Study/Finish-Line.aspx, accessed March 2014.
19. Brandon, "The Real Cost of Hiring the Wrong Employee."
20. "LexisNexis, www.lexisnexis.com, accessed March 2014; and Dave Larsen, "LexisNexis Wins Software Industry Award," *Dayton Daily News,* February 11, 2014.
21. Suzanne Lucas, "How Much Employee Turnover Really Costs You," *Inc.,* August 2013; and Jena MacGregor, "What It Costs to Replace a Twenty-Something," *The Washington Post,* August 6, 2013.
22. U.S. Department of Labor, www.dol.gov, accessed March 2014.
23. RandstadUSA, www.us.randstad.com, accessed March 2014.
24. Scott Levy, "Why Stellar Customer Service Is Key to Building Your Online Brand," *Entrepreneur,* December 23, 2013.
25. U.S. Department of Labor, www.doleta.gov, accessed March 2014.
26. GlobeSmart, www.globesmart.com, accessed March 2014.
27. McDonald's, www.mcdonalds.com, accessed March 2014.
28. Ross McCammon, "Guiding Lights," *Entrepreneur,* March 2013.
29. Jeffrey Dauksevich, "How to Be an Effective Mentor," *Entrepreneur,* December 27, 2013; and John Brandon, "How to Maximize the Benefits of Mentoring," *Inc.,* January 2014.
30. Daniel Bortz, "Ace Your Annual Review," *Money,* March 2014.
31. Sharon Wienbar, "Making Sense Out of Cents: Determining Employee Compensation," *Entrepreneur,* February 13, 2014.
32. Ronald J. Recardo and Diane Pricones, "Is Gainsharing for You?" www.qualitydigest.com, accessed March 2014.
33. Motley Fool Staff, "Q-and-A with Nucor CEO Dan DiMicco," *The Motley Fool,* www.fool.com, January 10, 2011.
34. Chad Terhune, "Health Premiums Expected to Rise for Many Small Firms under Obamacare," *Los Angeles Times,* February 25, 2014; and Joane Weiner, "Experts Disagree about Job Losses and the Moral Status of Obamacare," *The Washington Post,* February 26, 2014.
35. Amanda Greene, "Nine Companies with the Best Perks," www.womansday.com/life-9-companies-the-best-perks, accessed March 2014.
36. Scott Liebs, "You Can Buy Employee Happiness. (But Should You?) Companies That Offer Lavish Benefits Believe There Is a Return on Their Investment. The Challenge: Figuring Out How to Calculate It," *Inc.,* January 2014.
37. Gwen Moran, "Surviving the Open-Floor Plan," *Entrepreneur,* February 13, 2014.
38. Scott Benson, "Why Compressed Workweeks Can Be Great for Employers and Employees," *Huffington Post,* March 5, 2014.
39. Beth Braverman, "Be There—Even When You're Not," *CNNMoney.com,* March 2013.
40. Bill Kolbenschlag, "How to Keep Virtual Teams Connected," *Forbes,* March 5, 2014.
41. Anne Kates Smith, "Make Working at Home Work," *Kiplinger Personal Finance,* January 2013.

photo credits

Page 299: © Brad Swonetz/Redux; p. 302: © Tim Boyle/Bloomberg/Getty Images; p. 304: © Andersen Ross/The Image Bank/Getty Images; p. 307: © Monalyn Gracia/Fancy/age fotostock RF; p. 312: © Ben Margot/AP Images; p. 313: © AVAVA/iStock/360/Getty Images RF; p. 314: © Mike Brown/The Commercial Appeal/ AP Images; p. 315: NASA; p. 316: University of Exeter/Creative Commons, https://www .flickr.com/photos/26126239@N02/6441106901/ in/set-72157628245582169; p. 318: © Josh Rinehults/Getty Images RF; p. 320: © Paramount Pictures/Photofest; p. 321: © Guy Bubb/Gallo Images/Getty Images RF; p. 323: © Liam Norris/Cultura/Getty Images RF; p. 325: © Steve Cole/Getty Images RF.

Introduction to Managing Operations Across the Supply Chain

LEARNING OBJECTIVES   *After studying this chapter, you should be able to:*

LO1-1 Explain what operations management is and why it is important.

LO1-2 Describe the major decisions that operations managers typically make.

LO1-3 Explain the role of processes and "process thinking" in operations management.

LO1-4 Explain what the supply chain is and what it means to view operations management using a "supply chain perspective."

LO1-5 Identify the partners and functional groups that work together in operations management.

LO1-6 Define the planning activities associated with managing operations across the supply chain.

It Takes More than Cool Products to Make Apple Great

Apple often receives praise for its user-friendly and aesthetically pleasing product designs. But a less well-known contributor to Apple's success is its prowess in managing operations across its supply chain. This is the world of manufacturing, procurement, and logistics in which the chief executive officer, Tim Cook, excelled, earning him the trust of Steve Jobs. Apple has built a closed ecosystem where it exerts control over nearly every piece of the supply chain, from design to retail store. "Operations expertise is as big an asset for Apple as product innovation or marketing," says Mike Fawkes, the former supply-chain chief at Hewlett-Packard. "They've taken operational excellence to a level never seen before."

This operational edge is what enables Apple to handle massive product launches without having to maintain large, profit-sapping inventories. It's allowed a company often criticized for high prices to sell its iPad at a price that very few rivals can beat, while still earning a 25 percent margin on the device. Some of the basic elements of Apple's operational strategy include:

- Capitalize on volume. Because of its buying power, Apple gets big discounts on parts, manufacturing capacity, and air freight.
- Work closely with suppliers. Apple design guru Jony Ive and his engineers sometimes spend months living out of hotel rooms in order to be close to suppliers and manufacturers, helping to tweak the industrial processes and tools that translate prototypes into mass-produced devices.
- Focus on a few product lines, with little customization. Apple's unified strategy allows it to eliminate complexity and cost, while maximizing volume-based economies in its supply chain.
- Ensure supply availability and low prices. Apple makes big upfront payments to suppliers to lock in their capacity and to limit options for competitors.
- Keep a close eye on demand. By selling through its own retail stores, Apple can track demand by the store and by the hour; then it adjusts sales forecasts and production plans daily to respond quickly to demand changes.

Apple designs cool products. But its enormous profit margins—two to four times the profit margins of most other hardware companies—come in large part from its priority and focus on operations management.

This book, *Managing Operations Across the Supply Chain,* will help you to study "operations management" using a "supply chain" perspective. This perspective means that we will examine operational activities that take place *within firms* as well those *that cross firms' boundaries,* involving suppliers and customers of all types. This larger network of organizations makes up a firm's *supply chain.*

The Apple story illustrates the value of this broad perspective of operations management. The combination of excellence in both internal product design operations and external supply chain operations management makes Apple a dominant player in its industry. Operations management by definition spans a large number of activities that take place both inside and outside the business firm.

Prepare

What is operations management, and what is the supply chain?

Organize

A Broad Definition of Supply Chain Operations Management

    Important Decisions in Supply Chain Operations Management

    Differences in Goods and Services Operations

    Processes and Process Thinking

operations management
The management of processes used to design, supply, produce, and deliver valuable goods and services to customers.

supply chain The global network of organizations and activities involved in designing, transforming, consuming, and disposing of goods and services.

LO1-1 Explain what operations management is and why it is important.

A BROAD DEFINITION OF SUPPLY CHAIN OPERATIONS MANAGEMENT

Operations management is the management of processes used to design, supply, produce, and deliver valuable goods and services to customers.

Operations management includes the planning and execution of tasks that may be long-term (yearly) or short-term (daily) in nature. Operations managers interact with managers in other business functions, both inside and outside the operations managers' own company. Operations management thus spans the boundaries of any single firm, bringing together the activities of internal operations (i.e., internal to a given company) with the operations of customers, suppliers, and other partners around the world. In the future, operations located around the globe will be even more tightly interconnected than they are today. The supply chain concept can be used to describe connections among business partners.

A **supply chain** is the global network of organizations and activities involved in (1) designing a set of goods and services and their related processes, (2) transforming inputs into goods and services, (3) consuming these goods and services, and (4) disposing of these goods and services.

Think about all the different organizations located in different companies that are involved in converting raw materials into a delivered finished product. Dozens of organizations are involved in producing and delivering even a simple product like bottled water. Together, supply chain organizations perform all the value-creating activities required to innovate, plan, source, make, deliver, and return or dispose of a given set of products and services.[1] Other terms sometimes substituted for *supply chain* include *demand chain, extended enterprise, supply network,* or *supply web.* All of these terms reflect the idea that a supply chain involves connections and relationships among organizations that play various roles for a given set of products.

Operations management activities located throughout a supply chain create and enhance the value of goods and services by increasing their economic value (e.g., lowering delivered cost), functional value (e.g., improving product quality or convenience), and psychosocial value (e.g., improving product aesthetics and desirability). The following statements help define and describe operations management:

- Operations management is mainly concerned with how resources will be developed and used to accomplish business goals.
- Operations management is about designing, executing, and improving business processes.
- Operations management deals with processes that transform inputs including materials, information, energy, money, and even people into goods and services.
- Within a supply chain context, operations management brings together four major sets of players: the firm, customers, suppliers, and stakeholders.

---

[1]Supply Chain Council, *Integrated Supply Chain Performance Measurement: A Multi-Industry Consortium Recommendation,* Supply Chain Council Report #5566, p. 1.

- To be effective, operations management must be consistent with the strategic goals of the firm.
- Operations management is dynamic because of changes in customers' demands, resources, competition, and technologies.

relationships

To work in this increasingly interconnected world, you will need to understand the foundational concepts, functional groups, and integrated activities involved in managing operations located across a supply chain. The Get Real box below describes why operations management is important to all of us.

Even if you do not pursue a career in operations management, it will be important for you to understand and appreciate the fundamental challenges associated with managing operations well. First, the decisions you make as a worker in marketing, finance, accounting, human resources, or other areas will have an impact on, and be impacted by, operations. For example, suppose that you work in a hotel where managers want to buy new kiosks that will allow guests to check themselves into the hotel. The effects of this decision extend beyond operational issues such as labor costs and efficiency. The decision will also have implications for the use of capital (a finance concern), the type of

Automated check-in kiosks at a hotel.

GET REAL

Why You Need to Study Operations Management

Because it matters to people:
Operations management plays an important role in determining the quality of life for people around the world. New operational practices and technologies continue to radically improve the effectiveness of governments, not-for-profit institutions, and businesses in providing goods and services. Operations management also directly impacts sustainability issues including the environment, fair treatment of people, and safety. In doing so, operations management affects social systems and cultural norms, as well as the basic economic prosperity of people everywhere. Consider how your own life is affected. The speed with which organizations provide services to you determines the amount of leisure time you have. In an emergency, the speed and efficiency of a relief organization might even save your life. The cost and quality of products you consume affects your disposable income, your health, even your outlook on life. You can probably think of a good service experience that put a smile on your face, or a bad one that ruined your day! As an operations manager, you may someday have the opportunity and responsibility to positively affect your organization's success. In doing so, you may also be improving the quality of life of the firm's employees, its customers, and even society as a whole.

Because it matters to organizations:
Every product or service offering is a promise of some kind of benefit for someone. Organizations are successful only

when they can consistently deliver upon the promises that they make. Operations management determines how well such promises are fulfilled. Research shows that operationally excellent organizations consistently outperform their rivals in financial and other terms. For example, a recent study[1] showed that companies possessing excellent supply chain operations outperformed their nearest competitors in the following ways:

- 50 percent higher net profit margins
- 20 percent lower sales, general & administration (SG&A) expenses
- 12 percent lower average inventories
- 30 percent less working capital expenses
- Twice the return on assets (ROA)
- Twice the return on equity (ROE)
- 44 percent higher economic value added
- Twice the returns on stock prices
- 2.4 times the risk-weighted stock returns
- 46 percent greater market-value-to-assets ratio

These differences in performance are truly stunning, and highlight the important contributions that operations management makes to the financial well-being of a firm.

[1]M. L. Swink, R. Golecha, and T. Richardson, "Does Becoming a Top Supply Chain Company Really Pay Off? An Analysis of Top SCM Companies and Their Rivals," *Supply Chain Management Review*, March 2010, pp. 14–21.

service provided to customers (a marketing concern), and the training of employees (a human resource management concern). Managers of various functions cannot work in isolation if they hope to make decisions that are good for the overall success of the firm. Second, all activities, including marketing, finance, accounting, and so on, have operational elements to them. For example, think about the operational processes required to run a sales office. Managers in all functions need to understand the principles of operations management in order to keep their functional processes running effectively and efficiently.

Important Decisions in Supply Chain Operations Management

LO1-2 Describe the major decisions that operations managers typically make.

Operations managers get involved in answering certain questions, namely:

What?

- What types of activities and what types of goods or services are to be delivered by the system?
- What product features do our intended customers care about?
- What activities and resources are needed, and how should they be developed, allocated, and controlled?

How?

- How is the good or service to be designed, made, and delivered?
- How much should our transformation process be able to deliver (and under what conditions)?
- How should we measure and assess performance?

When?

- When should products be made, activities be carried out, services be delivered, or capacities/facilities come on line?

Where and Who?

- Where should certain activities be done, and who should do them: suppliers, partners, or the firm?

relationships

Operations managers answer these questions by defining both the structural and infrastructural aspects of the operations management system. Structural decisions affect physical resources such as capacity, facilities, technology, and the supply chain network. Once made, decisions in these areas determine what the operations management system can and cannot do well. Altering these decisions often requires significant investments and lots of time—often years. Infrastructural decisions affect the workforce, production planning and control, process innovation, and organization. Decisions in these areas determine what is done, when it is done, and who does it. Decisions in all of these areas are interrelated, making operations management a complex and cross-functional activity.

Differences in Goods and Services Operations

Operational activities exist in order to produce tangible goods and intangible services. Books, cars, and televisions are all tangible goods. In contrast, services like health care, banking, and entertainment are largely experiential or informational. For example, at a hair salon, you *consume* the expertise and labor of the hair stylist as part of the experience of getting a haircut. The experiences and information you receive at school form a service called *education*. Table 1-1 summarizes some of the important differences between goods and services.

Some businesses are mostly about producing goods (e.g., production of gasoline), and some are mostly about delivering services (e.g., financial consulting). However, most businesses integrate a mix of goods-producing and service-producing operations activities.

TABLE 1-1   Characteristics of Goods and Services

Goods	Services
Tangible	Intangible
Can be inventoried	Cannot be inventoried
Little customer contact (consumption is often separate from production)	Extensive customer contact (simultaneous production and consumption)
Long lead times	Short lead times
Often capital-intensive	Often labor-intensive
Quality easily assessed	Quality more difficult to assess (more perceptual)
Material is transformed	Information or the customer is transformed

There are key structural differences in operational processes designed to provide mostly goods versus mostly services. Chapter 5 discusses these differences in depth, but we will highlight a few important ones here. First, goods can be produced in advance and stored in inventory until a customer buys or consumes them. Since services are intangible, they cannot be stored. The production and consumption of a service usually occur at the same time. While goods-manufacturing operations can use inventory to smooth out imbalances between production capacity and customer demand, a producer of services must maintain enough capacity to meet demand during peak periods; otherwise, it must postpone (backlog) the demand. For example, when you go into a restaurant during its busy time and the greeter asks you to wait in the lounge, you become part of a backlog of demand. Service operations managers often use reservation and appointment systems to help customers avoid long wait times.

In services, customers frequently can observe the operational processes directly. In fact, the customer may take part in producing and consuming the service at the same time (think of your roles as codesigner and quality inspector in getting a haircut). On the other hand, the production of goods may require little contact with the customer.

Finally, operations managers can easily establish measurable quality standards for tangible goods to evaluate whether they work adequately, how they appear, and so on. Quality control is more difficult for services, as it is not always easy to objectively measure a service product's attributes. Service operations managers often evaluate both methods of delivery and customer perceptions. For example, a quality control inspector for a movie theater might study how workers interact with customers as they sell tickets or food to customers. In addition, they may periodically survey customers to gauge their levels of satisfaction.

In reality, there are very few pure goods and pure services. Most manufactured products also include services. When you buy a new car, for example, you may also buy financing, maintenance, and repair services. Many service products also include tangible items. A hospital, for example, provides medicines and bandages along with intangible diagnostic and treatment services.

student activity

Think of the last time you visited an amusement park (like Disney World). How many different goods and services did you consume as a part of your overall experience? How many of these products were "pure" goods and "pure" services? Which of these products was prepared before you ordered it, versus being prepared at the very time that you ordered it?

Because most firms deliver products that involve both goods and services, operations managers recognize the importance of delivering a **total product experience**. This term refers to all of the outputs of an operation, both goods and services, that are combined to define a customer's complete consumption experience. The experience includes all aspects of purchasing, consuming, and disposing of the product.

total product experience All the goods and services that are combined to define a customer's complete consumption experience.

8 **chapter 1** Introduction to Managing Operations Across the Supply Chain

Processes and Process Thinking

process A system of activities that transforms inputs into valuable outputs.

LO1-3 Explain the role of processes and "process thinking" in operations management.

Operations management is a *process*-oriented discipline. What, then, is a process? It is a system of activities that *transforms* inputs into valuable outputs. Processes use resources (workers, machines, money, and knowledge) to transform inputs (such as materials, energy, money, people, and data) into outputs (goods and services). For example, one uses a grill (a resource) and heat (an input) to convert a raw hamburger patty (an input) into a cooked hamburger (an output).

Processes can also transform information, or even people (customers), from one condition into another. In decision making, for example, managers transform data into actionable information and decisions. Think about how you are "transformed" by going to a movie—this is a process in which you are both an input and an output! Other processes transform things by transporting them from one location to another, or by storing them (e.g., a warehouse stores finished goods). Finally, some activities check or inspect work to make sure that it meets standards for quality, quantity, or timeliness.

Every organization can be described as a bundle of processes that connect different organizational groups. For example, companies use *design processes* to develop new goods and services and *strategic planning processes* to determine how the firm should compete. They use *production processes* to plan and execute the supply, manufacture, and delivery of goods and services to customers. Finally, companies use *evaluation processes* to measure and report how well they are meeting their goals or using their resources.

It is valuable to think about operations as *sets of processes and subprocesses* with many interrelationships and linkages. Consider the operations of an airport. There are flight-scheduling processes, ticketing processes, facilities-management processes, security processes, vendor-management processes, and on and on. The structure governing how these processes work together determines the ability of the airport to serve its customers.

We all have experienced organizations with complex, bureaucratic processes that seem incapable of providing a desired service in a timely manner. The design of a process should reflect what customers want. If customers want quick response, for example, then the process should be designed to be fast and flexible. In this case operations managers must identify and eliminate unnecessary or redundant steps, reduce distances between steps or activities, and diminish the time needed to complete each step. This connection between the process design and customers' desires must be maintained. If customers' desires change, then processes may also have to change.

An airport operation contains dozens of interrelated processes.

FIGURE 1-1
Foundational Concepts in Supply Chain Operations Management

Process thinking is so important that we have dedicated an entire section of this book to topics related to it. Figure 1-1 shows the conceptual building blocks of process thinking that are essential to the management of any operation. A separate chapter in this book addresses each building block. The bottom three blocks represent the foundational principles that describe how operational processes work, how product and process characteristics are intertwined, and how certain process structures are related to operational objectives. In order to make good decisions, operations managers need to understand the "physics" that govern processes, as well as understand how they relate to product design and development.

Building upon this foundational knowledge, operations managers can better understand how to make good decisions regarding product quality and the use of inventory (the second row of blocks in Figure 1-1). Product quality is a result of how people and technologies work together to execute processes. Inventory management can make processes more or less efficient, depending on whether the inventory is used wisely or unwisely.

The top block in Figure 1-1, "Managing Lean Systems," represents the application of all the aforementioned process-related concepts in ways that maximize the overall productivity of the operation. A lean operation produces maximum levels of efficiency and effectiveness using a minimal amount of resources.

lean operation An operation that produces maximum levels of efficiency and effectiveness using a minimal amount of resources.

OPERATIONS MANAGEMENT YESTERDAY AND TODAY: GROWTH OF THE SUPPLY CHAIN MANAGEMENT PERSPECTIVE

Many of the formal practices and concepts of operations management have their origins in the Industrial Revolution, which took place in the latter half of the 18th century. As an activity, however, operations management is much older. Signs of organized operations have been found in all ancient civilizations including Greece, Rome, and Egypt. Building the great pyramids was undoubtedly accomplished by means of organized operations, even if we don't know the exact nature of those operations.

Table 1-2 provides a brief history of operations management. Since the Industrial Revolution, modern operations management has evolved at different rates throughout the world. In America, the early 20th century witnessed a huge growth in demand and the rise of mass production. The latter half of the century was marked by standardization of operations practices and by fierce global competition. Today, continued globalization, the Internet, and numerous other technologies are radically transforming business operations.

The supply chain management perspective represents the latest technological shift in operations management. This now-dominant perspective is the result of certain forces in the marketplace, discussed below.

Prepare

Why has the supply chain perspective become important?

Organize

Operations Management Yesterday and Today: Growth of the Supply Chain Management Perspective

Advances in Technology and Infrastructure

Reduction in Governmental Barriers to Trade

Focus on Core Capabilities

Collaborative Networks

LO1-4 Explain what the supply chain is and what it means to view operations management using a "supply chain perspective."

TABLE 1-2   A Brief History of Operations Management

Operations Era		Technological Advances	Operations Management Span of Focus
1800–1850	Technical Capitalists	Improved manufacturing technology; interchangeable parts; locating factories on waterways and in industrial centers; emerging transportation network	Internal production
1850–1890	Mass Production	Emergence of local factory; movement to urban areas; introduction of steam and electrical power; new machines; economies of scale	Internal production
1890–1920	Scientific Management	More systematic approaches to operations management; moving assembly line; beginnings of process thinking	Internal production
1920–1960	Demand Growth	Increased automation; introduction of computers and quantitative analysis	Internal production
1960–1980	Global Competition	Just-in-time systems; emergence of statistical process control; early outsourcing	Internal production
1980–2000	World-Class Manufacturing	Increased computerization and information systems; world-class practices and benchmarks; greater global sourcing and need for supply chain coordination	Production, design, supply
2000–Present	E-commerce	Internet; enhanced communications and transportation technologies; integrated management across functions, including goods and services operations	Global supply chain

Operations management existed even in ancient times.

global

Advances in Technology and Infrastructure

Advances in communications, computers, and transportation technologies have enabled extensive connectivity and the growth of supply chain partnerships. With easier information transactions, there is less of a need to include all operations at one location or within one organizational boundary. Constant information sharing between supply chain partners improves efficiencies in planning, in material movements, and in the transfer of funds.

At the same time, growing transportation technologies and infrastructures have made the shipping of goods and people faster, more reliable, and more economical than in decades past. Transportation infrastructure (airports, train tracks, shipping docks, and highways) continues to be built in developing countries. This growing infrastructure improves reliability of deliveries to remote places, thus opening opportunities to work with new suppliers and to serve new markets.

Reduction in Governmental Barriers to Trade

In recent years we have witnessed incredible changes in governments and social systems around the world. More and more nations have moved away from centrally controlled economies to pursue free market systems. Russia, India, and China represent a few important examples. These falling political barriers have opened up new opportunities to develop global supply chains. While these global supply chains can offer improved product costs and quality, they can also be more complex and risky. Today, operations managers must often manage long pipelines of inventories that cross multiple country borders.

Focus on Core Capabilities

With new technologies and global sources of supply, firms are now able to focus attention on their core capabilities—that is, things they do well. A core capability is a unique set of skills that confers competitive advantages to a firm, because rival firms cannot easily duplicate them.

A focus on core capabilities leads a firm to concentrate on those few skills and areas of knowledge that make the firm distinct and competitive. The firm would then likely outsource other, noncore activities to suppliers who have advantages due to better skills or higher scale of operations. For example, Honda was one of the first companies to outsource many non-core activities such as component manufacturing, logistics, and other services. This allowed Honda to concentrate on design and assembly of motors and engines, its core capabilities.

The result of the core capabilities approach is supply chains in which each of the partnering organizations focuses on what it does best. The overall effect is to produce greater product value through higher quality and greater efficiencies. However, it also makes supply chain partners more interdependent.

Collaborative Networks

As firms become more reliant on their suppliers, the greatest improvements in product value are usually achieved through better coordination with these partners. However, when firms concentrate only on their immediate relationships, they address only a small portion of the total opportunity to improve the overall effectiveness of the system. For example, uncertainties in the availability of raw materials at a *supplier's* supplier can severely limit a firm's ability to deliver products to its customers. Problems like this are best avoided when partners across a supply chain network share their plans and capabilities, and work together to develop improvements. In addition, the creation of partnerships in integrated networks opens up opportunities to take advantage of complementary cost structures, the respective partners' technical expertise, market knowledge, and brand equities (reputations). By combining such assets, companies are able to make stronger product offerings together than they could individually.

VIEWING OPERATIONS MANAGEMENT FROM A SUPPLY CHAIN MANAGEMENT PERSPECTIVE

We began this chapter by noting that operations managers must coordinate a system of activities both inside and outside their firm's boundaries. The network of organizations that contains this system of activities is often referred to as a *supply chain*. So how then is "supply chain management" different from "operations management"?

Supply chain management is the design and execution of relationships and flows that connect the parties and processes across a supply chain. Recall that our definition of *operations management* is the management of processes used to design, supply, produce, and deliver valuable goods and services to customers.

As you can see, there is a substantial degree of overlap between the two definitions. Operations management focuses on managing *processes* (design, supply, production, delivery); supply chain management focuses on managing *relationships* and *flows* (flows of information, materials, energy, money, and people). Think of supply chain management as a way of viewing operations management. You can also think of the supply chain as a network of organizations in which operations activities are conducted.

core capability A unique set of skills that confers competitive advantages to a firm, because rival firms cannot easily duplicate them.

relationships

supply chain management The design and execution of relationships and flows that connect the parties and processes across a supply chain.

L01-5 Identify the partners and functional groups that work together in operations management.

Operations Management Partners Across the Supply Chain

Operations managers interact with three important groups that are external to the firm: (1) customers, (2) suppliers, and (3) stakeholders. Figure 1-2 illustrates how operations management links internal operational processes with the operational processes of customers and suppliers. The figure also identifies some of the points of interaction between operational groups and other business functional groups within the firm.

Customers

customers Parties that use or consume the products of operations management processes.

Customers include anyone (individuals or organizations) that uses or consumes the products of operations management processes. The firm cannot structure an effective or efficient operations management function unless it has clearly identified its customers. Types of customers can include *internal* customers, *intermediate* customers, and *final* customers. For example, consider a car manufacturer. A company-owned distribution center might be considered an internal customer of the manufacturing group; a dealership is an intermediate customer; and people who buy the car and drive it off the dealer's lot are the final customers, or consumers.

While each of these customer groups is important, it is beneficial for operations managers to identify *critical customers*. Critical customers have the greatest impact on product designs, sales, and future growth opportunities. Often, but not always, the consumer is the critical customer. For example, you are the consumer of this book, yet another customer (your professor) has had greater impact on the product design, sales, and growth opportunities for this product.

Suppliers

suppliers Parties that provide inputs to operational processes.

relationships

Figure 1-2 identifies important types of suppliers in the supply chain. Suppliers provide inputs to operational processes. The horizontal dimension of Figure 1-2 illustrates the flow of materials, information, and money related to the sourcing, making, and delivery of products. The vertical dimension of Figure 1-2 depicts suppliers of technologies and support services. From a single firm's perspective, there are multiple types of suppliers:

- *Upstream product suppliers* typically provide raw materials, components, and services directly related to manufacturing or service production processes.
- *Downstream product suppliers* typically provide enhancements to finished goods such as assembly, packaging, storage, and transportation services.
- *Resource and technology suppliers* provide equipment, labor, product and process designs, and other resources needed to support a firm's processes.
- *Aftermarket suppliers* provide product service and support such as maintenance, repair, disposal, or recycling.

Not shown in Figure 1-2 are a host of other suppliers who make up a part of the total supply chain, including suppliers of indirect goods and services such as mail delivery, health care benefits, cleaning services, and so on. Since suppliers provide so many of a firm's needed resources, technologies, raw materials, and services, the total portfolio of a firm's suppliers affects its success to a great extent.

Stakeholders

stakeholders Groups of people who have a financial or other interest in the well-being of an operation.

In addition to customers and suppliers, other groups of people also have an interest in the well-being (financial and otherwise) of an operation. Stakeholders include employees and unions, the local community, social groups (such as animals' rights or environmental concerns), government, and financial investors.

Why differentiate between customers, suppliers, and stakeholders? Stakeholders' demands often differ from the demands of customers or suppliers. For example, customers

FIGURE 1-2   Partners and Operations Functional Activities in the Supply Chain

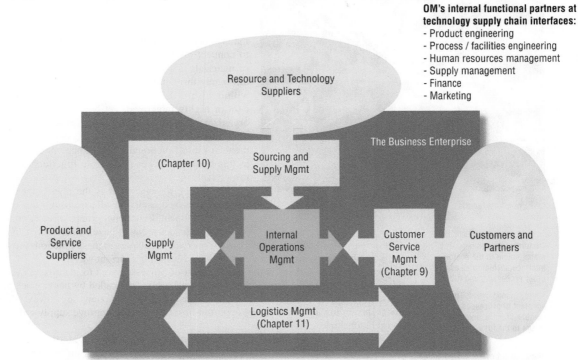

OM's internal functional partners at technology supply chain interfaces:
- Product engineering
- Process / facilities engineering
- Human resources management
- Supply management
- Finance
- Marketing

Resource and Technology Suppliers

The Business Enterprise

(Chapter 10)

Sourcing and Supply Mgmt

Product and Service Suppliers

Supply Mgmt

Internal Operations Mgmt

Customer Service Mgmt (Chapter 9)

Customers and Partners

Logistics Mgmt (Chapter 11)

OM's internal functional partners at upstream product supply chain interfaces:
- Supply management
- Finance
- Logistics management
- Warehousing/raw materials planning

OM's internal functional partners at downstream product supply chain interfaces:
- Marketing
- Sales and distribution
- Customer service/relationship management
- Logistics management
- Warehousing/finished goods materials planning

might care most about the price and quality of products, whereas some stakeholders might care most about environmental concerns. Like customers and suppliers, stakeholders can significantly affect how a firm operates.

Cross-Functional Relationships in Operations Management

We have already noted that operations managers must work closely with other functions in the firm. Managers making any operating decision should consider the decision's effects on other functions, including engineering, finance, marketing, human resources, and others. As shown in Figure 1-2, operations managers who work at the boundaries of the firm often work very closely with other functional groups. For example, an operations manager who works in supply management might work closely with finance managers to determine the most effective contract terms when purchasing equipment.

Some operations managers are primarily concerned with internal operations, such as manufacturing. These managers are always thinking about what operational capabilities are needed, and how to improve the cost, quality, and delivery of the products that the firm supplies to its customers. Other operations management groups work to integrate the internal operations of the firm with the external operations of supply chain partners. While Part 3 of this book specifically addresses these interfunctional relationships, we will provide a brief overview here.

sustainability

relationships

Flow of materials

customer management The management of the customer interface, including all aspects of order processing and fulfillment.

supply management The management of processes used to identify, acquire, and administer inputs to the firm.

logistics management The management of the movement of materials and information within, into, and out of the firm.

tier An upstream stage of supply.

Functional Activities That Connect Operations Managers

As shown in Figure 1-2, customer management, supply management, and logistics management activities serve to connect operational managers as they manage flows of materials and information throughout their firm, and ultimately throughout the entire supply chain. Processes within each of these functional areas may be independent or highly integrated, yet because of the divisional organizational structure that most firms use, most business managers tend to think of operations management in these functional terms. Chapters 9, 10, and 11 in this book discuss each of these functional activities, respectively.

Customer management is the management of the customer interface, including all aspects of order processing and fulfillment. Functional groups directly concerned with customer management have names such as *distribution, sales, order fulfillment,* and *customer service.* Managers in these functions are always thinking about ways to improve customer satisfaction in efficient ways.

Supply management is the management of processes used to identify, acquire, and administer inputs to the firm. Related functional groups are called by names such as *purchasing, sourcing,* and *procurement.* Managers in these functions are always thinking about insourcing and outsourcing opportunities, and ways to improve supply transactions and relationships.

Logistics management is the management of the movement of materials and information within, into, and out of the firm. Logistics functions go by names including *transportation/traffic management, warehousing, materials managers,* and so on. Managers in these functions are always thinking about ways to optimize these flows through better scheduling and the use of alternative transportation, storage, and information technologies.

An Example of Functional Relationships in a Supply Chain

Actual supply chains usually involve many processes including planning, sourcing, making, servicing, delivering, and so on. For example, consider the supply chain of a movie production company depicted in Figure 1-3. Boxes in the figure represent organizations or individuals; arrows represent flows of material, information, or people. To keep things simple, the figure shows only some of the major parties in the supply chain. You can probably easily think of other ones that are not included.

A movie production company's operations managers interact with many suppliers of goods and services that can be considered as either product-related or resource-related inputs. Accordingly, Figure 1-3 indicates stages of a product supply chain in the horizontal dimension, and stages of a resource/technology supply chain in the vertical dimension. Whether a supplier is a "product" supplier or a "resource" supplier is not always clear. Often, a single supplier may fit in both categories. For example, the director of a movie could be considered a resource in the sense that she brings creativity and knowledge to the moviemaking process. At the same time, her time and effort are consumed by the process of making the movie, and these could be considered to be product inputs. Usually, a product supplier provides an input that is fully consumed in the creation of a product or becomes part of the product (e.g., energy, raw materials, components). On the other hand, a resource or technology supplier provides an input that can be used again and again to create multiple products (e.g., information, product and process specifications, equipment, worker skills).

In a supply chain, each upstream stage of supply is known as a tier. The tier number refers to how directly the supplier works with the firm. A *first-tier* supplier provides goods and services directly to the firm. For example, the stock film wholesaler is a first-tier supplier

FIGURE 1-3   Partial Supply Chain Network for a Movie Production Company

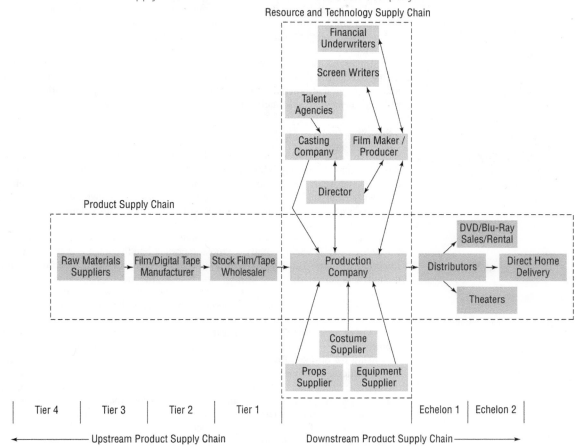

to the movie production company. A *second-tier* supplier provides inputs to the first-tier supplier, and so on. Each tier of the upstream supply chain could involve multiple suppliers for the same items or services. Also, a single supplier might provide inputs for multiple tiers of the

activity

student

Find a description of digital moviemaking technology on the Internet. Which of the stages and organizations depicted in Figure 1-3 are likely to be most affected by a shift to a completely digital process? How will the structure of the overall supply chain be changed?

supply chain. For example, the director in Figure 1-3 provides inputs to both the casting company and the movie production company.

Downstream stages of the supply chain are made up of layers of partners and customers commonly referred to as **echelons**. A single echelon might contain partners in locations all over the world. For example, there are usually many distributors for a given movie. These distributors can be thought of as suppliers of distribution services to the movie production company. The downstream supply chain can also be broken into different channels of distribution; theaters, direct/home delivery, and retail DVD/Blu-Ray sales are three channels shown in Figure 1-3.

Many different types of operations managers are needed in a movie production company. Supply managers help to identify and negotiate contracts with supply sources such as casting companies, directors, producers, equipment suppliers, film suppliers and so on. Internal

echelon A downstream stage of supply or consumption.

production managers are needed to schedule all moviemaking activities such as casting, shooting, and editing. Sales and distribution managers identify and negotiate terms with worldwide distributors of the film. Other logistics managers work out the means for transporting actors and crew and storing film and equipment throughout the various locations involved in making the film.

Similar roles are filled by operations managers at all kinds of firms. The Get Real box on the next page provides some examples of operations management job descriptions for undergraduate and graduate students. Operations managers' responsibilities can be quite exciting, as they are absolutely integral to the success of any organization.

The Changing Nature of Supply Chains

Supply chains are complex. Ultimately, all firms in an industry are connected to one another through links of sourcing, making, servicing, and delivery for different products in various markets. Adding to the complexity is the fact that the structures of supply chains are constantly changing in order to accommodate changes in the business environment. New suppliers emerge and old ones die out. Regulations, laws, and societal pressures change. Markets and technologies evolve. Consider, for example, the technological changes that are sweeping through the moviemaking industry. One could argue that the resource-technology supply chain is really the most important one for moviemakers to manage. The importance of the upstream product supply chain, which provides the medium upon which the movie is delivered, is diminishing rapidly as digital movie production and distribution are rapidly replacing film-based media. In other businesses, where standardized products are produced many times over, the product supply chain plays a more prominent role in a company's strategy.

sustainability

Most of us are aware of the increasing concerns of societies and governments over environmental issues such as pollution, global warming, and hazardous wastes. Expectations are also rising for business firms to behave in more socially responsible ways regarding their labor practices, involvement in communities, and promotion of the general welfare. These increasing pressures act as tremendously important drivers of change in supply chains today. For example, some operations managers who formerly procured supplies from faraway sources are now sourcing them locally in order to reduce the carbon dioxide pollution created by transportation of goods over long distances. This is such an important topic that we have dedicated an entire chapter to it (Chapter 16: Sustainable Operations Management). Additionally, you will encounter numerous examples addressing these issues throughout the book.

Levels of Operational Planning Across the Supply Chain

L01-6 Define the planning activities associated with managing operations across the supply chain.

To keep up with changes in supply chains and the business environment, the functional groups in operations management must periodically work together to plan out their actions. These plans include forecasts and decisions about what the demands on the system will be, what resources and inputs will be needed, how to deploy those resources, and how to process those inputs.

Figure 1-4 on page 18 shows the different levels and types of planning in operations management. Chapters in Parts 1 and 2 of this book address **strategic planning**, which includes high-level product and resource design decisions that define the overall operations objectives and capabilities for the firm and its partners. For example, strategic planning decisions would include what new products to develop, where to locate new plants, and what new technologies to buy. These types of decisions take a long time to implement, and the choices made put limits on the capacities and capabilities governing operational processes.

strategic planning A type of planning that addresses long-term decisions that define the operations objectives and capabilities for the firm and its partners.

tactical planning A type of planning that addresses intermediate-term decisions to target aggregate product demands and to establish how operational capacities will be used to meet them.

Chapters in Part 4 of this book address tactical and operational planning. These types of planning occur more frequently than strategic planning does. **Tactical planning** such as sales and operations planning seeks to identify and target customer demands for aggregate product families, and to establish the inventory and capacity plans needed to satisfy these

GET
REAL

Jobs in Operations Management

The following job descriptions provide examples of typical responsibilities of operations managers located in internal operations, customer management, supply management, and logistics management functions.

Typical job titles: Customer Program Manager, Enterprise Integration Leader, Commodity Manager, Procurement Specialist, Senior Global Commodity Specialist, Strategic Sourcing Commodity Leader, Project Manager for Supply Chain Information Systems, Production Team Leader, Materials Planning Manager, Logistics Specialist.

Typical job responsibilities:

- Choosing and developing suppliers.
- Designing and implementing systems and processes for improving the customer interface, reducing transaction costs, reducing inventories, and improving service levels.
- Sourcing materials, components, technologies, and services.
- Monitoring and managing inventory at all steps of the supply chain.
- Managing logistics, warehouses, distribution inventories, and service parts.
- Managing internal operations or service functions.
- Managing quality and Six Sigma projects throughout the supply chain.
- Strategically analyzing the supply chain to increase revenues, improve service, reduce cost, and ultimately improve profit.

Excerpts from actual job descriptions:

At a computer manufacturer: As part of the Americas Services Logistics team, Supply Chain Consultants design, develop, and improve processes throughout the company's industry leading logistics network as well as manage projects across multinational teams for the Americas region. The Supply Chain Consultant works on developing new concepts and strategies for the company's third-party logistics providers (3PLs) that enable greater product availability at lower costs and greater customer satisfaction. In addition to partnering with 3PLs, Supply Chain Consultants work closely with the company's world-renowned Enterprise Command Center in order to provide 24/7 critical logistics support and crisis resolution to millions of customers throughout the Americas. The general qualifications of a Supply Chain Consultant include:

- Strong analytical skills.
- Advanced verbal and written communication skills.
- Able to generate new and innovative solutions to complex problems.

- Strong knowledge of supply chain and service logistics concepts and practices, third-party logistics provider management experience preferred.
- Advanced understanding of processes and process improvement, Six Sigma experience preferred.
- Able to effectively negotiate with internal and external partners.
- Strong project management experience.
- Proven leadership skills.
- Unwavering customer focus.
- Bachelor's degree in Operations, Logistics, Engineering or Supply Chain Management with 3–4 years experience.

At a health care products company: Our Development Program in Operations is a fast-paced set of rotations that can turn you into a well-rounded, results-driven leader who is ready to move into a decision-making supervisory position. By gaining first-hand experience in our distribution centers and corporate/regional offices, you'll learn the necessary skills to manage our streamlined distribution process and help drive operational results and customer satisfaction. Our distribution centers across the country will offer you hands-on experience to help you develop your skills in project management, business process improvement, and labor management. We encourage and coach all participants to achieve outstanding results by giving them challenging and rewarding responsibilities. The Development Program in Operations lasts twenty-four months and offers rotations that concentrate on warehouse operations, inventory management, transportation, corporate operations and purchasing.

At a paper products company: Our co-op and internships will offer you a chance to explore the breadth of opportunities available in the supply chain while working on real projects such as process improvements in flow planning for finished products, raw materials and finishing supplies, space utilization and optimization analysis, or warehouse operations systems analysis. You will be provided meaningful work experiences that contribute to the overall strategic business goals of the company. You'll be treated and respected as a valuable contributor and given your own responsibilities and accountabilities. Your intern experience will include performance evaluations that provide you with valuable professional feedback to gauge your strengths and measure areas of improvement.

At a not-for-profit organization: As director of donated goods operations you will help the organization provide people who have disabilities and other barriers to employment with opportunities to become independent, self-supporting

Continued

Continued

citizens through training, work experience, and employment in the community. Position duties include:

- Develop short- and long-range plans for the donated goods operation to achieve service goals, budgeted revenue, and maximized contributed margin.
- Expand donated goods operation to new markets, new product lines, develop new sites and creative sales techniques to expand community and business donation base.
- Establish and monitor performance criteria for donated goods operation to enhance donated goods operations through increased efficiencies.

- Develop and manage inventory control system, a total quality improvement system, and e-commerce activities to assure customer satisfaction at all levels.
- Make recommendations to the President/CEO regarding the need for capital equipment additions or replacements.
- Contribute positively to the Executive Management Team. Promote positive image of the organization both internally and externally.
- Participate in and uphold the values and processes devoted to continuous quality improvement in all organizational operations.

You can find more operations management career information at:

www.careersinsupplychain.org
www.ism.ws/careercenter

FIGURE 1-4 Operations Management: Planning Activities Across the Supply Chain

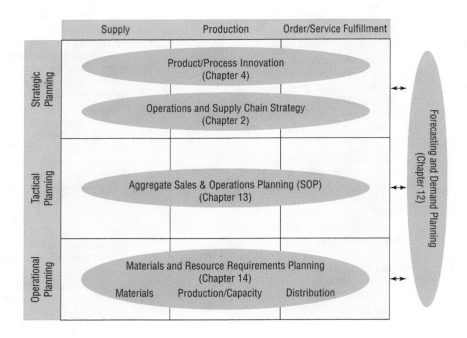

operational planning A type of planning that establishes short-term priorities and schedules to guide operational resource allocations.

overall demands. At the **operational planning** level, inventory and requirements planning activities address demands, materials, and capacities at the individual product level. Tactical planning usually spans months, whereas operational planning usually addresses weeks or days of activity. The chapters in Part 4 in this book also discuss planning approaches and technologies used in tactical and operational planning.

TABLE 1-3 A Content Map for This Book

Chapter	Relationships	Sustainability	Globalization
Part 1 Supply Chain: A Perspective for Operations Management			
1. Introduction to Managing Operations Across the Supply Chain	X	X	X
2. Operations and Supply Chain Strategy	X	X	X
Part 2 Foundations of Operations Management			
3. Managing Processes and Capacity	X	X	
4. Product/Process Innovation	X	X	X
5. Manufacturing and Service Process Structures	X	X	X
6. Managing Quality	X	X	X
7. Managing Inventories	X	X	X
8. Lean Systems	X		X
Part 3 Integrating Relationships Across the Supply Chain			
9. Customer Service Management	X		
10. Sourcing and Supply Management	X	X	X
11. Logistics Management	X	X	X
Part 4 Planning for Integrated Operations Across the Supply Chain			
12. Demand Planning: Forecasting and Demand Management	X		X
13. Sales and Operations Planning	X		X
14. Materials and Resource Requirements Planning	X		X
Part 5 Managing Change in Supply Chain Operations			
15. Project Management	X	X	X
16. Sustainable Operations Management–Preparing for the Future	X	X	X

HOW THIS BOOK IS STRUCTURED

Table 1-3 provides a content overview of this book, indicating the chapters in which critical operations management issues are addressed. Collectively, the five major parts of this book provide an introduction to the principles, programs, and practices of operations management:

- Part 1 provides an overview of operations management as a field, and describes its strategic role in a business from the perspective of supply chain management.
- Part 2 discusses foundational process-related concepts and principles that govern all operational processes.
- Part 3 deals with the primary functional relationships between internal operations management activities and other operational functions both inside and outside the firm.
- Part 4 discusses planning approaches and technologies used at different levels of operations decision making.

- Part 5 discusses how operations managers use projects, change programs, and technologies to shape the future of operations and supply chain management.

An overview and integration of the chapters contained in each part is provided at the beginning of each of the parts throughout this book.

CHAPTER SUMMARY

This chapter provides a broad overview and introduction to operations management. In discussing the scope and complexity of operations management, we have made the following points:

1. The goal of the modern firm is to develop and run an operations management system able to deliver superior product value to the firm's targeted consumers.

2. Operations management deals with the effective and efficient management of transformation processes. These processes include not only the making of products but also the design of products and related processes; sourcing of required materials and services; and delivery and management of relationships among customers, suppliers, and functions within the firm. As a system, operations management involves four major functional activities and their interactions: (1) customer relationships management, (2) internal operations (manufacturing and services) management, (3) supply management, and (4) logistics management.

3. The operations management system involves three major sets of partners outside the firm: (1) customers, (2) suppliers, and (3) stakeholders. Operations managers also work closely with other business functions within the firm.

4. The collective decisions made in areas of operations management determine the capabilities and success of the firm. In addition, the capabilities of a firm are heavily influenced by the capabilities of its suppliers.

5. For a number of reasons, the supply chain has grown to become a dominant way to look at operations management. Operations activities take place in various functional and geographic locations across a supply chain network. Whereas operations management is mainly about managing processes, supply chain management is mainly about managing flows and relationships.

6. Operations management is fundamentally dynamic; it is ever changing.

KEY TERMS

core capability   11
customer management   14
customers   12
echelon   15
lean operation   9
logistics management   14
operational planning   18

operations management   4
process   8
stakeholders   12
strategic planning   16
suppliers   12
supply chain   4

supply chain management   11
supply management   14
tactical planning   16
tier   14
total product experience   7

QUESTIONS

1. Review *Fortune* magazine's "Most Admired" American companies for 1959, 1979, 1999, and the most current year. (The issue normally appears in August each year.) Which companies have remained on the top throughout this period? Which ones have disappeared? What do you think led to the survival or demise of these companies?

2. Select two products that you have recently purchased; one should be a service and the other a manufactured good. Think about the process that you used to make the decision to purchase each item. What product characteristics were most important to you? What operational activities determine these characteristics?

3. What are the primary operations management decisions in each of the following corporations?
   a. Marriott Hotels and Resorts.
   b. A private golf and tennis club.
   c. Ben & Jerry's.
   d. ExxonMobil Corporation.

4. Consider the following processes that you frequently encounter as a college student:
   a. Enrolling in classes.
   b. Taking a class.
   c. Buying a ticket for a play, concert, or basketball game.

   Describe each process and its inputs, activities, and outputs. What is being converted or transformed in each process? Who are the customers, suppliers, and stakeholders for each process?

5. Recall the last time you went to a fast-food restaurant such as McDonald's. Describe all of the goods and services that make up your *total product experience*.

6. The following firms have long been seen as having strong competitive advantages:
   a. IBM
   b. Coca-Cola
   c. Xerox
   d. Walmart

   Read about one of these companies. Also draw from your experience as a customer to identify that company's competitive advantage. Discuss how operations management relates to the company's competitive advantage.

7. Why should a firm consider the position of stakeholders when evaluating operational alternatives? Consider the role of government and its impact. (*Hint:* Consider working conditions and pollution.)

8. Most people have worked as "operations managers" at some time. Describe a job or experience that you had that involved the management of a process.

CASE

Business Textbook Supply Chain

Dave Eisenhart, senior editor for Mountain Publishing, Inc., looked out his window as he considered the operational implications of the changes he had just heard discussed in the company's annual strategic planning meeting. The future looked to be both exciting and scary. As an editor for Mountain's business textbook division, Dave had recently witnessed major changes in his primary market. First, the body of knowledge in business school curricula had exploded over the past decade. It was getting harder and harder to cover all the content that any professor might want in a single textbook, while keeping the size of the book manageable. Second, Dave had noted that more and more schools were moving to modular course structures, including many shorter courses, sometimes as short as a week long. Third, a growing number of students preferred to buy their books from sources other than traditional bookstores, such as Amazon.com and other online sources.

At the same time, new technologies were changing the way that textbook content could be produced and delivered. Print technologies were improving the speed and quality of printing, so that it was easy to envision a day when books could be printed one copy at a time, "on demand." Mountain and other companies had already started to offer custom published books for professors who wanted to combine chapters and cases from several different sources into a single readings packet for their students. While the quality of these "books" (packets) did not match that of traditional hardbound texts, many professors and students valued the flexibility associated with this option.

Finally, e-books were slowly making an entrance into the market. While the percentage of books purchased in electronic form was currently very small, the potential seemed to be very large, if and when a standardized reader technology ever became widely accepted in the marketplace.

Dave began to think about the operational activities dispersed across Mountain's supply chain for traditional textbooks. On the upstream (input) side, Mountain worked with authors (usually professors), text editors, graphic artists, commercial printers, and other suppliers to edit, design, and produce books. After typically large print runs (up to three years of forecasted demand) were produced, transportation suppliers delivered the books to Mountain's distribution centers located around the country. Orders from bookstores and online retailers were filled from these distribution centers. For traditional textbooks, each of these players in the supply chain played a fairly clear role in creating value through the goods and services they provided. However, as Dave considered the market and technological changes currently under way, the operational value that each of these players provided became less clear.

Questions

1. Draw a diagram that illustrates the textbook supply chain from the publisher's point of view.

2. Who are the various customers for textbooks? What do these customers want in terms of goods and services related to textbooks? From the publisher's point of view, who is the critical customer?

3. Who are the major players in the supply chain? What operational roles do they play in terms of creating value for the critical customers?

4. Given the anticipated changes in the market and in product and process technologies, how do you envision each supply chain player's role changing in the future?

5. What advice would you give to Dave Eisenhart regarding long-term operational changes the firm should consider?

SELECTED READINGS & INTERNET SITES

Association of Operations Management
www.apics.org

Council of Supply Chain Management Professionals
www.cscmp.org

Institute for Supply Management
www.ism.ws

Goldratt, E. M., and J. Cox. *The Goal: A Process of Ongoing Improvement.* Great Barrington, MA: North River Press, 2004.

Friedman, T. L. *The World Is Flat.* New York: Farrar, Straus and Giroux, 2006.

Journal of Operations Management. Amsterdam: Elsevier Science, B.V., 1980–current.

Manufacturing & Service Operations Management: M&SOM. Linthicum, MD: Institute for Operations Research and Management Sciences, 1999–current.

Production and Operations Management: An International Journal of the Production and Operations Management Society/POMS. Baltimore, MD: Production and Operations Management Society, 1992–current.

Swamidass, P. (ed). *Encyclopedia of Production and Manufacturing Management.* Norwell, MA: Kluwer Academic Publishing, 2000.

Womack, J. P.; D. T. Jones; and D. Roos. *The Machine That Changed the World.* New York: Rawson Associates, 1990.

19

Using Securities Markets for Financing and Investing Opportunities

Learning Objectives

AFTER YOU HAVE READ AND STUDIED THIS CHAPTER, YOU SHOULD BE ABLE TO

LO 19-1   Describe the role of securities markets and of investment bankers.

LO 19-2   Identify the stock exchanges where securities are traded.

LO 19-3   Compare the advantages and disadvantages of equity financing by issuing stock, and detail the differences between common and preferred stock.

LO 19-4   Compare the advantages and disadvantages of obtaining debt financing by issuing bonds, and identify the classes and features of bonds.

LO 19-5   Explain how to invest in securities markets and set investment objectives such as long-term growth, income, cash, and protection from inflation.

LO 19-6   Analyze the opportunities stocks offer as investments.

LO 19-7   Analyze the opportunities bonds offer as investments.

LO 19-8   Explain the investment opportunities in mutual funds and exchange-traded funds (ETFs).

LO 19-9   Describe how indicators like the Dow Jones Industrial Average affect the market.

Getting to know **Mellody Hobson**

In some ways, making a stock trade in the modern age has become easy. Anybody with an e-mail address and a bank account can sign up with an online brokerage like E*Trade or Schwab and instantly start trading stocks from around the globe. However, having the ability to make *wise* trades is another matter.

Many people, hoping to understand investing, turn to experts like Mellody Hobson. As president of Ariel Investments, Hobson oversees assets of more than $9 billion. Hobson is interested in more than just her company's bottom line. As a staunch advocate for economic literacy and investor education, Hobson regularly contributes financial advice on radio, TV, and a column in *Black Enterprise Magazine*. She sits on the boards of prominent companies like DreamWorks Animation, Starbucks, and Estee Lauder. As a result, Hobson is considered to be one of the most intelligent and capable financial advisors in the industry. "She is the Picasso of questions," said DreamWorks CEO Jeff Katzenberg. "She can ask a question like nobody else. You have to find in yourself the answer to it. There's a real art to that."

Hobson was born the youngest of six children to a single mom in Chicago. She developed a strong work ethic, and was the first person in her family to attend college, graduating from Princeton University in 1991. She interned at Ariel Investments while in college and returned there to accept an entry-level position when she finished school. On her first day, Hobson received a crucial bit of advice from CEO John Rogers that still sticks with her: "John informed me that I would frequently find myself in the company of rich and successful people with big titles, lots of degrees and lots of experience," said Hobson. "And yet, my ideas could still be as good or even better."

Rogers's words encouraged Hobson as she rose through the ranks at Ariel. By 2000 she was appointed company president, placing her among the most prominent African American women in business. Under her watch Ariel Investments has grown to become the largest minority-owned mutual fund in the world.

Hobson has often said that her odds-defying rise to the top would not have been possible without a patient attitude. In fact, patience lies at the heart of Hobson's investment strategy at Ariel. True to its turtle logo, the company focuses on stocks and equity funds that will perform well in the long term, as opposed to risky but potentially lucrative short-term options. "For 30 years, we have been underscoring this idea of patient investing," said Hobson. "However, patience is not just our investment strategy but also how we build our business. Ariel is the only job I have ever had, and I have worked here more than 22 years. We live these values."

Expert investors like Mellody Hobson value sound judgment over just about anything else. But to be a successful investor, you need a little education on other important topics as well. In this chapter you'll learn about the many ways that money can be invested in securities markets.

Sources: Ben Lillie, "Be Color Brave, Not Color Blind: Mellody Hobson at TED2014," *TED Blog*, March 20, 2014; Mellody Hobson and Jeffrey Katzenberg, "The Best Advice I Ever Got," *Fortune*, November 1, 2013; Mellody Hobson, "Lean In Stories: Mellody Hobson on the Difference Between Assertive and Abrasive," *Blue Sky–Chicago Tribune*, December 7, 2013; and "Patient Investing: An Interview with Mellody Hobson," *Leaders Magazine*, January 2014.

Mellody Hobson
- President of Ariel Investments
- Expert investor
- Financial educator
www.arielinvestments.com/
@ArielFunds

name that **company**

If someone had bought 100 shares in this company when it was first available to the public in 1965, it would have cost $2,250. If he or she held on to the stock, the number of shares the person would have today would be 74,360 (after 12 stock splits) with a value of approximately $7.4 million. What is the name of this company? (Find the answer in the chapter.)

initial public offering (IPO)
The first public offering of a corporation's stock.

David and Tom Gardner, the Motley Fools, are passionate about spreading the message that securities markets can provide opportunities for all. The brothers have built their careers on providing high-quality financial information to investors regardless of education or income. Visit their website at www.fool.com for more information.

LO 19–1 Describe the role of securities markets and of investment bankers.

THE FUNCTION OF SECURITIES MARKETS

Securities markets—financial marketplaces for stocks, bonds, and other investments—serve two major functions. First, they assist businesses in finding long-term funding to finance capital needs, such as expanding operations, developing new products, or buying major goods and services. Second, they provide private investors a place to buy and sell securities (investments), such as stocks and bonds, that can help them build their financial future. In this chapter, we look at securities markets first from the perspective of funding for businesses and second as markets for private investors to buy and trade investments.

Securities markets are divided into primary and secondary markets. *Primary markets* handle the sale of *new* securities. This is an important point to understand. Corporations make money on the sale of their securities (stock) only once—when they sell it on the primary market. The first public offering of a corporation's stock is called an **initial public offering (IPO)**. After that, the *secondary market* handles the trading of these securities between investors, with the proceeds of the sale going to the investor selling the stock, not to the corporation whose stock is sold. For example, imagine your vegetarian restaurant, Very Vegetarian, has grown into a chain and your products are available in many retail stores throughout the country. You want to raise additional funds to expand further. If you offer 1 million shares of stock in your company at $10 a share, you can raise $10 million at this initial offering. However, after the initial sale, if Shareholder Jones decides to sell 100 shares of her Very Vegetarian stock to Investor Smith, Very Vegetarian collects nothing from that transaction. Smith buys the stock from Jones, not from Very Vegetarian. It is possible, however, for companies like Very Vegetarian to offer additional shares of stock for sale to raise additional capital.

As mentioned in Chapter 18, we can't overemphasize the importance of long-term funding to businesses. Given a choice, businesses normally prefer to meet their long-term financial needs by using retained earnings or borrowing funds either from a lending institution (bank, pension fund, insurance company) or corporate bond issue. However, if long-term funds are not available from retained earnings or lenders, a company may be able to raise capital by issuing corporate stock. (Recall from Chapter 18 that selling stock in the corporation is a form of *equity financing* and issuing corporate bonds is a form of *debt financing*.) Social networking giant Facebook's IPO in 2012 raised $16 billion for the company.[1] Visa, however, remains the largest U.S. IPO of the past 25 years raising $18 billion from its IPO in 2008. These sources of equity and bond financing are not available to all companies, especially small businesses.

Let's imagine you need further long-term financing to *expand* operations at Very Vegetarian. Your chief financial officer (CFO) says the company lacks sufficient retained earnings and she doesn't think it can secure the needed funds from a lending institution. She suggests that you offer shares of stock or issue corporate bonds to private investors to secure the funding. She warns, however, that issuing shares of stock or corporate bonds is not simple or automatic. To get approval for stock or bond issues you must make extensive financial disclosures and undergo detailed scrutiny by the U.S. Securities and Exchange Commission (SEC). Because of these requirements, your CFO recommends that the company turn to an investment banker for assistance. Let's see why.

The Role of Investment Bankers

Investment bankers are specialists who assist in the issue and sale of new securities. These large financial firms can help companies like Very Vegetarian prepare the extensive financial analyses necessary to gain SEC approval for bond or stock issues. Investment bankers can also *underwrite* new issues of stocks or bonds. That is, the investment banking firm buys the entire stock or bond issue at an agreed-on discount, which can be quite sizable, and then sells the issue to private or institutional investors at full price.

institutional investors are large organizations—such as pension funds, mutual funds, and insurance companies—that invest their own funds or the funds of others. Because of their vast buying power, institutional investors are a powerful force in securities markets.

Before we look at stocks and bonds as long-term financing and investment opportunities in more depth, it's important to understand stock exchanges—the places where stocks and bonds are traded.

> **investment bankers**
> Specialists who assist in the issue and sale of new securities.

> **institutional investors**
> Large organizations—such as pension funds, mutual funds, and insurance companies—that invest their own funds or the funds of others.

LO 19–2   Identify the stock exchanges where securities are traded.

STOCK EXCHANGES

As the name implies, a **stock exchange** is an organization whose members can buy and sell (exchange) securities on behalf of companies and individual investors. The New York Stock Exchange (NYSE) was founded in 1792 and was then primarily a floor-based exchange, which means trades physically took place on the floor of the stock exchange. Things changed in 2005 when the NYSE merged with Archipelago, a securities trading company that specialized in electronic trades. Two years later, it merged with Europe's Euronext exchange, and became the NYSE Euronext. In 2013, the Intercontinental Exchange (ICE) located in Atlanta purchased the NYSE Euronext for $8.2 billion.[2]

Today, the once active floor of the NYSE Euronext is now largely symbolic.[3] Most trading takes place on computers that can transact thousands of stock trades within seconds. In fact, trading stocks has become a very small part of the exchange's revenue.[4] The bulk of the company's revenue comes from selling complex financial contracts and market information to companies like Yahoo and Google that offer stock quotes as a service on their websites. They also earn revenue from fees paid by over 8,000 companies listed on the NYSE Euronext.[5]

> **stock exchange**
> An organization whose members can buy and sell (exchange) securities for companies and individual investors.

The NYSE Euronext was the largest floor-based exchange, where stock trades were made on the crowded floor of the exchange. Today stocks are bought and sold primarily on electronic networks. The illustration (on the right) of the exchange floor today seems deserted compared to the old days.

Not all securities are traded on registered stock exchanges. The **over-the-counter (OTC) market** provides companies and investors with a means to trade stocks not listed on the large securities exchanges. The OTC market is a network of several thousand brokers who maintain contact with one another and buy and sell securities through a nationwide electronic system. Trading is conducted between two parties directly, instead of through an exchange like the NYSE Euronext.

The **NASDAQ** (originally known as the National Association of Securities Dealers Automated Quotations) was the world's first electronic stock market. It evolved from the OTC market but is no longer part of it. The NASDAQ is an electronic-based network that links dealers so they can buy and sell securities electronically rather than in person. In 2007, the NASDAQ purchased the Swedish OMX Group and is now the NASDAQ OMX Group. It is the largest U.S. electronic stock trading market and has more trading volume than any electronic exchange in the world. The NASDAQ originally dealt mostly with smaller firms, but today well-known companies such as Facebook, Microsoft, Intel, Google, and Starbucks trade their stock on the NASDAQ. The NASDAQ also handles federal, state, and city government bonds and lists approximately 3,300 companies with a market value over $8 trillion.[6]

Adding a company to an exchange is a highly competitive undertaking, and the battle between the stock exchanges for a stock listing is often fierce.[7] If a company fails to meet the requirements of an exchange, the stock can be delisted from the exchange.[8] You can find the requirements for registering (listing) stocks on the NYSE Euronext and NASDAQ on their websites at www.nyx.com and www.nasdaqomx.com. The Spotlight on Small Business box discusses how the JOBS Act now gives small businesses access to public securities markets.

over-the-counter (OTC) market
Exchange that provides a means to trade stocks not listed on the national exchanges.

NASDAQ
A nationwide electronic system that links dealers across the nation so that they can buy and sell securities electronically.

Securities and Exchange Commission (SEC)
The federal agency that has responsibility for regulating the various stock exchanges.

Securities Regulations and the Securities and Exchange Commission

The **Securities and Exchange Commission (SEC)** is the federal agency responsible for regulating the various stock exchanges. The Securities Act of 1933 helps protect investors by requiring full disclosure of financial information by firms selling bonds or stock. The U.S. Congress passed this legislation to deal with the free-for-all atmosphere that existed in the securities markets during the 1920s and the early 1930s that helped cause the Great Depression. The Securities and Exchange Act of 1934 created the SEC.

Companies trading on the national exchanges must register with the SEC and provide it with annual updates. The 1934 act also established specific guidelines that companies must follow when issuing financial securities, such as stocks or bonds. For example, before issuing either stocks or bonds for sale to the public, a company must file a detailed registration statement with the

Giving Small Business a Jump on Funding

The most frequent complaint from small businesses is the lack of available financing. This scarcity of funding often thwarts any expansion or hiring plans small businesses may be considering. The goal of the Jumpstart Our Business Startups Act (JOBS Act) is to ease small business financing problems. In the JOBS Act, securities rules are streamlined to give small firms access to public securities markets. The Securities and Exchange Commission (SEC) was charged with adopting rules on general solicitations and equity crowdfunding.

The SEC altered securities laws in a number of ways. A brief summary includes:

- Raised from 500 to 2,000 the number of shareholders a company could have before it's required to register its stock with the SEC.

- Allows private companies to advertise to investors, but permits companies to accept funds only from individuals who earn more than $200,000 a year or have personal assets in excess of $1 million.

- Exempts emerging growth companies with gross revenues less than $1 billion from some of the stringent financial reporting rules of the Sarbanes-Oxley Act (see Chapter 17).

- Allows *equity* crowdfunding through investment brokers or portals, but limits the amount individuals with modest incomes or net worth can invest to a percentage of their annual income or assets.

- Expanded the ability of private companies to raise capital through limited stock offerings.

Many in the investment community have cheered the act's passage as a tremendous means for small businesses to generate needed funds. However, many investment analysts see major problems. One problem is the high number of small businesses that fail every year. Another is how investors will be able to resell stock when there is no broker or exchange to facilitate the sale. Still others have blasted the law as ripe for investment fraud. Time will tell if the JOBS Act is a boom or bust for many small businesses and investors.

Sources: Kathy Kristof, "Investor Beware," *Kiplinger's Personal Finance*, February 2014; Eric T. Wagner, "Equity Crowdfunding 101: Is It Right for Your Startup?" *Forbes*, March 18, 2014; and Kendall Almerico, "The JOBS Act Provision That Could Change IPOs Forever," *Entrepreneur*, February 21, 2014.

SEC that includes extensive economic and financial information. The condensed version of that registration document—called a **prospectus**—must be sent to prospective investors.

The 1934 act also established guidelines to prevent insiders within the company from taking advantage of privileged information they may have. *Insider trading* is using knowledge or information that individuals gain through their position that allows them to benefit unfairly from fluctuations in security prices. The key words here are *benefit unfairly*. Insiders within a firm are permitted to buy and sell stock in the company they work for, so long as they do not take unfair advantage of information unknown to the public.

Originally, the SEC defined the term *insider* rather narrowly as covering a company's directors and employees and their relatives. Today the term has been broadened to include just about anyone with securities information not available to the general public. Let's say the CFO of Very Vegetarian tells her next-door neighbor she is finalizing paperwork to sell the company to a large corporation, and the neighbor buys the stock based on this information. A court may well consider the purchase an insider trade. Penalties for insider trading can include fines or imprisonment.[9] For example, billionaire hedge fund manager Raj Rajaratnam was convicted of insider trading in a high-profile case in 2011. SAC Capital portfolio manager Matthew Martoma was convicted in 2014 in the largest insider-trading scheme ever, and could face 15 to 20 years in prison. The company paid $1.5 billion in fines.[10] Look at Figure 19.1 and test your skill in identifying insider trading.

prospectus
A condensed version of economic and financial information that a company must file with the SEC before issuing stock; the prospectus must be sent to prospective investors.

FIGURE 19.1 IS IT INSIDER TRADING OR NOT?

Insider trading involves buying or selling a stock on the basis of company information not available to the investing public. These hypothetical examples will give you an idea of what's legal and what's illegal. The answers are at the bottom of the box.

1. You work in research and development at a large company and have been involved in a major effort that should lead to a blockbuster new product coming to the market. News about the product is not public, and very few other workers even know about it. Can you purchase stock in the company?

2. Pertaining to the above situation, you are in a local coffee bar and mention to a friend about what's going on at the company. Another customer seated at an adjoining table overhears your discussion. Can this person legally buy stock in the company before the public announcement?

3. You work as an executive secretary at a major investment banking firm. You are asked to copy documents that detail a major merger about to happen that will keenly benefit the company being taken over. Can you buy stock in the company before the announcement is made public?

4. Your stockbroker recommends that you buy shares in a little-known company. The broker seems to have some inside information, but you don't ask any questions about his source. Can you buy stock in this company?

5. You work as a cleaning person at a major securities firm. At your job you come across information from the trash cans and computer printers of employees of the firm that provide detailed information about several upcoming deals the firm will be handling. Can you buy stock in the companies involved?

Answers: 1. No; 2. Yes; 3. No; 4. Yes; 5. No.

Foreign Stock Exchanges

Thanks to expanded communications and the relaxation of many legal barriers, investors can buy securities from companies almost anywhere in the world. If you uncover a foreign company you feel has great potential for growth, you can purchase shares of its stock with little difficulty from U.S. brokers who have access to foreign stock exchanges. Foreign investors can also invest in U.S. securities, and large foreign stock exchanges, like those in London and Tokyo, trade large amounts of U.S. securities daily. In addition to the London and Tokyo exchanges, other major stock exchanges are located in Shanghai, Sydney, Hong Kong, São Paolo, and Toronto. Stock exchanges have become active in Africa as well.[11]

Raising long-term funds using equity financing by issuing stock is an option many companies pursue. After the Test Prep, let's look in more depth at how firms raise capital by issuing stock.

Use LearnSmart to help retain what you have learned. Access your instructor's Connect course to check out LearnSmart, or go to learnsmartadvantage.com for help.

≣LEARNSMART

test **prep**

- What is the primary purpose of a securities exchange?
- What does NASDAQ stand for? How does this exchange work?

LO 19–3 Compare the advantages and disadvantages of equity financing by issuing stock, and detail the differences between common and preferred stock.

HOW BUSINESSES RAISE CAPITAL BY SELLING STOCK

Stocks are shares of ownership in a company. A **stock certificate** represents stock ownership. It specifies the name of the company, the number of shares owned, and the type of stock it represents. Companies, however, are not required to issue paper stock certificates to owners since stock is generally held electronically.

Stock certificates sometimes indicate a stock's *par value*, which is a dollar amount assigned to each share of stock by the corporation's charter. Today, since par values do not reflect the market value of the stock (what the stock is actually worth), most companies issue stock with a very low par value or no par value. **Dividends** are part of a firm's profits that the firm may (but is not required to) distribute to stockholders as either cash payments or additional shares of stock.[12] Dividends are declared by a corporation's board of directors and are generally paid quarterly.

stocks
Shares of ownership in a company.

stock certificate
Evidence of stock ownership that specifies the name of the company, the number of shares it represents, and the type of stock being issued.

dividends
Part of a firm's profits that the firm may distribute to stockholders as either cash payments or additional shares of stock.

Advantages and Disadvantages of Issuing Stock

Some advantages to a firm of issuing stock include:

- As owners of the business, stockholders never have to be repaid their investment.
- There's no legal obligation to pay dividends to stockholders; therefore, the firm can reinvest income (retained earnings) to finance future needs.
- Selling stock can improve the condition of a firm's balance sheet since issuing stock creates no debt. (A corporation may also buy back its stock to improve its balance sheet and make the company appear stronger financially.)[13]

Disadvantages of issuing stock include:

- As owners, stockholders (usually only common stockholders) have the right to vote for the company's board of directors. (Typically, one vote is granted for each share of stock.) Issuing new shares of stock can thus alter the control of the firm.
- Dividends are paid from profit after taxes and are not tax-deductible.
- The need to keep stockholders happy can affect managers' decisions.

Companies can issue two classes of stock: common and preferred. Let's see how these two forms of equity financing differ.

Issuing Shares of Common Stock

Common stock is the most basic form of ownership in a firm. In fact, if a company issues only one type of stock, by law it must be common stock. Holders of common stock have the right to (1) elect members of the company's board of directors and vote on important issues affecting the company and (2) share in the firm's profits through dividends, if approved by the firm's board of directors. Having voting rights in a corporation allows common stockholders to

common stock
The most basic form of ownership in a firm; it confers voting rights and the right to share in the firm's profits through dividends, if approved by the firm's board of directors.

538   PART 6   Managing Financial Resources

influence corporate policy because the board members they elect choose the firm's top management and make major policy decisions. Common stockholders also have a *preemptive right* to purchase new shares of common stock before anyone else. This allows common stockholders to maintain their proportional share of ownership in the company.

Issuing Shares of Preferred Stock

preferred stock
Stock that gives its owners preference in the payment of dividends and an earlier claim on assets than common stockholders if the company is forced out of business and its assets sold.

Owners of **preferred stock** are given preference in the payment of company dividends and must be paid their dividends in full before any common stock dividends can be distributed (hence the term *preferred*). They also have a prior claim on company assets if the firm is forced out of business and its assets sold. Normally, however, preferred stockholders do not get voting rights in the firm.

Preferred stock may be issued with a par value that becomes the base for a fixed dividend the firm is willing to pay. For example, if a preferred stock's par value is $50 a share and its dividend rate is 4 percent, the dividend is $2 a share. An owner of 100 preferred shares receives a fixed yearly dividend of $200 if dividends are declared by the board of directors.

Preferred stock can have other special features that common stock doesn't have.[14] For example it can be *callable*, which means preferred stockholders could be required to sell their shares back to the corporation. Preferred stock can also be converted to shares of common stock (but not the other way around), and it can be *cumulative*. That is, if one or more dividends are not paid when promised, they accumulate and the corporation must pay them in full at a later date before it can distribute any common stock dividends.[15]

Companies often prefer to raise capital by debt financing. One debt funding option frequently used by larger firms is issuing corporate bonds. Let's look at what's involved with issuing corporate bonds and how they differ from issuing stock.

test prep

- Name at least two advantages and two disadvantages of a company's issuing stock as a form of equity financing.
- What are the major differences between common stock and preferred stock?

Use LearnSmart to help retain what you have learned. Access your instructor's Connect course to check out LearnSmart, or go to learnsmartadvantage.com for help.

LEARNSMART

LO 19—4   Compare the advantages and disadvantages of obtaining debt financing by issuing bonds, and identify the classes and features of bonds.

HOW BUSINESSES RAISE CAPITAL BY ISSUING BONDS

A **bond** is a corporate certificate indicating that an investor has lent money to a firm (or a government). An organization that issues bonds has a legal obligation to make regular interest payments to investors and to repay the entire bond principal amount at a prescribed time. Let's further explore the language of bonds so you understand exactly how they work.

bond
A corporate certificate indicating that a person has lent money to a firm (or a government).

Learning the Language of Bonds

Corporate bonds are usually issued in units of $1,000 (government bonds can be in much larger amounts). The *principal* is the face value (dollar value) of a bond, which the issuing company is legally bound to repay in full to the bondholder on the **maturity date**. **Interest** is the payment the bond issuer makes to the bondholders to compensate them for the use of their money. If Very Vegetarian issues a $1,000 bond with an interest rate of 5 percent and a maturity date of 2025, it is agreeing to pay the bondholder a total of $50 interest each year until a specified date in 2025, when it must repay the full $1,000. Maturity dates can vary. Firms such as Disney, IBM, and Coca-Cola have issued so-called century bonds with 100-year maturity dates.[16]

maturity date
The exact date the issuer of a bond must pay the principal to the bondholder.

interest
The payment the issuer of the bond makes to the bondholders for use of the borrowed money.

Bond interest is sometimes called the *coupon rate,* a term that dates back to when bonds were issued as *bearer* bonds. The holder, or bearer, was considered the bond's owner. Back then, the company issuing the bond kept no record of changes in ownership. Bond interest was paid to whoever clipped coupons attached to the bond and sent them to the issuing company for payment. Today, bonds are registered to specific owners and changes in ownership are recorded electronically.

The interest rate paid by U.S. government bonds influences the bond interest rate businesses must pay. U.S. government bonds are considered safe investments, so they can pay lower interest. Figure 19.2 describes several types of government bonds that compete with U.S. corporate bonds in securities markets. Bond interest rates also vary according to the state of the economy, the reputation of the issuing company, and the interest rate for bonds of similar companies. Though bond interest is quoted for an entire year, it is usually paid in two installments, and the rate generally cannot be changed.

Bond rating organizations assess the creditworthiness of a corporation's bond issues. Independent rating firms such as Standard & Poor's, Moody's Investors Service, and Fitch Ratings rate bonds according to their degree of

FIGURE 19.2 TYPES OF GOVERNMENT SECURITIES THAT COMPETE WITH CORPORATE BONDS

U.S. government bond
Issued by the federal government; considered the safest type of bond investment

Treasury bill (T-bill)
Matures in less than a year; issued with a minimum denomination of $1,000

Treasury note
Matures in 10 years or less; sold in denominations of $1,000 up to $1,000,000

Treasury bond
Matures in 25 years or more; sold in denominations of $1,000 up to $1,000,000

Municipal bond
Issued by states, cities, counties, and other state and local government agencies; usually exempt from federal taxes

Yankee bond
Issued by a foreign government; payable in U.S. dollars

risk. Bonds can range from the highest quality to junk bonds (which we discuss later in this chapter). Figure 19.3 gives an example of the range of bond ratings issued by the ratings agencies.

Advantages and Disadvantages of Issuing Bonds

Bonds offer long-term financing advantages to an organization:

- Bondholders are creditors of the firm, not owners. They seldom vote on corporate matters; thus, management maintains control over the firm's operations.
- Bond interest is a business expense and tax-deductible to the firm (see Chapter 17).
- Bonds are a temporary source of funding. They're eventually repaid and the debt obligation is eliminated.
- Bonds can be repaid before the maturity date if they are *callable*. Bonds can also be converted to common stock. (We discuss both features below.)

Bonds also have financing drawbacks:

- Bonds increase debt (long-term liabilities) and may adversely affect the market's perception of the firm.
- Paying interest on bonds is a legal obligation. If interest is not paid, bondholders can take legal action to force payment.
- The face value of the bond must be repaid on the maturity date. Without careful planning, this obligation can cause cash flow problems when the repayment comes due.

Different Classes of Bonds

debenture bonds
Bonds that are unsecured (i.e., not backed by any collateral such as equipment).

Corporations can issue two different classes of corporate bonds. *Unsecured bonds*, usually called **debenture bonds**, are not backed by any specific collateral (such as land or equipment). Only firms with excellent reputations

Bond Rating Agencies			
Moody's	**Standard & Poor's**	**Fitch Ratings**	**Descriptions**
Aaa	AAA	AAA	Highest quality (lowest default risk)
Aa	AA	AA	High quality
A	A	A	Upper medium grade
Baa	BBB	BBB	Medium grade
Ba	BB	BB	Lower medium grade
B	B	B	Speculative
Caa	CCC, CC	CCC	Poor (high default risk)
Ca	C	DDD	Highly speculative
C	D	D	Lowest grade

FIGURE 19.3 BOND RATINGS: MOODY'S INVESTORS SERVICE, STANDARD & POOR'S INVESTOR SERVICE, AND FITCH RATINGS

and credit ratings can issue debenture bonds, due to the lack of security they provide investors. *Secured bonds*, sometimes called mortgage bonds, are backed by collateral such as land or buildings that is pledged to bondholders if interest or principal isn't paid when promised. A corporate bond issuer can choose to include different bond features. Let's look at some special features.

Special Bond Features

By now you should understand that bonds are issued with an interest rate, are unsecured or secured by some type of collateral, and must be repaid at their maturity date. This repayment requirement often leads companies (or governments) to establish a reserve account called a **sinking fund**. Its primary purpose is to ensure that enough money will be available to repay bondholders on the bond's maturity date. Firms issuing sinking-fund bonds periodically *retire* (set aside) some part of the principal prior to maturity so that enough funds will accumulate by the maturity date to pay off the bond. Sinking funds are generally attractive to both issuing firms and investors for several reasons:

sinking fund
A reserve account in which the issuer of a bond periodically retires some part of the bond principal prior to maturity so that enough capital will be accumulated by the maturity date to pay off the bond.

- They provide for an orderly retirement (repayment) of a bond issue.
- They reduce the risk the bond will not be repaid.
- They support the market price of the bond because they reduce the risk the bond will not be repaid.

A *callable bond* permits the bond issuer to pay off the bond's principal before its maturity date. This gives companies some discretion in their long-term forecasting. Suppose Very Vegetarian issued $10 million in 20-year bonds at 10 percent interest. Its yearly interest expense is $1 million ($10 million times 10 percent). If market conditions change and bonds of the same quality now pay only 7 percent, Very Vegetarian will be paying 3 percent, or $300,000 ($10 million times 3 percent), in excess interest yearly. The company could benefit by calling in (paying off) the old bonds and issuing new bonds at the lower rate. If a company calls a bond before maturity, it often pays investors a price above the bond's face value.

Investors can convert *convertible bonds* into shares of common stock in the issuing company. This can be an incentive for an investor because common stock value tends to grow faster than a bond. Therefore, if the value of the firm's common stock grows sizably over time, bondholders can compare the value of continued bond interest earned with the potential profit of a specified number of shares of common stock into which the bonds can be converted.[17]

Now that you understand the advantages and disadvantages of stocks and bonds as a financing tool from a company's perspective, let's explore the opportunities stocks and bonds provide for *investors*. First, though, check your progress with the Test Prep questions.

test **prep**

- Why are bonds considered a form of debt financing?
- What does it mean if a firm issues a 9 percent debenture bond due in 2025?
- Explain the difference between an unsecured and a secured bond.
- Why are convertible bonds attractive to investors?

Lo 19–5   Explain how to invest in securities markets and set investment objectives such as long-term growth, income, cash, and protection from inflation.

HOW INVESTORS BUY SECURITIES

Investing in stocks and bonds is not difficult. First, you decide what stock or bond you want to buy. After that, you find a brokerage firm authorized to trade securities to execute your order. A **stockbroker** is a registered representative who works for a brokerage firm as a market intermediary to buy and sell securities for clients. Stockbrokers place an order and negotiate a price. After the transaction is completed, the trade is reported to your broker, who notifies you. Today, large brokerage firms maintain automated order systems that allow brokers to enter your order the instant you make it. The order can be confirmed in seconds.

stockbroker
A registered representative who works as a market intermediary to buy and sell securities for clients.

*Online brokers like TD Ameritrade, Scottrade, and E*Trade specialize in providing information for investors. What are some of the features of this website that are designed to provide investment information?*

making **ethical decisions**

Money Going Up in Smoke

You recently received news that your Uncle Alex passed away after a long battle with lung cancer. To your surprise, he left you $25,000 in his will, saying you were his favorite nephew. You remember your uncle as a hard-working man who loved baseball and liked nothing better than to watch you pitch for your college team. Unfortunately, your uncle started smoking as a young man and eventually became a heavy chain-smoker. His doctors said that smoking was the primary cause of his lung cancer.

After receiving the inheritance, you wonder where to invest the money. Your old teammate, Jack, who is now a financial advisor, recommends that you buy stock in a well-known multinational firm that offers a good dividend and has solid global growth potential. He tells you the firm's primary product is tobacco, but assures you it produces many other products as well. You know Jack has your best interests at heart. You also believe Uncle Alex would like to see the money he left you grow. However, you wonder if a company that markets tobacco is an appropriate place to invest the inheritance from Uncle Alex. What are the ethical alternatives in this situation? What are the consequences of the alternatives? What will you do?

A stockbroker can also be a source of information about what stocks or bonds would best meet your financial objectives, but it's still important to learn about stocks and bonds on your own.[18] Investment analysts' advice may not always meet your specific expectations and needs.

Investing through Online Brokers

Investors can also choose from multiple online trading services to buy and sell stocks and bonds. TD Ameritrade, E*Trade, Charles Schwab, and Fidelity are among the leaders.[19] Investors who trade online are willing to do their own research and make investment decisions without the direct assistance of a broker. This allows online brokers the ability to charge much lower trading fees than traditional stockbrokers. The leading online services do provide important market information, such as company financial data, price histories of a stock, and analysts' reports. Often the level of information services you receive depends on the size of your account and your level of trading.

Whether you decide to use an online broker or to invest through a traditional stockbroker, remember that investing means committing your money with the hope of making a profit. The dot-com bubble in the early 2000s and the financial crisis that began in 2008 proved again that investing is a risky business.[20] Therefore, the first step in any investment program is to analyze your level of risk tolerance. Other factors to consider include your desired income, cash requirements, and need to hedge against inflation, along with the investment's growth prospects. The Making Ethical Decisions box describes an interesting stock investment decision.

You are never too young or too old to invest, but you should first ask questions and consider investment alternatives. Let's take a look at several strategies.

Choosing the Right Investment Strategy

Investment objectives change over the course of a person's life. A young person can better afford to invest in high-risk investment options, such as stocks, than can a person nearing retirement. Younger investors generally look for significant growth in the value of their investments over time. If stocks go into a tailspin and decrease in value, as they did in 2008, a younger person has time to wait for stock values to rise again. Older people, perhaps on a fixed income, lack the luxury of waiting and may be more inclined to invest in bonds that offer a steady return as a protection against inflation.

reaching beyond **our borders**

Global Stocks: Love Them or Leave Them

Concerns about the ups and downs of U.S. stocks may keep you from even thinking about investing in global stocks. If you also read the news about conflicts in Eastern Europe and the Middle East and natural disasters in Japan and Indonesia, the thought of investing globally may grow even less attractive. Your inclination is to forget about global stocks and play it safe with what may seem to be relatively secure U.S. securities. However, financial analysts generally recommend investing in some global stocks in order to diversify your investments.

Let's consider a few market facts that support their suggestion. If you research respected U.S. blue-chip stocks like Coca-Cola, IBM, and McDonald's, you will find they earn a large portion of their revenue from global markets. It's also important to note, at one time the United States accounted for over half of the global economy; today it accounts for about one-fourth. Economists also project developing economies in areas such as Asia and Africa will grow at a much faster pace than the United States.

Given the potential return, you would be remiss to not at least explore the opportunities that exist in global markets. However, like any investments, set your long-term financial goals and stay abreast of the daily news. Keep the following suggestions in mind as you consider global investments:

- Invest in familiar global companies with a solid reputation and record of performance. Companies like Honda (Japan), Nestlé (Switzerland), Samsung (South Korea), and Siemens (Germany) come to mind.
- Invest in only global stocks listed on U.S. exchanges. These companies must comply with U.S. accounting standards and rules of the SEC. American Depository Receipts (ADRs) are global stocks traded on U.S. exchanges and represent a set number of shares in a foreign company that are held on deposit at a U.S. bank.
- Invest in mutual and exchange-traded funds (ETFs), which offer a wide range of global opportunities. Many funds and ETFs have a mix of U.S. and foreign stocks. Others may focus strictly on specific countries such as China, on entire regions such as Africa, Asia, Europe, or Latin America, or on the entire world.
- Avoid Investing in stocks from countries with a history of currency problems or political instability.

Sources: Selena Maranjian, "Foreign Stocks with Dividends," *The Motley Fool*, January 2, 2014; Robert Schmansky, "How Much Should You Invest in International Stock Mutual Funds?" *Forbes*, August 8, 2013; and John Waggoner, "Investing: Simplify Life, Go Global, with Funds," *USA Today*, March 14, 2013.

Consider five key criteria when selecting investment options:

1. *Investment risk.* The chance that an investment will be worth less at some future time than it's worth now.
2. *Yield.* The expected return on an investment, such as interest or dividends, usually over a period of one year.
3. *Duration.* The length of time your money is committed to an investment.
4. *Liquidity.* How quickly you can get back your invested funds in cash if you want or need them.
5. *Tax consequences.* How the investment will affect your tax situation.

What's important in any investment strategy is the risk/return trade-off. Setting investment objectives such as *growth* (choosing stocks you believe will increase in price) or *income* (choosing bonds that pay consistent interest) should set the tone for your investment strategy.

Reducing Risk by Diversifying Investments

diversification
Buying several different investment alternatives to spread the risk of investing.

Diversification involves buying several different types of investments to spread the risk of investing. An investor may put 25 percent of his or her money into U.S. stocks that have relatively high risk but strong growth potential, another 25 percent in conservative government bonds, 25 percent in dividend-paying stocks that provide income, 10 percent in an international mutual fund (discussed later), and the rest in the bank for emergencies and other possible investment opportunities. By diversifying with such a *portfolio strategy* or *allocation model,* investors decrease the chance of losing everything they have invested.[21]

Both stockbrokers and certified financial planners (CFPs) are trained to give advice about the investment portfolio that would best fit each client's financial objectives. However, the more investors themselves read and study the market, the higher their potential for gain. A short course in investments can also be useful. Stocks and bonds are investment opportunities individuals can use to enhance their financial future. The Reaching Beyond Our Borders box discusses growing opportunities investors can find in global stocks. Before we look at stocks and bonds in depth, let's check your understanding with the Test Prep.

capital gains
The positive difference between the purchase price of a stock and its sale price.

test prep

- What is the key advantage of investing through online brokers? What is the key disadvantage?
- What is the primary purpose of diversifying investments?

LO 19–6   Analyze the opportunities stocks offer as investments.

INVESTING IN STOCKS

Buying stock makes investors part owners of a company. This means that as stockholders they can participate in its success. Unfortunately, they can also lose money if a company does not do well or the overall stock market declines.

Stock investors are often called bulls or bears according to their perceptions of the market. *Bulls* believe that stock prices are going to rise; they buy stock in anticipation of the increase. A bull market is when overall stock prices are rising. *Bears* expect stock prices to decline and sell their stocks in anticipation of falling prices. That's why, when stock prices are declining, the market is called a bear market.

The market price and growth potential of most stock depends heavily on how well the corporation is meeting its business objectives. A company that achieves its objectives offers great potential for **capital gains**, the positive difference between the price at which you bought a stock and what you sell it for. For example, an investment of $2,250 in 100 shares of McDonald's when the company first offered its stock to the public in 1965 would have grown to 74,360 shares (after the company's 12 stock splits) worth approximately $7.4 million as of year-end market close on December 31, 2013.[22] Now that's a lot of Big Macs!

Investors often select stocks depending on their investment strategy. Stocks issued by higher-quality companies such as Coca-Cola, Johnson & Johnson, and IBM are referred to as *blue-chip stocks* (a term derived from poker where the highest value chip was the blue chip). These stocks

It's fun to stop and enjoy a Dairy Queen sundae, especially if you own the company. Warren Buffett, America's most successful investor, built his fortune through prudent investing and is the second wealthiest person (after Bill Gates) in the United States. Rather than waiting until after his death, Buffett began giving the bulk of his fortune to the Gates Foundation in 2006. His annual donation is approximately $2 billion.

If you stroll through Times Square in New York City, you never have to wonder how stocks on the NASDAQ exchange are performing. The NASDAQ price wall continuously updates prices and the number of shares being traded. Originally, the NASDAQ dealt primarily with small companies; today, it competes with the NYSE Euronext for new stock listings.

stock splits
An action by a company that gives stockholders two or more shares of stock for each one they own.

buying stock on margin
Purchasing stocks by borrowing some of the purchase cost from the brokerage firm.

generally pay regular dividends and experience consistent price appreciation.

Stocks of corporations in emerging fields such as technology, biotechnology, or Internet-related firms, whose earnings are expected to grow at a faster rate than other stocks, are referred to as *growth stocks*. While riskier, growth stocks may offer the potential for higher returns. Stocks of public utilities are considered *income stocks* because they usually offer investors a high dividend yield that generally keeps pace with inflation. There are even *penny stocks*, representing ownership in companies that compete in high-risk industries like oil exploration. Penny stocks sell for less than $2 (some analysts say less than $5) and are considered risky investments.[23]

When purchasing stock, investors have choices when placing buy orders. A *market order* tells a broker to buy or sell a stock immediately at the best price available. A *limit order* tells the broker to buy or sell a stock at a specific price, if that price becomes available. Let's say a stock is selling for $40 a share. You believe the price will eventually go higher but could drop to $36 first. You can place a limit order at $36, so your broker will buy the stock at $36 if it drops to that price. If the stock never falls to $36, the broker will not purchase it for you.

Stock Splits

Brokers prefer stock purchases in *round lots* of 100 shares at a time. Investors, however, often cannot afford to buy 100 shares, and therefore often buy in *odd lots*, or fewer than 100 shares at a time. High per-share prices can induce companies to declare **stock splits**, in which they issue two or more shares for every one that's outstanding. If Very Vegetarian stock were selling for $100 a share, the firm could declare a two-for-one stock split. Investors who owned one share of Very Vegetarian would now own two, each worth only $50 (half as much as before the split).

Stock splits cause no change in the firm's ownership structure and no immediate change in the investment's value. Investors generally approve of stock splits, however, because they believe demand for a stock may be greater at $50 than at $100, and the price may then go up in the near future. A company cannot be forced to split its stock, and today stock splits are becoming less common.[24] Legendary investor Warren Buffett's firm, Berkshire Hathaway, has never split its Class A stock even when its per-share price surpassed $150,000. Google, however, decided to split its stock two-for-one after the stock price exceeded $1,000 per share, and credit card giant MasterCard split its stock ten-for-one as its stock price neared $900 per share.[25]

Buying Stock on Margin

Buying stock on margin means borrowing some of the stocks' purchase cost from the brokerage firm. The margin is the portion of the stocks' purchase price that investors must pay with their own money. The board of governors of the Federal Reserve System sets *margin rates* in the U.S. market. Briefly, if the margin rate is 50 percent, an investor who qualifies for a margin account may borrow up to 50 percent of the stock's purchase price from the broker.

Although buying on margin sounds like an easy way to buy more stocks, the downside is that investors must repay the credit extended by the broker, plus interest. If the investor's account goes down in value, the broker may issue a *margin call*, requiring the investor to come up with funds to cover the losses the account has suffered.[26] If the investor is unable to fulfill the margin call, the broker can legally sell off shares of the investor's stock to reduce the broker's chance of loss. Margin calls can force an investor to repay a significant portion of his or her account's loss within days or even hours. Buying on margin is thus a risky way to invest in stocks.

Understanding Stock Quotations

Publications like *The Wall Street Journal*, *Barron's*, and *Investor's Business Daily* carry a wealth of information concerning stocks and other investments. Your local newspaper may carry similar information as well. Financial websites like MSN Money, Yahoo! Finance, and CNBC carry up-to-the-minute information about companies that is much more detailed and only a click away. Take a look at Figure 19.4 to see an example of a stock quote from MSN Money for Microsoft. Microsoft trades on the NASDAQ exchange under the symbol MSFT. Preferred stock is identified by the letters *pf* following the company symbol. Remember, corporations can have several different preferred stock issues.

The information provided in the quote is easy to understand. It includes the highest and lowest price the stock traded for that day, the stock's high and low over the past 52 weeks, the dividend paid (if any), the stock's dividend yield (annual dividend as a percentage of the stock's price per share), important ratios like the price/earnings (P/E) ratio (the price of the stock divided by the firm's per-share earnings), and the earnings per share. Investors can also see the number of shares traded (volume) and the total market capitalization of the firm. More technical features, such as the stock's beta (which measures the degree of the stock's risk), may also appear. Figure 19.4 illustrates the stock's intraday trading (trading throughout the current day), but you can also click to see charts for different time periods. Similar information about bonds, mutual funds, and other investments is also available online.

You might want to follow the market behavior of specific stocks that catch your interest, even if you lack the money to invest in them. Many successful investors started in college by building hypothetical portfolios of stocks and tracking their performance. The more you know about investing before you

FIGURE 19.4 UNDERSTANDING STOCK QUOTATIONS

Microsoft Corporation (MSFT) - NasdaqGS ⭐ Follow

45.22 ↑0.27 (0.60%) 4:00PM EDT

After Hours : **45.20** ↓0.02 (0.04%) 5:59PM EDT

Prev Close:	44.95	Day's Range:	44.83 - 45.25
Open:	44.88	52wk Range:	30.95 - 45.71
Bid:	45.18 x 600	Volume:	22,272,025
Ask:	45.20 x 100	Avg Vol (3m):	28,677,000
1y Target Est:	47.00	Market Cap:	372.61B
Beta: .	0.68	P/E (ttm):	16.94
Earnings Date:	Oct 22 - Oct 27 (Est.)	EPS (ttm):	2.67
		Div & Yield:	1.12 (2.70%)

actually risk your money, the better. (The Developing Workplace Skills and Taking It to the Net exercises at the end of this chapter have exercises you can use for practice.)

LO 19–7   Analyze the opportunities bonds offer as investments.

INVESTING IN BONDS

Investors looking for guaranteed income and limited risk often turn to U.S. government bonds for a secure investment. These bonds have the financial backing and full faith and credit of the federal government. Municipal bonds are offered by local governments and often have advantages such as tax-free interest. Some may even be insured. Corporate bonds are a bit riskier and more challenging.

First-time corporate bond investors often ask two questions. The first is, "If I purchase a corporate bond, do I have to hold it until the maturity date?" No, you do not. Bonds are bought and sold daily on major securities exchanges (the secondary market we discussed earlier). However, if you decide to sell your bond to another investor before its maturity date, you may not get its face value. If your bond does not have features that make it attractive to other investors, like a high interest rate or early maturity, you may have to sell at a *discount*, that is, a price less than the bond's face value. But if other investors do highly value it, you may be able to sell your bond at a *premium*, a price above its face value. Bond prices generally fluctuate inversely with current market interest rates. This means *as interest rates go up, bond prices fall, and vice versa*. Like all investments, however, bonds have a degree of risk.

The second question is, "How can I evaluate the investment risk of a particular bond issue?" Standard & Poor's, Moody's Investors Service, and Fitch Ratings rate the risk of many corporate and government bonds (look back at Figure 19.3). In evaluating the ratings, recall the risk/return trade-off: The higher the risk of a bond, the higher the interest rate the issuer must offer. Investors will invest in a bond considered risky only if the potential return (interest) is high enough. In fact, some will invest in bonds considered junk.

Investing in High-Risk (Junk) Bonds

junk bonds
High-risk, high-interest bonds.

Although bonds are considered relatively safe investments, some investors look for higher returns through riskier high-yield bonds called **junk bonds**. Standard & Poor's, Moody's Investors Service, and Fitch Ratings define junk bonds as those with high risk *and* high default rates.[27] Junk bonds pay investors interest as long as the value of the company's assets remains high and its cash flow stays strong. Although the interest rates are attractive and often tempting, if the company can't pay off the bond, the investor is left with an investment that isn't worth more than the paper it's written on—in other words, junk.

Understanding Bond Quotations

Bond prices are quoted as a percentage of $1,000, and their interest rate is often followed by an *s* for easier pronunciation. For example, 9 percent bonds due in 2025 are called 9s of 25. Figure 19.5 is an example of a bond quote for Goldman Sachs from Yahoo! Finance. The quote highlights the bond's interest rate (coupon rate), maturity date, rating, current price, and whether it's callable. The more you know about bonds, the better prepared you will be to discuss your financial objectives with investment advisors and brokers and be sure their advice is consistent with your best interests and objectives.

GOLDMAN SACHS GROUP INC

OVERVIEW	
Price:	100.74
Coupon (%):	5.000
Maturity Date:	1-Oct-2014
Yield to Maturity (%):	-11.265
Current Yield (%):	4.963
Fitch Ratings:	A
Coupon Payment Frequency:	Semi-Annual
First Coupon Date:	1-Apr-2005
Type:	Corporate
Callable:	No

OFFERING INFORMATION	
Quantity Available:	13
Minimum Trade Qty:	1
Dated Date:	29-Sep-2004
Settlement Date:	15-Sep-2014

FIGURE 19.5
UNDERSTANDING BOND QUOTATIONS

LO 19–8 Explain the investment opportunities in mutual funds and exchange-traded funds (ETFs).

INVESTING IN MUTUAL FUNDS AND EXCHANGE-TRADED FUNDS

A **mutual fund** buys stocks, bonds, and other investments and then sells shares in those securities to the public. A mutual fund is like an investment company that pools investors' money and then buys stocks or bonds (for example) in many companies in accordance with the fund's specific purpose. Mutual fund managers are specialists who pick what they consider to be the best stocks and bonds available and help investors diversify their investments.

Mutual funds range from very conservative funds that invest only in government securities to others that specialize in emerging biotechnology firms, Internet companies, foreign companies, precious metals, and other investments with greater risk. Some funds will have a mix of investments like stocks and bonds. The number of mutual funds available today is staggering. For example, there were over 4,600 mutual funds investing in U.S. stocks in 2013.[28] Investors have invested over $13 trillion in mutual funds. Figure 19.6 gives you a list of some mutual fund investment options.

Young or new investors are often advised to buy shares in *index funds* that invest in a certain kind of stocks or bonds or in the market as a whole.[29] An index fund may focus on large companies, small companies, emerging countries, or real estate (real estate investment trusts, or REITs). One way to diversify your investments is by investing in a variety of index funds. A stockbroker, certified financial planner (CFP), or banker can help you find the option that best fits your investment objectives. The *Morningstar Investor* newsletter is an excellent resource for evaluating mutual funds, as are business publications such as *Bloomberg Businessweek*, *The Wall Street Journal*, *Money*, *Forbes*, *Investor's Business Daily*, and many others.

With mutual funds it's simple to change your investment objectives if your financial objectives change. For example, moving your money from a bond fund to a stock fund is no more difficult than making a phone call, clicking a mouse, or tapping your cellphone. Another advantage of mutual funds is that you can generally buy directly from the fund and avoid broker fees or

mutual fund
An organization that buys stocks and bonds and other investments, then sells shares in those securities to the public.

FIGURE 19.6 MUTUAL FUND OBJECTIVES

Mutual funds have a wide array of investment categories. They range from low-risk, conservative funds to others that invest in high-risk industries. Listed here are abbreviations of funds and what these abbreviations stand for.

AB	Investment-grade corporate bonds	MP	Stock and bond fund
AU	Gold oriented	MT	Mortgage securities
BL	Balanced	MV	Mid-cap value
EI	Equity income	NM	Insured municipal bonds
EM	Emerging markets	NR	Natural resources
EU	European region	PR	Pacific region
GL	Global	SB	Short-term corporate bonds
GM	General municipal bond	SC	Small-cap core
GT	General taxable bonds	SE	Sector funds
HB	Health/biotech	SG	Small-cap growth
HC	High-yield bonds	SM	Short-term municipal bonds
HM	High-yield municipal bonds	SP	S&P 500
IB	Intermediate-term corporate bonds	SQ	Specialty
IG	Intermediate-term government bonds	SS	Single-state municipal bonds
IL	International	SU	Short-term government bonds
IM	Intermediate-term municipal bonds	SV	Small-cap value
LC	Large-cap core	TK	Science & technology
LG	Large-cap growth	UN	Unassigned
LT	Latin America	UT	Utility
LU	Long-term U.S. bonds	WB	World bonds
LV	Large-cap value	XC	Multi-cap core
MC	Mid-cap core	XG	Multi-cap growth
MG	Mid-cap growth	XV	Multi-cap value

Sources: *The Wall Street Journal* and *Investor's Business Daily.*

commissions. However, check for fees and charges of the mutual fund because they can differ significantly. A *load fund*, for example, charges investors a commission to buy or sell its shares; a *no-load fund* charges no commission.[30]

It's important to check the long-term performance of the fund's managers; the more consistent the performance of the fund's management, the better. Mutual funds called *open-end funds* will accept the investments of any interested investors. *Closed-end funds*, however, limit the number of shares; once the fund reaches its target number, no new investors can buy into the fund.[31]

Exchange-traded funds (ETFs) resemble both stocks and mutual funds. They are collections of stocks, bonds, and other investments that are traded on securities exchanges, but are traded more like individual stocks than like mutual funds. Mutual funds, for example, permit investors to buy and sell shares only at the close of the trading day. ETFs can be purchased or sold at any time during the trading day just like individual stocks. Investors have invested over $1.6 trillion in ETFs.

The key points to remember about mutual funds and ETFs is that they offer small investors a way to spread the risk of stock and bond ownership and have their investments managed by a financial specialist for a fee. Financial advisors put mutual funds and ETFs high on the list of recommended investments, particularly for small or first-time investors.[32]

exchange-traded funds (ETFs)
Collections of stocks, bonds, and other investments that are traded on exchanges but are traded more like individual stocks than like mutual funds.

Understanding Mutual Fund Quotations

You can investigate the specifics of various mutual funds by contacting a broker or contacting the fund directly by phone or through its website. Business publications and online sources also provide information about mutual funds.

Look at the example of the Pimco High Income fund from Yahoo! Finance in Figure 19.7. The fund's name is listed in large letters. The quotation includes the price of the fund, as well as the previous day's closing price and the opening price. The chart also shows the 52-week range, the daily and average volumes, the earnings per share, and the dividend/yield.

Figure 19.8 evaluates bonds, stocks, mutual funds, and ETFs according to risk, income, and possible investment growth (capital gain).

Pimco High Income Fund Pimco Hi (PHK) - NYSE ★ Follow

13.01 ↑0.01(0.08%) 4:05PM EDT

Prev Close:	13.00	Day's Range:	12.95 - 13.02
Open:	12.99	52wk Range:	11.47 - 13.75
Bid:	12.94 x 1000	Volume:	527,469
Ask:	13.01 x 200	Avg Vol (3m):	639,641
1y Target Est:	N/A	Market Cap:	N/A
Beta:	N/A	P/E (ttm):	N/A
Next Earnings Date:	N/A	EPS (ttm):	-0.12
		Div & Yield:	1.06 (7.70%)

FIGURE 19.7
UNDERSTANDING MUTUAL FUND QUOTATIONS

Investment	Degree of risk	Expected income	Possible growth (capital gain)
Bonds	Low	Secure	Little
Preferred stock	Medium	Steady	Little
Common stock	High	Variable	Good
Mutual funds	Medium	Variable	Good
ETFs	Medium	Variable	Good

FIGURE 19.8
COMPARING INVESTMENTS

test prep

- What is a stock split? Why do companies sometimes split their stock?
- What does buying stock on margin mean?
- What are mutual funds and ETFs?
- What is the key benefit to investors in investing in a mutual fund or ETF?

Use LearnSmart to help retain what you have learned. Access your instructor's Connect course to check out LearnSmart, or go to learnsmartadvantage.com for help.

▤ LEARNSMART

LO 19–9 Describe how indicators like the Dow Jones Industrial Average affect the market.

UNDERSTANDING STOCK MARKET INDICATORS

Investors today have an enormous wealth of investment information available to them. Newspapers like *The Wall Street Journal, Barron's,* and *Investor's Business Daily* provide vast amounts of information about companies and global markets. Television networks like MSNBC and CNBC offer daily investment analysis and different viewpoints to assist investors. Websites like MSN Money and Yahoo! Finance offer financial information to investors free of charge that not long ago was available only to brokers for a hefty fee. But keep in mind that investing is an inexact science. Every time someone sells a stock, believing it will fall, someone else is buying it, believing its price will go higher.

You often hear business news reports include a comment like, "The Dow was up 90 points today in active trading." Ever wonder what that's all about? The **Dow Jones Industrial Average (the Dow)** is the average cost of 30 selected industrial stocks. The financial industry uses it to give an indication of the direction (up or down) of the stock market over time. Charles Dow began the practice of measuring stock averages in 1884, using the prices of 12 key stocks. In 1982, the Dow was broadened to include 30 stocks. The 12 original and the 30 current stocks in the Dow are illustrated in Figure 19.9. Do you recognize any of the 12 original companies?

Today, Dow Jones & Company substitutes new stocks in the Dow when it's deemed appropriate. In 1991, Disney was added to reflect the increased economic importance of the service sector. In 1999, the Dow added Home Depot and SBC Communications along with its first NASDAQ stocks, Intel and Microsoft. In 2013, Visa, Goldman Sachs, and Nike replaced Alcoa, Bank of America, and Hewlett-Packard.[33]

Critics argue that the 30-company Dow sample is too small to get a good statistical representation of the direction of the market over time. Many investors and analysts prefer to follow stock indexes like the Standard & Poor's 500 (S&P 500), which tracks the performance of 400 industrial, 40 financial, 40 public utility, and 20 transportation stocks. Investors also closely follow the NASDAQ average, which is quoted each trading day to show trends in this important exchange.

Staying abreast of the market will help you decide what investments seem most appropriate to your needs and objectives. Remember two key investment realities: Your personal financial objectives and needs change over time, and markets can be volatile. Let's look at market volatility and the challenges that present investors with new risks and opportunities.

Dow Jones Industrial Average (the Dow)
The average cost of 30 selected industrial stocks, used to give an indication of the direction (up or down) of the stock market over time.

FIGURE 19.9 THE ORIGINAL DOW AND CURRENT DOW

THE ORIGINAL DOW 12	THE 30 CURRENT DOW COMPANIES	
American Cotton Oil	American Express	JPMorgan Chase
American Sugar Refining Co.	AT&T	McDonald's
American Tobacco	Boeing	Merck
Chicago Gas	Caterpillar	Microsoft
Distilling & Cattle Feeding Co.	Chevron	3M
General Electric Co.	Cisco	Nike
Laclede Gas Light Co.	Coca-Cola	Pfizer
National Lead	DuPont	Procter & Gamble
North American Co.	ExxonMobil	Travelers
Tennessee Coal, Iron & Railroad Co.	General Electric	United Health Group
U.S. Leather	Goldman Sachs	United Technologies
U.S. Rubber Co.	Home Depot	Verizon
	IBM	Visa
	Intel	Wal-Mart Stores
	Johnson & Johnson	Walt Disney

Riding the Market's Roller Coaster

Throughout the 1900s, the stock market had its ups and downs, spiced with several major tremors. The first major crash occurred on Tuesday, October 29, 1929 (called Black Tuesday), when the stock market lost almost 13 percent of its value in a single day. This day, and the deep depression that followed, reinforced the reality of market volatility, especially to those who bought stocks heavily on margin. On October 19, 1987, the stock market suffered the largest one-day drop in its history, losing over 22 percent of its value. On October 27, 1997, investors again felt the market's fury. Fears of an impending economic crisis in Asia caused panic and widespread losses. Luckily, the market regained its strength after a short downturn.

After regaining strength in the late 1990s, the market again suffered misfortune in the early 2000s. All told, investors lost $7 trillion in market value from 2000 through 2002 due to the burst of the tech stock bubble. A recovery that started in the mid-2000s was cut short in 2008, when the financial crisis fueled a massive exodus from the stock market, resulting in record losses.

What caused the market turmoil of 1987, 1997, 2000–2002, and 2008? In 1987, many analysts agreed it was **program trading**, in which investors give their computers instructions to sell automatically to avoid potential losses, if the price of their stock dips to a certain point. On October 19, 1987, computers' sell orders caused many stocks to fall to unbelievable depths. The crash prompted the U.S. exchanges to create mechanisms called *curbs* and *circuit breakers* to restrict program trading whenever the market moves up or down by a large number of points in a trading day. A key computer is turned off and program trading is halted. If you watch programming on CNBC or MSNBC, you'll see the phrase *curbs in* appear on the screen.

Circuit breakers are more drastic than curbs and are triggered when the Dow falls 10, 20, or 30 percent in a day. That happened on October 27, 1997, when the market suffered an approximate 7 percent decline and the market closed for the day at 3:30 p.m. instead of 4:00. Many believe the 1997 market drop (caused by the financial crisis in Asia) could have been much worse without the trading restrictions. Depending on the rate of decline and the time of day, circuit breakers will halt trading for half an hour to two hours so traders have time to assess the situation.

program trading
Giving instructions to computers to automatically sell if the price of a stock dips to a certain point to avoid potential losses.

Investing in the stock market has never been for the faint of heart. The market seems to have continuous steep climbs and sharp falls. Do you have the risk tolerance to survive the wild market swings?

Huge swings in the market cause much anguish among Wall Street workers and people in general. What have we learned from market bubbles like those in technology and real estate?

In the late 1990s the stock market reached unparalleled heights only to collapse into a deep decline in 2000–2002. The bursting of the dot-com bubble was the primary reason. A bubble is caused when too many investors drive the price of something (in this case dot-com stocks) unrealistically high.

The dot-com crash was, unfortunately, accompanied by disclosures of financial fraud at companies such as WorldCom, Enron, and Tyco. Investors had trusted that the real value of these companies was fairly reflected in their financial statements. This trust was shattered when they found investment analysts often provided clients with wildly optimistic evaluations and recommendations about companies they knew were not worth their current prices.

After the financial downturn caused by the dot-com bubble, the stock market surged in the mid-2000s and set a new high. The market's growth was dramatic, especially in the real estate sector. From 2000 to 2006 prices of existing homes rose 50 percent; however, between 2006 and 2011, housing values fell $6.3 trillion. The real estate bubble was like the dot-com bubble before it: Investors believed that home prices would increase forever. Financial institutions reduced their lending requirements for buyers, homebuilders overbuilt, and buyers overspent, all sharing blame for the crisis. The government also contributed to the problem by requiring more mortgages be given to low- and moderate-income buyers, many with weak credit scores or no verification of income or assets. These *subprime* loans were pooled together and repackaged as mortgage-backed securities that were sold to investors (discussed in Chapter 20). What followed were huge numbers of foreclosures, the failure of government-sponsored mortgage giants Fannie Mae and Freddie Mac, and more than 350 bank failures.

The collapse of the real estate market caused the economy a combined loss of $8 trillion in housing and commercial property. Financial institutions, like Lehman Brothers, went out of business and Wall Street icon Merrill Lynch was purchased by Bank of America. With financial markets in the worst condition since the Great Depression and the economy in a deep recession, the federal government took action. Congress passed a $700 billion financial package called the Troubled Asset Relief Program (TARP) that allowed the Treasury Department to purchase or insure "troubled assets" to bolster banks and bail out the automotive industry and insurer American International Group (AIG). Unfortunately, in 2009 the economy continued to decline and unemployment grew to double digits, causing President Obama to encourage passage of an $800 billion economic stimulus package—a blend of tax cuts and increased government spending—that was intended to reduce unemployment and provide a "significant boost" to the crippled economy.

Since 2009, the economy has slowly recovered. Unfortunately, unemployment has remained high and consumers remain skeptical about the nation's economic future. Also, of the 5 million Americans who suffered foreclosure on their homes due to the financial crisis, many do not see owning another home as part of the "American Dream."[34] On the positive side, the amount of TARP funds the government spent did not approximate the $700 billion that was appropriated. The troubled banks repaid most of the money they received through TARP (with interest) and AIG repaid the government in full. The government did lose $10 billion when it sold its final shares of General Motors. Since then, the stock market has experienced growth and again moved to new highs.[35] What the future of the stock market will be remains to be seen.

Key Dodd-Frank Provisions

- Gave the government power to seize and shutter large financial institutions on the verge of collapse.
- Put derivatives and complicated financial deals (including those that packaged subprime mortgages) under strict governmental oversight.
- Required hedge funds to register with the SEC and provide information about trades and portfolio holdings.
- Created the Consumer Financial Protection Bureau to watch over the interests of American consumers by reviewing and enforcing federal financial laws.

FIGURE 19.10 CLEANING UP THE STREET
Key Provisions of the Dodd-Frank Wall Street Reform and Consumer Protection Act

Investing Challenges in the 21st-Century Market

As you can see from the previous section, in the stock market, what goes up may also go down. Financial markets will likely experience changes in the future that will only heighten investor risk. The financial crisis also reinforced the fact that the world's economies are closely linked. The United States was not the only nation affected by the financial crisis; financial markets in Europe, Asia, and South America felt the pain as well. Persistent challenges and even political and social change promise to make securities markets exciting but not stable places to be in the 21st century. Figure 19.10 highlights new government regulations designed to address some of these challenges.

Remember to diversify your investments, and be mindful of the risks of investing. Taking a long-term perspective is also a wise idea. There's no such thing as easy money or a sure thing. If you carefully research companies and industries, keep up with the news, and make use of investment resources—such as newspapers, magazines, newsletters, the Internet, TV programs, and college classes—the payoff can be rewarding over time.

test prep

- What does the Dow Jones Industrial Average measure? Why is it important?
- Why do the 30 companies comprising the Dow change periodically?
- Explain program trading and the problems it can create.

Use LearnSmart to help retain what you have learned. Access your instructor's Connect course to check out LearnSmart, or go to learnsmartadvantage.com for help.

LEARNSMART

summary

LO 19–1   Describe the role of securities markets and of investment bankers.

- **What opportunities do securities markets provide businesses and individual investors?**
  By issuing securities businesses are able to raise much-needed funding to help finance their major expenses. Individual investors can share in the success and growth of emerging or established firms by investing in them.

Access your instructor's Connect course to check out LearnSmart or go to learnsmartadvantage.com for help.

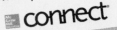

- **What role do investment bankers play in securities markets?**
Investment bankers are specialists who assist in the issue and sale of new securities.

LO 19–2   Identify the stock exchanges where securities are traded.

- **What are stock exchanges?**
Stock exchanges are securities markets whose members are engaged in buying and selling securities such as stocks and bonds.

- **What are the different exchanges?**
The NYSE Euronext lists the stock of over 8,000 companies. The NASDAQ is a telecommunications network that links dealers across the nation so that they can buy and sell securities electronically rather than in person. It is the largest U.S. electronic stock trading market. There are stock exchanges all over the world.

- **What is the over-the-counter (OTC) market?**
The OTC market is a system for exchanging stocks not listed on the national exchanges.

- **How are securities exchanges regulated?**
The Securities and Exchange Commission (SEC) regulates securities exchanges and requires companies that intend to sell bonds or stocks to provide a prospectus to potential investors.

- **What is insider trading?**
Insider trading is the use of information or knowledge that individuals gain that allows them to benefit unfairly from fluctuations in security prices.

LO 19–3   Compare the advantages and disadvantages of equity financing by issuing stock, and detail the differences between common and preferred stock.

- **What are the advantages and disadvantages to a firm of selling stock?**
The advantages of selling stock include the following: (1) the stock price never has to be repaid to stockholders, since they become owners in the company; (2) there is no legal obligation to pay stock dividends; and (3) the company incurs no debt, so it may appear financially stronger. Disadvantages of selling stock include the following: (1) stockholders become owners of the firm and can affect its management by voting for the board of directors; (2) it is more costly to pay dividends since they are paid in after-tax profits; and (3) managers may be tempted to make stockholders happy in the short term rather than plan for long-term needs.

- **What are the differences between common and preferred stock?**
Holders of common stock have voting rights in the company. In exchange for having no voting rights, preferred stockholders receive a fixed dividend that must be paid in full before common stockholders receive a dividend. Preferred stockholders are also paid back their investment before common stockholders if the company is forced out of business.

LO 19–4   Compare the advantages and disadvantages of obtaining debt financing by issuing bonds, and identify the classes and features of bonds.

- **What are the advantages and disadvantages of issuing bonds?**
The advantages of issuing bonds include the following: (1) management retains control since bondholders cannot vote; (2) interest paid on bonds is

tax-deductible; (3) bonds are only a temporary source of financing, and after they are paid off the debt is eliminated; (4) bonds can be paid back early if they are callable; and (5) sometimes bonds can be converted to common stock. The disadvantages of bonds include the following: (1) because bonds are an increase in debt, they may adversely affect the market's perception of the company; (2) the firm must pay interest on its bonds; and (3) the firm must repay the bond's face value on the maturity date.

- **What are the different types of bonds?**
  Unsecured (debenture) bonds are not supported by collateral, whereas secured bonds are backed by tangible assets such as mortgages, buildings, and equipment.

LO 19–5   Explain how to invest in securities markets and set investment objectives such as long-term growth, income, cash, and protection from inflation.

- **How do investors normally make purchases in securities markets?**
  Investors can purchase investments through market intermediaries called stockbrokers, who provide many different services. Online investing, however, has become extremely popular.

- **What are the criteria for selecting investments?**
  Investors should determine their overall financial objectives and evaluate investments according to (1) risk, (2) yield, (3) duration, (4) liquidity, and (5) tax consequences.

- **What is diversification?**
  Diversification means buying several different types of investments (government bonds, corporate bonds, preferred stock, common stock, global stock) with different degrees of risk. The purpose is to reduce the overall risk an investor would assume by investing in just one type of security.

LO 19–6   Analyze the opportunities stocks offer as investments.

- **What is a market order?**
  A market order tells a broker to buy or sell a security immediately at the best price available.

- **A limit order?**
  A limit order tells the broker to buy or sell if the stock reaches a specific price.

- **What does it mean when a stock splits?**
  When a stock splits, stockholders receive two (or more) shares of stock for each share they own. Each is worth half (or less) of the original share, so while the number of the shares increases, the total value of stockholders' holdings stays the same. Stockholders hope the lower per-share price that results may increase demand for the stock.

- **What does buying on margin mean?**
  An investor buying on margin borrows part (the percentage allowed to be borrowed is set by the Federal Reserve) of the cost of a stock from the broker to get shares of stock without immediately paying the full price.

- **What type of information do stock quotations give you?**
  Stock quotations provide the highest and lowest price in the last 52 weeks; the dividend yield; the price/earnings ratio; the total shares traded that day; and the closing price and net change in price from the previous day.

LO 19–7   Analyze the opportunities bonds offer as investments.

- **What is the difference between a bond selling at a discount and a bond selling at a premium?**
  In the secondary market a bond selling at a premium is priced above its face value. A bond selling at a discount sells below its face value.

- **What is a junk bond?**
  Junk bonds are high-risk (rated BB or below), high-interest debenture bonds that speculative investors often find attractive.

- **What information does a bond quotation give you?**
  A bond quotation gives the bond's interest rate (coupon rate), maturity date, rating, current price, and whether it's callable.

LO 19–8   Explain the investment opportunities in mutual funds and exchange-traded funds (ETFs).

- **How can mutual funds help individuals diversify their investments?**
  A mutual fund is an organization that buys stocks and bonds and then sells shares in those securities to the public, enabling individuals to invest in many more companies than they could otherwise afford.

- **What are ETFs?**
  Like mutual funds, ETFs are collections of stocks that are traded on securities exchanges, but they are traded more like individual stocks.

LO 19–9   Describe how indicators like the Dow Jones Industrial Average affect the market.

- **What is the Dow Jones Industrial Average?**
  The Dow Jones Industrial Average is the average price of 30 specific stocks that analysts use to track the direction (up or down) of the stock market.

key terms

bond 539	**initial public offering (IPO)** 532	**preferred stock** 538
buying stock on margin 546	**institutional investors** 533	**program trading** 553
capital gains 545	**interest** 539	**prospectus** 535
common stock 537	**investment bankers** 533	**Securities and Exchange Commission (SEC)** 534
debenture bonds 540	**junk bonds** 548	
diversification 544	**maturity date** 539	**sinking fund** 541
dividends 537	**mutual fund** 549	**stockbroker** 542
Dow Jones Industrial Average (the Dow) 552	**NASDAQ** 534	**stock certificate** 537
exchange-traded funds (ETFs) 550	**over-the-counter (OTC) market** 534	**stock exchange** 533
		stocks 537
		stock splits 546

critical thinking

1. Imagine you inherited $50,000 and you want to invest it to meet two financial goals: (*a*) to save for your wedding, which you plan to have in two years, and (*b*) to save for your retirement a few decades from now. How would you invest the money? Explain your answer.

2. If you are considering investing in the bond market, how could information provided by Standard & Poor's, Moody's Investors Service, and Fitch Ratings help you?

3. Why do companies like callable bonds? Why are investors generally not very fond of them?

4. If you were thinking about investing in the securities market, would you prefer individual stocks, mutual funds, or ETFs? Explain your choice by comparing the advantages and disadvantages of each.

5. Consider the companies added and subtracted from the Dow Jones Industrial Average over the past five years. (Go to www.djaverages.com, then proceed to Dow Jones Learning Center to learn more about these companies.) What types of companies were added and deleted? Why do you think the changes were made? Do you think new changes will be made in the next five years? Why?

---

developing **workplace skills**

Key: ● **Team**   ★ **Analytic**   ▲ **Communication**   ▣ **Technology**

1. Go to the websites of Charles Schwab (www.schwab.com), E*Trade ▣★▲
   (www.etrade.com), and TD Ameritrade (www.tdameritrade.com). Investigate each of these brokerage companies to compare their fees and what they offer in terms of research and advice. Which firm seems most appropriate to your investment objectives? Be prepared to defend your choice to the class.

2. Visit MSN Money or Yahoo! Finance and select six stocks for your ▣★▲
   portfolio—three from the NYSE and three from the NASDAQ. Track the stocks daily for three weeks using the graphs provided on the websites to see how market trends and information affected your stock's performance. Report your observations.

3. U.S. government bonds compete with corporations for investors' dollars. ▣★▲
   Check out the different types of bonds the federal government offers and list the types most appealing to you. (Hint: See www.treasurydirect.gov.) Be sure to check out TIPs.

4. See whether anyone in class is interested in forming an investment group. ●▣★▲
   If so, each member should choose one stock and one mutual fund or ETF. Record each student's selections and the corresponding prices. In two weeks measure the percentage of change in the investments and discuss the results.

5. Go to the websites of Charles Schwab (www.schwab.com), E*Trade ▣★▲
   (www.etrade.com), or TD Ameritrade (www.tdameritrade.com) and find two IPOs offered in the past year or so. Track the performance of each from its introduction to its present market price. Report your observations.

taking it to the **net**

PURPOSE

To evaluate and understand the advantages and disadvantages of ETFs.

EXERCISE

Exchange-traded funds (ETFs) are a low-cost, flexible way to diversify a portfolio. To learn more, go to Yahoo! Finance (www.finance.yahoo.com) and click on investing, then on the ETFs tab.

1. What are the pros and cons of investing in ETFs?

2. What are the five most actively traded ETFs?

3. Which ETFs grew the most in the last three years?

4. In which industry sectors or countries do these high-growth ETFs specialize?

video case   ⬛ connect

WHERE DID ALL MY MONEY GO?

We all hear about the importance of investing, but how do you know what the best investments are? Is there an objective source you can use to get investment advice? The answer is, yes, you can get much helpful and unbiased information from a company called Morningstar.

Most people choose between stocks and bonds. When you buy stocks, you buy part ownership of a firm. You can choose from large firms like AT&T and Microsoft or smaller firms. Morningstar can help you choose from the thousands of firms available.

One way to spread the risk of investing in stock is to diversify. That is, you can buy stock in a variety of firms in a variety of sectors. For example, you can buy stock in firms from other countries, in service firms, manufacturing firms, health care firms, and so on. One easy way to diversify is to buy mutual funds. Such funds buy a whole range of stocks and then sell you a portion of that fund. ETFs, or exchange-traded funds, are much like mutual funds, but you buy and sell them through stock exchanges much like you would buy individual shares of stock.

In the long run, most investment advisors recommend investing in stock. Yes, the stock market goes up and down, but they say, in the long run, stocks usually go up. Since young people can wait for years to sell their stock, investment advisors

like Morningstar would usually recommend stock (or mutual funds) to them.

Would Morningstar also be likely to recommend bonds? Sure. When you buy a bond, you are actually lending a company, the government, or some government agency money. The company (or the government) promises to return the money to you, plus interest. If the interest is high enough, such an investment makes sense. Of course, some companies are riskier than others, so the interest paid on bonds varies. Morningstar will help you choose bonds that are appropriate for you and your situation.

Almost everyone needs some investment advice. Morningstar has earned a reputation for being objective and helpful. This video is meant to reveal the benefits and drawbacks of investing. But stocks and bonds can earn you a nice return on your investment if you know what you are doing. If you don't know what you are doing, you can lose your savings rather quickly. Morningstar is just one source of information. You should explore as many sources as possible to learn about investing. Such sources include your textbook, your local newspaper, magazines such as *Money* and *Personal Finance*, and TV shows featuring financial news.

Everyone should have some money set aside (e.g., in a bank) for emergencies. Everyone should diversify their investments among stocks, bonds, real estate, and other investments, depending on their income and their willingness to assume risk.

Morningstar and other sources of advice are very important to your financial health. You have seen how some people believed that real estate could do nothing but go up. The recent real estate crash proved them wrong. The same is true of stocks, bonds, gold, oil, and other investments. They all involve risk, and expert advice is often wrong; but in any case, it pays to have the best, unbiased advice you can get, like that from Morningstar. It also helps to have several other sources of advice, including your own knowledge, gathered carefully over time.

THINKING IT OVER

1. Are you confident about investing in stocks, bonds, mutual funds, ETFs, and other investments? What sources of information would you use to make a decision about investments?

2. Should you totally rely on Morningstar or any other investment advice service or should you search out several sources of advice? How can you know what advice is best?

3. Given what you've read in this text and from other sources, would you recommend that your fellow students' first investment be in stocks, bonds, mutual funds, ETFs, real estate, or some other investments? Why?

notes

1. Katie Roof, "Big Tech IPOs for 2014," *Forbes*, December 23, 2013.
2. Nandini Sukumar, "BME May Evaluate NYSE Technology Units, Won't Buy Euronext Stake," *Bloomberg Businessweek*, February 24, 2014; and Steven M. Sears, "Master of the Markets," *Barron's*, February 10, 2014.
3. "The End of the Street," *The Economist*, November 16, 2013.
4. Bradley Hope and Keiko Morris, "NYSE's New York City Footprint May Shrink," *The Wall Street Journal*, February 17, 2014.
5. NYSE Euronext, www.nyx.com, accessed May 2014.
6. NASDAQ OMX, www.nasdaqomx.com, accessed May 2014.
7. Chris Dieterich, "Big Board Scores One for Humans," *The Wall Street Journal*, January 5, 2014; and Sam Mamudi and Ari Levy, "NASDAQ Offers an IPO Alternative," *Bloomberg Businessweek*, February 13, 2014.
8. Dan Stumpf, "U.S. Public Companies Rise Again," *The Wall Street Journal*, February 5, 2014.
9. Peter J. Henning, "Paying the Price for Insider Trading Profits," *The New York Times*, February 24, 2014.
10. Christopher M. Matthews, "Prosecutors Tell Jury to Convict Martoma, As Insider Trading Trial Nears End," *The Wall Street Journal*, February 3, 2014; and Michelle Celarier, "Ex-SAC Martoma Asks Judge to Toss Guilty Verdict," *New York Post*, February 24, 2014.
11. "Bull Runs Free in African Stock Markets," *USA Today*, May 27, 2013.
12. Shirley A. Lazo, "Global Payouts Hit $1 Trillion," *Barron's*, March 1, 2014.
13. Kopin Tan, "Buyback Bonbons," *Barron's*, January 6, 2014.
14. "Common and Preferred Stock: What's the Difference," *The Motley Fool*, February 23, 2014.
15. Tom Konrad, "Power REIT's Preferred Stock Offering: A Hedge That Pays 7.75%," *Forbes*, February 7, 2014.
16. Katy Burne, "Bankers Pitch 100-Year Bonds," *The Wall Street Journal*, August 23, 2010; Vivianne Sander, Michael Mackenzie, and Henny Sander, "Verizon Eyes Maturities of 100 Years for Bonds," *Financial Times*, September 7, 2013; and Katie Linsell, "EDF's Borrowing Exceeds $12 Billion This Week with 100-Year Bond," *Bloomberg News*, January 17, 2014.
17. William Baldwin, "Six Ways to Inflation-Proof Your Bonds," *Forbes*, March 2, 2011; and 4 Ways Bonds Can Fit into Your Portfolio," *Forbes*, February 9, 2012.
18. Kevin Harlan, "The Changing Broker Scene Offers Options for Traders," *Investor's Business Daily*, April 25, 2011; and Eve Kaplan, "The Difference between a Stockbroker, Financial Advisor and Planner Explained," *Forbes*, March 15, 2012.
19. Selena Maranjian, "How to Find the Best Online Brokers," *The Motley Fool*, June 25, 2013; and Ken Hoover and Donald Gold, "Research, Stock Trading Tools Sharpen at Top Brokers," November 25, 2013.
20. Carolyn Bigda, "Happy Fifth Birthday, Mr. Bull," *Kiplinger's Personal Finance*, March 2014.
21. Ryan Caldbeck, "Successful Venture Investing: The Importance of Understanding Risks, and Diversification," *Forbes*, February 19, 2014.
22. McDonald's www.mcdonalds.com/aboutmcdonalds/stocksplit, accessed May 2014.
23. Andrew Tangel, "'Massive Trading Suspensions' Highlight Threat of Penny Stock Fraud," *Los Angeles Times*, February 3, 2014.
24. Ben Levisohn, "Splits Dive; Cheap Stocks Thrive," *Barron's*, January 6, 2014.
25. Dakin Campbell and Elizabeth Dexheimer, "MasterCard Boosts Dividend 83%, Announces 10 for 1 Stock Split," *Bloomberg Personal Finance*, December 10, 2013; and Alistar Barr, "Google Hits Record on Revenue Gain, Stock Split," *USA Today*, January 30, 2014.
26. "Motley Fool—Buying on Margin Is a Tightrope Deal," *The Columbus Dispatch*, February 2, 2014.
27. Michael Aneiro, "Junk Yields: Too Low for Comfort," *Barron's*, January 6, 2014; and Vivianne Rodrigues, "Taper Time-Bomb Hits High U.S. Yield Debt," *Financial Times*, February 10, 2014.
28. Rob Silverblatt, "Are There Too Many Mutual Funds?" *U.S. News & World Report*, June 10, 2013.
29. Jia Lynn Yung, "Warren Buffett Reveals the One Stock Fund You Need to Invest In," *The Washington Post*, February 24, 2014.
30. Jeff Sommer, "Give Fees an Inch and They'll Take a Mile," *The New York Times*, March 1, 2014.

31. Andrew Bary, "The Case for Closed-End Funds," *Barron's*, December 23, 2013.

32. Patrick Graham, "Wealth Advisor: Embracing ETFs Over Index Mutual Funds," *The Wall Street Journal*, February 21, 2014; and David Ning, "Signs Index Funds Aren't for You," *U.S. News & World Report*, February 26, 2014.

33. Jeffrey R. Kosnett, "The Dow Loves Dividends," *Kiplinger's Personal Finance*, December 2013; and Rodney Brooks, John Waggoner, and Matt Krantz, "Dow 30 Adds Goldman Sachs, Nike, and Visa," *USA Today*, September 10, 2013.

34. V. Dionne Hayes, Peyton Craighill, and Scott Clement, "For More People, the American Dream Does Not Include a Home of Their Own," *The Washington Post*, March 1, 2014.

35. Stan Choe, "Five Years into Bull Market, Returns Can Be Deceiving," *The Boston Globe*, March 2, 2014.

photo credits

B

Using Technology to Manage Information

Learning Objectives

AFTER YOU HAVE READ AND STUDIED THIS BONUS CHAPTER, YOU SHOULD BE ABLE TO

B-1   Outline the changing role of business technology.

B-2   List the types of business information, identify the characteristics of useful information, and discuss how data are stored and analyzed.

B-3   Compare the scope of the Internet, intranets, extranets, and virtual private networks and explain how broadband technology enabled the evolution to Web 2.0 and 3.0.

B-4   Explain virtual networking and discuss the benefits and drawbacks for cloud computing.

B-5   Evaluate the human resource, security, privacy, and stability issues affected by information technology.

Getting to know **Jack Dorsey**

Technology innovators strive to change the ways we communicate and manage information through hardware, software, and the Internet. Today's tech experts often move from company to company, hoping that one of their new ventures turns into "the next big thing."

Programmer and entrepreneur Jack Dorsey discovered a way to make "the next big thing"—twice. In 2006 he co-founded the microblogging site Twitter. He also launched Square, a service that allows businesses to accept debit and credit card payments through mobile devices. These revolutionary enterprises made Dorsey a billionaire by the time he turned 35.

Before he took the tech world by storm, Dorsey was just a data-obsessed kid from St. Louis, Missouri. Using his father's CB radio and a police scanner, he would spend hours tracking the city's police and emergency personnel. Dorsey's dad bought him a computer so he could record and analyze the movements further. After learning a coding language, Dorsey constructed a program that graphically showed the movements of all the vehicles. Dorsey devoted his full attention to the hypnotizing program. "It's a rush," said Dorsey. "You forget to sleep. You forget to eat. I just felt so great, because, Oh, I can actually build something that enables me to see the city." But Dorsey knew that an important element was missing from the program: people. "I could see ambulances, I could see black cars, but I was missing the individuals," said Dorsey.

Transferring the real world into a virtual landscape became Dorsey's ultimate goal. He explored the idea further as a computer science and math student at the Missouri University of Science and Technology. Meanwhile, the car-tracking software he created as a kid got the attention of a bike-messenger start-up in New York. Dorsey left the Midwest in his junior year to join the company while going to New York University. He eventually moved to San Francisco to start his own web-based taxi dispatching service, but the dot-com bust of the late-1990s ended that dream.

Dorsey spent the next few years coding at various companies. He also trained as a massage therapist, developed a secure ticketing system for the tourist ferry to Alcatraz Island, and even briefly studied fashion design. No matter what he did, though, Dorsey couldn't stop thinking about his people-free mapping program. By the mid-2000s, his obsession with SMS text messaging and the growing influence of social media had finally given him a solution to his problem. One day when he was sitting with two friends, Dorsey asked, "What if we used SMS to report what you're doing, and also to receive news of what everyone else is doing?" The trio soon set to work on a messaging service that could keep people connected through small bursts of information. They named the service Twitter after the way a cell phone vibrates when receiving a message. At first many people wondered why they would want to limit their communication to just 140 characters. As the years went by, however, hundreds of millions were drawn to Twitter's ability to plug into an international conversation with other users, companies, and celebrities.

Despite the social network's runaway success, Dorsey wasn't finished disrupting things. His mobile-payment company Square recently struck a deal with Starbucks, which will soon use the service in its more than 7,000 American stores. In fact, as developers like Jack Dorsey and tech companies continue to change the face of the digital landscape, it's possible that even the most entrenched technologies could become obsolete in a few years. In this bonus chapter you'll learn about how this ever-changing tech world affects business.

Sources: D. T. Max, "Two-Hit Wonder," *The New Yorker*, October 21, 2013; Seth Stevenson, "Simplicity and Order For All," *The Wall Street Journal*, October 26, 2012; Jake Tapper and Sherisse Pham, "Jack Dorsey on His Desire to Be Mayor of New York City, Steve Jobs, and Being a Bachelor," *CNN*, March 21, 2013; Tim Bradshaw, "Jack Dorsey: Twitter Star Seeking Investors," *Financial Times*, October 4, 2013.

Jack Dorsey
- Co-founder of Twitter
- Founder of Square
- Programmer, pioneer

www.twitter.com

@jack

name that **company**

This company used social media to build its business. Its customers design new products, name them, and enter them in the company's database. Customers may even make YouTube commercials that are featured on the company's video wall. If other customers buy the new product, the creator gets a small store credit. Name that company. (Find the answer in the chapter.)

LO B–1　Outline the changing role of business technology.

THE ROLE OF INFORMATION TECHNOLOGY

The importance of business knowledge is nothing new—what is newer is the recognition of the need to manage it like any other asset. To manage knowledge, a company needs to share information efficiently throughout the organization and to implement systems for creating new knowledge. This need is constantly leading to new technologies that support the exchange of information among staff, suppliers, and customers. Studies have shown that data-driven decision making (i.e., collecting data, analyzing it, and using it to make crucial decisions, like whether to create a new product or service) lifts productivity 5 percent higher than decision making based on experience and intuition.[1]

Evolution from Data Processing to Business Intelligence

To understand technology today, it is helpful to review how we got here.

data processing (DP)
Name for business technology in the 1970s; included technology that supported an existing business and was primarily used to improve the flow of financial information.

- In the 1970s, business technology was known as **data processing (DP)**. (Although many people use the words *data* and *information* interchangeably, they mean different things. *Data* are raw, unanalyzed, and unorganized facts and figures. *Information* is processed and organized data that managers can use for decision making.) The primary purpose of data processing was to improve the flow of financial information. Data processing employees were support staff who rarely came in contact with customers.

information systems (IS)
Technology that helps companies do business; includes such tools as automated teller machines (ATMs) and voice mail.

- In the 1980s, business technology became known as **information systems (IS)** when it moved out of the back room and into the center of the business. Its role changed from *supporting* the business to *doing* business. Customers began to interact with a wide array of technological tools, from automated teller machines (ATMs) to voice mail. As business increased its use of information systems, it became more dependent on them.

- Until the late 1980s, business technology was just an addition to the existing way of doing business. Keeping up-to-date was a matter of using new technology on old methods. But things started to change when businesses applied new technology to new methods. Business technology then became known as **information technology (IT)**, and its role became to *change* business by storing, retrieving, and sending information efficiently.

information technology (IT)
Technology used to store, retrieve, and send information efficiently.

- In the 1990s, the introduction of the World Wide Web changed the way that people interacted with one another and information. Online services such as Google offered a new way of accessing information. In addition, bluetooth technology created conveniences by providing wireless communication systems to replace cables that typically connected devices, thus freeing people to access information wherever they wanted.

- In the 2000s, as this technology became more sophisticated, it became better known as **business intelligence (BI) or analytics**. BI refers to a variety of software applications used to analyze an organization's raw data and derive useful insights from it. BI activities include data mining (which we discuss later in this chapter), online analytical processes, querying, and reporting.[2] Knowledge is information charged with enough intelligence to make it relevant and useful. Knowledge technology adds a layer of intelligence to filter appropriate information and deliver it when it is needed.

BI changes the traditional flow of information. Instead of an individual going to the database, the database comes to the individual. Managers can put a new employee at a workstation using BI training software and let the system take over everything from laying out a checklist of the tasks required on a shift to providing answers and insights that once would have taken up a supervisor's time.

BI helps businesspeople focus on what's important: deciding how to react to problems and opportunities. For example, imagine you're a sales rep who just closed a big deal. While you celebrate your success, the finance department is upset because your customer never pays on time, which costs the company a lot of money. BI could provide you that insight so that you could negotiate different payment terms with the customer, thus connecting sales activity to financial requirements in a seamless process.

Technology changes react with one another to create more change. Maintaining the flexibility to successfully integrate these changes is crucial to business survival. Packard Bell and Kodak once dominated their industries, but failed to compete effectively and lost market share. In the case of Kodak, even though it invented the first digital camera, the company was concerned that digital photography would eat into its traditional film business. So Kodak decided to continue to focus on film rather than digital cameras, a decision that eventually led to the company's bankruptcy.[3] Both Packard Bell and Kodak had size and money, but not flexibility.

Knowledge sharing is at the heart of keeping pace with change. Of course, it can be difficult to predict which new technologies will be successful. For a fun look at the worst tech predictions of all time, see Figure B.1.

Obviously, the role of the IT staff has changed as technology itself has improved and evolved. The chief information officer (CIO) has moved out of the back room and into the boardroom, and now spends less time worrying about keeping systems running and more time finding ways to boost business by applying technology to purchasing decisions, operational strategy, and marketing and sales. Today the role of the CIO is to help the business use technology to communicate better with others, while offering better service and lower costs.[4]

How Information Technology Changes Business

Time and place have always been at the center of business. Customers once had to go to the business during certain hours to satisfy their needs. For example, people went to the store to buy clothes. They went to the bank to arrange for a loan. Businesses decided when and where they did business with them. Today, IT allows businesses to deliver goods and services whenever and wherever the customer wants them. You can order books and clothes, arrange a home mortgage loan, and buy music or a car online, anytime you choose.

The Fire Phone, Amazon's first entry into the smartphone market, offers a unique feature called Firefly. Imagine noticing your friend sporting a cool new headset. With just a click of a button, Firefly will identify the headset and show you all the purchasing info you need—including reviews, of course. Another click and it's on the way to your home—all before you've had a chance to reconsider whether you really need that headset. Can you see how Firefly helps buyers buy?

business intelligence (BI) or analytics
The use of data analytic tools to analyze an organization's raw data and derive useful insights from it.

FIGURE B.1 THE WORST TECH PREDICTIONS OF ALL TIME
You can't be right all the time. Here are a few quotes from technology leaders who got it wrong—*way* wrong.

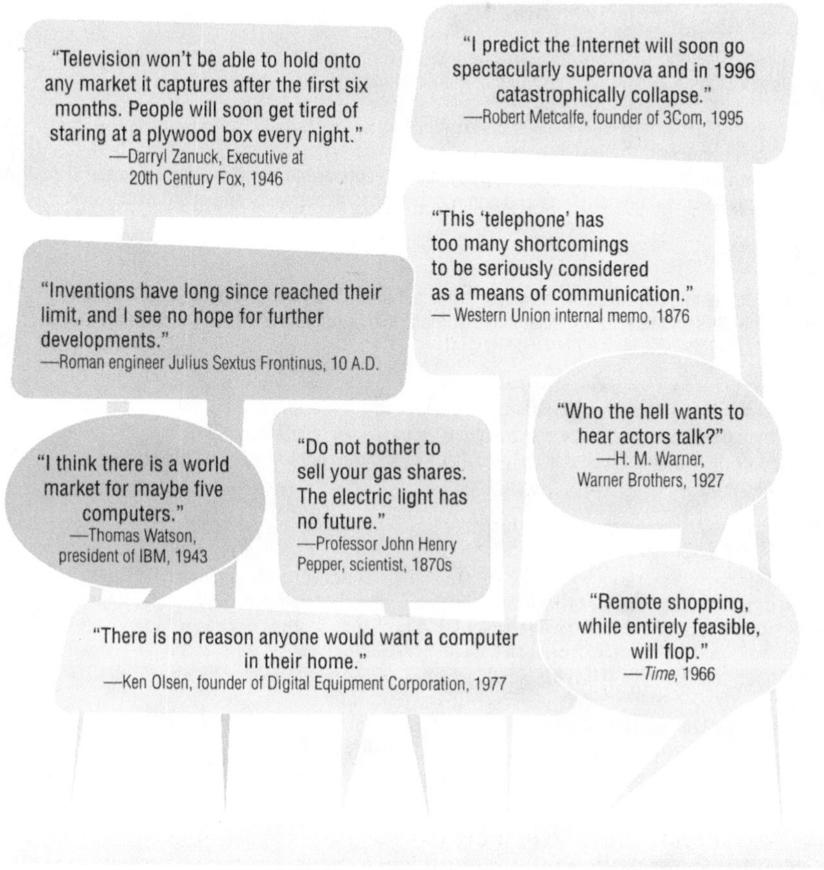

"Television won't be able to hold onto any market it captures after the first six months. People will soon get tired of staring at a plywood box every night."
—Darryl Zanuck, Executive at 20th Century Fox, 1946

"I predict the Internet will soon go spectacularly supernova and in 1996 catastrophically collapse."
—Robert Metcalfe, founder of 3Com, 1995

"Inventions have long since reached their limit, and I see no hope for further developments."
—Roman engineer Julius Sextus Frontinus, 10 A.D.

"This 'telephone' has too many shortcomings to be seriously considered as a means of communication."
— Western Union internal memo, 1876

"I think there is a world market for maybe five computers."
—Thomas Watson, president of IBM, 1943

"Do not bother to sell your gas shares. The electric light has no future."
—Professor John Henry Pepper, scientist, 1870s

"Who the hell wants to hear actors talk?"
—H. M. Warner, Warner Brothers, 1927

"There is no reason anyone would want a computer in their home."
—Ken Olsen, founder of Digital Equipment Corporation, 1977

"Remote shopping, while entirely feasible, will flop."
—*Time*, 1966

Sources: David Zeiler, "The 10 Worst Tech Predictions of All Time," *Money Morning*, www.moneymorning.com, accessed June 2014; and Mark Spoonauer, "10 Worst Tech Predictions of All Time," *Labtop*, August 7, 2013.

Consider how IT has changed the entertainment industry. Forty-five years ago, you had to go to a movie theater if you wanted to see a movie. Forty years ago, you could wait for it to be on television. Thirty years ago, you could wait for it to be on cable television. Twenty-five years ago, you could go to a video store and rent it. Now you can order video on demand by satellite, cable, or WiFi or download it to watch on your TV, computer, smartphone, iPad, or other device whenever and wherever you wish.

As IT broke time and location barriers, it created new organizations and services that are independent of location. For example, **NASDAQ** is an electronic stock exchange without trading floors where buyers and sellers make trades by computer. Smartphones, laptops, and tablets allow you access to people and information as if you were in the office. That independence brings work to people instead of people to work.

The way people do business drastically changes when companies increase their technological capabilities. Electronic communications can provide substantial time savings. E-mail and texting have put an end to tedious games of telephone tag and are far faster than paper-based correspondence. Internet and intranet communications using shared documents and other methods allow contributors to work on a common document without time-consuming meetings. See Figure B.2 for other examples of how information technology is changing business.

Organization

Technology is breaking down corporate barriers, allowing functional departments or product groups (including factory workers) to share critical information instantly.

Operations

Technology shrinks cycle times, reduces defects, and cuts waste. Service companies use technology to streamline ordering and communication with suppliers and customers.

Staffing

Technology eliminates layers of management and cuts the number of employees. Companies use computers and telecommunication equipment to create "virtual offices" with employees in various locations.

New products

Information technology cuts development cycles by feeding customer and marketing comments to product development teams quickly so that they can revive products and target specific customers.

Customer relations

Customer service representatives can solve customers' problems instantly by using company-wide databases to complete tasks from changing addresses to adjusting bills. Information gathered from customer service interactions can further strengthen customer relationships.

New markets

Since it is no longer necessary for customers to walk down the street to get to stores, online businesses can attract customers to whom they wouldn't otherwise have access.

FIGURE B.2 HOW INFORMATION TECHNOLOGY IS CHANGING BUSINESS
This table shows a few ways that information technology is changing businesses, their employees, suppliers, and customers.

test **prep**

- How has the role of information technology changed since the days when it was known as data processing?
- How has information technology changed the way we do business?

LO B–2   List the types of business information, identify the characteristics of useful information, and discuss how data are stored and analyzed.

TYPES OF INFORMATION

Today, information flows into and through an organization from many different directions. The types of information available to businesses today include:

- *Business process information.* This includes all transaction data gathered at the point of sale as well as information gained through operations like enterprise resource planning, supply chain management, and customer relationship management systems.
- *Physical-world observations.* These result from the use of radio frequency identification (**RFID**) devices, miniature cameras, wireless access, global positioning systems, and sensor technology—all of which have to do with where people or items are located and what they are doing.

Advances in retinal scanning technology allow companies like Kimberly Clark to track how many seconds a person spends looking at different packaging designs for paper towels. Retinal scanning simulations aid marketers in determining what will attract customers the most. What other ways can you think of for businesses to make use of biometric technology?

Computer chips cost pennies apiece and can be found in a wide range of products, including credit cards, printer ink cartridges, baseballs, tire valves, running shoes, vacuum cleaners, and even beer mugs. That's right—Mitsubishi has produced a "smart" beer mug that senses when it is time for a refill and sends a signal to the bartender.

- *Biological data.* Forms of identification include improved fingerprinting technology and biometric devices that scan retinas, recognize faces and voices, and analyze DNA. Although such information usually serves security purposes, it can also be used to customize products and services by tracking shoppers' eyes in stores.[5]

- *Public data.* Free and accessible, public data include the electronic traces we leave when posting to the Internet, sending e-mail, and using instant messaging. More and more, public data are being stored, shared, or sold.

- *Data that indicate personal preferences or intentions.* Online shoppers leave a trail of information that can reveal personal likes and dislikes.

The volume and complexity of all these data and information are staggering. Computing systems can search through text, numbers, audio, and video—and identify, categorize, and refine relevant opinions on any topic imaginable.

Managing Information

Even before the use of computers, managers had to sift through mountains of information to find what they needed to help them make decisions. Today, businesspeople are faced with *infoglut,* an overabundance of data. Have you seen the classic episode of TV's *I Love Lucy* with Lucy and Ethel working in a factory on the candy line? Everything was going OK until the candy started coming too fast for them. Then mayhem broke loose. That's what's happening to many managers today, with information instead of candy. Too much information can confuse issues rather than clarify them.

How can managers keep from getting buried in the infoglut? Stepping back to gain perspective is the key. It is important to identify the four or five key goals you wish to reach, and eliminate information not related to them. That can cut the information flow by half. As we were gathering information for this chapter, we collected hundreds of print journal articles and found thousands more online. Feeling the pressure of information overload, we identified the objectives we wanted the chapter to help you accomplish and eliminated all the articles that didn't address those objectives. As we further refined our objectives, the huge file gradually dropped to a manageable size.

Obviously, not all the information that ends up on your desk will be useful. The usefulness of management information depends on four characteristics:

1. *Quality.* Quality means that the information is accurate and reliable. When the clerk at a fast-food restaurant enters your order into the cash register, it may be automatically fed to a computer that calculates the day's sales and profits as soon as the store closes. The sales and expense data must be accurate, or the rest of the calculations will be wrong. Quality can be a real problem when a large number of calculations are based on questionable sales forecasts rather than actual sales.

2. *Completeness.* There must be enough information to allow you to make a decision, but not so much as to confuse the issue. Today, as we have noted, the problem is often too much information rather than too little.

3. *Timeliness*. Information must reach managers quickly. E-mail and texting can let marketing, engineering, and production know about a problem with a product the same day the salesperson hears about it, so customer complaints can be handled instantly if possible, or certainly within a day. Product changes can be made on the spot using computer-integrated manufacturing, as discussed in Chapter 9.

4. *Relevance*. Different managers have different information needs. Since information systems often provide too much data, managers must learn which questions to ask to get the answers they seek.

Remember, though, that you can never read everything available. Set objectives for yourself, and do the best you can.

Organizing E-Mail and Electronic Files

Even though many businesspeople communicate through real-time technology, such as instant messaging, videoconferencing, or Internet relay chats, e-mail is still a dominant method of communication, particularly when sending attached electronic files. Today's information management tools make it easier than ever for individuals and small businesses to organize information. Here are some tips for sorting e-mail and electronic files so that you can find what you need easily and quickly:[6]

1. *Use your e-mail program's organizing tools.* Most e-mail programs allow you to create folders for specific topics, projects, or clients. As you work through your in-box, move the messages you want to keep to the appropriate folders. Archive your old e-mail monthly. Figure B.3 offers suggestions for ways to reduce the number of distractions caused by sending and receiving e-mail.

2. *Use consistent file names.* Save related materials across multiple software programs under the same name, and file them together. Perhaps you've been assigned to work with a team of other students to create a sample business plan for this course. You could save all files (whether e-mail, spreadsheets, PowerPoint, or Word documents) with a file name that begins "Business Plan Project" and store them in one folder in "My Documents."

- Turn off all electronic alerts.
- Limit the number of times you check e-mail to no more than a few times a day.
- Delete garbage messages (i.e., spam, junk mail, etc.) first.
- Reply immediately only to urgent alerts and messages that take less than 2 minutes to write a response and save the rest for later.
- Set a specific time (i.e., at the end of the workday) to respond to remaining messages.
- Limit use of the reply-all button.
- Use an automatic out-of-office message such as "I will be offline until after 5 p.m. Please call me if you have an urgent message." This will give you time to focus on work while letting others know not to expect a reply soon.
- Don't limit your communication to e-mail or texting. Communicating by phone or in person can sometimes save time and build relationships.

Sources: Joanna Stern, "Cellphone Users Check Phones 150x/Day and Other Internet Fun Facts," *ABC News*, www.abcnews.com, May 29, 2013; "Get More Done by Only Checking Email Twice a Day," *Time Management Ninja*, www.timemanagementninja.com, accessed June 2014; and Bob Sullivan and Hugh Thomas, "Brain Interrupted," *The New York Times*, May 3, 2013.

FIGURE B.3 TAMING ELECTRONIC COMMUNICATION INTERRUPTIONS
Typical office workers are interrupted every 11 minutes, and it takes them about 25 minutes to return to the original task. Studies show that people don't really multitask, but rather toggle rapidly between tasks, and there are costs involved in doing so. So much interruption undermines workers' attention spans, increases stress, and decreases job satisfaction and creativity. Here are a few hints to reduce the number of electronic distractions.

3. *Use online backup services.* Backup, backup, backup—we've all heard how important it is to back up our files, but we often forget to follow through. Don't risk an avoidable loss. As the cost of online storage continues to drop, backing up files to online services such as Dropbox can be a very cost-effective way to protect your files.

4. *Use desktop search software.* Finding files can be easier with a desktop search software program like Google Desktop or Windows Live Search. Google Desktop has an enterprise version for midsize companies. Larger companies also have access to Google but may need to pay for additional tech support.

Big Data and Data Analytics

Chances are that some program is keeping track of every click you make online, every movement you make as you shop in stores, every restaurant you go to for lunch—even what you eat. Collecting such data isn't enough; you have to derive meaning from it. And when you collect more data, you need more storage. How do businesses store and organize a data glut so that it eventually becomes useful information? The answer for many companies is data analytics. **Data analytics** is the process of collecting, organizing, storing, and analyzing large sets of data ("big data") in order to identify patterns and other information that is most useful to the business now and for making future decisions.[7]

One part of data analytics is *data mining,* a technique for looking for hidden patterns and previously unknown relationships among the data. The legendary example is a study by a retail chain that revealed a spike in beer sales coinciding with a spike in diaper sales on weekdays between 5:00 and 7:00 p.m. The conclusion that thirsty dads pick up diapers on the way home from work prompted store managers to consider moving the diapers next to the beer to boost sales. The retailer never did pair the Heineken with the Huggies, but the story led to a new science of tracking what's selling where and who's buying it. For example, because data mining showed Walmart that U.S. consumers like to buy Pop-Tarts (particularly strawberry) just before a hurricane hits, the company makes sure they're available in the right place at the right time.

The lesson here is that companies can gain a competitive advantage with high-quality data that support management decisions. Companies can better target their goods and service, attract new customers, and adjust prices. Figure B.4 offers a few examples of sectors that benefit from big data and data analytics.

Of course, when so much data and such powerful analytic tools are used by so many companies, mistakes are bound to happen. For example, an out-of-print book was recently listed on Amazon as having 17 copies available: 15 used from $35.54 and two new from $23,698,655.93 (plus $3.99 shipping). The astronomical price was the result of two sellers' automated programs that each raised the book price based on the other's price. While the only thing these two sellers lost in this automated bidding war was a book sale, another Amazon seller, a T-shirt company called Solid Gold Bomb, didn't fare so well.

Solid Gold Bomb uses a program that takes libraries of words that are used in popular phrases, such as "Keep Calm and Carry On," and automatically mixes them with other popular words. It then designs a T-shirt emblazoned with the new phrase (it doesn't actually print the shirt until someone orders it) and automatically posts it on Amazon. You can imagine the public relations nightmare when the shirt "Keep Calm and Rape a Lot" was posted for sale. Since it was all done automatically, no one at Solid Gold Bomb had actually seen the listing until the complaints poured in. The company's reputation was damaged by a T-shirt that never actually existed. The lesson to be learned is that companies must make certain that the applications they use to analyze data are not flawed.[8]

Data analytics
The process of collecting, organizing, storing, and analyzing large sets of data ("big data") in order to identify patterns and other information that is most useful to the business now and for making future decisions.

FIGURE B.4 EXAMPLES OF SECTORS THAT BENEFIT FROM BIG DATA AND DATA ANALYTICS

E-commerce
Online sellers can analyze cart data to change prices for people who leave items behind in order to attract them back to the site and follow through on the purchase.

Retail
Stores such as Target can tell from a woman's previous purchases that she's pregnant. It can then send her coupons and other promotions for baby products. It can analyze the data a little more and promote similar products to the grandparents-to-be.

Real estate
Beach house rental agents can target vacation promotions to people who buy sunscreen frequently.

Law enforcement
Video cameras in light fixtures collect and feed data to software that can spot long lines, recognize license plates, and even identify suspicious activity, sending alerts to the appropriate staff. Sensors in the fixtures can pinpoint a gunshot, sense an earthquake or dangerous gas, or spot a person stopping at various cars in a parking lot.

Health care
Smartphones with motion sensors can detect early signs of Parkinson's disease.

Sources: Adam Tanner, "How Much Did You Pay for That Lipstick?" *Forbes*, April 14, 2014; "Dynamic Data," *Fortune*, October 7, 2013; Diane Cardwell, "At Newark Airport the Lights Are On, and They're Watching You," *The New York Times*, February 17, 2014; Philip Atiba Goff, "Can Big Data Transform Social Justice," *CNN*, www.cnn.com, May 2, 2014; and "Tech," *The Kiplinger Letter*, May 23, 2014.

test prep

- **What types of information are available to businesses today?**
- **What are the four characteristics of information that make it useful?**
- **What is data mining and how do businesses use it?**

LO B–3   Compare the scope of the Internet, intranets, extranets, and virtual private networks and explain how broadband technology enabled the evolution to Web 2.0 and 3.0.

THE HEART OF KNOWLEDGE MANAGEMENT: THE INTERNET

You already know the Internet is a network of computer networks that evolved from a one-to-one communications tool to a one-to-many broadcast communication tool. Today it is the *heart of knowledge management*. Internet users can point and click their way from site to site with complete freedom. But what if you don't want just anybody to have access to your website? You might create an intranet, extranet, or virtual private network.

Intranets   An **intranet** is a companywide network, closed to public access, that uses Internet-type technology. To prevent unauthorized outsiders (particularly

intranet
A companywide network, closed to public access, that uses Internet-type technology.

the competition) from accessing their sites, companies can construct a firewall between themselves and the outside world. A firewall can consist of hardware, software, or both. Firewalls allow only authorized users to access the intranet. Some companies use intranets only to publish employee phone lists and policy manuals, while others create interactive applications that fully exploit the technology's possibilities. They allow employees to update their addresses or submit company forms such as supply requisitions, time sheets, or payroll forms online, eliminating paper handling and speeding decision making.[9]

Extranets   Many businesses choose to open their intranets to other, selected companies and even customers, through the use of extranets. An **extranet** is a semiprivate network that lets more than one company access the same information or allows people on different servers to collaborate. Now almost all companies can use extranets for electronic data interchange (EDI) functions like sharing data and processing orders, specifications, invoices, and payments.

Notice that we described an extranet as a semiprivate network. This means that outsiders cannot access the network easily, but since an extranet does use public lines, knowledgeable hackers can gain unauthorized access. Most companies want a network as private and secure as possible, so they use dedicated lines (lines reserved solely for the network).

Dedicated lines are expensive, however, and they limit extranet use only to computers directly linked to those lines. What if your company needs to link securely with another firm or an individual for just a short time? Installing dedicated lines in this case would be too expensive and time-consuming. Virtual private networks are a solution.

Virtual Private Networks   A **virtual private network (VPN)** is a private data network that creates secure connections, or "tunnels," over regular Internet lines. It gives users the same capabilities as an extranet at much lower cost by using shared public resources rather than private ones. Just as phone companies provide secure shared resources for voice messages, VPNs provide the same secure sharing of public resources for data. This allows for on-demand networking: An authorized user can join the network for any desired function at any time, for any length of time, while keeping the corporate network secure. You probably use a VPN when you log on to your school's website. VPNs are commonplace in schools across the country that want to allow only affiliated students and faculty access to accounts like Blackboard (an online tool used to enhance teaching and learning, share course documentation and register for courses). If you don't have access to a corporate VPN, you can easily set up an account at a public VPN provider like WiTopia, StrongVPN, or Hotspot Shield.[10]

How do users log on to an organization's network? They do so through an *enterprise portal* that centralizes information and transactions and serves as an entry point to a variety of resources, such as e-mail, financial records, schedules, and employment and benefits files. Portals can even include streaming video of the company's day care center. They are more than simply web pages with links. They identify users and allow them access to areas of the intranet according to their roles: customers, suppliers, employees, and so on. They make information available in one place so that users don't have to deal with a dozen different web interfaces.

The challenge to the chief information officer (CIO) is to integrate resources, information, reports, and so on—all of which may be in a variety of places—so that they appear seamless to the user.

Broadband Technology

The more traffic on the Internet, the slower connections become. Tools to unlock these traffic jams include **broadband technology**, a continuous connection to the Internet that allows users to send and receive mammoth video, voice, and data

---

extranet
A semiprivate network that uses Internet technology and allows more than one company to access the same information or allows people on different servers to collaborate.

virtual private network (VPN)
A private data network that creates secure connections, or "tunnels," over regular Internet lines.

broadband technology
Technology that offers users a continuous connection to the Internet and allows them to send and receive mammoth files that include voice, video, and data much faster than ever before.

files faster than ever before. Even though broadband in the United States is dramatically faster than old dial-up connections, its average speed of 9.8 megabits per second is snail-like compared to the 22.1 and 13.3 averages of South Korea and Japan, respectively.[11] President Obama has made improving and expanding broadband technology a priority of his administration.[12] As people use more and more bandwidth to stream videos on services like Netflix or music on apps like Pandora, Internet service providers have begun to place caps on the amount of broadband consumers can use. Right now this isn't a problem for most users since average usage is well below the current caps, but as more mobile devices and services come online, the more likely broadband will become a consumption-based service (i.e., you pay for the broadband you use).

Net Neutrality   Today there is plenty of debate about "net neutrality" and the Federal Communication Commission's (FCC) role in regulating it.[13] One issue is defining what net neutrality even is. Some say it is treating all traffic on the Internet the same, whether it's e-mail from your mom or web page traffic on Google. Others say net neutrality is treating all the same type of content the same way, whether it's a video of frolicking kittens or a video of an ongoing surgery. Still others say net neutrality is nothing more than forbidding ISPs from blocking specific websites or services.[14] As video streaming services like Netflix and Amazon increasingly hog the lines, the debate over how the existing broadband should be distributed and who should regulate the distribution should go on for quite some time. What does this mean to you? If ISPs can charge for speed, deep-pocketed companies like Netflix and Amazon can pay the fees (passing them on to you, the customer, of course); and low-budget and start-up sites are likely to lose customers unwilling to travel at slower speeds, reducing competition and innovation. It is also possible that ISPs can begin charging people to go to certain websites; the more money you're willing to pay, the more sites you'll have access to. Rich customers and poor customers will get two different webs.[15]

Meanwhile new services like Google Fiber, a high-speed fiber network up to 100 times faster than average connections, give us hope that broader pipes may be on the horizon.[16]

How the existing broadband should be distributed and who should regulate the distribution are major concerns today. Why does it matter how broadband is divided and distributed? Some people are concerned that ISPs will charge customers to go to certain websites: the more money you're willing to pay,' the more and better sites you'll have access to. Rich customers and poor customers could get two different webs. Other people say that it's only fair that whoever uses the most broadband should pay the most. What do you think?

Internet2   Even with broadband technology, scientists and other scholars who access, transmit, and manipulate complex mathematical models, data sets, and other digital elements need a faster solution. Their answer? Create a private Internet reserved for research purposes only. **Internet2** runs more than 22,000 times faster than today's public infrastructure, and supports heavy-duty applications such as videoconferencing, collaborative research, distance education, digital libraries, and full-body simulations known as tele-immersion.[17] A key element of Internet2 is a network called very-high-speed backbone network service (vBNS), which was set up in 1995 as a way to link government supercomputer centers and a select group of universities. The power of Internet2 makes it possible for a remote medical specialist to assist in a medical operation over the Internet without having the connection deteriorate as, say, home users watch *House of Cards*.

Internet2 became available to only a few select organizations in late 1997, but there are now more than 500 member universities, government agencies, corporations, and laboratories in over 100 countries.[18] Whereas the public Internet divides bandwidth equally among users (if there are 100 users, they each get to use 1 percent of the available bandwidth), Internet2 is more capitalistic. Users who are willing to pay more can use more bandwidth.

Internet2
The private Internet system that links government supercomputer centers and a select group of universities; it runs more than 22,000 times faster than today's public infrastructure and supports heavy-duty applications.

Some fear that Internet2 may soon be overrun by undergrads engaged in video streaming and other resource-hogging pursuits. But the designers of Internet2 are thinking ahead. Not only do they expect Internet history to repeat itself; they are counting on it. They are planning to filter Internet2 technology out to the wider Internet community in such a way that there is plenty of room on the road for all of us—at a price, of course.

Social Media and Web 2.0

For businesses, social media provide an array of opportunities and challenges. They are an inexpensive way to gain exposure. Most important, they give businesses tools to collaborate with consumers on product development, service enhancement, and promotion. Until now, using social media has been optional for most businesses. However, many believe that businesses that do not have a social media presence will not survive. We're not talking just about a Facebook page with an occasional update. Successful businesses will have a social media ecosystem and comprehensive strategy where every part of the organization collaborates and where customers are part of the conversation instantly.

Adam Kidron, co-founder of Manhattan hamburger restaurant 4food, says he wouldn't be in business if it were not for social media. The restaurant is based on customization. Customers choose the type of bun (i.e., bagel, multigrain, brioche, pumpernickel, etc.), donut-shaped burger (i.e., beef, lamb, egg, turkey, salmon, veggie, sausage, etc.), "scoop" to fill the donut hole (i.e., avocado and chili mango, potato and chorizo hash, etc.), and then finally the cheese and condiments. Social media become part of the fundamental product when a customer creates a new product and they use their own mobile device or one of the iPads placed around the restaurant to create a name for

FIGURE B.5 TIPS FOR USING SOCIAL MEDIA TO PARTNER WITH CUSTOMERS
Using social media is about trusting your brand and identity to your customers, partners, and the world at large. The world is going to do things with your brand, whether or not you participate in the process. Here are some tips to keep in mind.

- **If your competition is using social media, you had better be using it too.** More than 50 percent of Twitter users say that they follow companies, brands, or products on social networks.

- **Let the network mature and develop a comprehensive social media strategy.** Don't just set up a network and immediately begin exploiting it. For example, when the list of online supporters started to grow, the Obama fund-raisers wanted to immediately tap them for contributions. They were persuaded to wait until his e-mail team created an environment that let people know they were part of the campaign.

- **Take customers' comments seriously and establish two-way communication.** People expect to be listened to. If you respond, they'll keep coming back. Post questions and surveys.

- **Ask your customers to answer common questions.** Asking your most active fans and advocates to answer common questions is an effective way of acknowledging the value of loyal customers while adding credibility to information about your product or service.

- **Be authentic.** You have to talk directly with your customers, not just make an announcement as you would in a press release. Keep it authentic and you'll build a personality around your company and your brand.

- **Make your corporate site social.** Provide social sharing opportunities by offering share buttons, tweet widgets, and Facebook like buttons to make it easier to share across social networks.

Sources: Stephanie Frasco, "100 Facts about Twitter, and Why They Matter to Your Business," *Social Media Today,* www.socialmediatoday.com, September 26, 2013; "Effective Social Media Strategies—Four Tips, Four Benefits," Oracle, www.oracle.com, accessed June 2014; and Cindy King, "10 Social Media Tips to Enhance Your Marketing," *Social Media Examiner,* www.socialmediaexaminer.com, March 12, 2014.

their burger and save it in 4food's database. If they like the burger, they can post their creation directly to Twitter or Facebook. If they *really* like the burger, they can create a YouTube commercial that is shown on the restaurant's giant video wall along with Twitter feeds. If another customer buys the burger, the creator gets a 25-cent credit on his or her 4food account.[19]

It is inevitable that at some point a company is going to suffer some negative social media buzz. For example, when McDonald's introduced its new Happy Meal mascot, Happy, the company was hit with a storm of social media criticism about the weird-looking guy. What did McDonald's do? Well, it just acknowledged it and tweeted back with an image of Happy reading all the negative comments on his laptop. After the image was sent to McDonald's 2.5 million Twitter followers and 31 million Facebook friends, a social media monitoring tool showed that there were 190 positive comments to every one negative comment about Happy. Soon there were no comments at all. The lesson to be learned here is that all businesses and organizations should monitor and respond quickly to social chatter. When bad buzz happens, a company should identify the source and nature of the buzz and develop a quick response to contain it.[20]

Figure B.5 offers suggestions to consider when using social media in business. The most important thing to remember is that the social media have to serve a unique purpose and not be just gimmicky add-ons.

Social networking is the best example of what tech publisher Tim O'Reilly dubbed "Web 2.0." **Web 2.0** is the set of tools that allow people to build social and business connections, share information, and collaborate on projects online with user-generated sites like blogs, wikis, social networking sites and other online communities, and virtual worlds. (In this context, *Web 1.0* refers to corporate-generated sites like Google and Amazon.) YouTube and the microblogging site Twitter are among the largest Web 2.0 businesses, where ordinary people create all the content.

Web 2.0
The set of tools that allow people to build social and business connections, share information, and collaborate on projects online (including blogs, wikis, social networking sites and other online communities, and virtual worlds).

Web 3.0

Another generation of web innovators has expanded the utility of the web so that it enables an unprecedented level of intelligence in almost all applications. The objective is to pull data in real time, as needed. As you pull data, the system learns about you and your interests and pushes information it "thinks" you might like toward you.[21] Known as Web 3.0, this technology represents a shift in how people interact with the web, and vice versa.[22] Those who describe Web 1.0 as the Static Web and Web 2.0 as the Social Web, describe Web 3.0 as the Personal Web. You could think of Web 3.0 as Web 2.0 with a brain. **Web 3.0** technology is made up of three basic components: semantic web, mobile web, and immersive Internet, which are all leading to what many call the Internet of Things.[23]

Web 3.0
A combination of technologies that adds intelligence and changes how people interact with the web, and vice versa (consists of the semantic web, mobile web, and immersive Internet).

Semantic Web   The semantic web refers to powerful intelligent decision-making applications.[24] For example, Amdocs is a company that interacts with customers on behalf of its clients in service industries such as telecom, health care, utilities, and insurance. This requires the Amdocs representatives to have real-time knowledge from internal sources—such as service disruptions and policy management—and external forces, such as social trends and competitive offers. Using Web 3.0 semantic technologies, Amdocs combines information from a variety of sources in real time to anticipate the reason for a customer's call. Responses can be made 30 percent faster, which makes customers happy.[25]

Mobile Web   The mobile web allows users to use the web as they move from one device to another and one location to another. Location-based services are tied to devices that can track a user's whereabouts and suggest

Wearable technology such as Google Glass, smart watches and other hands-free technology may change the way we communicate, and how we work and play. Some Google Glass Explorers (as the first adopters are called) have encountered negative reactions from other people. For example, some people want them to leave or take the glasses off, since the wearers could be taking photos or videos of them. What do you think the benefits and drawbacks of Google Glass are?

places, like restaurants or shops, in the area. You can get a message from Starbucks offering you a discount on a latte as you walk by the door. If you do drop in the store, you can use an app on your smartphone to pay for your drink. Because so many customers use multiple devices throughout the day, it is important that a business uses the same design in apps for all types of computers, phones, and tablets. Then users will be able to rely on consistent, high-quality access no matter what type of device they're using. Users can be frustrated or annoyed when they can't find what they need or where they were earlier.[26]

Immersive Internet   The immersive Internet includes virtual worlds, augmented reality, and 3D environments. The use of virtual worlds, simulations, augmented reality, and multiplayer gaming technologies is expected to increase dramatically for learning in the next few years. For example, Intel's Real Sense technology recognizes gestures and facial features, which allows it to understand movement and emotions. It recognizes foregrounds and backgrounds, which allows it to enhance interactive reality; and it can scan items in three dimensions. The use of gestures, voice, and touch encourages children to become more active participants in learning games. In a game based on Scholastic's Clifford the Big Red Dog, kids can use arm and hand motions, talk, and touch to move within the game and learn core literacy skills while playing. For us bigger kids, Intel is working with DreamWorks animation to bring users new experiences with characters and content. The Real Sense technology is also expected to bring 3D scanning and printing to mainstream users, allowing them to easily and affordably create 3D items.[27]

Internet of Things   The Internet connects more people faster than ever before, and mobile devices let people be online all of the time. However, it's not just phones and tablets that connect us to the Internet. There are so many other things that connect us that the term the "Internet of Things (IoT) has become popular in mainstream media. IoT refers to technology that enables ordinary objects to be connected to the Internet by using sensors, cameras, software, databases, and massive data centers.[28] There are WiFi-based home automation networks that automatically cool or heat your home, turn the lights on and off, and change the controls on your garage doors, from your smartphone or computer. A technology called Echo can monitor your home's water, gas, and electricity consumption and reward you for conserving. Wearables such as smart watches or conductive fibers woven into the fabric of your workout clothes can monitor your breathing and heart rate, count your steps, and send the information to your phone.[29]

Soon every part of our lives will be quantifiable and we could be even more accountable for our decisions. For example, skipping the gym too many times may prompt your gym shoes to auto tweet to your health insurance network, which may decide to increase your premiums. While this may seem futuristic, there are many companies today that get measurable results by analyzing data collected from networked things. For example, John Deere can do remote, wireless diagnostics of tractors and combines, saving farmers days of down time. Union Pacific reduced the number of train derailments caused by failed bearings by 75 percent using near-real-time analysis of data collected by sensors along the tracks.[30]

Who's the "Boss" of the Internet?

The U.S. Defense Department created the first computer network in the late 1960s; and Tim Berners-Lee, a software engineer in a physics lab in Switzerland, invented the World Wide Web in 1990.[31] But who controls the Internet now? Well, the U.S. Commerce Department controls the root server for the domain name system, a digital directory that tells your computer where to go when you type in a web address, including ".gov" or ".edu." This gives the U.S. hazy ownership rights to the Internet. The U.S. created the Internet Corporation for Assigned Names and Numbers (ICANN) in 1998 to keep the management of networks in the hands of a private sector system of committees representing multiple stakeholders including companies, academics, and governments.

The U.S. government agreed to work with ICANN to give away all of its ownership of the Internet to the private sector by sometime in 2015. Some people believe that the U.S. giving up Internet ownership will give countries like Russia and China the ability to convince other countries to add regulatory power that would limit access to certain sites as they tried to do in 2013.[32] Others believe the opposite is true, that giving up U.S. ownership weakens Russia's and China's argument that the Internet is controlled by one country.[33] To date, the U.S. has been successful in building a coalition of nations that agrees the Internet should be free of government regulations or restrictions on free speech.[34] What does this mean to you? It could mean that someday the Internet would be very different than it is today; you may not be free to go where you want or say what you want on the Internet. On the other hand, the coalition may remain strong enough to keep the Internet open to everyone. We'll have to wait and see.

test prep

- How do computer networks change the way employees gather information?
- What is the Internet of Things?

LO B–4 Explain virtual networking and discuss the benefits and drawbacks for cloud computing.

VIRTUAL NETWORKING AND CLOUD COMPUTING

Computers can be networked a couple of ways: by hardware (i.e., cables, switches, etc.) or by software. For every computer a company has in its hardware-based network, an array of potential problems lurks in the shadows, from time-wasting crashes to crippling viruses. To remedy this, many companies have turned to **virtual networking**, a process that allows software-based networked computers to run multiple operating systems and programs, and share storage. Virtual networking can be either external or internal. *External networking* treats the network as a single pool of resources that can all be accessed regardless of its physical components (i.e., networked computers share the resources of all the other computers on the network). *Internal networking*

virtual networking
A process that allows software-based networked computers to run multiple operating systems and programs, and share storage.

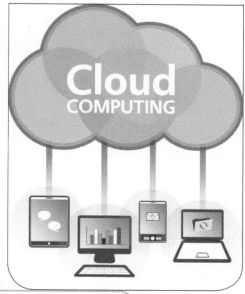

Cloud computing changes the way people and businesses use technology. Since their data are stored in the cloud rather than locked on their computers, users are free to access the data from anywhere with any device rather than only from their own personal computers. How has cloud computing changed the way you access your programs and files?

cloud computing
A form of virtualization in which a company's data and applications are stored at offsite data centers that are accessed over the Internet (the cloud).

shares the resources of one central computer with all the networked computers.[35] You might think of external networking as being decentralized and internal networking as being centralized.

Companies that want to virtualize but not to store all those data in their own offices need only look to the sky for a solution called **cloud computing**. This technology stores a company's data and applications at offsite data centers, accessed over the Internet.[36] The data aren't necessarily stored in a single data center; portions could be in a series of centers anywhere in the world. The data are easily accessible from any computer with an Internet connection. Vendors like Amazon, Google, Apple, and IBM offer cloud computing for a monthly pay-as-you-go fee.[37]

There are three types of cloud computing: (1) *private* clouds (wholly behind a firewall), *public* clouds (run on remote computers), and (3) *hybrid* clouds (consist of a private cloud for essential tasks, but use a public cloud as needed).[38]

The advantages of cloud computing include:[39]

1. **Reduced software costs.** Most software is free because the service provider supplies it. No more paying for upgrades or spending time installing all those patches since they're installed in the cloud.

2. **Improved security.** Offsite centers provide full and regular backups of data, etc., which is something many small businesses fail to do regularly.

3. **Flexible capacity.** Sometimes businesses need large chunks of capacity during peak demand periods, but much less at other times. Cloud computing allows the company to rent only what it needs when it needs it. If its needs increase, it just rents more. This is especially important to growing businesses that don't know what their needs will be.

4. **Lower equipment costs.** Since applications run in the cloud and not on your desk, you don't need to buy expensive equipment.

5. **Easier access.** Since you access all of your documents in the cloud via the Internet, it is much easier to share documents and make sure that everyone is working with the latest version.

Of course, cloud computing has its disadvantages as well. Primarily these involve concerns about security, stability, and control of data.[40] (We'll discuss these issues in more detail later in the chapter.) Popular cloud-storage service Dropbox suffered a 3-hour outage in early 2014 and another outage a few months later. Its 100 million customers were temporarily locked out of their files.[41] Dropbox was also accused of misleading users about the security and privacy of their files.[42] VMware provides a service that lets IT managers control the data on private and public clouds so that they can enjoy the cost savings and flexibility of cloud services, but still maintain control over security.

test **prep**

- How do computer networks change the way employees manage information?

- What are the benefits and drawbacks of cloud computing?

LO B–5   Evaluate the human resource, security, privacy, and stability issues affected by information technology.

EFFECTS OF INFORMATION TECHNOLOGY ON MANAGEMENT

The increase of information technology has affected management greatly and will continue to do so. Four major issues today are human resource changes, security threats, privacy concerns, and stability.

Human Resource Issues

We talked in Chapter 8 about tall versus flat organization structures. Computers often eliminate middle-management functions and thus flatten organization structures.

Human resource managers need to recruit employees who know how to use the new technology or train those who already work in the company. The speed at which technology has advanced has created a generational divide in terms of tech skills among different-aged workers. This creates greater challenges when it comes to recruitment and training. Companies often hire consultants instead of internal staff to address these concerns. Outsourcing technical training allows them to concentrate on their core businesses.

Perhaps the most revolutionary effect of computers and the Internet is telecommuting. Using computers linked to the company's network, mobile employees can transmit their work to the office from anywhere as easily as they can walk to the boss's office. Naturally, that decreases travel time and overall costs, and often increases productivity. Having fewer employees in the office also means that a company can get by with smaller, and therefore less expensive, office space than before.

Telecommuting enables men and women to work while staying home with small children or elders. It has also been a tremendous boon for workers with disabilities. Employees who can work after hours on their home computers, rather than staying late at the office, report lowered stress and improved morale. Telecommuting is most successful among people who are self-starters, who don't have home distractions, and whose work doesn't require face-to-face interaction with co-workers.

Electronic communication can never replace face-to-face communication for creating enthusiasm and team spirit, however. Even as telecommuting has grown in popularity, some telecommuters report that a consistent diet of long-distance work leaves them feeling dislocated or left out of the loop. Some miss the energy of social interaction or dislike the intrusion of work into what is normally a personal setting. Often people working from home don't know when to turn the work off. Some companies are therefore using telecommuting only as a part-time alternative. In fact, industry now defines telecommuting as working at home a minimum of two days a week.

Figure B.6 illustrates how information technology changes the way managers and workers interact. For additional information about telecommuting and home-based workers, review Chapters 6 and 11.

Telecommuting is one of the biggest human resource boons of the wireless age, but some employees are better suited to its demands than others. Do you have what it takes?

FIGURE B.6 WHEN INFORMATION TECHNOLOGY ALTERS THE WORKPLACE

MANAGERS MUST	WORKERS MUST
• Instill commitment in subordinates rather than rule by command and control.	• Become initiators, able to act without management direction.
• Become coaches, training workers in necessary job skills, making sure they have resources to accomplish objectives, and explaining links between a job and what happens elsewhere in the company.	• Become financially literate so that they can understand the business implications of what they do and changes they suggest.
• Give greater authority to workers over scheduling, priority setting, and even compensation.	• Learn group interaction skills, including how to resolve disputes within their work group and how to work with other functions across the company.
• Use new information technologies to measure workers' performance, possibly based on customer satisfaction or the accomplishment of specific objectives.	• Develop new math, technical, and analytical skills to use newly available information on their jobs.

Security Issues

"Secure" information may be at risk from hackers who break into companies' networks; from employees who steal it; or from companies' own incompetence, poor gatekeeping, or sloppy procedures. Computer security is more complicated today than ever, as smartphones and the networks they run on, social networks and online games, and USB storage devices (flash drives and memory cards) become hackers' targets. When information was processed on mainframes, the single data center was easier to control because there was limited access to it. Today, however, computers are accessible not only in all areas within the company but also in all areas of other companies with which the firm does business.

virus
A piece of programming code inserted into other programming to cause some unexpected and, for the victim, usually undesirable event.

Viruses   An ongoing security threat is the spread of computer viruses over the Internet. A **virus** is a piece of programming code inserted into other programming that usually lies dormant until triggered to cause some unexpected and, for the victim, usually undesirable event. Users pick up viruses by unknowingly downloading infected programming over the Internet or sharing an infected USB storage device. Often the source of the infected file is unaware of the virus. Some viruses are playful messages ("Kilroy was here!"), but some can be quite harmful, erasing data or causing your hard drive to crash. Programs such as Norton AntiVirus inoculate your computer so that it doesn't catch a known virus. But because new viruses are being developed constantly, antivirus programs may have only limited success. Thus it is important to keep your antivirus protection up-to-date and, more important, practice safe computing by not downloading files from unknown sources.

Hackers   If a business stores customer data, it is subject to laws and regulations regarding the proper protection of these data. Many smaller businesses that don't have the manpower to handle security concerns might consider hiring a managed security services provider (MSSP) like Alert Logic or Perimeter E-Security.[43] MSSPs can install and manage firewalls, virtual private networks, web filtering and antispam programs, security intelligence services, and wireless and mobile functions. Even with all of this security protection, it is still possible that hackers can get through. Perhaps you were one of the tens of millions who had to get new credit or debit cards and monitor their credit reports when hackers breached Target's system and stole credit and debit card numbers. Target is now offering new credit cards with chip-and-pin technology to prevent further fraud.[44]

Some security experts advise businesses to assume that their systems have been breached and take the fight to the hackers. They recommend using methods that will frustrate the hackers and drive up their cost in order to deter them from future hacking. These methods include planting false information on their systems to mislead data thieves, and creating decoys that gather information about intruders. CloudFare offers a service called Maze, which it describes as "a virtual labyrinth of gibberish and gobbledygook."[45] Bottom line is that businesses that store data will need stronger and smarter tools to protect themselves from hackers.

Phishing   *Phishing* is another type of online security threat. A scammer will embellish an e-mail message with a stolen logo for a well-recognized brand such as eBay, PayPal, or Citibank that makes the message look authentic. Phishing messages often state something like "Account activation required" or "Your account will be canceled if you do not verify." When the victims click the link contained in the message, they are sent to a phony website that takes their personal information and uses it to commit fraud. The best way to avoid a phishing scam is never to access a website through a link in an e-mail message. Instead, open a new window and go to the home page of the company's website directly.

As more people log on to the Internet, the number of legal issues surrounding its use will likely increase. Today, copyright and pornography laws are entering into the virtual world. Other legal questions relate to intellectual property and contract disputes, online sexual and racial harassment, and the use of electronic communication to promote crooked sales schemes. Cybercrimes cost the United States billions of dollars a year.[46]

Cyberterrorism   Until September 11, 2001, corporate and government security officials worried mostly about online theft, credit card fraud, and hackers. Today, however, they are most concerned about *cyberterrorism*. Terrorist hackers could shut down the entire communications, money supply, electricity, and transportation systems. Recently hackers tried to get control of the CIA's main computer, and there were a string of denial of service attacks on other government computers. Although these sophisticated cyberattacks inconvenienced governmental agencies and had little impact on day-to-day public life, many are increasingly worried about an attack on the energy sector. In fact, the most sophisticated cyberthreat yet, called the Mask, was detected by an Internet security company in 2014 and has taken over thousands of IP addresses in dozens of countries. Its most likely target is oil and natural gas companies.[47]

The Critical Infrastructure Protection Board, a part of the U.S. Department of Homeland Security, was created after September 11, 2001, to devise a plan for improving the security of the United States' critical infrastructure. The agency needs the cooperation of businesses across the country, because 85 percent of the system it needs to protect is in the private sector. Companies have been reluctant to file reports about security breaches, however,

Were you one of the tens of millions who had to get a new credit or debit card when hackers breached Target's system and stole credit and debit card numbers? What can you do to protect yourself from loss when someone steals your vital information from a third party? How did the hacking affect Target's relationship with you and other customers? How did it affect the company's finances?

for fear the public will lose faith in their ability to protect their assets. To encourage the sharing of such information, Congress passed the Critical Infrastructure Information Act of 2002, assuring businesses that any information they provide the Department of Homeland Security will remain secret through an exemption from the Freedom of Information Act. This is only a start on what is likely to be a long effort to improve security technologies.

Privacy Issues

The increasing use of technology creates major concerns about privacy. In 2013, Edward Snowden leaked classified documents to the media regarding NSA's tactics in tracking U.S. citizens, international governments, and companies. Snowden's revelations changed the public conversation about privacy and security.[48]

You don't need to be the target of a criminal investigation to have your e-mail or phone calls snooped, and you're being watched by many more entities than the government. Of course, we've already talked about how your online clicks are monitored by private industry.[49] In addition, many U.S. companies scan employee e-mail regularly, and it's legal. They look for trade secrets, non-work-related traffic, harassing messages, and conflicts of interest. Any hacker with a desire to read your thoughts can also trap and read your messages, most of which are unencrypted. Some e-mail systems, such as Lotus Notes, can encrypt e-mail to keep corporate messages private. If you use browser-based e-mail, you can obtain a certificate that has an encryption key from a company such as VeriSign. Legitimate users who want to decrypt your mail need to get an unlocking key.

The Internet presents increasing threats to your privacy, as more personal information is stored in computers and more people are able to access it, legally or not. Some websites allow people to search for vehicle ownership from a license number or to find other individuals' real estate property records. One key question in the debate over protecting our privacy is "Isn't this personal information already public anyway?" Civil libertarians have long fought to keep certain kinds of information available to the public. If access to such data is restricted on the Internet, wouldn't we have to reevaluate our policies on all public records? Privacy advocates don't think so. After all, the difference is that the Internet makes obtaining personal information *too* easy. Would your neighbors or friends even consider going to the appropriate local agency and sorting through public documents for hours to find your driving records or to see your divorce settlement? Probably not. But they might dig into your background if all it takes is a few clicks of a button.

Many web servers track the online movements of users willing to swap such personal details for free access to online information. Site owners can share your data with others without your permission. Websites also often send **cookies** to your computer that stay on your hard drive. These are pieces of information such as registration data (name and password) or user preferences that the browser sends back to the server whenever you return to that website. Some software, known as spyware, can be installed on your computer without your knowledge. The spyware can then infect your system with viruses and track your online behavior.

Do you mind someone watching over your shoulder while you're on the web? Tim Berners-Lee, the researcher who invented the World Wide Web, led

How many of the online and mobile apps that you use track your whereabouts (both your physical location and where you go online) and share that information with third parties? Probably more than you think.

cookies
Pieces of information, such as registration data or user preferences, sent by a website over the Internet to a web browser that the browser software is expected to save and send back to the server whenever the user returns to that website.

the development of a way to prevent you from receiving cookies without your permission. His Platform for Privacy Preferences, or P3, allows a website to automatically send information on its privacy policies.[50] With P3 you can set up your web browser to communicate only with those websites that meet certain criteria. You need to decide how much information about yourself you are willing to give away. Remember, we are living in an information economy, and information is a commodity—that is, an economic good with a measurable value.[51]

Stability Issues

Although technology can provide significant increases in productivity and efficiency, instability has a significant impact on business. Candy maker Hershey discovered the Halloween trick was on it one year when the company couldn't get its treats to stores on time. Failure of its new $115 million computer system disrupted shipments, and retailers were forced to order Halloween candy from other companies, leaving Hershey with a 12 percent decrease in sales that quarter.

What's to blame? Experts say it is a combination of computer error; human error; malfunctioning software; and an overly complex marriage of software, hardware, and networking equipment. Some systems are launched too quickly to be bug-proof, and some executives don't have the technical knowledge to challenge computer specialists. As critical as technology is to business, some of it is not built for rigorous engineering, and some people aren't properly trained to use it. As things get more complex, we will probably be prone to more errors.

TECHNOLOGY AND YOU

If you're beginning to think being computer illiterate may be occupational suicide, you're getting the point. As information technology eliminates old jobs while creating new ones, it will be up to you to learn and maintain the skills you need to be certain you aren't left behind. And, who knows, maybe you can find a job like Gabi Gregg did. MTV appreciated so much the trust and passion she shared with her many Twitter followers that it offered her a job. It made her MTV first "TJ" in order to help "amplify the voice of our audience as part of the global conversation." She loves her new job, and the $100,000 a year salary isn't bad either!

test prep

- How has information technology changed the way people work?
- What management issues have been affected by the growth of information technology?

Use LearnSmart to help retain what you have learned. Access your instructor's Connect course to check out LearnSmart, or go to learnsmartadvantage.com for help.

≣ LEARNSMART

summary

Access your instructor's Connect course to check out LearnSmart or go to learnsmartadvantage.com for help.

LO B–1 Outline the changing role of business technology.

- **What have been the various names and roles of business technology since 1970?**
  In the 1970s, business technology was called data processing (DP) and its role was to support existing business. In the 1980s, its name became information systems (IS) and its role changed to doing business. In the 1990s, business technology became information technology (IT) and its role now is to change business. As technology became more sophisticated in the 2000s, it became known as business intelligence (or analytics) and includes data mining, online analytical processes, querying, and reporting.

- **How does information technology change business?**
  Information technology has minimized the importance of time and place to businesses. Firms that are independent of time and location can deliver products and services whenever and wherever convenient for the customer. See Figure B.6 for examples of how information technology changes business.

- **What is business intelligence?**
  Business intelligence refers to a variety of software applications that analyze an organization's raw data and take out useful insights from it.

LO B–2 List the types of business information, identify the characteristics of useful information, and discuss how data are stored and analyzed.

- **What types of information are available to businesses today?**
  The types of information available to businesses today include (1) business process information, (2) physical-world observations, (3) biological data, (4) public data, and (5) data that indicate personal preferences or intentions.

- **How can you deal with information overload?**
  The most important step in dealing with information overload is to identify your four or five key goals. Eliminate information that will not help you meet them.

- **What makes information useful?**
  The usefulness of management information depends on four characteristics: quality, completeness, timeliness, and relevance.

- **What is big data and data analytics?**
  Data analytics is the process of collecting, organizing, storing, and analyzing large sets of data ("big data") in order to identify patterns and other information that is most useful to the business now and for making future decisions. Data mining is the part of data analytics that involves looking for hidden patterns and previously unknown relationships among the data.

LO B–3 Compare the scope of the Internet, intranets, extranets, and virtual private networks and explain how broadband technology enabled the evolution to Web 2.0 and 3.0.

- **What information technology is available to help business manage information?**
  The heart of information technology involves the Internet, intranets, extranets, and virtual private networks. The Internet is a massive network of thousands of smaller networks open to everyone with a computer and a modem.

An intranet is a companywide network protected from unauthorized entry by outsiders. An extranet is a semiprivate network that allows more than one company to access the same information. A virtual private network is a private data network that creates secure connections, or "tunnels," over regular Internet lines.

- **What is Web 2.0?**
  Web 2.0 is the set of tools that allows people to build social and business connections, share information, and collaborate on projects online with user-generated sites like blogs, wikis, social networking sites and other online communities, and virtual worlds. YouTube and Twitter are among the largest Web 2.0 businesses, where ordinary people create all the content.

- **What is Web 3.0?**
  Web 3.0 is technology that adds a level of intelligence to interacting with the Web. It could be described as the Personal Web, whereas Web 1.0 can be thought of as the Static Web and Web 2.0 as the Social Web. Web 3.0 is made up of three basic components: the semantic web, the mobile web, and the immersive Internet, which are all leading to what many call the Internet of Things.

- **What is the Internet of Things?**
  Internet of Things refers to technology that enables ordinary objects to be connected to the Internet by using sensors, cameras, software, databases, and massive data centers.

 LO B–4   Explain virtual networking and discuss the benefits and drawbacks for cloud computing.

- **What is virtual networking?**
  Virtual networking is a process that allows software-based networked computers to run multiple operating systems and programs, and share storage. Virtual networking can be either external or internal. *External networking* treats the network as a single pool of resources that can all be accessed regardless of its physical components (i.e., networked computers share the resources of all the other computers on the network). *Internal networking* shares the resources of one central computer with all the networked computers.

- **What is cloud computing and what are its benefits and drawbacks?**
  Cloud computing is technology that stores a company's data and applications at offsite data centers, accessed over the Internet. Its benefits are reduced software costs, improved security, flexible capacity, lower equipment costs, and easier access. The drawbacks of cloud computing are concerns about security, stability, and control of data.

LO B–5   Evaluate the human resource, security, privacy, and stability issues affected by information technology.

- **What effect has information technology had on business management?**
  Computers eliminate some middle management functions and thus flatten organization structures. Computers also allow employees to work from their own homes. On the negative side, computers sometimes allow information to fall into the wrong hands. Concern for privacy is an issue affected by the vast store of information available on the Internet. Finding the balance between freedom to access private information and individuals' right to maintain privacy will require continued debate.

key terms

broadband technology 10	**extranet** 10	**virtual networking** 15
business intelligence (BI) **or analytics** 3	**information systems** **(IS)** 2	**virtual private network** **(VPN)** 10
cloud computing 16	**information** **technology (IT)** 2	**virus** 18
cookies 20		**Web 2.0** 13
data analytics 8	**Internet2** 11	**Web 3.0** 13
data processing (DP) 2	**intranet** 9	

critical thinking

1. What information, either for your personal life or for your job, would you like to receive exactly when and where you need it?

2. What are the implications for world trade given the ability firms and government organizations now have to communicate across borders so easily?

3. How will the introduction and integration of more and more devices into the Internet of Things affect your life? Do you think they will widen or narrow the gap between the haves and have-nots (rich and poor people)?

developing **workplace skills**

Key: ● **Team**   ★ **Analytic**   ▲ **Communication**   ▣ **Technology**

● ▣ ▲ ★ 1. Imagine you have $2,000 to buy or upgrade a computer system. Research hardware and software in computer magazines and on websites such as ZDNet (www.zdnet.com). Visit a computer store or shop online to find the best value. List what you would buy, and write a summary explaining your choices.

▣ ▲ ★ 2. Interview someone who bought a computer to use in his or her business. Ask why he or she bought that specific computer and how it is used. Ask about any problems that occurred during the purchase process or in installing and using the system. What would the buyer do differently next time? What software does he or she find especially useful?

▣ ▲ ★ 3. Describe one computer glitch you've experienced and what you did to resolve it. Discuss the consequences of the interruption (lost data, decreased productivity, increased stress). What steps have you taken to prevent a recurrence of the problem you faced?

● ▣ ★ 4. Choose a topic that interests you and use two search engines to find information about it online. Narrow your search using the tips offered by the search engine. Did both search engines find the same websites? If not, how were their results different? Which engine found the most appropriate information?

5. How has technology changed your relationship with specific businesses or organizations such as your bank, your school, and your favorite places to shop? Has it strengthened or weakened your relationship? Has technology affected your relationship with your family, friends, and community? Take a sheet of paper and write down how technology has helped build your business and personal relationships on one side. On the other side, list how technology has weakened those relationships. What can you and others do to use technology more effectively to reduce any negative impact?

taking it to the **net**

PURPOSE

To identify how the Internet of Things (IoT) uses connected devices to gather and analyze data to provide information useful to both businesses and individuals.

EXERCISE

Go to http://postscapes.com/what-exactly-is-the-internet-of-things-infographic and scroll through the infographic "What Exactly Is the Internet of Things?"

1. IoT is driven by a combination of what three components? Give three examples of each of them.

2. List three smart devices and applications created by the interaction of the three components of IoT identified in question 1.

3. How is IoT impacting business?

notes

1. John Naughton, "We're All Being Mined for Data—but Who Are the Real Winners?" *The Guardian,* June 7, 2014.
2. Ryan Mulcahy, "Business Intelligence Definition and Solutions," *CIO,* www.cio.com, accessed June 2014.
3. "Kodak Files for Bankruptcy, No More Kodak Moments," *Business Today,* www.businesstoday.com, accessed June 2014.
4. Ernest von Simson, "The New Role of the CIO," *Bloomberg Businessweek,* May 22, 2013; and Shane O'Neill, "Digital Business Skills: Most Wanted List," *InformationWeek,* May 1, 2014.
5. Scott Young, "Bringing Eye-Tracking to the Stores," *Perception Research Services,* www.prservices.com, accessed June 2014.
6. Jilly Duffy, "Get Organized: How to Clean Out Your Inbox," *PCMagazine,* September 23, 2013; and Jennifer Forker, "Tips to Organize Your Email and Other Digital Clutter," *Huffington Post,* March 5, 2013.
7. Brady Dale, "In Brooklyn, a Grasp at Giving 'Big Data' Meaning," *CNN Money,* April 28, 2014; Irving Wladawsky-Berger, "Data-Driven Decision Making: Promises and Limits," *The Wall Street Journal,* September 27, 2013; and Katherine Noyes, "IBM Stakes Its Claim in 'Scale-Out' Storage for Big Data," *CNN Money,* May 14, 2014.
8. Joshua Klein, "When Big Data Goes Bad," *CNN Money,* November 5, 2013.
9. Juan Carlos Perez, "Badgeville Aims to Make Child's Play Out of Software Deployment," *PC World,* June 10, 2014.
10. Roland Waddilove, "How to Set Up a VPN Service to Surf the Web Anonymously," *PC World,* May 19, 2014.
11. Emil Protalinski, "Akamai: Average Internet Speed Grew 29% Year-over-Year to 3.6 Mbps," *The Next Web,* www.tnw.com, accessed June 2014.
12. National Broadband Plan, www.broadband.gov, accessed June 2014.
13. David Nicklaus, Todd Shields, and Chris Strohm, "FCC Advances Fast Lane Rules," *St. Louis Post-Dispatch,* May 16, 2014.
14. Nancy Scola, "Five Myths about Net Neutrality," *The Washington Post,"* June 12, 2014.
15. Betsy Issacson, "Web 3.0: What the Web Could Look Like without Net Neutrality," *Huffington Post,* January 25. 2014.
16. Fiber Google, www.fiber.google.com, accessed June 2014.
17. Jim Clayman, "Internet2 CIO to Discuss the Emerging Higher Education Community Cloud at Three Rivers Systems' Annual Global Users Conference," *St. Louis Post-Dispatch,* June 8, 2014.
18. Internet2, www.internet2.edu, accessed June 2014.
19. 4food, www.4food.com, accessed June 2014.
20. *Randy Hlavac, "Because We're Happy: Using Social Media to Turn Audiences Around," Forbes,* June 3, 2014.

21. Anjana Ahuja, "Thinking Machines Are Ripe for a World Take-over," *Financial Times*, June 10, 2014.
22. Trish Winters, "Web 3.0," *Bitcoin Magazine*, www.bitcoinmagazine.com, April 25, 2014; and Harry Siegel, "Humanity, We Had a Good Run," *The New York Daily News*, June 9, 2014.
23. Anthony Wing Cosner, "Famo.us Part I: New Concepts Will Increase the Flow of Highly Dynamic Web 3.0 Apps," *Forbes*, May 27, 2014.
24. World Wide Web Consortium, www.w3c.org, accessed June 2014.
25. *PR Newswire*, "Amdocs Announces Self-Optimizing Networks Solution for Customer Experience-Driven Network Automation," *Web 2.0 Journal*, web2.sys-con.com, February 10, 2014.
26. George Glover, "Why Responsive Web Design Is the Cornerstone to Any Mobile Strategy," *Business 2 Community*, www.business2community.com, June 2, 2014.
27. "Intel Brings Immersive, Human Interaction to Devices in 2014," *The Wall Street Journal*, January 6, 2014; Bob Tita, "How 3-D Printing Works," *The Wall Street Journal*, June 11, 2013; and Mark Jenkins, "3-D Printing Can Make Everyone a Designer," *Washington Post*, March 15, 2013.
28. Lori Kozlowski, "Everthing Is Connected: What "The 'Internet of Things' Means Now," *Forbes*, April 23, 2014; and Stuart Dredge, "10 Things We Learned from Pew Research's Internet of Things Report," *The Guardian*, May 14, 2014.
29. "An Uncommon Thread," *The Economist*," March 8., 2014.
30. Chris Murphy, "Internet of Things: What's Holding Us Back," *InformationWeek*, www.informationweek.com, May 5, 2014.
31. "Who Invented the Internet?" *History*, www.history.com, December 18, 2013; and *World Wide Web Foundation*, www.webfoundation.org, accessed June 2014.
32. Todd Shields, "House Republicans Question U.S. Plan to Give Up Internet Control," *Bloomberg Businessweek*, April 2, 2014; and Brendan Greeley, "The U.S. Gives Up Its Control of the Free Speech Internet," *Bloomberg Businessweek*, March 17, 2014.
33. Emma Woollacott, "U.S. Government Cedes Control of the Internet," *Forbes*, March 15, 2014.
34. Tom Risen, "The U.S. Gives the Internet to the World," *U.S. News & World Report*, March 17, 2014.
35. Network Virtualization, *Webopedia*, www.webopedia.com, accessed June 2014; and Kurt Marko, "Network Virtualization: The Final Piece of the Private Cloud," *Forbes*, March 25, 2014.
36. Quentin Hardy, "Cloud Computing, in Translation," *The New York Times*, June 11, 2014.
37. David Kramer, "A Layman's Guide to Cloud Computing," *Huffington Post*, June 12, 2014.
38. Quentin Hardy, "The Era of Cloud Computing," *The New York Times*, June 11, 2014; and "Migration: A Planned, Structured Cloud Approach," *CIO.*, www.cio.com, June 11, 2014.
39. Joe McKendrick, "5 Benefits of Cloud Computing You Aren't Likely to See in a SalesBrochure," *Forbes*, July 12, 2013; Ian Stone, "Cloud Computing Enables Businesses to Discover Their Entrepreneurial Spirit," *The Guardian*, April 15, 2014; and "Cloud Computing Industry Analysis and Infographic: Companies Overspend on Infrastructure by 30% or More," *PRWeb*, www.prweb.com, June 3, 2014.
40. Archana Venkatraman, "Advantages and Disadvantages of Cloud Computing," *ComputerWeekly*, www.computerweekly.com, accessed June 2014; and Mikal E. Belicove, "Will the Cloud Rain on My Parade?," *Entrepreneur*, August 2013.
41. Zack Whittaker, "Dropbox Hit by Outage; File Sync Busted," *ZDNet*, www.zdnet.com, March 14, 2014.
42. Warwick Ashford, "Dropbox Can Be Hacked, Say Security Researchers," *ComputerWeekly*, www.computerweekly.com, August 29, 2014.
43. C. J. Ariottta, "Top Emerging Managed Security Service Providers," *MSPMentor*, www.mspmentor.com, January 14, 2013.
44. Shan Li, "Target Hires New Security Chief from General Motors after Security Breach," *Los Angeles Times*, June 11, 2014.
45. "Firewalls and Firefights," *The Economist*, August 10, 2013.
46. "SIRF's Up," *The Economist*, November 30, 2014.
47. Christopher Harress, "Obama Says Cyberterrorism Is the Country's Biggest Threat, U.S. Government Assembles 'Cyber Warriors,'" *International Business Times*, February 18, 2014.
48. Daniel Terdiman, "The Most Anticipated SXSW Talk in Years, Snowden Fires Up Austin," *CNet*, www.cnet.com, March 10, 2014.
49. Josh Gerstein and Stephanie Simon, "Who Watches the Watchers? Big Data Goes Unchecked," *Politico*, www.politico.com, May 14, 2014.
50. Platform for Privacy Preferences, www.w3.org/P3P, accessed June 2014.
51. "Hiding from Big Data," *The Economist*, June 7, 2014.

photo credits

Page B-1: © Nancy Kaszerman/Zumapress.com/ Newscom; p. B-3: © Ted S. Warren/AP Images; p. B-6: © Anthony Lee/caia image/Alamy RF; p. B-11: © Martin McCarthy/iStock/360/Getty Images RF; p. B-14: © epa european pressphoto agency b.v./Alamy; p. B-16: © liewy/iStock/360/ Getty Images RF; p. B-17: © pixdeluxe/iStock/360/ Getty Images RF; p. B-19: © The Detroit Free Press/MCT/Getty Images; p. B-20: © Design Pics Inc./Alamy RF.

Chapter

1

What Do We Mean by Leadership?

Introduction

In the spring of 1972, an airplane flew across the Andes mountains carrying its crew and 40 passengers. Most of the passengers were members of an amateur Uruguayan rugby team en route to a game in Chile. The plane never arrived. It crashed in snow-covered mountains, breaking into several pieces on impact. The main part of the fuselage slid like a toboggan down a steep valley, coming to rest in waist-deep snow. Although a number of people died immediately or within a day of the impact, the picture for the 28 survivors was not much better. The fuselage offered little protection from the extreme cold, food supplies were scant, and a number of passengers had serious injuries from the crash. Over the next few days, several surviving passengers became psychotic and several others died from their injuries. The passengers who were relatively uninjured set out to do what they could to improve their chances of survival.

Several worked on "weatherproofing" the wreckage; others found ways to get water; and those with medical training took care of the injured. Although shaken by the crash, the survivors initially were confident they would be found. These feelings gradually gave way to despair as search and rescue teams failed to find the wreckage. With the passing of several weeks and no sign of rescue in sight, the remaining passengers decided to mount expeditions to determine the best way to escape. The most physically fit were chosen to go on the expeditions because the thin mountain air and the deep snow made the trips difficult. The results of the trips were both frustrating and demoralizing: the expedition members determined they were in the middle of the Andes mountains, and walking out to find help was believed to be impossible. Just when the survivors thought nothing worse could possibly happen, an avalanche hit the wreckage and killed several more of them.

The remaining survivors concluded they would not be rescued, and their only hope was for someone to leave the wreckage and find help. Three of the fittest passengers were chosen for the final expedition, and everyone else's work was directed toward improving the expedition's chances of success. The three expedition members were given more food and were exempted from routine survival activities; the rest spent most of their energies securing supplies for the trip. Two months after the plane crash, the expedition members set out on their final attempt to find help. After hiking for 10 days through some of the most rugged terrain in the world, the expedition stumbled across a group of Chilean peasants tending cattle. One of the expedition members stated, "I come from a plane that fell in the mountains. I am Uruguayan . . ." Eventually 14 other survivors were rescued.

When the full account of their survival became known, it was not without controversy. It had required extreme and unsettling measures: the survivors had lived only by eating the flesh of their deceased comrades. Nonetheless, their story is one of the most moving survival dramas of all time, magnificently told by Piers Paul Read in *Alive*.[1] It is a story of tragedy and courage, and it is a story of leadership.

Perhaps a story of survival in the Andes is so far removed from everyday experience that it does not seem to hold any relevant lessons about leadership for you personally. But consider some of the basic issues the Andes survivors faced: tension between individual and group goals, dealing with the different needs and personalities of group members, and keeping hope alive in the face of adversity. These issues are not so different from those facing many groups we're a part of. We can also look at the Andes experience for examples of the emergence of informal leaders in groups. Before the flight, a boy named Parrado was awkward and shy, a "second-stringer" both athletically and socially. Nonetheless, this unlikely hero became the best loved and most respected among the survivors for his courage, optimism, fairness, and emotional support. Persuasiveness in group decision making also was an important part of leadership among the Andes survivors. During the difficult discussions preceding the agonizing decision to survive on the flesh of their deceased comrades, one of the rugby players made his reasoning clear: "I know that if my dead body could help you stay alive, then I would want you to use it. In fact, if I do die and you don't eat me, then I'll come back from wherever I am and give you a good kick in the ass."[2]

*Lives of great men all remind us
We can make our lives sublime
And, departing, leave behind us
Footprints on the sands of time.*

Henry Wadsworth Longfellow

What Is Leadership?

The Andes story and the experiences of many other leaders we'll introduce to you in a series of profiles sprinkled throughout the chapters provide numerous examples of leadership. But just what *is* leadership?

The halls of fame are open wide and they are always full. Some go in by the door called "push" and some by the door called "pull."

Stanley Baldwin, British prime minister in the 1930s

Remember the difference between a boss and a leader: a boss says, "Go!"—a leader says, "Let's go!"

E. M. Kelly

People who do research on leadership disagree more than you might think about what leadership really is. Most of this disagreement stems from the fact that **leadership** is a complex phenomenon involving the leader, the followers, and the situation. Some leadership researchers have focused on the personality, physical traits, or behaviors of the leader; others have studied the relationships between leaders and followers; still others have studied how aspects of the situation affect how leaders act. Some have extended the latter viewpoint so far as to suggest there is no such thing as leadership; they argue that organizational successes and failures often get falsely attributed to the leader, but the situation may have a much greater impact on how the organization functions than does any individual, including the leader.[3]

Perhaps the best way for you to begin to understand the complexities of leadership is to see some of the ways leadership has been defined. Leadership researchers have defined leadership in many different ways:

- The process by which an agent induces a subordinate to behave in a desired manner.[4]
- Directing and coordinating the work of group members.[5]
- An interpersonal relation in which others comply because they want to, not because they have to.[6]
- The process of influencing an organized group toward accomplishing its goals.[7]
- Actions that focus resources to create desirable opportunities.[8]
- Creating conditions for a team to be effective.[9]
- The ability to get results and the ability to build teams; these represent the what and the how of leadership.[10]
- A complex form of social problem solving.[11]

As you can see, definitions of leadership differ in many ways, and these differences have resulted in various researchers exploring disparate aspects of leadership. For example, if we were to apply these definitions to the Andes survival scenario described earlier, some researchers would focus on the behaviors Parrado used to keep up the morale of the survivors. Researchers who define leadership as influencing an organized group toward accomplishing its goals would examine how Parrado managed to convince the group to stage and support the final expedition. One's definition of leadership might also influence just *who* is considered an appropriate leader for study. Thus each group of researchers might focus on a different aspect of leadership, and each would tell a different story regarding the leader, the followers, and the situation.

Although having many leadership definitions may seem confusing, it is important to understand that there is no single correct definition. The various definitions can help us appreciate the multitude of factors that affect leadership, as well as different perspectives from which to view it. For example, in the first definition just listed, the word *subordinate* seems to confine leadership to downward influence in hierarchical relationships; it seems to exclude informal leadership. The second definition emphasizes the directing and controlling aspects of leadership, and thereby may deemphasize emotional aspects of leadership. The emphasis placed in the third definition on subordinates' "wanting to" comply with a leader's wishes seems to exclude any kind of coercion as a leadership tool. Further, it becomes problematic to identify ways in which a leader's actions are really leadership if subordinates voluntarily comply when a leader with considerable potential coercive power merely asks others to do something without explicitly threatening them. Similarly, a key reason behind using the phrase *desirable opportunities* in one of the definitions was precisely to distinguish between leadership and tyranny. And partly because there are many different definitions of leadership, there is also a wide range of individuals we consider leaders. In addition to stories about leaders and leadership we will sprinkle through this book, we will highlight several in each chapter in a series of Profiles in Leadership. The first of these is Profiles in Leadership 1.1, which highlights Peter Jackson.

All considered, we find that defining leadership as "the process of influencing an organized group toward accomplishing its goals" is fairly comprehensive and helpful. Several implications of this definition are worth further examination.

Leadership Is Both a Science and an Art

Saying leadership is both a science and an art emphasizes the subject of leadership as a field of scholarly inquiry, as well as certain aspects of the practice of leadership. The scope of the science of leadership is reflected in the number of studies—approximately 8,000—cited in an authoritative reference work, *Bass & Stogdill's Handbook of Leadership: Theory, Research, and Managerial Applications.*[12] However, being an expert on leadership research is neither necessary nor sufficient for being a good leader. Some managers may be effective leaders without ever having taken a course or training program in leadership, and some scholars in the field of leadership may be relatively poor leaders themselves.

However, knowing something about leadership research is relevant to leadership effectiveness. Scholarship may not be a prerequisite for leadership effectiveness, but understanding some of the major research findings can help individuals better analyze situations using a variety of perspectives. That, in turn, can tell leaders how to be more effective. Even so, because skills in analyzing and responding to situations vary greatly across leaders, leadership will always remain partly an art as well as a science.

Any fool can keep a rule. God gave him a brain to know when to break the rule.
General Willard W. Scott

Peter Jackson

PROFILES IN LEADERSHIP 1.1

When Peter Jackson read *The Lord of the Rings* trilogy at the age of 18, he couldn't wait until it was made into a movie; 20 years later he made that movie himself. In 2004 *The Lord of the Rings: The Return of the King* took home 11 Academy Awards, winning the Oscar in every category for which it was nominated. This tied the record for the most Oscars ever earned by one motion picture. Such an achievement might seem unlikely for a producer/director whose film debut was titled *Bad Taste,* which it and subsequent works exemplified in spades. Peter Jackson made horror movies so grisly and revolting that his fans nicknamed him the "Sultan of Splatter." Nonetheless, his talent was evident to discerning eyes—at least among horror film aficionados. *Bad Taste* was hailed as a cult classic at the Cannes Film Festival, and horror fans tabbed Jackson as a talent to follow.

When screenwriter Costa Botes heard that *The Lord of the Rings* would be made into a live action film, he thought those responsible were crazy. Prevailing wisdom was that the fantastic and complex trilogy simply could not be believably translated onto the screen. But he also believed that "there was no other director on earth who could do it justice" (Botes, 2004). And do it justice he obviously did. What was it about the "Sultan of Splatter's" leader-ship that gave others such confidence in his ability to make one of the biggest and best movies of all time? What gave him the confidence to even try? And what made others want to share in his vision?

Peter Jackson's effectiveness as a leader has been due in large part to a unique combination of personal qualities and talents. One associate, for example, called him "one of the smartest people I know," as well as a maverick willing to buck the establishment. Jackson is also a tireless worker whose early successes were due in no small part to the combination of his ambition and dogged perseverance (Botes, 2004). His initial success was driven largely by his budding genius in making films on a low budget and with virtually no other staff. In reading others' comments who worked with him on the *LOTR* project, however, it's clear that his leadership continued to develop over the years. It was his ability to communicate a shared vision and inspire such extraordinary work from an incredibly large staff that made *LOTR* so spectacularly successful.

Not one to rest on his laurels, in 2012 Jackson released the first installment of *The Hobbit*, another technologically standard-breaking and popular film trilogy.

Source: Adapted from Costa Botes, *Made in New Zealand: The Cinema of Peter Jackson,* NZEDGE.com, May 2004.

Highlight 1.1 provides further perspective on how the art and science of leadership are represented in somewhat distinctive research traditions.

Leadership Is Both Rational and Emotional

Leadership involves both the rational and emotional sides of human experience. Leadership includes actions and influences based on reason and logic as well as those based on inspiration and passion. We do not want to cultivate merely intellectualized leaders who respond with only logical predictability. Because people differ in their thoughts and feelings, hopes and dreams, needs and fears, goals and ambitions, and strengths and weaknesses, leadership situations can be complex. People are both rational and emotional, so leaders can use rational techniques and emotional appeals to influence followers, but they must also weigh the rational and emotional consequences of their actions.

A democracy cannot follow a leader unless he is dramatized. A man to be a hero must not content himself with heroic virtues and anonymous action. He must talk and explain as he acts—drama.

William Allen White, American writer and editor, *Emporia Gazette*

The Academic and Troubadour Traditions of Leadership Research

HIGHLIGHT 1.1

On a practical level, leadership is a topic that almost everyone is interested in at one time or another. People have a vested interest in who is running their government, schools, company, or church, and because of this interest thousands of books and articles have been written about the topic of leadership. Curphy and Hogan believe these works can be divided into two major camps. The **academic tradition** consists of articles that use data and statistical techniques to make inferences about effective leadership. Because the academic tradition is research based, for the most part these findings are written for other leadership researchers and are virtually uninterpretable to leadership *practitioners*. As such, leadership practitioners are often unfamiliar with the research findings of the academic tradition.

The second camp of leadership literature is the **troubadour tradition**. These books and articles often consist of nothing more than the opinions or score-settling reminiscences of former leaders. Books in the troubadour tradition, such as *Who Moved My Cheese?*, *What the CEO Wants You to Know*, *Winning*, and *Lead Like Jesus: Lessons from the Greatest Leadership Role Model of all Time*, are wildly popular, but it is difficult to separate fact from fiction or determine whether these opinions translate to other settings. People who are unfamiliar with the findings of the academic tradition and the limitations of the troubadour tradition find it difficult to differentiate research findings from opinion.

Perhaps the biggest challenge to improving the practice of leadership is to give practitioners timely, easily digestible, research-grounded advice on how to effectively lead others. The knowledge accumulated from 90 years of leadership research is of tremendous value, yet scientists have paid little attention to the ultimate consumers of their work—leaders and leaders-to-be. Leadership practitioners often want fast answers about how to be more effective or successful and understandably turn to popular books and articles that *appear* to provide timely answers to their practical concerns. Unfortunately, however, the claims in the popular literature are rarely based on sound research; they oversimplify the complexities of the leadership process; and many times they actually offer bad advice. Relatively little weight is given to well-researched leadership studies, primarily because the arcane requirements of publishing articles in scholarly journals make their content virtually unreadable (and certainly uninteresting) to actual leadership practitioners. One of the primary objectives of this book is to make the results of leadership research more usable for leaders and leaders-to-be.

Sources: G. J. Curphy, M. J. Benson, A. Baldrica, and R. T. Hogan, *Managerial Incompetence* (unpublished manuscript, 2007); G. J. Curphy, "*What We Really Know about Leadership (But Seem Unwilling to Implement)*" (presentation given to the Minnesota Professionals for Psychology and Applied Work, Minneapolis, MN, January 2004); R. T. Hogan, *Personality and the Fate of Organizations* (Mahwah, NJ: Lawrence Erlbaum Associates, 2007).

A full appreciation of leadership involves looking at both these sides of human nature. Good leadership is more than just calculation and planning, or following a checklist, even though rational analysis can enhance good leadership. Good leadership also involves touching others' feelings; emotions play an important role in leadership too. Just one example of this is the civil rights movement of the 1960s, which was based on emotions as well as on principles. Dr. Martin Luther King Jr. inspired many people to action; he touched people's hearts as well as their heads.

Aroused feelings, however, can be used either positively or negatively, constructively or destructively. Some leaders have been able to inspire others to deeds of great purpose and courage. On the other hand, as images of Adolf Hitler's mass rallies or present-day angry mobs attest, group frenzy can readily become group mindlessness. As another example, emotional appeals by the Reverend Jim Jones resulted in approximately 800 of his followers volitionally committing suicide.

The mere presence of a group (even without heightened emotional levels) can also cause people to act differently than when they are alone. For example, in airline cockpit crews, there are clear lines of authority from the captain down to the first officer (second in command) and so on. So strong are the norms surrounding the authority of the captain that some first officers will not take control of the airplane from the captain even in the event of impending disaster. Foushee[13] reported a study wherein airline captains in simulator training intentionally feigned incapacitation so the response of the rest of the crew could be observed. The feigned incapacitations occurred at a predetermined point during the plane's final approach in landing, and the simulation involved conditions of poor weather and visibility. Approximately 25 percent of the first officers in these simulated flights allowed the plane to crash. For some reason, the first officers did not take control even when it was clear the captain was allowing the aircraft to deviate from the parameters of a safe approach. This example demonstrates how group dynamics can influence the behavior of group members even when emotional levels are *not* high. (Believe it or not, airline crews are so well trained that this is *not* an emotional situation.) In sum, it should be apparent that leadership involves followers' feelings and nonrational behavior as well as rational behavior. Leaders need to consider *both* the rational and the emotional consequences of their actions.

Leadership and Management

In trying to answer "What is leadership?" it is natural to look at the relationship between leadership and management. To many, the word **management** suggests words like *efficiency, planning, paperwork, procedures, regulations, control,* and *consistency.* Leadership is often more associated with words like *risk taking, dynamic, creativity, change,* and *vision.* Some say leadership is fundamentally a value-choosing, and thus a value-laden, activity, whereas management is not. Leaders are thought to *do the right things,* whereas managers are thought to *do things right.*[14,15] Here are some other distinctions between managers and leaders:[16]

- Managers administer; leaders innovate.
- Managers maintain; leaders develop.
- Managers control; leaders inspire.

If you want some ham, you gotta go into the smokehouse.

Huey Long, governor of Louisiana, 1928–1932

- Managers have a short-term view; leaders, a long-term view.
- Managers ask how and when; leaders ask what and why.
- Managers imitate; leaders originate.
- Managers accept the status quo; leaders challenge it.

Zaleznik[17] goes so far as to say these differences reflect fundamentally different personality types: leaders and managers are basically different kinds of people. He says some people are managers *by nature;* other people are leaders *by nature.* One is not better than the other; they are just different. Their differences, in fact, can be useful because organizations typically need both functions performed well. For example, consider again the U.S. civil rights movement in the 1960s. Dr. Martin Luther King Jr. gave life and direction to the civil rights movement in America. He gave dignity and hope of freer participation in national life to people who before had little reason to expect it. He inspired the world with his vision and eloquence, and he changed the way we live together. America is a different nation today because of him. Was Dr. Martin Luther King Jr. a leader? Of course. Was he a manager? Somehow that does not seem to fit, and the civil rights movement might have failed if it had not been for the managerial talents of his supporting staff. Leadership and management complement each other, and both are vital to organizational success.

With regard to the issue of leadership versus management, the authors of this book take a middle-of-the-road position. We think of leadership and management as closely related but distinguishable functions. Our view of the relationship is depicted in Figure 1.1, which shows leadership and management as two overlapping functions. Although some functions performed by leaders and managers may be unique, there is also an area of overlap. In reading Highlight 1.2, do you see more good management in the response to the 1906 San Francisco earthquake, more good leadership, or both?

FIGURE 1.1
Leadership and
Management
Overlap

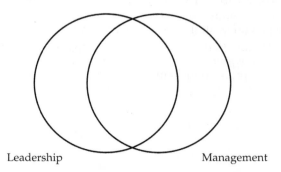

Leadership   Management

The Response of Leadership to a Natural Disaster

HIGHLIGHT 1.2

Much has been written about the inadequate response of local, state, and federal agencies to Hurricane Katrina. It may be instructive to compare the response of government agencies to a natural disaster on a different coast a century earlier: the San Francisco earthquake and fire of 1906.

While the precipitant disaster was the earthquake itself, much destruction resulted from the consequent fire, one disaster aggravating the impact of the other. Because of the earthquake, utility poles throughout the city fell, taking the high-tension wires they were carrying with them. Gas pipes broke; chimneys fell, dropping hot coals into thousands of gallons of gas spilled by broken fuel tanks; stoves and heaters in homes toppled over; and in moments fires erupted across the city. And because the earthquake's first tremors also broke water pipes throughout the city, fire hydrants everywhere suddenly went dry, making fighting the fires virtually impossible. In objective terms, the disaster is estimated to have killed as many as 3,000 people, rendered more than 200,000 homeless, and by some measures caused $195 billion in property loss as measured by today's dollars.

How did authorities respond to the crisis when there were far fewer agencies with presumed response plans to combat disasters, and when high-tech communication methods were unheard of? Consider these two examples:

- The ranking officer assigned to a U.S. Army post in San Francisco was away when the earthquake struck, so it was up to his deputy to help organize the army's and federal government's response. The deputy immediately cabled Washington, D.C., requesting tents, rations, and medicine. Secretary of War William Howard Taft, who would become the next U.S. president, responded by immediately dispatching 200,000 rations from Washington State. In a matter of days, every tent in the U.S. Army had been sent to San Francisco, and the longest hospital train in history was dispatched from Virginia.

- Perhaps the most impressive example of leadership initiative in the face of the 1906 disaster was that of the U.S. Post Office. It recovered its ability to function in short order without losing a single item that was being handled when the earthquake struck. And because the earthquake had effectively destroyed the city's telegraphic connection (telegrams inside the city were temporarily being delivered by the post office), a critical question arose: How could people struck by the disaster communicate with their families elsewhere? The city postmaster immediately announced that all citizens of San Francisco could use the post office to inform their families and loved ones of their condition and needs. He further stipulated that for outgoing private letters *it would not matter whether the envelopes bore stamps.* This was what was needed: Circumstances demanded that people be able to communicate with friends and family whether or not they could find or pay for stamps.

Perhaps this should remind us that modern leadership is not necessarily better leadership, and that leadership in government is not always bureaucratic and can be both humane and innovative.

Source: Adapted from S. Winchester, *A Crack in the Edge of the World: America and the Great California Earthquake of 1906* (New York: Harper Perennial, 2006).

The Romance of Leadership

HIGHLIGHT 1.3

This text is predicated on the idea that leaders can make a difference. Interestingly, though, while businesspeople generally agree, not all scholars do.

People in the business world attribute much of a company's success or failure to its leadership. One study counted the number of articles appearing in *The Wall Street Journal* that dealt with leadership and found nearly 10 percent of the articles about representative target companies addressed that company's leadership. Furthermore, there was a significant positive relationship between company performance and the number of articles about its leadership; the more a company's leadership was emphasized in *The Wall Street Journal,* the better the company was doing. This might mean the more a company takes leadership seriously (as reflected by the emphasis in *The Wall Street Journal*), the better it does.

However, the study authors were skeptical about the real utility of leadership as a concept.

They suggested leadership is merely a romanticized notion—an obsession people want and need to believe in. Belief in the potency of leadership may be a cultural myth that has utility primarily insofar as it affects how people create meaning about causal events in complex social systems. The behavior of leaders, the authors contend, does not account for much of the variance in an organization's performance. Nonetheless, people seem strongly committed to a basic faith that individual leaders shape organizational destiny for good or ill.

As you read this book and come to appreciate how many factors affect a group's success *besides* the talents of the individual leader, you might pay a price for that understanding. As you appreciate the *complexity* of leadership more, the *romance* of leadership might slightly diminish.

Source: J. R. Meindl, S. B. Ehrlich, and J. M. Dukerich, "The Romance of Leadership," *Administrative Science Quarterly* 30 (1985), pp. 78–102.

Leadership Myths

Few things pose a greater obstacle to leadership development than certain unsubstantiated and self-limiting beliefs about leadership. Therefore, before we begin examining leadership and leadership development in more detail, we will consider what they are not. We will examine several beliefs (we call them myths) that stand in the way of fully understanding and developing leadership.

Myth: Good Leadership Is All Common Sense

At face value, this myth says one needs only common sense to be a good leader. It also implies, however, that most if not all of the studies of leadership reported in scholarly journals and books only confirm what anyone with common sense already knows.

The problem, of course, is with the ambiguous term *common sense*. It implies a common body of practical knowledge about life that virtually any reasonable person with moderate experience has acquired. A simple experiment, however, may convince you that common sense may be less common than you think. Ask a few friends or acquaintances whether the old folk wisdom "Absence makes the heart grow fonder" is true or false. Most will say it is true. After that ask a different group whether the old folk wisdom "Out of sight, out of mind" is true or false. Most of that group will answer true as well, even though the two proverbs are contradictory.

A similar thing sometimes happens when people hear about the results of studies concerning human behavior. On hearing the results, people may say, "Who needed a study to learn that? I knew it all the time." However, several experiments[18,19] showed that events were much more surprising when subjects had to guess the outcome of an experiment than when subjects were told the outcome. What seems obvious after you know the results and what you (or anyone else) would have predicted beforehand are not the same thing. Hindsight is always 20/20.

The point might become clearer with a specific example; read the following paragraph:

> After World War II, the U.S. Army spent enormous sums of money on studies only to reach conclusions that, many believed, should have been apparent at the outset. One, for example, was that southern soldiers were better able to stand the climate in the hot South Sea islands than northern soldiers were.

If you miss seven balls out of ten, you're batting three hundred and that's good enough for the Hall of Fame. You can't score if you keep the bat on your shoulder.

Walter B. Wriston, chairman of Citicorp, 1970–1984

This sounds reasonable, but there is a problem: the statement here is exactly contrary to the actual findings. Southerners were no better than northerners in adapting to tropical climates.[20] Common sense can often play tricks on us.

Put a little differently, one challenge of understanding leadership may be to know when common sense applies and when it does not. Do leaders need to act confidently? Of course. But they also need to be humble enough to recognize that others' views are useful, too. Do leaders need to persevere when times get tough? Yes. But they also need to recognize when times change and a new direction is called for. If leadership were nothing more than common sense, there should be few, if any, problems in the workplace. However, we venture to guess you have noticed more than a few problems between leaders and followers. Effective leadership must be something more than just common sense.

Myth: Leaders Are Born, Not Made

Some people believe being a leader is either in one's genes or not; others believe that life experiences mold the individual and that no one is born a leader. Which view is right? In a sense, both and neither. Both views are right in that innate factors as well as formative experiences influence many sorts of behavior, including leadership. Yet both views are wrong to the extent they imply leadership is *either* innate *or* acquired; what matters more is how these factors *interact*. It does not seem useful, we believe, to think of the world as composed of two mutually exclusive types of people, leaders and nonleaders. It is more useful to address how each person can make the most of leadership opportunities he or she faces.

It may be easier to see the pointlessness of asking whether leaders are born or made by looking at an alternative question of far less popular interest: Are *college professors* born or made? Conceptually the issues are the same, and here too the answer is that every college professor is both born *and* made. It seems clear enough that college professors are partly "born" because (among other factors) there is a genetic component to intelligence, and intelligence surely plays some part in becoming a college professor (well, at least a *minor* part!). But every college professor is also partly "made." One obvious way is that college professors must have advanced education in specialized fields; even with the right genes one could not become a college professor without certain requisite experiences. Becoming a college professor depends partly on what one is born with and partly on how that inheritance is shaped through experience. The same is true of leadership.

More specifically, research indicates that many cognitive abilities and personality traits are at least partly innate.[21] Thus natural talents or characteristics may offer certain advantages or disadvantages to a leader. Consider physical characteristics: A man's above-average height may increase others' tendency to think of him as a leader; it may also boost his own self-confidence. But it doesn't make him a leader. The same holds true for psychological characteristics that seem related to leadership. The stability of certain characteristics over long periods (for example, at school reunions people seem to have kept the same personalities we remember them as having years earlier) may reinforce the impression that our basic natures are fixed, but different environments nonetheless may nurture or suppress different leadership qualities.

Myth: The Only School You Learn Leadership from Is the School of Hard Knocks

Some people skeptically question whether leadership can develop through formal study, believing instead it can be acquired only through actual experience. It is a mistake, however, to think of formal study and learning from experience as mutually exclusive or antagonistic. In fact, they complement each other. Rather than ask whether leadership develops from formal study or from real-life experience, it is better to ask what kind of study will help students learn to discern critical lessons about leadership from their own experience. Approaching the issue in such a way recognizes the vital role of experience in leadership development, but it also admits that certain kinds of study and training can improve a person's ability to discern important lessons about leadership

Never reveal all of yourself to other people; hold back something in reserve so that people are never quite sure if they really know you.
Michael Korda, author, editor

Progress always involves risks. You can't steal second base and keep your foot on first.
Frederick B. Wilcox

from experience. It can, in other words, accelerate the process of learning from experience.

We argue that one advantage of formally studying leadership is that formal study provides students with a variety of ways of examining a particular leadership situation. By studying the different ways researchers have defined and examined leadership, students can use these definitions and theories to better understand what is going on in any leadership situation. For example, earlier in this chapter we used three different leadership definitions as a framework for describing or analyzing the situation facing Parrado and the survivors of the plane crash, and each definition focused on a different aspect of leadership. These frameworks can similarly be applied to better understand the experiences one has as both a leader and a follower. We think it is difficult for leaders, particularly novice leaders, to examine leadership situations from multiple perspectives; but we also believe developing this skill can help you become a better leader. Being able to analyze your experiences from multiple perspectives may be the greatest single contribution a formal course in leadership can give you. Maybe you can reflect on your own leadership over a cup of coffee in Starbucks as you read about the origins of that company in Profiles in Leadership 1.2.

Howard Schultz

PROFILES IN LEADERSHIP 1.2

Starbucks began in 1971 as a very different company than we know it as today. The difference is due in large part to the way its former CEO, Howard Schultz, reframed the kind of business Starbucks should be. Schultz joined Starbucks in 1981 to head its marketing and retail store operations. While on a trip to Italy in 1983, Schultz was amazed by the number and variety of espresso bars there—1,500 in the city of Turin alone. He concluded that the Starbucks stores in Seattle had missed the point: *Starbucks should be not just a store but an experience—a gathering place.*

Everything looks clearer in hindsight, of course, but the Starbucks owners resisted Schultz's vision; Starbucks was a retailer, they insisted, not a restaurant or bar. Schultz's strategic reframing of the Starbucks opportunity was ultimately vindicated when—after having departed Starbucks to pursue the same idea with another company—Schultz had the opportunity to purchase the whole Starbucks operation in Seattle, including its name.

Despite today's pervasiveness of Starbucks across the world, however, and the seeming obviousness of Schultz's exemplary leadership, the Starbucks story has not been one of completely consistent success. After Schultz retired as Starbucks CEO when it was a global megabrand, the company's performance suffered to the point Schultz complained that it was "losing its soul." He was asked to return as CEO in 2008 and has tried to resurrect Starbucks by bringing new attention to the company's operating efficiency and by admitting, in effect, that some of his own earlier instinctive approach to company strategy and management would no longer be sufficient for the new global scale of Starbucks operation. In fact, Schultz discovered the challenges and the road to recovery even more daunting than he expected. Leadership—even for one with a proven track record—is never easy.

The Interactional Framework for Analyzing Leadership

Perhaps the first researcher to formally recognize the importance of the leader, follower, and situation in the leadership process was Fred Fiedler.[22] Fiedler used these three components to develop his contingency model of leadership, a theory of leadership that will be discussed in more detail in Chapter 13. Although we recognize Fiedler's contributions, we owe perhaps even more to Hollander's[23] transactional approach to leadership. We call our approach the **interactional framework.**

Several aspects of this derivative of Hollander's approach are worthy of additional comment. First, as shown in Figure 1.2, the framework depicts leadership as a function of three elements—the **leader,** the **followers,** and the **situation.** Second, a particular leadership scenario can be examined using each level of analysis separately. Although this is a useful way to understand the leadership process, we can understand the process even better if we also examine the **interactions** among the three elements, or lenses, represented by the overlapping areas in the figure. For example, we can better understand the leadership process if we not only look at the leaders and the followers but also examine how leaders and followers affect each other in the leadership process. Similarly, we can examine the leader and the situation separately, but we can gain even further understanding of the leadership process by looking at how the situation can constrain or facilitate a leader's actions and how the leader can change different aspects of the situation to be more effective. Thus a final important aspect of the framework is that leadership is the result of a complex set of interactions among the leader, the followers, and the situation. These complex interactions may be why broad generalizations about leadership are problematic: many factors influence the leadership process (see Highlight 1.3 on page 11).

FIGURE 1.2
An Interactional Framework for Analyzing Leadership

Source: Adapted from E. P. Hollander, *Leadership Dynamics: A Practical Guide to Effective Relationships* (New York: Free Press, 1978).

An example of one such complex interaction between leaders and followers is evident in what have been called in-groups and out-groups. Sometimes there is a high degree of mutual influence and attraction between the leader and a few subordinates. These subordinates belong to the **in-group** and can be distinguished by their high degree of loyalty, commitment, and trust felt toward the leader. Other subordinates belong to the **out-group.** Leaders have considerably more influence with in-group followers than with out-group followers. However, this greater degree of influence has a price. If leaders rely primarily on their formal authority to influence their followers (especially if they punish them), then leaders risk losing the high levels of loyalty and commitment followers feel toward them.[24]

The Leader

This element examines primarily what the leader brings *as an individual* to the leadership equation. This can include unique personal history, interests, character traits, and motivation.

Leaders are *not* all alike, but they tend to share many characteristics. Research has shown that leaders differ from their followers, and effective leaders differ from ineffective leaders, on various personality traits, cognitive abilities, skills, and values.[25-30] Another way personality can affect leadership is through temperament, by which we mean whether a leader is generally calm or is instead prone to emotional outbursts. Leaders who have calm dispositions and do not attack or belittle others for bringing bad news are more likely to get complete and timely information from subordinates than are bosses who have explosive tempers and a reputation for killing the messenger.

Another important aspect of the leader is how he or she achieved leader status. Leaders who are appointed by superiors may have less credibility with subordinates and get less loyalty from them than leaders who are elected or emerge by consensus from the ranks of followers. Often emergent or elected officials are better able to influence a group toward goal achievement because of the power conferred on them by their followers. However, both elected and emergent leaders need to be sensitive to their constituencies if they wish to remain in power.

More generally, a leader's experience or history in a particular organization is usually important to her or his effectiveness. For example, leaders promoted from within an organization, by virtue of being familiar with its culture and policies, may be ready to "hit the job running." In addition, leaders selected from within an organization are typically better known by others in the organization than are leaders selected from the outside. That is likely to affect, for better or worse, the latitude others in the organization are willing to give the leader; if the leader is widely respected for a history of accomplishment, she may be given more latitude than a newcomer whose track record is less well known. On the other hand, many people tend to give new leaders a fair chance to succeed, and newcomers to an organization

Chapter 1 *What Do We Mean by Leadership?* **17**

often take time to learn the organization's informal rules, norms, and "ropes" before they make any radical or potentially controversial decisions.

A leader's legitimacy also may be affected by the extent to which followers participated in the leader's selection. When followers have had a say in the selection or election of a leader, they tend to have a heightened sense of psychological identification with her, but they also may have higher expectations and make more demands on her.[31] We also might wonder what kind of support a leader has from his own boss. If followers sense their boss has a lot of influence with the higher-ups, subordinates

"I'll be blunt, coach. I'm having a problem with this 'take a lap' thing of yours . . ."

Source: © *Tribune Media Services, Inc. All Rights Reserved. Reprinted with permission.*

18   Part One   *Leadership Is a Process, Not a Position*

> *I must follow the people. Am I not their leader?*
> **Benjamin Disraeli, 19th-century British prime minister**

may be reluctant to take their complaints to higher levels. On the other hand, if the boss has little influence with higher-ups, subordinates may be more likely to make complaints to these levels.

The foregoing examples highlight the sorts of insights we can gain about leadership by focusing on the individual leader as a level of analysis. Even if we were to examine the individual leader completely, however, our understanding of the leadership process would be incomplete.

The Followers

> *The crowd will follow a leader who marches twenty steps in advance; but if he is a thousand steps in front of them, they do not see and do not follow him.*
> **Georg Brandes**

Followers are a critical part of the leadership equation, but their role has not always been appreciated, at least in empirical research (but read Highlight 1.4 to see how the role of followers has been recognized in literature). For a long time, in fact, "the common view of leadership was that leaders actively led and subordinates, later called followers, passively and obediently followed."[32] Over time, especially in the last century, social change shaped people's views of followers, and leadership theories gradually recognized the active and important role that followers play in the leadership process.[33] Today it seems natural to accept the important role

The *First* Band of Brothers

HIGHLIGHT 1.4

Many of you probably have seen, or at least heard of, the award-winning series *Band of Brothers* that followed a company of the famous 101st Airborne division during World War II. You may not be aware that an earlier band of brothers was made famous by William Shakespeare in his play *Henry V*.

In one of the most famous speeches by any of Shakespeare's characters, the young Henry V tried to unify his followers when their daring expedition to conquer France was failing. French soldiers followed Henry's army along the rivers, daring them to cross over and engage the French in battle. Just before the battle of Agincourt, Henry's rousing words rallied his vastly outnumbered, weary, and tattered troops to victory. Few words of oratory have ever better bonded a leader with his followers than Henry's call for unity among "we few, we happy few, we band of brothers."

Hundreds of years later, Henry's speech is still a powerful illustration of a leader who emphasized the importance of his followers. Modern leadership concepts like vision, charisma, relationship orientation, and empowerment are readily evident

in Henry's interactions with his followers. Here are the closing lines of Henry's famous speech:

> *From this day to the ending of the world,*
> *But we in it shall be remembered—*
> *We few, we happy few, we band of brothers;*
> *For he today that sheds his blood with me*
> *Shall be my brother; be he ne'er so vile,*
> *This day shall gentle his condition;*
> *And gentlemen in England now-a-bed*
> *Shall think themselves accurs'd they were not here,*
> *And hold their manhoods cheap whiles any speaks*
> *That fought with us upon Saint Crispin's day.*

Shakespeare's insights into the complexities of leadership should remind us that while modern research helps enlighten our understanding, it does not represent the only, and certainly not the most moving, perspective on leadership to which we should pay attention.

Source: N. Warner, "Screening Leadership through Shakespeare: Paradoxes of Leader–Follower Relations in *Henry V* on Film," *The Leadership Quarterly* 18 (2007), pp. 1–15.

A Student's Perspective on Leadership and Followership

HIGHLIGHT 1.5

Krista Kleiner, a student at Claremont-McKenna College and active in its Kravis Leadership Institute, has offered these reflections on the importance for both students and college administrators of taking seriously the opportunities provided in the classroom for developing leadership and followership skills.

She notes that the admissions process to college (as well, we might add, as postcollege job searches) typically places significant emphasis on a person's leadership experience and abilities. Usually this is reflected in something like a list of "leadership positions held." Unfortunately, however, this system tends to overemphasize the mere acquisition of leadership titles and pays insufficient attention to the domain that is the most central and common element of student life: the classroom learning environment. Outstanding learning, she argues, is to a significant degree a collaborative experience between the formal leader (the teacher) and the informal followers (the students). The learning experience is directly enhanced by the degree to which effective participation by students contributes to their classroom groups, and this requires good leadership and good followership. The quality of one's contribution to the group could be assessed via peer surveys, the results of which would be made available to the teacher. The surveys would assess dimensions of student contributions like these:

- Which students displayed particularly helpful leadership in work groups you participated in, and what did they do that was effective?

- Which students displayed particularly helpful followership in work groups you participated in that supported or balanced the leadership that emerged in the group or that was helpful to fellow group members?

- How have you contributed to the learning experience of your peers through your leadership–followership role in the classroom? How have you grown as a constructive leader and constructive follower through these experiences?

We hope these ideas challenge you to be a leader in your own student life and especially in this leadership course.

Source: K. Kleiner, "Rethinking Leadership and Followership: A Student's Perspective," in R. Riggio, I. Chaleff, and J. Lipman-Blumen (eds.), *The Art of Followership: How Great Followers Create Great Leaders and Organizations* (San Francisco: Jossey-Bass, 2008), pp. 89–93.

All men have some weak points, and the more vigorous and brilliant a person may be, the more strongly these weak points stand out. It is highly desirable, even essential, therefore, for the more influential members of a general's staff not to be too much like the general.

Major General Hugo Baron von Freytag-Loringhoven, anti-Hitler conspirator

followers play. Highlight 1.5 suggests some interesting interactions between leadership and followership in an arena familiar to you.

One aspect of our text's definition of leadership is particularly worth noting in this regard: Leadership is a social influence process shared among *all* members of a group. Leadership is not restricted to the influence exerted by someone in a particular position or role; followers are part of the leadership process, too. In recent years both practitioners and scholars have emphasized the relatedness of leadership and **followership.** As Burns[34] observed, the idea of "one-man leadership" is a contradiction in terms.

Obvious as this point may seem, it is also clear that early leadership researchers paid relatively little attention to the roles followers play in the leadership process.[35,36] However, we know that the followers' expectations, personality traits, maturity levels, levels of competence, and motivation affect the leadership process too. Highlight 1.6 describes a systematic approach to classifying different kinds of followers that has had a major impact on research.[37-40]

Followership Styles

HIGHLIGHT 1.6

The concept of different styles of leadership is reasonably familiar, but the idea of different styles of followership is relatively new. The very word *follower* has a negative connotation to many, evoking ideas of people who behave like sheep and need to be told what to do. Robert Kelley, however, believes that followers, rather than representing the antithesis of leadership, are best viewed as collaborators with leaders in the work of organizations.

Kelley believes that different types of followers can be described in terms of two broad dimensions. One of them ranges from **independent, critical thinking** at one end to **dependent, uncritical thinking** on the other end. According to Kelley, the best followers think for themselves and offer constructive advice or even creative solutions. The worst followers need to be told what to do. Kelley's other dimension ranges from whether people are **active followers** or **passive followers** in the extent to which they are engaged in work. According to Kelley, the best followers are self-starters who take initiative for themselves, whereas the worst followers are passive, may even dodge responsibility, and need constant supervision.

Using these two dimensions, Kelley has suggested five basic styles of followership:

1. *Alienated followers* habitually point out all the negative aspects of the organization to others. While alienated followers may see themselves as mavericks who have a healthy skepticism of the organization, leaders often see them as cynical, negative, and adversarial.

2. *Conformist followers* are the "yes people" of organizations. While very active at doing the organization's work, they can be dangerous if their orders contradict societal standards of behavior or organizational policy. Often this style is the result of either the demanding and authoritarian style of the leader or the overly rigid structure of the organization.

3. *Pragmatist followers* are rarely committed to their group's work goals, but they have learned not to make waves. Because they do not like to stick out, pragmatists tend to be mediocre performers who can clog the arteries of many organizations. Because it can be difficult to discern just where they stand on issues, they present an ambiguous image with both positive and negative characteristics. In organizational settings, pragmatists may become experts in mastering the bureaucratic rules which can be used to protect them.

4. *Passive followers* display none of the characteristics of the exemplary follower (discussed next). They rely on the leader to do all the thinking. Furthermore, their work lacks enthusiasm. Lacking initiative and a sense of responsibility, passive followers require constant direction. Leaders may see them as lazy, incompetent, or even stupid. Sometimes, however, passive followers adopt this style to help them cope with a leader who expects followers to behave that way.

5. *Exemplary followers* present a consistent picture to both leaders and co-workers of being independent, innovative, and willing to stand up to superiors. They apply their talents for the benefit of the organization even when confronted with bureaucratic stumbling blocks or passive or pragmatist co-workers. Effective leaders appreciate the value of exemplary followers. When one of the authors was serving in a follower role in a staff position, he was introduced by his leader to a conference as "my favorite subordinate because he's a loyal 'No-Man.' "

Exemplary followers—high on both critical dimensions of followership—are essential to organizational success.

Leaders, therefore, would be well advised to select people who have these characteristics and, perhaps even more importantly, *create the conditions that encourage these behaviors.*

Source: Adapted from R. Kelley, *The Power of Followership* (New York: Doubleday Currency, 1992).

The nature of followers' motivation to do their work is also important. Workers who share a leader's goals and values, and who feel intrinsically rewarded for performing a job well, might be more likely to work extra hours on a time-critical project than those whose motivation is solely monetary.

Even the number of followers reporting to a leader can have significant implications. For example, a store manager with three clerks working for him can spend more time with each of them (or on other things) than can a manager responsible for eight clerks and a separate delivery service; chairing a task force with 5 members is a different leadership activity than chairing a task force with 18 members. Still other relevant variables include followers' trust in the leader and their degree of confidence that he or she is interested in their well-being. Another aspect of followers' relations to a leader is described in Profiles in Leadership 1.3.

Paul Revere

PROFILES IN LEADERSHIP 1.3

A fabled story of American history is that of Paul Revere's ride through the countryside surrounding Boston, warning towns that the British were coming so local militia could be ready to meet them. As a result, when the British did march toward Lexington on the following day, they faced unexpectedly fierce resistance. At Concord the British were beaten by a ragtag group of locals, and so began the American Revolutionary War.

It has been taken for granted by generations of Americans that the success of Paul Revere's ride lay in his heroism *and* in the self-evident importance of the news itself. A little-known fact, however, is that Paul Revere was not the only rider that night. A fellow revolutionary by the name of William Dawes had the same mission: to ride simultaneously through a separate set of towns surrounding Boston to warn them that the British were coming. He did so, carrying the news through just as many towns as Revere did. But his ride was not successful; those local militia leaders weren't aroused and did not rise up to confront the British. If they had been, Dawes would be as famous today as Paul Revere.

Why was Revere's ride successful when Dawes's ride was not? Paul Revere started a word-of-mouth epidemic, and Dawes did not, *because of differing kinds of relationships the two men had with others.* It wasn't, after all, the nature of the news itself that proved ultimately important so much as the nature of the men who carried it. Paul Revere was a gregarious and social person—what Malcolm Gladwell calls a *connector.* Gladwell writes that Revere was "a fisherman and a hunter, a cardplayer and a theater-lover, a frequenter of pubs and a successful businessman. He was active in the local Masonic Lodge and was a member of several select social clubs." He was a man with a knack for always being at the center of things. So when he began his ride that night, it was Revere's nature to stop and share the news with anyone he saw on the road, and he would have known who the key players were in each town to notify.

Dawes was not by nature so gregarious as Revere, and he did not have Revere's extended social network. It's likely he *wouldn't* have known whom to share the news with in each town and whose doors to knock on. Dawes did notify some people, but not enough to create the kind of impact that Revere did. Another way of saying this is simply to note that the people Dawes notified didn't know *him* the way that Revere was known by those *he* notified.

It isn't just the information or the ideas you have as a leader that make a difference. It's also whom you know, and how many you know—and what they know about you.

Source: Adapted from Malcolm Gladwell, *The Tipping Point* (New York: Little, Brown and Company, 2002).

22   Part One   *Leadership Is a Process, Not a Position*

> *Never try to teach a pig to sing; it wastes your time and it annoys the pig.*
>
> **Paul Dickson, baseball writer**

In the context of the interactional framework, the question "What is leadership?" cannot be separated from the question "What is followership?" There is no simple line dividing them; they merge. The relationship between leadership and followership can be represented by borrowing a concept from topographical mathematics: the Möbius strip. You are probably familiar with the curious properties of the Möbius strip: when a strip of paper is twisted and connected in the manner

Source: © *Tribune Media Services, Inc. All Rights Reserved. Reprinted with permission.*

FIGURE 1.3
The Leadership/
Followership
Möbius Strip

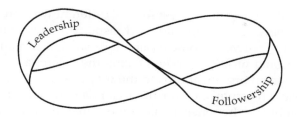

depicted in Figure 1.3, it has only one side. You can prove this to yourself by putting a pencil to any point on the strip and tracing continuously. Your pencil will cover the entire strip (that is, both "sides"), eventually returning to the point at which you started. To demonstrate the relevance of this curiosity to leadership, cut a strip of paper. On one side write *leadership*, and on the other side write *followership*. Then twist the strip and connect the two ends in the manner of the figure. You will have created a leadership/followership Möbius strip wherein the two concepts merge, just as leadership and followership can become indistinguishable in organizations.[41]

This does not mean leadership and followership are the same thing. When top-level executives were asked to list qualities they most look for and admire in leaders and followers, the lists were similar but not identical.[42] Ideal leaders were characterized as honest, competent, forward-looking, and inspiring; ideal followers were described as honest, competent, independent, and cooperative. The differences could become critical in certain situations, as when a forward-looking and inspiring subordinate perceives a significant conflict between his own goals or ethics and those of his superiors. Such a situation could become a crisis for the individual and the organization, demanding a choice between leading and following.

As the complexity of the leadership process has become better understood, the importance placed on the leader–follower relationship itself has undergone dynamic change.[43,44] One reason for this is an increasing pressure on all kinds of organizations to function with reduced resources. Reduced resources and company downsizing have reduced the number of managers and increased their span of control, which in turn leaves followers to pick up many of the functions traditionally performed by leaders. Another reason is a trend toward greater power sharing and decentralized authority in organizations, which create greater interdependence among organizational subunits and increase the need for collaboration among them. Furthermore, the nature of problems faced by many organizations is becoming so complex and the changes are becoming so rapid that more and more people are required to solve them.

These trends suggest several different ways in which followers can take on new leadership roles and responsibilities in the future. For one thing, followers can become much more proactive in their stance toward organizational problems. When facing the discrepancy between the way things are in an organization and the way they could or should be, followers can play an active and constructive role collaborating with leaders in solving problems. In general, making organizations better is a task that needs to be "owned" by followers as well as by leaders. With these changing roles for followers, it should not be surprising to find that qualities of good followership are statistically correlated with qualities typically associated with good leadership. One recent study found positive correlations between the followership qualities of active engagement and independent thinking and the leadership qualities of dominance, sociability, achievement orientation, and steadiness.[45]

In addition to helping solve organizational problems, followers can contribute to the leadership process by becoming skilled at "influencing upward." Because followers are often at the levels where many organizational problems occur, they can give leaders relevant information so good solutions are implemented. Although it is true that some leaders need to become better listeners, it is also true that many followers need training in expressing ideas to superiors clearly and positively. Still another way followers can assume a greater share of the leadership challenge in the future is by staying flexible and open to opportunities. The future portends more change, not less, and followers who face change with positive anticipation and an openness to self-development will be particularly valued and rewarded.[46]

Thus, to an ever-increasing degree, leadership must be understood in terms of both leader variables and follower variables, as well as the interactions among them. But even that is not enough—we must also understand the particular situations in which leaders and followers find themselves.

The Situation

The situation is the third critical part of the leadership equation. Even if we knew all we could know about a given leader and a given set of followers, leadership often makes sense only in the context of how the leader and followers interact in a particular situation (see Profiles in Leadership 1.4 and 1.5).

This view of leadership as a complex interaction among leader, follower, and situational variables was not always taken for granted. To the contrary, most early research on leadership was based on the assumption that leadership is a general personal trait expressed independently of the situation in which the leadership is manifested. This view, commonly known as the **heroic theory**, has been largely discredited

You've got to give loyalty down, if you want loyalty up.

Donald T. Regan, former CEO and White House chief of staff

Aung San Suu Kyi

PROFILES IN LEADERSHIP 1.4

In 1991 Aung San Suu Kyi already had spent two years under house arrest in Burma for "endangering the state." That same year she won the Nobel Peace Prize. She was not released from house arrest until 2010, and in 2012 was elected to Parliament. Like Nelson Mandela, Suu Kyi is an international symbol of heroic and peaceful resistance to government oppression.

Until the age of 43, Suu Kyi led a relatively quiet existence in England as a professional working mother. Her life changed dramatically in 1988 when she returned to her native country of Burma to visit her sick mother. That visit occurred during a time of considerable political unrest in Burma. Riot police had recently shot to death hundreds of demonstrators in the capital city of Rangoon (the demonstrators had been protesting government repression). Over the next several months, police killed nearly 3,000 people who had been protesting government policies.

When hundreds of thousands of pro-democracy demonstrators staged a protest rally at a prominent pagoda in Rangoon, Suu Kyi spoke to the crowd. Overnight she became the leading voice for freedom and democracy in Burma.

Today she is the most popular and influential leader in her country.

What prepared this woman, whose life was once relatively simple and contented, to risk her life by challenging an oppressive government? What made her such a magnet for popular support? Impressive as Aung San Suu Kyi is as a populist leader, it is impossible to understand her effectiveness purely in terms of her own personal characteristics. It is impossible to understand it independent of her followers—the people of Burma. Her rapid rise to prominence as the leading voice for democracy and freedom in Burma must be understood in terms of the living link she represented to the country's greatest modern hero—her father. He was something of a George Washington figure in that he founded the Burmese Army in 1941 and later made a successful transition from military leadership to political leadership. At the height of his influence, when he was the universal choice to be Burma's first president, he was assassinated. Suu Kyi was two years old. Stories about his life and principles indelibly shaped Suu Kyi's own life, but his life and memory also created a readiness among the Burmese people for Suu Kyi to take up her father's mantle of leadership.

but for a long time represented the dominant way of conceptualizing leadership.[47]

In the 1950s and 1960s a different approach to conceptualizing leadership dominated research and scholarship. It involved the search for effective leader *behaviors* rather than the search for universal *traits* of leadership. That approach proved too narrow because it neglected important contextual, or situational, factors in which presumably effective or ineffective behaviors occur. Over time, the complexities of interactions among leader, follower, and situational variables increasingly have been the focus of leadership research.[48] (See Chapters 6, 7, and 13 for more detailed discussions of leader attributes, leader behaviors, and formal theories of leadership that examine complex interdependencies between leader, follower, and situational variables.) Adding the situation to the mix of variables that make up leadership is complicated. The

Bill Gates's Head Start

PROFILES IN LEADERSHIP 1.5

Belief in an individual's potential to overcome great odds and achieve success through talent, strength, and perseverance is common in America, but usually there is more than meets the eye in such success stories. Malcolm Gladwell's best seller *Outliers* presents a fascinating exploration of how situational factors contribute to success in addition to the kinds of individual qualities we often assume are all-important. Have you ever thought, for example, that Bill Gates was able to create Microsoft because he's just brilliant and visionary?

Well, let's take for granted he *is* brilliant and visionary—there's plenty of evidence of that. The point here, however, is that's not always enough (and maybe it's *never* enough). Here are some of the things that placed Bill Gates, with all his intelligence and vision, at the right time in the right place:

- Gates was born to a wealthy family in Seattle that placed him in a private school for seventh grade. In 1968, his second year there, the school started a computer club—even before most *colleges* had computer clubs.

- In the 1960s virtually everyone who was learning about computers used computer cards, a tedious and mind-numbing process. The computer at Gates's school, however, was linked to a mainframe in downtown Seattle. Thus in 1968 Bill Gates was practicing computer programming via time-sharing as an eighth grader; few others in the world then had such opportunity, whatever their age.

- Even at a wealthy private school like the one Gates attended, however, funds ran out to cover the high costs of buying time on a mainframe computer. Fortunately, at about the same time, a group called the Computer Center Corporation was formed at the University of Washington to lease computer time. One of its founders, co-incidentally a parent at Gates's own school, thought the school's computer club could get time on the computer in exchange for testing the company's new software programs. Gates then started a regular schedule of taking the bus after school to the company's offices, where he programmed long into the evening. During one seven-month period, Gates and his fellow computer club members averaged eight hours a day, seven days a week, of computer time.

- When Gates was a high school senior, another extraordinary opportunity presented itself. A major national company (TRW) needed programmers with specialized experience—exactly, as it turned out, the kind of experience the kids at Gates's school had been getting. Gates successfully lobbied his teachers to let him spend a spring doing this work in another part of the state for independent study credit.

- By the time Gates dropped out of Harvard after his sophomore year, he had accumulated more than *10,000 hours* of programming experience. It was, he's said, a better exposure to software development than anyone else at a young age could have had—and all because of a lucky series of events.

It appears that Gates's success is at least partly an example of the right person being in the right place at just the right time.

Source: Malcolm Gladwell, *Outliers: The Story of Success* (New York: Little, Brown and Company, 2008).

situation may be the most ambiguous aspect of the leadership framework; it can refer to anything from the specific task a group is engaged in to broad situational contexts such as the remote predicament of the Andes survivors. One facet of the complexity of the situation's role in leadership is examined in Highlight 1.7.

Decision Making in a Complex World

HIGHLIGHT 1.7

Decision making is a good example of how leaders need to behave differently in various situations. Until late in the 20th century, decision making in government and business was largely based on an implicit assumption that the world was orderly and predictable enough for virtually all decision making to involve a series of specifiable steps: assessing the facts of a situation, categorizing those facts, and then responding based on established practice. To put that more simply, decision making required managers to *sense, categorize,* and *respond.*

The Situation	The Leader's Job
Simple: predictable and orderly; right answers exist.	Ensure that proper processes are in place, follow best practices, and communicate in clear and direct ways.
Complex: flux, unpredictability, ambiguity, many competing ideas, lots of unknowns.	Create environments and experiments that allow patterns to emerge; increase levels of interaction and communication; use methods that generate new ideas and ways of thinking among everyone.

That process is actually still effective in simple contexts characterized by stability and clear cause-and-effect relationships that are readily apparent. Not all situations in the world, however, are so simple, and new approaches to decision making are needed for situations that have the elements of what we might call complex systems: large numbers of interacting elements, nonlinear interactions among those elements by which small changes can produce huge effects, and interdependence among the elements so that the whole is more than the sum of the parts. The challenges of dealing with the threat of terrorism are one example of the way complexity affects decision making, but it's impacting how we think about decision making in business as well as government. To describe this change succinctly, the decision-making process in complex contexts must change from sense, categorize, and respond to probe, sense, and respond.

In other words, making good decisions is about both *what* decisions one makes and understanding the role of the situation in affecting *how* one makes decisions.

Source: D.F. Snowden and M.E. Boone, "A Leader's Framework for Decision Making," *Harvard Business Review*, November 2007, pp. 69–76.

Illustrating the Interactional Framework: Women in Leadership Roles

Not long ago if people were asked to name a leader they admired, most of the names on the resulting list could be characterized as "old white guys." Today the names on that same list would be considerably more heterogeneous. That change—which we certainly consider progress—represents a useful illustration of the power of using the interactional framework to understand the complexities of the leadership process.

A specific example is women in leadership roles, and in this section we'll examine the extent to which women have been taking on new leadership roles, whether there are differences in the effectiveness of men and women in leadership roles, and what explanations have been offered for differences between men and women in being selected for and succeeding in positions of leadership. This is an area of considerable academic research and popular polemics, as evident in many recent articles in the popular press that claim a distinct advantage for women in leadership roles.[49]

It is clear that women are taking on leadership roles in greater numbers than ever before. On the other hand, the actual percentage of women in leadership positions has stayed relatively stable. For example, a report released in 2010 by the U.S. Government Accountability Office indicated that women comprised an estimated 40 percent of managers in the U.S. workforce in 2007 compared with 39 percent in 2000.[50] And the percentage of women in top executive positions is considerably less encouraging. In a 2009 study by the nonprofit organization Catalyst, women made up only 13.5 percent of senior executive positions; almost 30 percent of companies in the Fortune 500 had no women in those top positions.[51]

Although these statistics are important and promising, problems still exist that constrain the opportunity for capable women to rise to the highest leadership roles in organizations. Many studies have considered this problem, a few of which we'll examine here.

One recent study reported that a higher percentage of women executives now receive on-the-job mentoring than men. The same study, however, found that the mentors of those women executives had less organizational influence and clout than did the mentors of their male counterparts. While such mentoring can still provide invaluable psycho-social support for personal and professional development, it does not seem sufficient to assure promotion to higher level jobs (mentoring will be explored in greater detail in the next chapter).[52] Another recent study examined differences in the networking patterns of men and women. Compared to men, women's trust in each other tends to decrease when work situations become more professionally risky. Such a pattern of behavior could potentially become a kind of self-imposed promotion disadvantage by women on themselves.[53]

In a classic study of sex roles, Schein[54,55] demonstrated how bias in sex role stereotypes created problems for women moving up through managerial roles. Schein asked male and female middle managers to complete a survey in which they rated various items on a five-point scale in terms of how characteristic they were of men in general, women in general, or successful managers. Schein found a high correlation between the ways both male and female respondents perceived "males" and "managers," but no correlation between the ways the respondents perceived "females" and "managers." It was as though being a manager was defined by attributes thought of as masculine.

Furthermore, it does not appear that the situation has changed much over the past two decades. In 1990 management students in the United

States, Germany, and Great Britain, for example, still perceived successful middle managers in terms of characteristics more commonly ascribed to men than to women.[56] A 2011 meta-analysis of studies of gender stereotyping continued to find strong evidence of a tendency for leadership to be viewed as culturally masculine. It involved sophisticated statistical analyses of the results of 40 separate studies similar to Schein's paradigm of *think manager–think male*; of 22 other studies that looked at gender stereotyping in an *agency-communion* paradigm; and of a third group of 7 studies that looked at stereotyping through the lens of occupational stereotyping. The study concluded that a strong masculine stereotype of leadership continues to exist in the workplace and that it will continue to challenge women for some time to come.[57] One area where views *do* seem to have changed over time involves women's perceptions of their own roles. In contrast to the earlier studies, women today see as much similarity between "female" and "manager" as between "male" and "manager."[58] To women, at least, being a woman and being a manager are not contradictory.

There have been many other studies of the role of women in management. In one of these, *Breaking the Glass Ceiling,*[59] researchers documented the lives and careers of 78 of the highest-level women in corporate America. A few years later the researchers followed up with a small sample of those women to discuss any changes that had taken place in their leadership paths. The researchers were struck by the fact that the women were much like the senior men they had worked with in other studies. Qualitatively, they had the same fears: They wanted the best for themselves and for their families. They wanted their companies to succeed. And not surprisingly, they still had a drive to succeed. In some cases (also true for the men) they were beginning to ask questions about life balance—was all the sacrifice and hard work worth it? Were 60-hour workweeks worth the cost to family and self?

More quantitatively, however, the researchers expected to find significant differences between the women who had broken the glass ceiling and the men who were already in leadership positions. After all, the popular literature and some social scientific literature had conditioned them to expect that there is a feminine versus a masculine style of leadership, the feminine style being an outgrowth of a consensus/team-oriented leadership approach. Women, in this view, are depicted as leaders who, when compared to men, are better listeners, more empathic, less analytical, more people oriented, and less aggressive in pursuit of goals.

In examining women in leadership positions, the researchers collected behavioral data, including ratings by both self and others, assessment center data, and their scores on the California Psychological Inventory. Contrary to the stereotypes and popular views, however, there were no statistically significant differences between men's and women's leadership styles. Women and men were equally analytical, people oriented, forceful, goal oriented, empathic, and skilled at listening. There were other differences between the men and women, however, beyond the question of leadership styles. The researchers did find (and these results must be interpreted cautiously because of the relatively small numbers involved) that women had significantly lower well-being scores, their commitment to the organizations they worked for was more guarded than that of their male counterparts, and the women were much more likely to be willing to take career risks associated with going to new or unfamiliar areas of the company where women had not been before.

Continued work with women in corporate leadership positions has both reinforced and clarified these findings. For example, the lower scores for women in general well-being may reflect the inadequacy of their support system for dealing with day-to-day issues of living. This is tied to the reality for many women that in addition to having roles in their companies they remain chief caretakers for their families. Further, there may be additional pressures of being visibly identified as proof that the organization has women at the top.

Other types of differences—particularly those around "people issues"—are still not evident. In fact, the hypothesis is that such supposed differences may hinder the opportunities for leadership development of women in the future. For example, turning around a business that is in trouble or starting a new business are two of the most exciting opportunities a developing leader has to test her leadership abilities. If we apply the "women are different" hypothesis, the type of leadership skills needed for successful completion of either of these assignments may leave women off the list of candidates. However, if we accept the hypothesis that women and men are more alike as leaders than they are different, women will be found in equal numbers on the candidate list.

Research on women leaders from medium-sized, nontraditional organizations has shown that successful leaders don't all come from the same mold. Such women tended to be successful by drawing on their shared experience as women, rather than by adhering to the "rules of conduct" by which men in larger and more traditional organizations have been successful.[60] Survey research by Judith Rosener identified several differences in how men and women described their leadership experiences. Men tended to describe themselves in somewhat transactional terms, viewing leadership as an exchange with subordinates for services rendered. They influenced others primarily through their organizational position and authority. The women, on the other hand, tended to describe themselves in transformational terms. They helped subordinates develop commitment to broader goals than their own self-interest, and they described their influence more in terms of personal characteristics like charisma and interpersonal skill than mere organizational position.

According to Rosener, such women leaders encouraged participation and shared power and information, but went far beyond what is commonly thought of as participative management. She called it **interactive leadership.** Their leadership self-descriptions reflected an approach based on enhancing others' self-worth and believing that the best performance results when people are excited about their work and feel good about themselves.

How did this interactive leadership style develop? Rosener concluded it was due to these women's socialization experiences and career paths. As we have indicated, the social role expected of women has emphasized that they be cooperative, supportive, understanding, gentle, and service-oriented. As they entered the business world, they still found themselves in roles emphasizing these same behaviors. They found themselves in staff, rather than line, positions, and in roles lacking formal authority over others so that they had to accomplish their work without reliance on formal power. What they had to do, in other words, was employ their socially acceptable behavioral repertoire to survive organizationally.

What came easily to women turned out to be a survival tactic. Although leaders often begin their careers doing what comes naturally and what fits

"That's what they all say, honey."

Source: © Tom Cheney, The New Yorker Collection, www.cartoonbank.com.

32 Part One *Leadership Is a Process, Not a Position*

within the constraints of the job, they also develop their skills and styles over time. The women's use of interactive leadership has its roots in socialization, and the women interviewees believe that it benefits their organizations. Through the course of their careers, they have gained conviction that their style is effective. In fact, for some it was their own success that caused them to formulate their philosophies about what motivates people, how to make good decisions, and what it takes to maximize business performance.

Rosener has called for organizations to expand their definitions of effective leadership—to create a *wider* band of acceptable behavior so both men and women will be freer to lead in ways that take advantage of their true talents. There is further discussion of stereotype-based "bands of acceptable behavior" in Highlight 1.8.

The Narrow Band of Acceptable Behavior

HIGHLIGHT 1.8

One of the most important factors that seems to impede the advance of women and other minorities into leadership roles is bias. A bias that might be labeled "the narrow band of acceptable behavior" is depicted below.

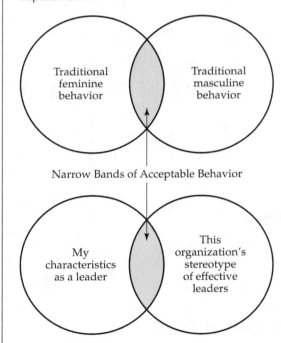

Narrow Bands of Acceptable Behavior

The characteristics and behaviors in the right-hand circle are those associated with traditional masculine behavior, and the characteristics and behaviors in the left-hand circle are those associated with traditional feminine behavior. The narrow band of overlap between the two circles can be thought of as a "hoop" women executives need to pass through.

The concept of a narrow band of acceptable behavior is not limited to women. It may be applied to any individual's deviation from organizationally defined standards. The more a person looks like, acts like, dresses like, and talks like other leaders in the organization, the wider the band of acceptable behavior (the greater the overlap of the two circles). The less one looks like, acts like, dresses like, and talks like other leaders in the organization (some aspects of which, such as gender and race, are beyond a person's control) the narrower the band of acceptable behavior. One implication of this view is that an individual who differs in obvious ways from the prototypical image of a leader (as with gender) has less "wiggle room" available; it's as though there are already one or two strikes against that person. It's like walking a tightrope.

Source: Adapted from A. M. Morrison, R.P. White, and E. Van Velsor, *Breaking the Glass Ceiling* (Reading, MA: Addison-Wesley, 1987).

A more recent study sheds additional light on factors that affect the rise of women in leadership positions.[61] It identifies four general factors that explain the shift toward more women leaders.

The first of these is that *women themselves have changed*. That's evident in the ways women's aspirations and attitudes have become more similar to those of men over time. This is illustrated in findings about the career aspirations of female university students;[62] in women's self-reports of traits such as assertiveness, dominance, and masculinity;[63,64] and in the value that women place on characteristics of work such as freedom, challenge, leadership, prestige, and power.[65] The second factor is that *leadership roles have changed*, particularly with regard to a trend toward less stereotypically masculine characterizations of leadership. Third, *organizational practices have changed*. A large part of this can be attributed to legislation prohibiting gender-based discrimination at work, as well as changes in organizational norms that put a higher priority on results than on an "old boy" network. Finally, the *culture has changed*. This is evident, for example, in the symbolic message often intended by appointment of women to important leadership positions, one representing a departure from past practices and signaling commitment to progressive change.

Finally, in addition to the glass ceiling, another recently identified challenge for women is called the **glass cliff**. The glass cliff refers to the intriguing finding that female candidates for an executive position are *more* likely to be hired than equally qualified male candidates when an organization's performance is declining. At first that may seem like good news for women, but the picture is not quite so positive. When an organization's performance is declining, there is inherently an increased risk of failure. The increased likelihood of women being selected in those situations may actually reflect a greater willingness to put women in precarious positions;[66] it could also, of course, represent an increased willingness to take some chances when nothing else seems to be working.

There Is No Simple Recipe for Effective Leadership

To fill the gaps between leadership research and practice, this book will critically review major findings about the nature of leadership as well as provide practical advice for improving leadership. As our first step in that journey, the next chapter of the book will describe how leadership develops through experience. The remainder of the book uses the leader–follower–situation interaction model as a framework for organizing and discussing various theories and research findings related to leadership. In this study, it will become clear that while there is no simple recipe for effective leadership, there *are* many different paths to effective leadership.

Little things affect little minds.

Benjamin Disraeli, British prime minister, 1874–1880

As noted previously, it is important to understand how the three domains of leadership interact—how the leader, the followers, and the situation are all part of the leadership process. Understanding their interaction is necessary before you can draw valid conclusions from the leadership you observe around you. When you see a leader's behavior (even when it may appear obviously effective or ineffective to you), you should not automatically conclude something good or bad about the leader, or what is the right way or wrong way leaders should act. You need to think about the effectiveness of that behavior in *that* context with *those* followers.

As obvious as this advice sounds, we often ignore it. Too frequently we look at just the leader's behavior and conclude that he or she is a good leader or a bad leader apart from the context. For example, suppose you observe a leader soliciting advice from subordinates. Obviously it seems unreasonable to conclude that good leaders always ask for advice or that leaders who do not frequently ask for advice are not good leaders. The appropriateness of seeking input from subordinates depends on many factors, such as the nature of the problem or the subordinates' familiarity with the problem. Perhaps the subordinates have a lot more experience with this particular problem, and soliciting their input is the correct action to take in this situation.

Consider another example. Suppose you hear that a leader did not approve a subordinate's request to take time off to attend to family matters. Was this bad leadership because the leader did not appear to be taking care of her people? Was it good leadership because she did not let personal matters interfere with the mission? Again, you cannot make an intelligent decision about the leader's actions by looking at the behavior itself. You must always assess leadership in the context of the leader, the followers, and the situation.

The following statements about leaders, followers, and the situation make these points a bit more systematically:

- A leader may need to respond to various followers differently in the same situation.
- A leader may need to respond to the same follower differently in different situations.
- Followers may respond to various leaders quite differently.
- Followers may respond to each other differently with different leaders.
- Two leaders may have different perceptions of the same followers or situations.

All of these points lead to one conclusion: the right behavior in one situation is not necessarily the right behavior in another situation. It does *not* follow, however, that any behavior is appropriate in any situation. Although we may not be able to agree on the one best behavior in a given situation, we often can agree on some clearly inappropriate behaviors.

Saying that the right behavior for a leader depends on the situation is not the same thing as saying it does not matter what the leader does. It merely recognizes the complexity among leaders, followers, and situations. This recognition is a helpful first step in drawing meaningful lessons about leadership from experience.

Summary

We have defined leadership as the process of influencing an organized group toward achieving its goals. The chapter also looked at the idea that leadership is both a science and an art. Because leadership is an immature science, researchers are still struggling to find out what the important questions in leadership are; we are far from finding conclusive answers to them. Even individuals with extensive knowledge of leadership research may be poor leaders. Knowing what to do is not the same as knowing when, where, and how to do it. The art of leadership concerns the skill of understanding leadership situations and influencing others to accomplish group goals. Formal leadership education may give individuals the skills to better understand leadership situations, and mentorships and experience may give individuals the skills to better influence others. Leaders must also weigh both rational and emotional considerations when attempting to influence others. Leadership sometimes can be accomplished through relatively rational, explicit, rule-based methods of assessing situations and determining actions.

Nevertheless, the emotional side of human nature must also be acknowledged. Leaders are often most effective when they affect people at both the emotional level and the rational level. The idea of leadership as a whole-person process can also be applied to the distinction often made between leaders and managers. Although leadership and management can be distinguished as separate functions, there is considerable overlap between them in practice.

Leadership is a process in which leaders and followers interact dynamically in a particular situation or environment. Leadership is a broader concept than that of leaders, and the study of leadership must involve more than just the study of leaders as individuals. The study of leadership must also include two other areas: the followers and the situation. In addition, the interactive nature of these three domains has become increasingly important in recent years and can help us to better understand the changing nature of leader–follower relationships and the increasing complexity of situations leaders and followers face. Because of this complexity, now, more than ever before, effective leadership cannot be boiled down to a simple recipe. It is still true, however, that good leadership makes a difference, and it can be enhanced through greater awareness of the important factors influencing the leadership process.

36   Part One   *Leadership Is a Process, Not a Position*

Key Terms

leadership, *4*
academic tradition, *7*
troubadour
    tradition, *7*
management, *8*
interactional
    framework, *15*
leader, *15*

followers, *15*
situation, *15*
interactions, *15*
in-group, *16*
out-group, *16*
followership, *19*
independent, critical
    thinking, *20*

dependent, uncritical
    thinking, *20*
active followers, *20*
passive followers, *20*
heroic theory, *24*
interactive
    leadership, *30*
glass cliff, *33*

Questions

1. We say leadership involves influencing organized groups toward goals. Do you see any disadvantages to restricting the definition to organized groups?

2. How would you define *leadership*?

3. Are some people the "leader type" and others not the "leader type"? If so, what in your judgment distinguishes them?

4. Identify several "commonsense" notions about leadership that, to you, are self-evident.

5. Does every successful leader have a valid theory of leadership?

6. Would you consider it a greater compliment for someone to call you a good manager or a good leader? Why? Do you believe you can be both?

7. Do you believe leadership can be studied scientifically? Why or why not?

8. To the extent that leadership is an art, what methods come to mind for improving one's "art of leadership"?

9. According to the interactional framework, effective leader behavior depends on many variables. It follows that there is no simple prescription for effective leader behavior. Does this mean effective leadership is merely a matter of opinion or subjective preference?

10. Generally leaders get most of the credit for a group's or an organization's success. Do you believe this is warranted or fair?

11. What are some other characteristics of leaders, followers, and situations you could add to those listed in Figure 1.2?

Activities

1. Describe the best leader you have personally known or a favorite leader from history, a novel, or a movie.

2. In this activity you will explore connotations of the words *leadership* and *management.* Divide yourselves into small groups and have each group brainstorm different word associations to the terms *leader* and *leadership* or *manager* and *management.* In addition, each group should discuss whether they would prefer to work for a manager or for a leader, and why. Then the whole group should discuss similarities and differences among the respective perceptions and feelings about the two concepts.

Minicase

Richard Branson Shoots for the Moon

The Virgin Group is the umbrella for a variety of business ventures ranging from air travel to entertainment. With close to 200 companies in over 30 countries, it is one of the largest companies in the world. At the head of this huge organization is Richard Branson. Branson founded Virgin over 30 years ago and has built the organization from a small student magazine to the multibillion-dollar enterprise it is today.

Branson is not your typical CEO. Branson's dyslexia made school a struggle and sabotaged his performance on standard IQ tests. His teachers and tests had no way of measuring his greatest strengths—his uncanny knack for uncovering lucrative business ideas and his ability to energize the ambitions of others so that they, like he, could rise to the level of their dreams.

Richard Branson's true talents began to show themselves in his late teens. While a student at Stowe School in England in 1968, Branson decided to start his own magazine, *Student.* Branson was inspired by the student activism on his campus in the 1960s and decided to try something different. *Student* differed from most college newspapers or magazines; it focused on the students and their interests. Branson sold advertising to major corporations to support his magazine. He included articles by ministers of Parliament, rock stars, intellectuals, and celebrities. *Student* grew to become a commercial success.

In 1970 Branson saw an opportunity for *Student* to offer records cheaply by running ads for mail-order delivery. The subscribers to *Student* flooded the magazine with so many orders that his spin-off discount music venture proved more lucrative than the magazine subscriptions. Branson recruited the staff of *Student* for his discount music business. He built a small recording studio and signed his first artist. Mike Oldfield recorded "Tubular Bells" at Virgin in 1973; the album sold 5 million copies, and Virgin Records and the Virgin brand name were born. Branson has gone on to start his own airline (Virgin Atlantic Airlines was launched in 1984), build hotels (Virgin Hotels started in 1988), get into the personal finance business (Virgin Direct Personal Finance Services was launched in 1995), and even enter the cola wars (Virgin Cola was introduced in 1994). And those are just a few highlights of the Virgin Group—all this while Branson has attempted to break world speed records for crossing the Atlantic Ocean by boat and by hot air balloon.

As you might guess, Branson's approach is nontraditional—he has no giant corporate office or staff and few if any board meetings. Instead he keeps each enterprise small and relies on his skills of empowering people's ideas to fuel success. When a flight attendant from Virgin Airlines approached him with her vision of a wedding business, Richard told her to go do it. He even put on a wedding dress himself to help launch the publicity. Virgin Brides was born. Branson relies heavily on the creativity of his staff; he is more a supporter of new ideas than a creator of them. He encourages searches for new business ideas everywhere he goes and even has a spot on the Virgin website called "Got a Big Idea?"

In December 1999 Richard Branson was awarded a knighthood in the Queen's Millennium New Year's Honours List for "services to entrepreneurship." What's next on Branson's list? It's Virgin Galactic, Branson's company designed in part to make space tourism available to private citizens. He has announced that the company's first space flight will take place in 2013 on its *Spaceship Two* traveling 62 miles above the earth. The first passengers will be Branson himself and his two adult sons; you can take a later flight yourself for a mere $200,000 for a two-hour trip. Not everyone is convinced that space tourism can become a fully fledged part of the travel industry, but with Branson behind the idea it just might fly.

1. Would you classify Richard Branson as a manager or a leader? What qualities distinguish him as one or the other?

2. As mentioned earlier in this chapter, followers are part of the leadership process. Describe the relationship between Branson and his followers.

3. Identify the myths of leadership development that Richard Branson's success helps to disprove.

Sources: http://www.johnshepler.com/articles/branson.html;
http://www.wma.com/richard_branson/summary/;
http://www.virgin.com/aboutvirgin/allaboutvirgin/thewholestory/;
http://www.virgin.com/aboutvirgin/allaboutvirgin/whosrichardbranson/;
http://www.qksrv.net/click-310374-35140;
http://www.guardian.co.uk/space/article/0,14493,1235926,00.html.

End Notes

1. P. P. Read, *Alive* (New York: J. B. Lippincott, 1974).

2. Ibid., p. 77.

3. J. R. Meindl and S. B. Ehrlich, "The Romance of Leadership and the Evaluation of Organizational Performance," *Academy of Management Journal* 30 (1987), pp. 90–109.

4. W. G. Bennis, "Leadership Theory and Administrative Behavior: The Problem of Authority," *Administrative Science Quarterly* 4 (1959), pp. 259–60.

5. F. Fiedler, *A Theory of Leadership Effectiveness* (New York: McGraw-Hill, 1967).

6. R. K. Merton, *Social Theory and Social Structure* (New York: Free Press, 1957).

7. C. F. Roach and O. Behling, "Functionalism: Basis for an Alternate Approach to the Study of Leadership," in *Leaders and Managers: International Perspectives on Managerial Behavior and Leadership*, eds. J. G. Hunt, D. M. Hosking, C. A. Schriesheim, and R. Stewar (Elmsford, NY: Pergamon, 1984).

8. D. P. Campbell, *Campbell Leadership Index Manual* (Minneapolis: National Computer Systems, 1991).

9. R. C. Ginnett, "Team Effectiveness Leadership Model: Identifying Leverage Points for Change," *Proceedings of the 1996 National Leadership Institute Conference* (College Park, MD: National Leadership Institute, 1996).

10. G. J. Curphy and R. T. Hogan, *The Rocket Model: Practical Advice for Building High Performing Teams* (Tulsa, OK: Hogan Press, 2012).

11. M. D. Mumford, S. J. Zaccaro, F. D. Harding, T. O. Jacobs, and E. A. Fleishman, "Leadership Skills for a Changing World," *Leadership Quarterly* 11, no. 1 (2000), pp. 11–35.

12. B. M. Bass, *Bass and Stogdill's Handbook of Leadership,* 3rd ed. (New York: Free Press, 1990).

13. H. C. Foushee, "Dyads and Triads at 35,000 Feet: Factors Affecting Group Process and Aircrew Performance," *American Psychologist* 39 (1984), pp. 885–93.

14. W. G. Bennis and B. Nanus, *Leaders: The Strategies for Taking Charge* (New York: Harper & Row, 1985).

15. A. Zaleznik, "The Leadership Gap," *Washington Quarterly* 6, no. 1 (1983), pp. 32–39.

16. W. G. Bennis, *On Becoming a Leader* (Reading, MA: Addison-Wesley, 1989).

17. Zaleznik, "The Leadership Gap."

18. P. Slovic and B. Fischoff, "On the Psychology of Experimental Surprises," *Journal of Experimental Social Psychology* 22 (1977), pp. 544–51.

19. G. Wood, "The Knew-It-All-Along Effect," *Journal of Experimental Psychology: Human Perception and Performance* 4 (1979), pp. 345–53.

20. P. E. Lazarsfeld, "The American Soldier: An Expository Review," *Public Opinion Quarterly* 13 (1949), pp. 377–404.

21. For example, A. Tellegen, D. T. Lykken, T. J. Bouchard, K. J. Wilcox, N. L. Segal, and S. Rich, "Personality Similarity in Twins Reared Apart and Together," *Journal of Personality and Social Psychology* 54 (1988), pp. 1031–39.

22. Fiedler, *A Theory of Leadership Effectiveness.*

23. E. P. Hollander, *Leadership Dynamics: A Practical Guide to Effective Relationships* (New York: Free Press, 1978).

24. G. B. Graen and J. F. Cashman, "A Role-Making Model of Leadership in Formal Organizations: A Developmental Approach," in *Leadership Frontiers,* eds. J. G. Hunt and L. L. Larson (Kent, OH: Kent State University Press, 1975).

25. R. M. Stogdill, "Personal Factors Associated with Leadership: A Review of the Literature," *Journal of Psychology* 25 (1948), pp. 35–71.

26. R. M. Stogdill, *Handbook of Leadership* (New York: Free Press, 1974).

27. R. T. Hogan, G. J. Curphy, and J. Hogan, "What We Know about Personality: Leadership and Effectiveness," *American Psychologist* 49 (1994), pp. 493–504.

28. R. G. Lord, C. L. DeVader, and G. M. Allinger, "A Meta-Analysis of the Relationship between Personality Traits and Leadership Perceptions: An Application of Validity Generalization Procedures," *Journal of Applied Psychology* 71 (1986), pp. 402–10.

29. R. M. Kanter, *The Change Masters* (New York: Simon & Schuster, 1983).

30. E. D. Baltzell, *Puritan Boston and Quaker Philadelphia* (New York: Free Press, 1980).

31. E. P. Hollander and L. R. Offermann, "Power and Leadership in Organizations," *American Psychologist* 45 (1990), pp. 179–89.

32. S. D. Baker, "Followership: The Theoretical Foundation of a Contemporary Construct," *Journal of Leadership & Organizational Studies* 14, no. 1 (2007), p. 51.

33. Baker, "Followership."

34. J. M. Burns, *Leadership* (New York: Harper & Row, 1978).

35. B. M. Bass, *Bass and Stogdill's Handbook of Leadership*, 3rd ed. (New York: Free Press, 1990).

36. Stogdill, *Handbook of Leadership*.

37. C. D. Sutton and R. W. Woodman, "Pygmalion Goes to Work: The Effects of Supervisor Expectations in the Retail Setting," *Journal of Applied Psychology* 74 (1989), pp. 943–50.

38. L. I. Moore, "The FMI: Dimensions of Follower Maturity," *Group and Organizational Studies* 1 (1976), pp. 203–22.

39. T. A. Scandura, G. B. Graen, and M. A. Novak, "When Managers Decide Not to Decide Autocratically: An Investigation of Leader-Member Exchange and Decision Influence," *Journal of Applied Psychology* 52 (1986), pp. 135–47.

40. C. A. Sales, E. Levanoni, and D. H. Saleh, "Satisfaction and Stress as a Function of Job Orientation, Style of Supervision, and the Nature of the Task," *Engineering Management International* 2 (1984), pp. 145–53.

41. Adapted from K. Macrorie, *Twenty Teachers* (Oxford: Oxford University Press, 1984).

42. J. M. Kouzes and B. Z. Posner, *The Leadership Challenge: How to Get Extraordinary Things Done in Organizations* (San Francisco: Jossey-Bass, 1987).

43. R. Lippitt, "The Changing Leader–Follower Relationships of the 1980s," *Journal of Applied Behavioral Science* 18 (1982), pp. 395–403.

44. P. Block, *Stewardship* (San Francisco: Berrett-Koehler, 1992).

45. G. F. Tanoff and C. B. Barlow, "Leadership and Followership: Same Animal, Different Spots?" *Consulting Psychology Journal: Practice and Research*, Summer 2002, pp. 157–65.

46. P. M. Senge, *The Fifth Discipline: The Art and Practice of the Learning Organization* (New York: Doubleday/Currency, 1990).

47. V. Vroom and A. G. Jago, "The Role of the Situation in Leadership," *American Psychologist* 62, no. 1 (2007), pp. 17–24.

48. Vroom and Jago, "The Role of the Situation in Leadership."

49. For example, M. Conlin, "The New Gender Gap: From Kindergarten to Grad School, Boys Are Becoming the Second Sex," *BusinessWeek*, May 26, 2003.

50. GAO, Women in Management: Female Managers' Representation, Characteristics, and Pay, GAO-10-1064T (Washington, D.C.: September 28, 2010).

51. http://catalyst.org/press-release/161/2009-catalyst-census-of-the-fortune-500-reveals-women-missing-from-critical-business-leadership. 10/05/2010.

52. H. Ibarra, N. M. Carter, and C. Silva, "Why Men Still Get More Promotions Than Women," *Harvard Business Review*, September 2010, pp. 80–85.

53. D. Bevelander and M. J. Page, "Ms. Trust: Gender, Networks and Trust—Implications for Management and Education," *Academy of Management Learning & Education* 10, no. 4 (2011), pp. 623–42.

54. V. Schein, "The Relationship between Sex Role Stereotypes and Requisite Management Characteristics," *Journal of Applied Psychology* 57 (1973), pp. 95–100.

55. V. Schein, "Relationships between Sex Role Stereotypes and Requisite Management Characteristics among Female Managers, *Journal of Applied Psychology* 60 (1975), pp. 340–44.

56. V. Schein and R. Mueller, "Sex Role Stereotyping and Requisite Management Characteristics: A Cross Cultural Look," *Journal of Organizational Behavior* 13 (1992), pp. 439–47.

57. A. M. Koenig, A. H. Eagly, A. A. Mitchell, and T. Ristikari, "Are Leader Stereotypes Masculine? A Meta-analysis of Three Research Paradigms," *Psychological Bulletin* 137, no. 4, (2011), pp. 616–42.

58. O. C. Brenner, J. Tomkiewicz, and V. E. Schein, "The Relationship between Sex Role Stereotypes and Requisite Management Characteristics Revisited," *Academy of Management Journal* 32 (1989), pp. 662–69.

59. A. M. Morrison, R. P. White, and E. Van Velsor, *Breaking the Glass Ceiling* (Reading, MA: Addison-Wesley, 1987).

60. J. B. Rosener, "Ways Women Lead," *Harvard Business Review* 68 (1990), pp. 119–25.

61. A. H. Eagly and L. L. Carli, "The Female Leadership Advantage: An Evaluation of the Evidence," *The Leadership Quarterly* 14 (2003), pp. 807–34.

62. A. W. Astin, S. A. Parrrott, W. S. Korn, and L. J. Sax, *The American Freshman: Thirty Year Trends* (Los Angeles: Higher Education Research Institute, University of California, 1997).

63. J. M. Twenge, "Changes in Masculine and Feminine Traits over Time: A Meta-analysis," *Sex Roles* 36 (1997), pp. 305–25.

64. J. M. Twenge, "Changes in Women's Assertiveness in Response to Status and Roles: A Cross-Temporal Meta-analysis, 1931–1993," *Journal of Personality and Social Psychology* 81 (2001), pp. 133–45.

65. A. M. Konrad, J. E. Ritchie, Jr., P. Lieb, and E. Corrigall, "Sex Differences and Similarities in Job Attribute Preferences: A Meta-analysis," *Psychological Bulletin* 126 (2000), pp. 593–641.

66. S. A. Haslam and M. K. Ryan, "The Road to the Glass Cliff: Differences in the Perceived Suitability of Men and Women for Leadership Positions in Succeeding and Failing Organizations," *The Leadership Quarterly* 19 (2008), pp. 530–46.

3

Doing Business in Global Markets

Learning Objectives

AFTER YOU HAVE READ AND STUDIED THIS CHAPTER, YOU SHOULD BE ABLE TO

LO 3-1   Discuss the importance of the global market and the roles of comparative advantage and absolute advantage in global trade.

LO 3-2   Explain the importance of importing and exporting, and understand key terms used in global business.

LO 3-3   Illustrate the strategies used in reaching global markets and explain the role of multinational corporations.

LO 3-4   Evaluate the forces that affect trading in global markets.

LO 3-5   Debate the advantages and disadvantages of trade protectionism.

LO 3-6   Discuss the changing landscape of the global market and the issue of offshore outsourcing.

Getting to Know **Leila Janah**

For decades U.S. companies have outsourced work overseas to countries known for providing cheap labor. The practice is controversial. While it saves businesses money, that's often the only benefit. Not only may it hurt job creation domestically, outsourcing can also overload foreign job markets with underpaid work that often offers little chance for advancement.

Leila Janah saw this problem firsthand when she befriended a call center employee working in India. The young man took a long commute to his job from one of Mumbai's worst slums, which was the only place he could afford. "I knew there were more people like him capable of doing quality work," says Janah. She then came up with the idea for Samasource, a nonprofit "microwork" company that helps young men and women in developing countries earn extra income in order to rise out of poverty.

The bulk of the work provided by Samasource involves simple, computer-related tasks—such as tagging images, moderating comments on websites, and transcribing interviews. These jobs normally end up in countries like India and the Philippines through large outsourcing corporations. Unlike these companies, however, Samasource carefully selects potential employees based on the skills they lack, not the ones they have already. "The criteria for selecting agents is that they must be between the ages of 18 and 30, have no formal work experience, and are currently earning less than a living wage," says Janah. "Agents are then provided free, specialized technology training, soft skills training, and project-specific training before beginning work." Samasource's contracts with companies like Google, Microsoft and eBay have helped more than 4,000 people and their families rise above the poverty line. In fact, a recent study projected that by 2020 more than 2.9 million people will be employed through "impact sourcing" companies like Samasource.

Janah's commitment to combating world poverty has been her driving force since her teenage years. She earned a $10,000 scholarship, which funded a trip to Ghana to teach English. Janah continued to travel the world while also studying at Harvard University. After graduating with a degree in economic development, she took a job with the World Bank that made her question traditional methods of providing aid. "The more time I spent in developing countries, and the more time I spent talking to poor people, I realized what they want more than anything is a good job," says Janah. "We spend billions on international aid annually, but we don't find ways to connect people to dignified work."

Janah hopes that Samasource will change that. The nonprofit currently operates 16 centers in nine countries and is always expanding. One of Samasource's most ambitious projects is SamaUSA, a pilot program the company recently launched in San Francisco. This 80-hour training program teaches marketable computer skills to community-college students from low-income neighborhoods and helps them find online work. In the end, though, much of the nonprofit's future success depends on outside companies choosing to work with Samasource instead of other outsourcing services. "We tell [clients], 'You're going to spend this money on an outsourcing company anyway—why not end poverty and save the world without spending more money than you already spend?'" says Janah.

Leila Janah is an example of an emerging global businessperson. She has learned to speak other languages, understands cultural and economic differences, and knows how to adapt to changes successfully. This chapter explains the opportunities and challenges businesspeople like Janah face every day in dealing with the dynamic environment of global business.

Leila Janah
- Founder and CEO of Samasource
- Fights world poverty and trains unskilled workers
- Finds jobs for newly trained workers

www.samasource.org

@samasource

Sources: Jason Ankeny, "The 7 Most Powerful Women to Watch in 2014: The Humanitarian," *Entrepreneur*, January 3, 2014; Catherine Dunn, "40 Under 40: Leila Janah," *Forbes*, September 19, 2013; Visi R. Talik, "'Rising Star' Leila Janah on Fighting Poverty," *The Wall Street Journal*, November 29, 2012; and "A Letter from Leila Janah, Founder and CEO," www.samasource.org, accessed February 2014.

name that **company**

This Swiss-based company has many foreign subsidiaries including Jenny Craig (weight management), Ralston Purina, Chef America (maker of Hot Pockets), and Dreyer's Ice Cream in the United States, as well as Perrier in France. The company employs over 328,000 people and has operations in almost every country in the world. Name that company. (Find the answer in the chapter.)

LO 3–1   Discuss the importance of the global market and the roles of comparative advantage and absolute advantage in global trade.

THE DYNAMIC GLOBAL MARKET

Have you dreamed of traveling to cities like Paris, London, Rio de Janeiro, or Moscow? Today, over 90 percent of the companies doing business globally believe it's important for their employees to have experience working in other countries.[1] The reason is not surprising—although the United States is a market of over 317 *million* people, there are over 7.1 *billion* potential customers in the 194 countries that make up the global market.[2] That's too many people to ignore! (See Figure 3.1 for a map of the world and important statistics about world population.)

Today U.S. consumers buy billions of dollars' worth of goods from China.[3] United Parcel Service (UPS) has experienced double-digit market growth in its global operations and Walmart operates more than 350 stores in Africa.[4] The National Basketball Association (NBA) played eight preseason games in Europe, Asia, and South America in 2013 and the National Football League (NFL) plans to play three games in London's Wembley Stadium in 2014.

FIGURE 3.1 WORLD POPULATION BY CONTINENT

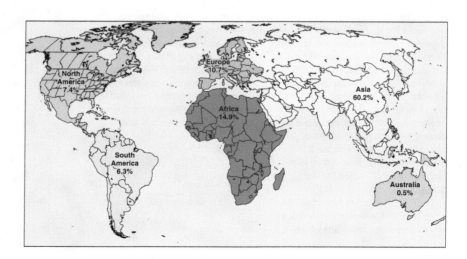

It may not be what the rest of the world calls "football," but American football is attracting an audience outside the United States. London's Wembley Stadium has been home to the NFL's International Series since 2007. What cultural factors must U.S. sports franchises overcome in order to increase popularity abroad?

NBC paid $250 million to telecast three full seasons of England's Barclays Premier Soccer League in the United States.[5] U.S. film stars Matt Damon, Tom Cruise, and Meryl Streep draw crowds to movie theaters around the globe.[6]

Because the global market is so large, it is important to understand the language used in global trade. For example, **importing** is buying products from another country. **Exporting** is selling products to another country. As you might suspect, competition among exporting nations is intense. The United States is the largest importing nation in the world and is the second-largest exporting nation, behind China.[7]

This chapter will familiarize you with global business and its many challenges. As competition in global markets intensifies, the demand for students with training in global business is almost certain to grow.

WHY TRADE WITH OTHER NATIONS?

No nation, not even a technologically advanced one, can produce all the products its people want and need. Even if a country did become self-sufficient, other nations would seek to trade with it to meet the needs of their own people. Some nations, like Venezuela and Russia, have an abundance of natural resources but limited technological know-how. Other countries, such as Japan and Switzerland, have sophisticated technology but few natural resources. Global trade enables a nation to produce what it is most capable of producing and buy what it needs from others in a mutually beneficial exchange relationship. This happens through the process called free trade.[8]

Free trade is the movement of goods and services among nations without political or economic barriers. It has become a hotly debated concept.[9] In fact, many in the United States take the position "fair trade, not free trade."[10] Figure 3.2 offers some of the pros and cons of free trade.

importing
Buying products from another country.

exporting
Selling products to another country.

free trade
The movement of goods and services among nations without political or economic barriers.

FIGURE 3.2 THE PROS AND CONS OF FREE TRADE

PROS	CONS
• The global market contains over 7 billion potential customers for goods and services. • Productivity grows when countries produce goods and services in which they have a comparative advantage. • Global competition and less-costly imports keep prices down, so inflation does not curtail economic growth. • Free trade inspires innovation for new products and keeps firms competitively challenged. • Uninterrupted flow of capital gives countries access to foreign investments, which help keep interest rates low.	• Domestic workers (particularly in manufacturing-based jobs) can lose their jobs due to increased imports or production shifts to low-wage global markets. • Workers may be forced to accept pay cuts from employers, who can threaten to move their jobs to lower-cost global markets. • Moving operations overseas because of intense competitive pressure often means the loss of service jobs and growing numbers of white-collar jobs. • Domestic companies can lose their comparative advantage when competitors build advanced production operations in low-wage countries.

The Theories of Comparative and Absolute Advantage

Countries exchange more than goods and services, however. They also exchange art, sports, cultural events, medical advances, space exploration, and labor. Comparative advantage theory, suggested in the early 19th century by English economist David Ricardo, was the guiding principle that supported the idea of free economic exchange.[11] **Comparative advantage theory** states that a country should sell to other countries those products it produces most effectively and efficiently, and buy from other countries those products it cannot produce as effectively or efficiently. The United States has a comparative advantage in producing goods and services, such as software and engineering services.[12] In contrast, it lacks a comparative advantage in growing coffee or making shoes; thus, we import most of the shoes and coffee we consume. By specializing and trading, the United States and its trading partners can realize mutually beneficial exchanges.

A country has an **absolute advantage** if it can produce a specific product more efficiently than all other countries. Absolute advantage does not last forever; global competition causes absolute advantages to fade. Today there are very few instances of absolute advantage in global markets.

comparative advantage theory
Theory that states that a country should sell to other countries those products that it produces most effectively and efficiently, and buy from other countries those products that it cannot produce as effectively or efficiently.

absolute advantage
The advantage that exists when a country produces a specific product more efficiently than all other countries.

 LO 3–2 Explain the importance of importing and exporting, and understand key terms used in global business.

GETTING INVOLVED IN GLOBAL TRADE

People interested in a job in global business often think they are limited to firms like Boeing, Caterpillar, or IBM, which have large multinational accounts. However, real global job potential may be with small businesses. In the United States, only 1 percent of the 30 million small businesses export yet they account for about 30 percent of the total U.S. exports.[13] In 2010,

President Obama challenged small businesses to think big and help double exports by 2015. With the support of the U.S. Department of Commerce, U.S. exports increased significantly but not quite at the level the president requested.[14]

Getting started globally is often a matter of observing, being determined, and taking risks. In a classic story, several years ago a U.S. traveler in an African country noticed there was no ice available for drinks or for keeping foods fresh. Research showed there was no ice factory for hundreds of miles, yet the market seemed huge. The man returned to the United States, found some investors, and returned to Africa to build an ice-making plant. The job was tough; much negotiation was necessary with local authorities (much of which was done by local citizens and businesspeople who knew the system). But the plant was built, and this forward-thinking entrepreneur gained a considerable return on his idea, while the people gained a needed product.

Importing Goods and Services

Students attending colleges and universities abroad often notice that some products widely available in their countries are unavailable or more expensive elsewhere. By working with producers in their native country, finding some start-up financing, and putting in long hours of hard work, many have become major importers while still in school.

Howard Schultz, CEO of Starbucks, found his opportunity while traveling in Milan, Italy. Schultz was enthralled with the ambience, the aroma, and especially the sense of community in the Italian neighborhood coffee and espresso bars that stretched across the country. He felt such gathering places would be great in the United States. Schultz bought the original Starbucks coffee shop in Seattle and transformed it according to his vision.[15] Because the Italian coffee bars caught his attention, U.S. coffee lovers now know what a grande latte is.

Exporting Goods and Services

Who would think U.S. firms could sell beer in Germany, home of so many good beers? Well, some of Munich's most famous beer halls now have American outposts where you can buy U.S. beers like Samuel Adams Boston Lager.[16] If this surprises you, imagine selling sand in the Middle East. Meridan Group exports a special kind of sand used in swimming pool filters that sells well there.

The fact is, you can sell just about any good or service used in the United States to other countries—and sometimes the competition is not nearly so intense as it is at home. For example, you can sell snowplows to Saudi Arabians, who use them to clear sand off their driveways. As Chinese women develop more sophisticated beauty routines, companies like Mary Kay are increasing their presence in China.[17] Exporting also provides a terrific boost to the U.S. economy. C. Fred Bergsten, founding director of the Peterson Institute for International Economics, states that U.S. exports of $1.5 trillion goods and services create approximately 10 million well-paid jobs in our economy. He also estimates that every $1 billion in additional U.S. exports generates over 7,000 jobs at home.[18] But selling in global markets and adapting products to global customers are by no means easy tasks. We discuss key forces that affect global trading later in this chapter.

Things may not have started off "pretty" for Ugly Dolls, a venture founded almost by accident, but the two-person company has grown into a global business selling its products in over 1,000 stores around the world. The original dolls have been joined by accessories, books, calendars, action figures, and T-shirts. Does a career in exporting or importing sound appealing to you?

If you are interested in exporting, send for "The Basic Guide to Exporting," a brochure from the U.S. Government Printing Office, Superintendent of Documents, Washington, DC 20402. More advice is available at websites such as those sponsored by the U.S. Department of Commerce (www.doc.gov), the Bureau of Export Administration (www.bea.gov), the Small Business Administration (www.sba.gov), and the Small Business Exporters Association (www.sbea.org).

Measuring Global Trade

In measuring global trade, nations rely on two key indicators: balance of trade and balance of payments. The **balance of trade** is the total value of a nation's exports compared to its imports measured over a particular period. A *favorable* balance of trade, or **trade surplus**, occurs when the value of a country's exports exceeds that of its imports. An *unfavorable* balance of trade, or **trade deficit**, occurs when the value of a country's exports is less than its imports. It's easy to understand why countries prefer to export more than they import. If I sell you $200 worth of goods and buy only $100 worth, I have an extra $100 available to buy other things. However, I'm in an unfavorable position if I buy $200 worth of goods from you and sell you only $100.

The **balance of payments** is the difference between money coming into a country (from exports) and money leaving the country (for imports) plus money flows coming into or leaving a country from other factors such as tourism, foreign aid, military expenditures, and foreign investment. The goal is to have more money flowing into the country than out—a *favorable* balance of payments. Conversely, an *unfavorable* balance of payments exists when more money is flowing out of a country than coming in.

In the past, the United States exported more goods and services than it imported. However, since 1975 it has bought more goods from other nations than it has sold and thus has a trade deficit. Today, the United States runs its highest trade deficit with China.[19] Nonetheless the United States remains one of the world's largest *exporting* nations even though the U.S. exports a much lower *percentage* of its products than other countries, such as China, Germany, and Japan. (Figure 3.3 lists the major trading countries in the world and the leading U.S. trading partners.)

balance of trade
The total value of a nation's exports compared to its imports measured over a particular period.

trade surplus
A favorable balance of trade; occurs when the value of a country's exports exceeds that of its imports.

trade deficit
An unfavorable balance of trade; occurs when the value of a country's imports exceeds that of its exports.

balance of payments
The difference between money coming into a country (from exports) and money leaving the country (for imports) plus money flows from other factors such as tourism, foreign aid, military expenditures, and foreign investment.

 connect

 iSee It! Need help understanding balance of trade? Visit your Connect e-book video tab for a brief animated explanation.

FIGURE 3.3 THE LARGEST EXPORTING NATIONS IN THE WORLD AND THE LARGEST U.S. TRADE PARTNERS

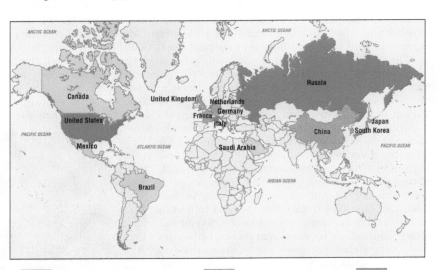

World's Largest Exporting Nations   Top U.S. Trading Partners   Both

In supporting free trade, the United States, like other nations, wants to make certain global trade is conducted fairly. To ensure a level playing field, countries prohibit unfair trade practices such as dumping. **Dumping** is selling products in a foreign country at lower prices than those charged in the producing country. This predatory pricing tactic is sometimes used to reduce surplus products in foreign markets or to gain a foothold in a new market. Some governments may even offer financial incentives to certain industries to sell goods in global markets for less than they sell them at home. China, Brazil, and Russia, for example, have been penalized for dumping steel in the United States. U.S. laws against dumping are specific and require foreign firms to price their products to include 10 percent overhead costs plus an 8 percent profit margin. Now that you understand some of the basic terms used in global business, we can look at different strategies for entering global markets. First, let's assess your progress so far.

dumping
Selling products in a foreign country at lower prices than those charged in the producing country.

test **prep**

- What are two of the main arguments favoring the expansion of U.S. businesses into global markets?
- What is comparative advantage, and what are some examples of this concept at work in the United States?
- How are a nation's balance of trade and balance of payments determined?
- What is meant by the term *dumping* in global trade?

Use LearnSmart to help retain what you have learned. Access your instructor's Connect course to check out LearnSmart, or go to learnsmartadvantage.com for help.

≡LEARNSMART

LO 3–3 Illustrate the strategies used in reaching global markets and explain the role of multinational corporations.

STRATEGIES FOR REACHING GLOBAL MARKETS

Businesses use different strategies to compete in global markets. The key strategies include licensing, exporting, franchising, contract manufacturing, international joint ventures and strategic alliances, foreign subsidiaries, and foreign direct investment. Each provides different economic opportunities, along with specific commitments and risks. Figure 3.4 places the strategies on

FIGURE 3.4 STRATEGIES FOR REACHING GLOBAL MARKETS

a continuum showing the amount of commitment, control, risk, and profit potential associated with each strategy. Take some time to look over the information in Figure 3.4 before you continue.

Licensing

licensing
A global strategy in which a firm (the licensor) allows a foreign company (the licensee) to produce its product in exchange for a fee (a royalty).

A firm (the licensor) may decide to compete in a global market by **licensing** the right to manufacture its product or use its trademark to a foreign company (the licensee) for a fee (a royalty). A company with an interest in licensing generally sends company representatives to the foreign company to help set up operations. The licensor may also assist or work with a licensee in such areas as distribution, promotion, and consulting.

A licensing agreement can benefit a firm in several ways. First, the firm can gain revenues it would not otherwise have generated in its home market. Also, foreign licensees often must purchase start-up supplies, materials, and consulting services from the licensing firm. Coca-Cola has entered into global licensing agreements with over 300 licensees that have extended into long-term service contracts that sell over $1 billion of the company's products each year.[20] Service-based companies are also active in licensing. For example, retailer Frederick's of Hollywood recently entered into a licensing agreement with Emirates Associated Business Group to build and operate Frederick's of Hollywood stores in the Middle East.

A final advantage of licensing is that licensors spend little or no money to produce and market their products. These costs come from the licensee's pocket. Therefore, licensees generally work hard to succeed. However, licensors may also experience problems. Often a firm must grant licensing rights to its product for an extended period, 20 years or longer. If a product experiences remarkable growth in the foreign market, the bulk of the revenues belong to the licensee. Perhaps even more threatening is that the licensing firm is actually selling its expertise. If a foreign licensee learns the company's technology or product secrets, it may break the agreement and begin to produce a similar product on its own. If legal remedies are not available, the licensing firm may lose its trade secrets, not to mention promised royalties.

Warner Bros. has licensed many companies to make products related to successful film franchises like The Hobbit. *Do you think* Hobbit-*licensed products will maintain their global popularity with new generations of viewers?*

Exporting

To meet increasing global competition, the U.S. Department of Commerce created Export Assistance Centers (EACs). EACs provide hands-on exporting assistance and trade-finance support for small and medium-sized businesses that wish to directly export goods and services. An EAC network exists in more than 100 U.S. cities and 80 countries, with further expansion planned.[21]

U.S. firms that are still hesitant can engage in *indirect* exporting through specialists called export-trading companies (or export-management companies) that assist in negotiating and establishing trading relationships. An export-trading company not only matches buyers and sellers from different countries but also deals with foreign customs offices, documentation,

and even weights and measures conversions to ease the process of entering global markets. It also can assist exporters with warehousing, billing, and insuring. If you are considering a career in global business, export-trading companies often provide internships or part-time opportunities for students.

Franchising

Franchising is a contractual agreement whereby someone with a good idea for a business sells others the rights to use the business name and sell a product or service in a given territory in a specified manner. Franchising is popular domestically and globally. (We discuss it in depth in Chapter 5.) Major U.S. franchisors such as Subway, Holiday Inn, and Dunkin' Donuts have many global units operated by foreign franchisees, but global franchising isn't limited to large franchisors. For example, Rocky Mountain Chocolate Factory, a Colorado-based producer of premium chocolates, has agreements with the Al Muhairy Group of the United Arab Emirates and plans to open two stores in Saudi Arabia in 2015. In the Middle East, chocolate is considered a gourmet luxury much like caviar in the United States.[22] Foreign franchisors also may look to expand to the U.S. market. Guatemala-based Pollo Campara opened its first restaurant franchise in the U.S. in 2002, and Vietnamese entrepreneur Ly Qui Trung introduced his Pho24 franchises to the United States in 2012.

Franchisors have to be careful to adapt their product or service to the countries they serve. Yum! Brands has 40,000 of its KFC, Taco Bell, and Pizza Hut restaurants in 130 countries around the world.[23] It learned quickly that preferences in pizza toppings differ globally. Japanese customers, for example, enjoy squid and sweet mayonnaise pizza. In the company's KFC restaurants in China, the menu is chicken with Sichuan spicy sauce and rice, egg soup, and a "dragon twister" (KFC's version of a traditional Beijing duck wrap).[24] Read the nearby Reaching Beyond Our Borders box that highlights another global franchise champion, McDonald's.

Tired of studying and want a quick snack? How about a piping hot Domino's pizza with potatoes and corn topped with mayo? Domino's serves pizzas around the globe that appeal to different tastes (the mayo pizza is a hit in Japan). How can franchises ensure their products are appropriate for global markets?

Contract Manufacturing

In **contract manufacturing** a foreign company produces private-label goods to which a domestic company then attaches its own brand name or trademark. For example, contract manufacturers make circuit boards and components used in computers, printers, smartphones, medical products, airplanes, and consumer electronics for companies such as Dell, Xerox, and IBM. Nike has more than 800 contract factories around the world that manufacture all its footwear and apparel. The worldwide contract manufacturing business is estimated to be a $250 billion industry that's expected to grow to $325 billion soon.[25]

Contract manufacturing enables a company to experiment in a new market without incurring heavy start-up costs such as building a manufacturing plant. If the brand name becomes a success, the company has penetrated a new market with relatively low risk. A firm can also use contract manufacturing temporarily to meet an unexpected increase in orders, and, of course, labor costs are often very low. Contract manufacturing falls under the broad category of *outsourcing*, which we defined in Chapter 1 and will discuss in more depth later in this chapter.

contract manufacturing
A foreign company's production of private-label goods to which a domestic company then attaches its brand name or trademark; part of the broad category of outsourcing.

reaching beyond **our borders**

www.mcdonalds.com

McDonald's: Over 100 Cultures Served

For decades McDonald's has been the undisputed king of global food franchising. With more than 34,000 restaurants in over 118 countries, Mickey D's serves more than 69 million customers every day.

So how did McDonald's become such a global powerhouse? It certainly didn't get there through hamburgers alone. Since it first began expanding overseas, McDonald's has been careful to include regional tastes on its menus along with the usual Big Mac and French fries. For instance, in Thailand patrons can order the Samurai Burger, a pork-patty sandwich marinated in teriyaki sauce and topped with mayonnaise and a pickle. If fish is more your taste, try the Ebi Filet-o shrimp sandwich from Japan.

McDonald's is also careful to adapt its menus to local customs and culture. In Israel, all meat served in the chain's restaurants is 100 percent kosher beef. The company also closes many of its restaurants on the Sabbath and religious holidays. McDonald's pays respect

МакЭкспресс

to religious sentiments in India as well by not including any beef or pork on its menu. For more examples, go to www.mcdonalds.com and explore the various McDonald's international franchises websites. Notice how the company blends the culture of each country into the restaurant's image.

McDonald's main global market concern as of late has been Asia. So far McDonald's strategy seems to be working. In Shanghai the company's Hamburger University attracts top-level college graduates to be trained for management positions. Only about eight out of every 1,000 applicants makes it into the

program, an acceptance rate even lower than Harvard's! McDonald's is reaching out further in Asia and in 2014 opened its first store in Vietnam. The Vietnamese location in Ho Chi Minh City is the country's very first drive-thru restaurant. Bringing McDonald's to Vietnam is a dream come true for Henry Nguyen, founder of Good Day Hospitality, who has been wanting to introduce the brand to Vietnam for over a decade. Nguyen brought in 20 top McDonald's employees from Australia to help aid in the opening while also sending prospective Vietnamese employees to Queensland to learn the ropes in a real-life restaurant setting. In the end, one can only hope that McDonald's remains dedicated to quality as it continues adapting and expanding into the global market.

Sources: Erin Smith, "Some McSkills to Share," *The Warwick Daily News,* February 4, 2014; Kate Taylor, "New Year, New Expansion: McDonald's to Open First Restaurant in Vietnam," *Entrepreneur,* December 23, 2013; Vivian Giang, "McDonald's Hamburger University: Step inside the Most Exclusive School in the World," *Business Insider,* April 7, 2012; and McDonald's, www.mcdonalds .com, accessed February 2014.

International Joint Ventures and Strategic Alliances

joint venture

A partnership in which two or more companies (often from different countries) join to undertake a major project.

A **joint venture** is a partnership in which two or more companies (often from different countries) join to undertake a major project. Joint ventures are often mandated by governments such as China as a condition of doing business in their country. For example, Disney and state-owned Shanghai Shendi Group entered a joint venture to create a Disneyland theme park in Shanghai that is expected to open in 2015.[26]

Joint ventures are developed for many different reasons. Marriott International and AC Hotels in Spain entered a joint venture to create AC Hotels by Marriott to increase their global footprint and future growth.[27] PepsiCo, as part of its Performance with Purpose global vision, agreed to joint ventures with Tata Global Beverages of India to develop packaged health and wellness beverages for the mass consumer market in India and the Strauss Group in Mexico to provide fresh dips and spreads.[28] Joint ventures can also be truly unique, such as the University of Pittsburgh's Medical Center and the Italian government's joint venture that brought a new medical transplant center to Sicily. The transplant center in Palermo called ISMETT recently celebrated its fifteenth year of operation.[29] The benefits of international joint ventures are clear:

1. Shared technology and risk.
2. Shared marketing and management expertise.
3. Entry into markets where foreign companies are often not allowed unless goods are produced locally.

The drawbacks of joint ventures are not so obvious but are important. One partner can learn the other's technology and business practices and then use what it has learned to its own advantage. Also, a shared technology may become obsolete, or the joint venture may become too large to be as flexible as needed.

The global market has also fueled the growth of strategic alliances. A **strategic alliance** is a long-term partnership between two or more companies established to help each company build competitive market advantages. Unlike joint ventures, strategic alliances don't share costs, risks, management, or even profits. Such alliances provide broad access to markets, capital, and technical expertise. Thanks to their flexibility, strategic alliances can effectively link firms from different countries and firms of vastly different sizes. Hewlett-Packard has strategic alliances with Hitachi and Samsung, and Coca-Cola and Nestlé have had an alliance since early 1990 to distribute ready-to-drink tea and coffee.

Foreign Direct Investment

Foreign direct investment (FDI) is the buying of permanent property and businesses in foreign nations. The most common form of FDI is a **foreign subsidiary**, a company owned in a foreign country by another company, called the *parent company*. The subsidiary operates like a domestic firm, with production, distribution, promotion, pricing, and other business functions under the control of the subsidiary's management. The subsidiary also must observe the legal requirements of both the country where the parent firm is located (called the *home country*) and the foreign country where the subsidiary is located (called the *host country*).

The primary advantage of a subsidiary is that the company maintains complete control over any technology or expertise it may possess. The major shortcoming is the need to commit funds and technology within foreign boundaries. Should relationships with a host country falter, the firm's assets could be *expropriated* (taken over by the foreign government). Swiss-based Nestlé has many foreign subsidiaries. The consumer-products giant spent billions of dollars acquiring foreign subsidiaries such as Jenny Craig (weight management), Ralston Purina, Chef America (maker of Hot Pockets), and Dreyer's Ice Cream in the United States as well as Perrier in France. Nestlé employs over 328,000 people and has operations in almost every country in the world.[30]

Nestlé is a **multinational corporation**, one that manufactures and markets products in many different countries and has multinational stock

strategic alliance
A long-term partnership between two or more companies established to help each company build competitive market advantages.

foreign direct investment (FDI)
The buying of permanent property and businesses in foreign nations.

foreign subsidiary
A company owned in a foreign country by another company, called the *parent company*.

multinational corporation
An organization that manufactures and markets products in many different countries and has multinational stock ownership and multinational management.

The United States has been and remains a popular global spot for foreign direct investment. Global automobile manufacturers like Toyota, Honda, and Mercedes have spent millions of dollars building facilities in the United States, like the Mercedes plant in Tuscaloosa, Alabama, pictured here. Do you consider a Mercedes made in Alabama to be an American car or a German car?

FIGURE 3.5 THE LARGEST MULTINATIONAL CORPORATIONS IN THE WORLD

COMPANY	COUNTRY	WEBSITE
1. Royal Dutch Shell	Netherlands	shell.com
2. Wal-Mart Stores	United States	walmart.com
3. ExxonMobil	United States	exxonmobil.com
4. Sinopec Group	China	Sinopecgroup.com
5. China National Petroleum	China	cnpc.com.cn
6. BP	Britain	bp.com
7. State Grid	China	sgcc.com.cn
8. Toyota Motor	Japan	toyota.co.jp
9. Japan Post Holdings	Japan	japanpost.jp
10. Chevron	United States	chevron.com

Source: *Fortune*, July 25, 2013.

ownership and management. Multinational corporations are typically extremely large corporations like Nestlé, but not all large global businesses are multinationals. For example, a corporation could export everything it produces, deriving 100 percent of its sales and profits globally, and still not be a multinational corporation. Only firms that have *manufacturing capacity* or some other physical presence in different nations can truly be called multinational. Figure 3.5 lists the 10 largest multinational corporations in the world.

A growing form of foreign direct investment is the use of **sovereign wealth funds (SWFs)**, investment funds controlled by governments holding investment stakes in foreign companies. SWFs from the United Arab Emirates, Singapore, and China have purchased interests in many U.S. companies. Norway, with a population of 5 million people, is the world's richest SWF with assets of approximately $830 billion.[31] The size of SWFs ($6 trillion globally) and government ownership make some fear they might be used for achieving geopolitical objectives, gaining control of strategic natural resources, or obtaining sensitive technologies. Thus far this has not been a problem. In fact during the Great Recession, SWFs injected billions of dollars into struggling U.S. companies.[32] Many economists argue that foreign investment through SWFs is a vote of confidence in the U.S. economy and a way to create thousands of U.S. jobs.

Entering global business requires selecting an entry strategy that best fits your business goals. The different strategies we've discussed reflect different levels of ownership, financial commitment, and risk. However, this is just the beginning. You should also be aware of market forces that affect a business's ability to thrive in global markets. After the Test Prep, we'll discuss them.

sovereign wealth funds (SWFs)
Investment funds controlled by governments holding investment stakes in foreign companies.

Use LearnSmart to help retain what you have learned. Access your instructor's Connect course to check out LearnSmart, or go to learnsmartadvantage.com for help.

🔲LEARNSMART

test **prep**

- What are the advantages to a firm of using licensing as a method of entry in global markets? What are the disadvantages?
- What services are usually provided by an export-trading company?
- What is the key difference between a joint venture and a strategic alliance?
- What makes a company a multinational corporation?

LO 3–4   Evaluate the forces that affect trading in global markets.

FORCES AFFECTING TRADING IN GLOBAL MARKETS

The hurdles to success are higher and more complex in global markets than in domestic markets. Such hurdles include dealing with differences in sociocultural forces, economic and financial forces, legal and regulatory forces, and physical and environmental forces. Let's analyze each of these market forces to see how they challenge even the most established and experienced global businesses.

Sociocultural Forces

The word *culture* refers to the set of values, beliefs, rules, and institutions held by a specific group of people. Culture can include social structures, religion, manners and customs, values and attitudes, language, and personal communication. (See the Spotlight on Small Business box for a story about how one entrepreneur is attempting to appeal to the changing values in China as newly affluent consumers desire luxury U.S. products.) If you hope to get involved in global trade, it's critical to be aware of the cultural differences among nations. Unfortunately, while the United States is a multicultural nation, U.S. business-people are often accused of *ethnocentricity*, an attitude that your own culture is superior to other cultures.

In contrast, many foreign companies are very good at adapting to U.S. culture. Think how effectively German, Japanese, and Korean carmakers adapted to U.S. drivers' wants and needs in the auto industry. In contrast, for many years U.S. auto producers didn't adapt automobiles to drive on the left side of the road and printed owner's manuals only in English. Liberia, Myanmar, and the United States are the only nations in the world that have not conformed to the metric system of measurement. Let's look at other hurdles U.S. businesses face in adapting to social and cultural differences in global markets.

Religion is an important part of any society's culture and can have a significant impact on business operations. Consider the violent clashes between religious communities in India, Pakistan, and the Middle East—clashes that have wounded these areas' economies. Even successful global companies can be affected by ignoring religious implications in making business decisions. For example, in honor of nations competing in the World Cup in 1994, both McDonald's and Coca-Cola reprinted the flags of the participating countries on their packaging. Muslims were offended when the Saudi Arabian flag was put on their packaging because the flag's design contained the Muslim Sha-hada (the Muslim declaration of faith), and Muslims believe their holy writ should never be wadded up and thrown away. Both companies learned from this experience that understanding religious implications in the global market is important.

In a similar classic story, a U.S. manager in Islamic Pakistan toured a new plant under his control. While the plant was in full operation, he went to his office to make some preliminary production forecasts. Suddenly all the machinery in the plant stopped. The manager rushed out, suspecting a power failure, only to find his production workers on their prayer rugs. Upon learn-ing that Muslims are required to pray five times a day, he returned to his office and lowered his production estimates.

Understanding sociocultural differences is also important in managing employees. In some Latin American countries, workers believe managers are in positions of authority to make decisions concerning the well-being of the

spotlight on **small business**

www.yaofamilywines.com

From Setting Picks to Picking Grapes

Although Americans love to watch sports, professional athletes often receive criticism for collecting enormous paychecks. After all, some sports stars make more money in a single season than many educators or nurses would see in a lifetime. But matters can change drastically for athletes once their playing days end. Suddenly skills that you've spent your entire life honing are obsolete, often leading to confusion over what to do next.

When faced with this problem, the groundbreaking former NBA center Yao Ming opted to use his resources to start a business. Although this is a common post-retirement tactic for many athletes, Yao didn't unveil a line of

athletic wear or open a chain of sports bars. Instead, he established a high-end winery in California's famous Napa Valley. Although many wealthy Chinese celebrities have bought vineyards, Yao has set himself apart by building a brand from scratch

rather than investing in an existing operation. A national hero in China, Yao Family Wines uses the name recognition of its seven-and-half-foot founder to appeal to the nation's growing consumer class. Yao's wines are intentionally expensive: the cheapest vintage goes for about $87 while the priciest bottle, Yao Ming Family Reserve, lists for more than $1,000. With premium brands still a rarity in China, Yao could end up being just as influential in the Chinese business world as he was on the basketball court.

Sources: Jason Chow, "Yao Ming's Napa Winery Stoops to Conquer China's Middle Class," *The Wall Street Journal*, September 5, 2013; and Michelle FlorCruz, "Yao Ming's Wine Company Sets Sights on China's Growing Middle Class," *International Business Times*, September 6, 2013.

workers under their control. Consider the U.S. manager in Peru who was unaware of this cultural characteristic and believed workers should participate in managerial functions. He was convinced he could motivate his workers to higher levels of productivity by instituting a more democratic decision-making style. Workers instead began quitting in droves. When asked why, they said the new manager did not know his job and was asking the workers what to do. All stated they wanted to find new jobs, since this company was doomed due to its incompetent management.

Even today, many U.S. companies still fail to think globally, not understanding that something like the color of flowers can have different meanings in different cultures. A sound philosophy is: *Never assume what works in one country will work in another.* Intel, Nike, IBM, Apple, KFC, and Walmart have developed brand names with widespread global appeal and recognition, but even they often face difficulties.[33] To get an idea of the problems companies have faced with translations of advertising globally, take a look at Figure 3.6.

Economic and Financial Forces

Economic differences can muddy the water in global markets. In Qatar, annual per capita income is over $100,000, the highest in the world. In economically strapped Ethiopia and Haiti, per capita income is barely over $1,200. It's difficult for us to imagine buying chewing gum by the stick. Yet this behavior is commonplace in economically depressed nations like Haiti, where customers can afford only small quantities. You might suspect with over 1.2 billion potential customers, India would be a dream market for a company like Coca-Cola. Unfortunately, Indians consume only 12 eight-ounce bottles of Coke per person a year due to low per-capita income.[34] Financially, Mexicans shop with pesos, Chinese with yuan (also known as renminbi), South Koreans with won,

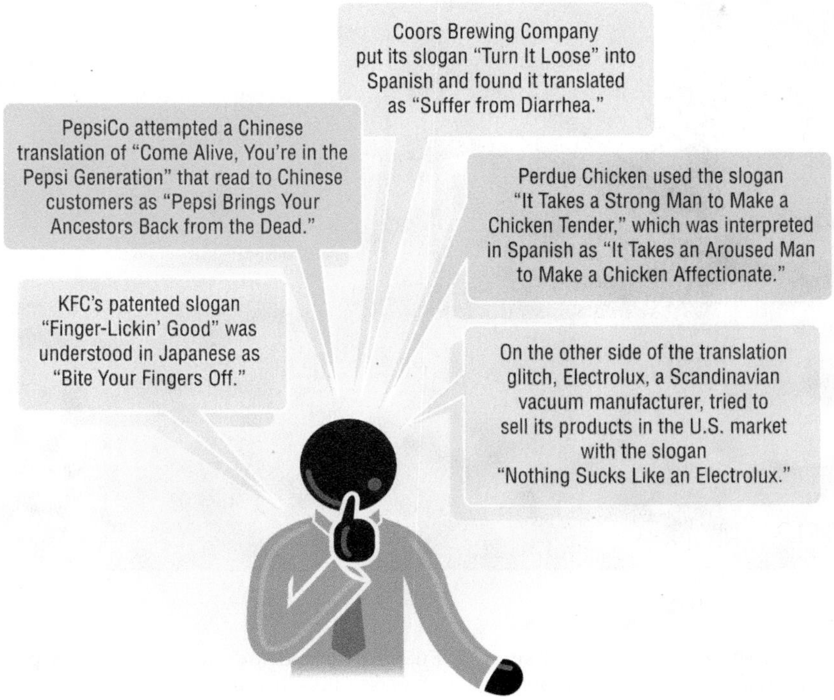

> Coors Brewing Company put its slogan "Turn It Loose" into Spanish and found it translated as "Suffer from Diarrhea."

> PepsiCo attempted a Chinese translation of "Come Alive, You're in the Pepsi Generation" that read to Chinese customers as "Pepsi Brings Your Ancestors Back from the Dead."

> Perdue Chicken used the slogan "It Takes a Strong Man to Make a Chicken Tender," which was interpreted in Spanish as "It Takes an Aroused Man to Make a Chicken Affectionate."

> KFC's patented slogan "Finger-Lickin' Good" was understood in Japanese as "Bite Your Fingers Off."

> On the other side of the translation glitch, Electrolux, a Scandinavian vacuum manufacturer, tried to sell its products in the U.S. market with the slogan "Nothing Sucks Like an Electrolux."

FIGURE 3.6 OOPS, DID WE SAY THAT?
A global marketing strategy can be very difficult to implement. Look at the problems these well-known companies encountered in global markets.

Japanese with yen, and U.S. consumers with dollars. Among currencies, globally, the U.S. dollar is considered a dominant and stable currency.[35] However, it doesn't always retain the same market value. In a global transaction today, a dollar may be exchanged for eight pesos; tomorrow you may get seven. The **exchange rate** is the value of one nation's currency relative to the currencies of other countries.

Changes in a nation's exchange rates have effects in global markets. A *high value of the dollar* means a dollar is trading for more foreign currency than previously. Therefore, foreign products become cheaper because it takes fewer dollars to buy them. However, U.S.-produced goods become more expensive because of the dollar's high value. Conversely, a *low value of the dollar* means a dollar is traded for less foreign currency—foreign goods become more expensive because it takes more dollars to buy them, but U.S. goods become cheaper to foreign buyers because it takes less foreign currency to buy them.

Global financial markets operate under a system called *floating exchange rates,* which means that currencies "float" in value according to the supply and demand for them in the global market for currency. This supply and demand is created by global currency traders who develop a market for a nation's currency based on the country's perceived trade and investment potential.

Changes in currency values can cause many problems globally.[36] For instance, labor costs for multinational corporations like Nestlé, General Electric, and Sony can vary considerably as currency values shift, causing them to juggle production from one country to another. The same is true for

exchange rate
The value of one nation's currency relative to the currencies of other countries.

When the dollar is "up," foreign goods and travel are a bargain for U.S. consumers. When the dollar trades for less foreign currency, however, foreign tourists like these often flock to U.S. cities to enjoy relatively cheaper vacations and shopping trips. Do U.S. exporters profit more when the dollar is up or when it is down?

medium-sized companies like H.B. Fuller, a global industrial adhesives provider from St. Paul, Minnesota, which has 4,000 employees in 43 countries. Like its larger counterparts, H.B. Fuller uses currency fluctuations to its advantage in dealing with its global markets.[37]

Currency valuation problems can be especially harsh on developing economies. At times a nation's government will intervene and readjust the value of its currency, often to increase the export potential of its products. **Devaluation** lowers the value of a nation's currency relative to others. Argentina and Venezuela both devalued their currencies in 2014 to try to alleviate severe economic problems in both countries.[38] Sometimes, due to a nation's weak currency, the only way to trade is *bartering*, the exchange of merchandise for merchandise or service for service with no money traded.[39]

Countertrading is a complex form of bartering in which several countries each trade goods or services for other goods or services. Let's say a developing country such as Jamaica wants to buy vehicles from Ford Motor Company in exchange for bauxite, a mineral compound that is a source of aluminum ore. Ford does not need Jamaican bauxite, but it does need compressors. In a countertrade, Ford may trade vehicles to Jamaica, which trades bauxite to another country, say India, which exchanges compressors with Ford. All three parties benefit and avoid some of the financial problems and currency constraints in global markets. Estimates are that countertrading accounts for over 20 percent of all global exchanges, especially with developing countries.[40]

devaluation
Lowering the value of a nation's currency relative to other currencies.

countertrading
A complex form of bartering in which several countries may be involved, each trading goods for goods or services for services.

Legal and Regulatory Forces

In any economy, the conduct and the direction of business are firmly tied to the legal and regulatory environment. In global markets, no central system of law exists, so different systems of laws and regulations may apply in different places. This makes conducting global business difficult as businesspeople navigate a sea of laws and regulations that are often inconsistent. Antitrust rules, labor relations, patents, copyrights, trade practices, taxes, product liability, child labor, prison labor, and other issues are governed differently country by country.

U.S. businesses must follow U.S. laws and regulations in conducting business globally, although legislation such as the Foreign Corrupt Practices Act of 1978 can create competitive disadvantages. This law prohibits "questionable" or "dubious" payments to foreign officials to secure business contracts.[41] That runs contrary to practices in some countries, where corporate or government bribery is not merely acceptable but perhaps the only way to secure a lucrative contract. The Organization for Economic Cooperation and Development (OECD) and Transparency International have led a global effort to fight corruption and bribery in global business, with limited success.[42] Figure 3.7 shows a partial list of countries where bribery or other unethical business practices are most common.

The cooperation and sponsorship of local businesspeople can help a company penetrate the market and deal with laws, regulations, and bureaucratic barriers in their country.

Physical and Environmental Forces

Physical and environmental forces certainly affect a company's ability to conduct global business. Some developing countries have such primitive transportation and storage systems that international distribution is ineffective, if not impossible, especially for perishable food. Add unclean water and lack of effective sewer systems, and you can see the intensity of the problem.

Technological differences also influence the features of exportable products. For example, residential electrical systems in most developing countries do not match those of U.S. homes, in kind or capacity. Computer and Internet use in many developing countries is thin or nonexistent. These facts make for a tough environment for business in general and for e-commerce in particular. After the Test Prep, we'll explore how another force, trade protectionism, affects global business.

FIGURE 3.7 COUNTRIES RATED HIGHEST ON CORRUPT BUSINESS

1. Somalia
2. North Korea
3. Afghanistan
4. Sudan
5. South Sudan
6. Libya
7. Iraq
8. Uzbekistan
9. Turkmenistan
10. Syria

Source: Transparency International, 2014.

---

test prep ✓✓

- What are four major hurdles to successful global trade?
- What does *ethnocentricity* mean, and how can it affect global success?
- How would a low value of the dollar affect U.S. exports?
- What does the Foreign Corrupt Practices Act prohibit?

Use LearnSmart to help retain what you have learned. Access your instructor's Connect course to check out LearnSmart, or go to learnsmartadvantage.com for help.

📖 LEARNSMART

LO 3–5   Debate the advantages and disadvantages of trade protectionism.

TRADE PROTECTIONISM

As we discussed in the previous section, sociocultural, economic and financial, legal and regulatory, and physical and environmental forces are all challenges to global trade. What is often a much greater barrier to global trade, however, is trade protectionism. **Trade protectionism** is the use of

trade protectionism
The use of government regulations to limit the import of goods and services.

Some workers believe that too many U.S. jobs have been lost due to the growing number of imported products. Should governments protect their industries by placing tariffs on imported products? Why or why not?

tariff
A tax imposed on imports.

import quota
A limit on the number of products in certain categories that a nation can import.

embargo
A complete ban on the import or export of a certain product, or the stopping of all trade with a particular country.

government regulations to limit the import of goods and services. Advocates of protectionism believe it allows domestic producers to survive and grow, producing more jobs. Other countries use protectionist measures because they are wary of foreign competition in general. To understand how protectionism affects global business, let's briefly review a bit of global economic history.

Business, economics, and politics have always been closely linked. Economics was once referred to as *political economy,* indicating the close ties between politics (government) and economics. In the 17th and 18th centuries, businesspeople and government leaders endorsed an economic policy called *mercantilism.*[43] The idea was for a nation to sell more goods to other nations than it bought from them, that is, to have a favorable balance of trade. According to mercantilists, this resulted in a flow of money to the country that sold the most globally. The philosophy led governments to implement **tariffs**, taxes on imports, making imported goods more expensive to buy.

There are two kinds of tariffs: protective and revenue. *Protective tariffs* (import taxes) raise the retail price of imported products so that domestic goods are more competitively priced. These tariffs are meant to save jobs for domestic workers and keep industries—especially infant industries that have companies in the early stages of growth—from closing down because of foreign competition. *Revenue tariffs* are designed to raise money for the government.

An **import quota** limits the number of products in certain categories a nation can import. The United States has import quotas on a number of products, including sugar and shrimp, to protect U.S. companies and preserve jobs. Nations also prohibit the export of specific products. Antiterrorism laws and the U.S. Export Administration Act of 1979 prohibit exporting goods such as high-tech weapons that could endanger national security. An **embargo** is a complete ban on the import or export of a certain product, or the stopping of all trade with a particular country. Political disagreements have caused many countries to establish embargoes, such as the U.S. embargo against Cuba, in effect since 1962.

Nontariff barriers are not as specific or formal as tariffs, import quotas, and embargoes but can be as detrimental to free trade.[44] For example, India imposes a number of restrictive standards like import licensing, burdensome product testing requirements, and lengthy customs procedures that inhibit the sale of imported products. China omits many American-made products from its government catalogs that specify what products may be purchased by its huge government sector. Other trade barriers detail exactly how a product must be sold in a country or may insist on local content requirements that require that some part of a product be produced domestically. For example, even though we have a free-trade agreement with South Korea, nontariff barriers still restrict the import of U.S. cars there. Barriers such as the size of the engine and strict emission standards limit the number of U.S. cars that can be sold in the country. South Korea on the other hand sells almost 1.3 million cars to the United States.

Would-be exporters might view such trade barriers as good reasons to avoid global trade, but overcoming constraints creates business opportunities. Next, we'll look at organizations and agreements that attempt to eliminate trade barriers.

The World Trade Organization

In 1948, government leaders from 23 nations formed the **General Agreement on Tariffs and Trade (GATT)**, a global forum for reducing trade restrictions on goods, services, ideas, and cultural programs. In 1986, the Uruguay Round of the GATT convened to renegotiate trade agreements. After eight years of meetings, 124 nations voted to lower tariffs an average of 38 percent worldwide and to expand new trade rules to areas such as agriculture, services, and the protection of patents.

The Uruguay Round also established the **World Trade Organization (WTO)** to mediate trade disputes among nations. The WTO, headquartered in Geneva, is an independent entity of 159 member nations whose purpose is to oversee cross-border trade issues and global business practices.[45] Trade disputes are presented by member nations with decisions made within a year, rather than languishing for years as in the past; member nations can appeal a decision.

The WTO has not solved all global trade problems. Legal and regulatory differences (discussed above) often impede trade expansion. Also a wide gap persists between developing nations (80 percent of the WTO membership) and industrialized nations like the United States. The WTO meetings in Doha, Qatar, begun in 2001 to address dismantling protection of manufactured goods, eliminating subsidies on agricultural products, and overturning temporary protectionist measures, have still not resulted in any significant agreements.[46]

This Indian family used to use bullocks to pull their plow, but had to sell them because the cost to maintain the animals is now too high. Do you think a Doha resolution regarding tariff protection would help families like these?

Common Markets

An issue not resolved by the GATT or the WTO is whether common markets create regional alliances at the expense of global expansion. A **common market** (also called a *trading bloc*) is a regional group of countries with a common external tariff, no internal tariffs, and coordinated laws to facilitate exchange among members. The European Union (EU), Mercosur, the Association of Southeast Asian Nations (ASEAN) Economic Community, and the Common Market for Eastern and Southern Africa (COMESA) are common markets.

The EU began in the late 1950s as an alliance of six trading partners (then known as the Common Market and later the European Economic Community). Today it is a group of 28 nations (see Figure 3.8) with a population of over 500 million and a GDP of $17.2 trillion. Though the EU is represented as a unified body in the WTO, the economies of six members (Germany, France, United Kingdom, Italy, Spain, and the Netherlands) account for over three-fourths of the EU's GDP.

European unification was not easy, but in 1999 the EU took a significant step by adopting the euro as a common currency. The euro has helped EU businesses save billions by eliminating currency conversions and has challenged the U.S. dollar's dominance in global markets. Eighteen member nations now use the euro as their common currency. In 2013, the EU faced debt, deficit, and growth problems due to financial difficulties in member nations Greece, Italy, Portugal, and Spain that required bailout assistance.[47] EU officials moved forward with broad economic policies to ensure the financial stability of the union. Even though the EU faces challenges going

General Agreement on Tariffs and Trade (GATT)
A 1948 agreement that established an international forum for negotiating mutual reductions in trade restrictions.

World Trade Organization (WTO)
The international organization that replaced the General Agreement on Tariffs and Trade and was assigned the duty to mediate trade disputes among nations.

common market
A regional group of countries that have a common external tariff, no internal tariffs, and a coordination of laws to facilitate exchange; also called a *trading bloc*. An example is the European Union.

FIGURE 3.8 MEMBERS OF THE EUROPEAN UNION
Current EU members are highlighted in yellow. Countries that have applied for membership are in orange. Iceland (not shown) is also an EU candidate.

forward, it still considers economic integration among member nations as the way to compete globally against major competitors like the United States and China.

Mercosur unites Brazil, Argentina, Paraguay, Uruguay, Venezuela and associate members Bolivia, Chile, Colombia, Ecuador, and Peru in a trading bloc that encompasses more than 275 million people. The EU and Mercosur have hopes of finalizing a trade agreement in 2014 that would expand the movement of goods and services between the two trading blocs.[48]

The ASEAN Economic Community was established in 1967 in Thailand to create economic cooperation among its five original members (Indonesia, Malaysia, the Philippines, Singapore, and Thailand). ASEAN has expanded to include Brunei, Cambodia, the Lao People's Democratic Republic, Myanmar, and Vietnam, creating a trade association with a population of approximately 620 million and a GDP of $2.2 trillion.[49] COMESA is a 19-member African trading bloc. In 2008, COMESA joined with the Southern African Development Community (SADC) and the East Africa Community (EAC) to form an expanded free-trade zone that has a GDP of $624 billion and a population of 527 million.[50]

The North American and Central American Free Trade Agreements

North American Free Trade Agreement (NAFTA)
Agreement that created a free-trade area among the United States, Canada, and Mexico.

A widely debated issue of the early 1990s was the **North American Free Trade Agreement (NAFTA)**, which created a free-trade area among the United States, Canada, and Mexico. Opponents warned of the loss of U.S. jobs and capital. Supporters predicted NAFTA would open a vast new market for U.S. exports and create jobs and market opportunities in the long term. In reality,

NAFTA did not cause the huge job losses feared by many nor did it achieve the large economic gains predicted.[51]

NAFTA's objectives were to (1) eliminate trade barriers and facilitate cross-border movement of goods and services, (2) promote conditions of fair competition, (3) increase investment opportunities, (4) provide effective protection and enforcement of intellectual property rights (patents and copyrights), (5) establish a framework for further regional trade cooperation, and (6) improve working conditions in North America. Today, the three NAFTA countries have a combined population of over 460 million and a gross domestic product (GDP) of over $18 trillion.

After 20 years in existence, NAFTA remains a debated issue.[52] On the positive side, trade volume in goods and services among the three partners expanded from $289 billion in 1994 to over $1.2 trillion today. However, the major gains in trade were in the early years of the agreement.[53] On the negative side, in the United States, of the 680,000 manufacturing jobs that have been lost since enacting NAFTA in 1994, many were lost to Mexico. In Mexico, promises to close the wage gap with the U.S., boost job growth, fight poverty, and improve environmental controls have largely failed.[54] Illegal immigration remains a major problem between the two nations. Still, NAFTA controversies have not changed the U.S. commitment to free-trade agreements.

In 2005 the Central American Free Trade Agreement (CAFTA) was signed into law, creating a free-trade zone with Costa Rica, the Dominican Republic, El Salvador, Guatemala, Honduras, and Nicaragua. The United States is also considering an agreement with eleven Pacific-Rim nations called the Trans-Pacific Partnership and a massive free-trade deal with the EU called the Transatlantic Trade and Investment Partnership.[55]

Common markets and free-trade areas will be debated far into the future. While some economists resoundingly praise such efforts, others are concerned the world is dividing into major trading blocs (EU, NAFTA, etc.) that will exclude poor and developing nations. After the Test Prep, we'll look at the future of global trade and address the issue of outsourcing.

test **prep**

- What are the advantages and disadvantages of trade protectionism and of tariffs?
- What is the primary purpose of the WTO?
- What is the key objective of a common market like the EU?
- What three nations comprise NAFTA?

Use LearnSmart to help retain what you have learned. Access your instructor's Connect course to check out LearnSmart, or go to learnsmartadvantage.com for help.

LEARNSMART

LO 3–6 Discuss the changing landscape of the global market and the issue of offshore outsourcing.

THE FUTURE OF GLOBAL TRADE

Global trade opportunities grow more interesting and more challenging each day. After all, over 7 billion potential customers are attractive. However, terrorism, nuclear proliferation, rogue states, income inequality, and other issues cast a dark shadow on global markets. Let's conclude this chapter by looking at issues certain to influence global markets, and perhaps your business career.

With more than 1.3 billion people and incredible exporting prowess, China has transformed the world economic map. China is the world's largest exporter and the second largest economy. Its rise has happened over a relatively short period of time, with the value of Chinese trade roughly doubling every four years over the last three decades.[56] Not long ago, foreign direct investment in China was considered risky and not worth the risk. In 2013, China attracted $117 billion in foreign direct investment.[57] Today, over 400 of the Fortune 500 companies (the world's largest companies) have invested in China. According to Goldman Sachs Group and the London Center for Economic and Business Research, China could overtake the United States as the world's largest economy by 2028.[58]

Since 2009 China has been the largest motor vehicle market in the world with sales and production topping nearly 22 million vehicles in 2013.[59] It's estimated that by 2030, there could be more cars on the road in China than all the cars in the world today. Walmart began operations in China in 1996 and now has over 390 stores with plans to open more. Even newcomers like IMAX Corporation are expanding in this fast-growing market. IMAX currently has 150 movie theaters with plans to grow to 400 by 2018.

Many view China as a free trader's dream, where global investment and entrepreneurship will lead to wealth. However, concerns remain about China's one-party political system, human rights abuses, currency issues, and increasing urban population growth. China's underground economy also generates significant product piracy and counterfeiting, although the country has been more responsive to these problems since its admission to the WTO. With the global economy continuing to grow, China will be a key driver of the world economy along with the United States, the EU, and Japan.

While China attracts most of the attention in Asia, India's population of 1.2 billion presents a tremendous opportunity. With nearly 575 million of its population under 25, India's working-age population will continue to grow while the United States, China, and the EU expect a decline in the 2020s. Already India has seen huge growth in information technology and biotechnology, and its pharmaceutical business is expected to grow to $30 billion, a jump of over 150 percent by 2020. Still, it remains a nation with difficult trade laws and an inflexible bureaucracy.[60]

China's economy is booming, and a highly educated middle class with money to spend is emerging, especially in the cities. Many observers believe China will continue its growth and play a major role in the global economy. Are U.S. firms prepared to compete?

Russia is an industrialized nation with large reserves of oil, gas, and gold that became a member of the WTO in 2012. Multinationals like Chevron, ExxonMobil, and BP have invested heavily in developing Russia's oil reserves. However, Russia's economy slowed when world oil prices declined and the government admitted that growth prospects for the economy were not strong for the next two decades.[61] Unfortunately, Russia is plagued by political, currency, and social problems and is considered by Transparency International as the world's most corrupt major economy.

Brazil is an emerging nation that along with China, India, and Russia was projected to be one of the wealthier global economies by 2030. In fact, the term *BRIC* has been used as an acronym for the economies of Brazil, Russia, India, and China. Today, Brazil is the largest economy in South America and the seventh-largest economy in the world with well-developed agriculture, mining, manufacturing, and service sectors. Along with Russia, Brazil was expected to dominate the global market as a supplier of raw materials. China and India were predicted to be leading global suppliers of manufactured goods and services. Unfortunately, the past few years have been tough times for Brazil's economy with growing inflation and slow growth. Still, its growing consumer market of over 200 million people is a target for major exporters like the United States and China.

The *BRIC* economies are certainly not the only areas of opportunity in the global market. The developing nations of Asia, including Indonesia, Thailand, Singapore, the Philippines, Korea, Malaysia, and Vietnam, also offer great potential for U.S. businesses. Africa, especially South Africa, has only begun to emerge as a center for global economic growth. Business today is truly global and your role in it is up to you.

The Challenge of Offshore Outsourcing

Outsourcing, as noted in Chapter 1, is the process whereby one firm contracts with other companies, often in other countries, to do some or all of its functions. In the United States, companies have outsourced payroll functions, accounting, and some manufacturing operations for many years. However, the shift to primarily low-wage global markets, called *offshore outsourcing*, remains a major issue in the United States. This is especially true as the growth in U.S. jobs has lagged since the financial crisis began in 2008. Take a look at the pros and cons of offshore outsourcing in Figure 3.9.

As lower-level manufacturing became more simplified, U.S. companies such as Levi Strauss and Nike outsourced manufacturing offshore. Today, economists suggest, we have moved into the "second wave" of offshore outsourcing, shifting from product assembly to design and architecture. This process has proved more disruptive to the U.S. job market than the first, which primarily affected manufacturing jobs. Today, increasing numbers of skilled, educated, middle-income workers in service-sector jobs such as accounting, law, finance, risk management, health care, and information technology have seen their jobs outsourced offshore. While loss of jobs is a major concern, it's not the only worry. Nations such as China have a spotty safety record in manufacturing toys, food, and drugs. Today, concerns are mounting about companies like Medtronic and Siemens shifting production of sensitive medical devices such as MRI and CT machines to China. IBM is setting up research facilities in offshore locations. U.S. airlines have even outsourced airline maintenance to countries such as El Salvador. India at one time was the center for telemarketing, data entry, call centers, billing, and low-end software development. Today—with its well-educated, deep pool of scientists, software engineers, chemists, accountants, lawyers, and physicians—India is providing more sophisticated services. For

FIGURE 3.9 THE PROS AND CONS OF OFFSHORE OUTSOURCING

PROS	CONS
• Less-strategic tasks can be outsourced globally so that companies can focus on areas in which they can excel and grow. • Outsourced work allows companies to create efficiencies that in fact let them hire more workers. • Consumers benefit from lower prices generated by effective use of global resources and developing nations grow, thus fueling global economic growth.	• Jobs may be lost permanently and wages fall due to low-cost competition offshore. • Offshore outsourcing may reduce product quality and can therefore cause permanent damage to a company's reputation. • Communication among company members, with suppliers, and with customers becomes much more difficult.

example, radiologists from Wipro Health Science read CAT scans and MRIs for many U.S. hospitals. Some medical providers are shifting surgical procedures to India and other nations. The nearby Making Ethical Decisions box offers an interesting ethical question about this process.

As technical talent grows around the globe, offshore outsourcing will increase. To stay competitive, education and training will be critical for U.S. workers to preserve the skill premium they possess today and to stay ahead in the future.

Globalization and Your Future

Whether you aspire to be an entrepreneur, a manager, or some other type of business leader, think globally in planning your career. By studying foreign languages, learning about foreign cultures, and taking business courses (including a global business course), you can develop a global perspective on your future. As you progress through this text, keep two things in mind: globalization is real, and economic competition promises to intensify.

Also keep in mind that global market potential does not belong only to large, multinational corporations. Small and medium-sized businesses have a world of opportunity in front of them. In fact, these firms are often better prepared to leap into global markets and react quickly to opportunities than are large businesses. Finally, don't forget the potential of franchising, which we examine in more detail in Chapter 5.

Use LearnSmart to help retain what you have learned. Access your instructor's Connect course to check out LearnSmart, or go to learnsmartadvantage.com for help.

test prep

- What are the major threats to doing business in global markets?
- What key challenges must India and Russia face before becoming global economic leaders?
- What does the acronym *BRIC* stand for?
- What are the two primary concerns associated with offshore outsourcing?

www.medicaltourism.com

making **ethical decisions**

Making Your Operation Your Vacation

The Affordable Care Act (ACA) may bring some relief to astronomical insurance costs. But as premiums continue to rise at home, overseas in countries like Thailand, Colombia, and India, health care is not only affordable, it's also high quality. For instance, in the United States it would cost Patrick Follett, an avid skier, at least $65,000 for his hip replacement surgery. Unlike some Americans, Follett had medical insurance and would have part of the procedure covered. However, it would have still cost him at least $10,000 out-of-pocket. Follett, like 1.6 million other Americans, started looking for treatment elsewhere. In March of 2012, he underwent surgery in Mexico and was back on the California ski slopes in March of 2013. His total bill: $10,000, all of which was covered by his company.

Right now, few American companies include medical tourism in their health care plans, but some of the larger companies like Aetna and WellPoint are working with companies to include international coverage. It's even expected to become a booming industry with worldwide annual growth estimated between 20 and 30 percent. Would it be ethical to force patients to travel thousands of miles and be separated from friends and family in a time of crisis in order to save money?

Sources: Medical Tourism Association, "Medical Tourism Sample Surgery Cost Chart," www.medicaltourismassociation.com/en/for-patients.html, accessed March 2014; Kevin Gray, "Medical Tourism: Overseas and Under the Knife," *Men's Journal*, November 2013; and Elisabeth Rosenthal "The Growing Popularity of Having Surgery Overseas," *The New York Times*, August 6, 2013.

summary

LO 3–1 Discuss the importance of the global market and the roles of comparative advantage and absolute advantage in global trade.

- **Why should nations trade with other nations?**
(1) No country is self-sufficient, (2) other countries need products that prosperous countries produce, and (3) natural resources and technological skills are not distributed evenly around the world.

- **What is the theory of comparative advantage?**
The theory of comparative advantage contends that a country should make and then sell those products it produces most efficiently but buy those it cannot produce as efficiently.

- **What is absolute advantage?**
Absolute advantage exists if a country produces a specific product more efficiently than any other country. There are few examples of absolute advantage in the global market today.

LO 3–2 Explain the importance of importing and exporting, and understand key terms used in global business.

- **What kinds of products can be imported and exported?**
Though it is not necessarily easy, just about any product can be imported or exported.

- **What terms are important in understanding world trade?**
Exporting is selling products to other countries. *Importing* is buying products from other countries. The *balance of trade* is the relationship of exports to imports. The *balance of payments* is the balance of trade plus

other money flows such as tourism and foreign aid. *Dumping* is selling products for less in a foreign country than in your own country. See the Key Terms list after this Summary to be sure you know the other important terms.

LO 3–3   Illustrate the strategies used in reaching global markets and explain the role of multinational corporations.

- **What are some ways in which a company can engage in global business?**
  Ways of entering world trade include licensing, exporting, franchising, contract manufacturing, joint ventures and strategic alliances, and direct foreign investment.

- **How do multinational corporations differ from other companies that participate in global business?**
  Unlike companies that only export or import, multinational corporations also have manufacturing facilities or other physical presence abroad.

LO 3–4   Evaluate the forces that affect trading in global markets.

- **What are some of the forces that can discourage participation in global business?**
  Potential stumbling blocks to global trade include sociocultural forces, economic and financial forces, legal and regulatory forces, and physical and environmental forces.

LO 3–5   Debate the advantages and disadvantages of trade protectionism.

- **What is trade protectionism?**
  Trade protectionism is the use of government regulations to limit the import of goods and services. Advocates believe it allows domestic producers to grow, producing more jobs. The key tools of protectionism are tariffs, import quotas, and embargoes.

- **What are tariffs?**
  Tariffs are taxes on foreign products. Protective tariffs raise the price of foreign products and protect domestic industries; revenue tariffs raise money for the government.

- **What is an embargo?**
  An embargo prohibits the importing or exporting of certain products.

- **Is trade protectionism good for domestic producers?**
  That is debatable. Trade protectionism offers pluses and minuses.

- **Why do governments continue such practices?**
  The theory of mercantilism started the practice of trade protectionism and it has persisted, though in a weaker form, ever since.

LO 3–6   Discuss the changing landscape of the global market and the issue of offshore outsourcing.

- **What is offshore outsourcing? Why is it a major concern for the future?**
  Outsourcing is the purchase of goods and services from outside a firm rather than providing them inside the company. Today, more businesses are outsourcing manufacturing and services offshore. Many fear that growing numbers of jobs in the United States will be lost due to offshore outsourcing and that the quality of products produced could be inferior.

Access your instructor's Connect course to check out LearnSmart or go to learnsmartadvantage.com for help.

connect

key terms

absolute advantage 64
balance of payments 66
balance of trade 66
common market 79
comparative advantage theory 64
contract manufacturing 69
countertrading 76
devaluation 76
dumping 67
embargo 78
exchange rate 75
exporting 63

foreign direct investment (FDI) 71
foreign subsidiary 71
free trade 63
General Agreement on Tariffs and Trade (GATT) 79
importing 63
import quota 78
joint venture 70
licensing 67
multinational corporation 71

North American Free Trade Agreement (NAFTA) 80
sovereign wealth funds (SWFs) 72
strategic alliance 71
tariff 78
trade deficit 66
trade protectionism 77
trade surplus 66
World Trade Organization (WTO) 79

critical thinking

1. About 95 percent of the world's population lives outside the United States, but many U.S. companies, especially small businesses, still do not engage in global trade. Why not? Do you think more small businesses will participate in global trade in the future? Why or why not?

2. Countries like the United States that have a high standard of living are referred to as *industrialized nations*. Countries with a lower standard of living and quality of life are called *developing countries* (or *underdeveloped* or *less developed countries*). What factors prevent developing nations from becoming industrialized nations?

3. What can businesses do to prevent unexpected problems in dealing with sociocultural, economic and financial, legal and regulatory, and physical and environmental forces in global markets?

4. How would you justify the use of revenue or protective tariffs in today's global market?

developing workplace skills

Key: ● Team   ★ Analytic   ▲ Communication   ▣ Technology

1. Find out firsthand the global impact on your life. How many different countries' names appear on the labels in your clothes? How many languages do your classmates speak? List the ethnic restaurants in your community. Are they family-owned or corporate chains?   ▲

2. Call, e-mail, or visit a local business that imports foreign goods (perhaps a wine or specialty foods importer). Ask the owner or manager about the business's participation in global trade, and compile a list of the advantages and disadvantages he or she cites. Compare notes with your classmates about their research.   ▲★

3. Visit four or five public locations in your community such as schools, hospitals, city/county buildings, or airports. See how many signs are posted in different languages (don't forget the restrooms) and look for other multilingual information, such as brochures or handouts. Do any of the locations fly flags from different nations? In what other ways do they recognize   ★

the diversity of employees or students? What does your search tell you about your community?

 4. Suppose Representative I. M. Wright delivers a passionate speech at your college on tariffs. He argues tariffs are needed to
   a. Protect our young industries.
   b. Encourage consumers to buy U.S.-made products because it's patriotic.
   c. Protect U.S. jobs and wages.
   d. Achieve a favorable balance of trade and balance of payments.

   Do you agree with Representative Wright? Evaluate each of his major points and decide whether you consider it valid. Be sure to justify your position.

 5. Form an imaginary joint venture with three classmates and select a product, service, or idea to market to a specific country. Have each team member select a key global market force in that country (sociocultural, economic and financial, legal and regulatory, or physical and environmental) to research. Have each report his or her findings. Then, as a group, prepare a short explanation of whether the market is worth pursuing.

taking it to the net

PURPOSE
To compare the shifting exchange rates of various countries and to predict the effects of such exchange shifts on global trade.

EXERCISE
One of the difficulties of engaging in global trade is the constant shift in exchange rates. How much do exchange rates change over a 30-day period? Research this by choosing five currencies (say, the euro, the British pound, the Japanese yen, the Mexican peso, the Saudi Arabian riyal) and recording their exchange rates relative to the U.S. dollar for 30 days. The rates are available on the Internet at Yahoo Finance's Currency Center (http://finance.yahoo.com/currency). At the end of the tracking period, choose a company and describe what effects the currency shifts you noted might have on this company's trade with each of the countries or areas whose currency you chose.

video case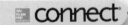

ELECTRA BICYCLE COMPANY

Doing business in global markets can be tricky, but the benefits that come from overseas success justify much of the risk. That's what Electra Bicycle Company's founders discovered after their business's growth suddenly halted. Throughout the early 2000s, many bicycle manufacturers concentrated on producing mountain and speed bikes while discontinuing casual models. Benno Baziger and Jeano Erforth of Electra didn't follow the fad, though, choosing instead to stick with cool, upright bikes perfect for cruising city streets.

The company thrived for years thanks to their unique "comfort bikes." However, major competitors like Schwinn eventually took notice and began making their own sleek street bikes. Electra's explosive growth halted, and the company's two founders searched for a solution. To grow further, the pair knew they would have to enter the global marketplace. They went on a search for places where their vintage sense of style and up-to-date technology would give them a comparative advantage against their bigger competitors.

Electra eventually settled on Taiwan as the site for its overseas manufacturing site. From Taiwan, the California-based company can simply export bikes to neighboring Asian countries like China where bikes are most popular. They can in turn feed their domestic demand by importing bikes into the U.S., a practice that is actually cheaper for Electra than producing bikes on their home soil. This outsourcing of production to a foreign manufacturing plant helps Electra keep its costs down. If labor costs increase or instability flares up between Taiwan and China, Electra could move its production to a less turbulent location.

Such unexpected problems represent just a few of the hurdles companies can face when they go global. For example, laws against motorized bikes forced Electra to tweak the design for its Townie Go model in order to make the bike acceptable in some foreign markets. Despite these issues, global commerce puts companies on the radar of millions of new customers. This immense access can make all the additional effort needed for going global worth it. In fact, Electra now sells more than 100,000 bikes each year.

Electra's success eventually brought it to the attention of Trek, a multinational corporation with offices in Wisconsin, the UK, and Germany. The conglomerate bought Electra, which can now use Trek's established distribution network to reach new markets more quickly and effectively. Letting their parent company worry about matters like capitalization and manufacturing infrastructure allows Electra to focus on other things, such as designing stylish bikes that are easy to ride and fun to own by people all over the world.

THINKING IT OVER

1. What major advantages did Electra gain by using a contract manufacturer in Taiwan to produce its bikes?

2. When Electra produced its bikes in Taiwan, did the company have to follow the laws of Taiwan or the laws of the United States?

3. What major forces impact Electra (or any global producer) in trading in global markets?

notes

1. Robert J. Thomas, Joshua Bellin, Claudy Jules, and Nandani Lynton, "Developing Tomorrow's Global Leaders," *Sloan Management Review,* Fall 2013; and Gregory C. Unruh and Angel Cabera, "Join the Global Elite," *Harvard Business Review,* May 2013.

2. "World Population Clock," U.S. Census Bureau, www.census.gov/ipc/www/popclockworld.html, accessed April 2014; and WorldAtlas.com, accessed April 2014.

3. Russell Flannery, "What Can be Done about the Big U.S. Trade Deficit with China?" *Forbes,* August 3, 2013; and Paul Davidson, "U.S. Trade Deficit Drops to 4-Year Low," *USA Today,* January 7, 2014.

4. *UPS.com,* accessed April 23, 2014; *Walmart.com,* accessed April 23, 2014; and Janice Kew, "Walmart Brand Favored in Massmarts Africa Growth," *Bloomberg Personal Finance,* April 16, 2013.

5. Ira Boudway, "Soccer Will Not Stop Arriving," *Bloomberg Businessweek,* January 2, 2014.

6. Pamela McClintock and Stuart Kemp, "The 21 Surprising Hollywood Actors Whose Names Sell Movies Overseas," *The Hollywood Reporter,* September 12, 2013.

7. World Bank, www.worldbank.org, accessed April 2014; World Trade Organization, www.wto.org, accessed April 2014; and Gordon Chang, "Is China Really the World's No. 1 Trader?" *Forbes,* January 12, 2014.

8. Matthew J. Slaughter, "Exports Sagging? Try Some Free Trade," *The Wall Street Journal,* January 23, 2013.

9. "Free Trade and Secrecy Don't Mix," *Bloomberg Businessweek,* December 1, 2013.

10. Joshua Kurlantzick, "Farewell to the Age of Free Trade," *Bloomberg Businessweek,* December 22, 2013.

11. Robert Skidelsky, "In a World Based on Free Trade, Love Will Cost You," *Global Times,* January 23, 2014.

12. Donald Lessard, Rafael Lucea, and Luis Vives, "Building Your Company's Capabilities Through Global Expansion," *MIT Sloan Management Review,* Winter 2013.

13. International Trade Administration, www.trade.gov, accessed April 2014.

14. Bryan Lowry, Tanvi Misra, and Katie Peralta, "U.S. Exports Rise but Are Likely to Fall Short of Obama's Goal," *McClatchy DC,* December 30, 2013.

15. Alexandra Wolfe, "Howard Schultz: What Next Starbucks?" *The Wall Street Journal,* September 27, 2013.

16. Greg Kitsock, "Beer: Brewers Find It Can Be Bright in Helles," *The Washington Post,* January 7, 2014.

17. Carolyn Berg, "Holding a Mirror to China's Economy Through Cosmetics," *China Daily USA,* October 15, 2013.

18. C. Fred Bergston, "How Best to Boost U.S. Exports," *The Washington Post,* February 3, 2010; and Barry Wood, "An Interview with C. Fred Bergsten, Evangelist for the Open Economy," *The Washington Post,* April 19, 2013.

19. Paul Davidson, "U.S. Trade Deficit Drops to 4-Year Low," *USA Today,* January 7, 2014; and Rob Hotakainen, "U.S. Exports on Record Pace but So Is Trade Deficit with China," *Miami Herald,* January 7, 2014.

20. www.goldmarks.com, accessed April 2014.

21. www.Export.gov, accessed April 2014; and www.sba.gov, accessed April 2014.

22. "Rocky Mountain Chocolate Factory, Inc. Reports Improved Third Quarter Operating Results," *The Wall Street Journal,* January 21, 2014.

23. "Yum Brands' World Hunger Relief Efforts Result in Record-Breaking $37 Million in Cash and Food Donations," *The Wall Street Journal,* January 9, 2014.

24. AnnaLisa Kraft, "Crazy Food You Can't Get Here," *The Motley Fool,* January 4, 2014.

25. Flextronics, www.flextronics.com, accessed May 2012.
26. Zhou Wenting, "Full Steam Ahead for Shanghai Disney in 2015," *China Daily USA,* January 24, 2014.
27. Alby Gallum, "European Hotel Chain Coming to River North," *Crain Chicago Business,* January 24, 2014.
28. "Pepsi Announces Plans for $5 Billion Investment in Mexico," *The Wall Street Journal,* January 24, 2014.
29. Sean D. Hamill, "How UPMC's Overseas Operation Blossomed in 14 Years," *Pittsburgh Post-Gazette,* May 30, 2010; and University of Pittsburgh Medical Center, www .upmc.com, accessed April 2014.
30. *CNNMoney,* www.cnnmoney.com, accessed April 2014; and Nestlé, www.nestle.com, accessed 2014.
31. Vivienne Walt, "Norway's Trillion Dollar Oil Problem," *Fortune Magazine,* January 16, 2014.
32. Ashley Stahl, "The Promise and Perils of Sovereign Wealth Funds," *Forbes,* December 19, 2013; and "More Money than Thor," *The Economist,* September 14, 2013.
33. Susan Bergfield, "4 Countries Walmart Can't Conquer," *MSN Money,* October 15, 2013; Walter Loeb, "Walmart: What Happened in India?" *Forbes,* October 16, 2013; and Agustino Fontevecchia, "IBM Falls Off Cliff as Q3 Sales Fall on Services and Hardware Weakness," *Forbes,* October 16, 2013.
34. Nikhul Gulati and Rumman Ahmed, "India Has 1.2 Billion People but Not Enough Drink Coke," *The Wall Street Journal,* July 13, 2012; and Coca-Cola, www.cocacola.com, accessed April 2014.
35. "In Dollars They Trust," *The Economist,* April 27, 2013.
36. Simon Kennedy, "Developed Economies Seen Fighting Off Emerging Market Contagion," *Bloomberg Businessweek,* January 27, 2014.
37. H.B. Fuller, www.hbfuller.com, accessed April 2014.
38. Taos Turner, Ken Parks, and Juan Foreno, "Crisis Squeeze Two Latin Leaders," *The Wall Street Journal,* January 26, 2014; and Jonathan Gilbert, Simon Romero, and William Neuman, "Erosian of Argentine Peso Sends a Shudder Through Latin America," *The New York Times,* January 24, 2014.
39. Christina LeBeau, "Rules of the Trade," *Entrepreneur,* February 2014.
40. www.wto.com, accessed April 2014.
41. Crayton Harrison, "Hewlett-Packard in Advanced Talks to Resolve U.S. Bribery Probes," *Bloomberg Businessweek,* December 30, 2013; and Chris Isidore, "SEC Expands Probe into Overseas Hiring by U.S. Banks," *CNN Money,* November 27, 2013.
42. Alexandra Wrage, "What Companies Can't Do about Corruption," *Forbes,* January 24, 2014.
43. "What Was Mercantilism?" *The Economist,* August 23, 2013; and Nathan Lewis, "Keynes and Rottbard Agreed: Today's Economics Is Mercantilism," *Forbes,* January 23, 2014.
44. "The Hidden Persuaders: Protectionism Can Take Many Forms, Not All of Them Obvious," *The Economist,* October 12, 2013.
45. www.wto.org, accessed April 2014; and "Unaccustomed Victory," *The Economist,* December 14, 2013.
46. David Nicklaus, "WTO Talks Could Boost Trade by $1 Trillion," *St. Louis Post Dispatch,* December 8, 2013; and "Life After Doha," *The Economist,* December 14, 2013.
47. Emma Ross Thomas,"EU Says Spain Should Improve Bank Monitoring as Bailout Ends," *Bloomberg Businessweek,* January 29, 2014; and Juergen Baetz, "EU Seeks to Make Mega-Banks Less Risky," *Bloomberg Businessweek,* January 29, 2014.
48. "EU-Mercosur Trade Talks: Strategic Patience Runs Out," *The Economist,* December 14, 2013; and Uruguay: CFK Must Improve EU Trade Offer," *Buenos Aires Herald,* January 22, 2014.
49. Association of Southeast Asian Nations, www.aseansec.org, accessed April 2014.
50. Common Market for Eastern and Southern Africa, www .comesa.int, accessed April 2014.
51. "Briefing NAFTA at 20: Ready to Take Off Again?" *The Economist,* January 4, 2014; and Mark Glassman, "NAFTA 20 Years After: Neither Miracle nor Disaster," *Bloomberg Businessweek,* December 30, 2013.
52. "Deeper, Better, NAFTA," *The Economist,* January 4, 2014.
53. www.uschamber.com, accessed April 2014; and "Deeper, Better, NAFTA."
54. Mark Stevenson, "20 Years after NAFTA, a Changed Mexico," *The Boston Globe,* January 3, 2014; and Alfredo Conchado, "20 Years after NAFTA, Mexico Has Transformed," *The Dallas Morning News,* January 1, 2014.
55. "Free Trade Deals such as the Trans-Pacific Partnership Help the United States," *The Washington Post,* January 16, 2014; and Christian Oliver and Shawn Donnan, "Brussels Wants Finance Rules Back in the U.S. Trade Pact," *Financial Times,* January 27, 2014.
56. Jamil Anderlini and Lucy Hornby, "China Overtakes U.S. as World's Largest Goods Trader," *Financial Times,* January 10, 2014.
57. Liyan Qi and Grace Zhu, "China's Capital Inflows, Foreign Direct Investment Rose in 2013," *The Wall Street Journal,* January 16, 2014.
58. www.goldmansachs.com, accessed April 2014; and Morris Beschloss, "Will China Overtake U.S. GDP World Leadership by 2028?" *The Desert Sun (Gannett),* January 23, 2014.
59. Samuel Shen and Norihiko Shirozu, "China Auto Market Seen Cruising to Another Strong Year," *Reuters,* January 12, 2014.
60. "Can India Become a Great Power?" *The Economist,* March 30, 2013; and Philip Stephens, "India Still a Contender in the Asian Race," *Financial Times,* January 30, 2014.
61. Paul Hannon, "EBRD Reduces Investment in Russia," *The Wall Street Journal,* January 15, 2014; and Mark Adomanis, "Russia's Economic Performance Is Actually Very Similar to Other East European Countries," *Forbes,* January 20, 2014.

photo credits

Page 61: Postcode Lottery Green Challenge/Creative Commons, https://www.flickr.com/photos/post-codelotterygreenchallenge/8202992042; p. 63: © Sang Tan/AP Images; p. 65: Peter Rivera/Creative Commons, https://www.flickr.com/photos/riverap1/3258668503; p. 68: © Rex Features/AP Images; p.69: Courtesy of Domino's Pizza;

p. 70: © Andrey Rudakov/Bloomberg/Getty Images; p. 71: © imago stock&people/Newscom; p. 74: Courtesy of Yao Family Winery, © George Rose Photography; p. 76: © Eyecandy Images/age fotostock RF; p. 78: © Tom Williams/Roll Call/Getty Images; p. 79: © Sam Panthaky/AFP/Getty Images; p. 82: © Imaginechina/Corbis.